WEAVING THE VISIONS

New Patterns in Feminist Spirituality

edited by

**Judith Plaskow
and Carol P. Christ**

1817

Harper & Row, Publishers, San Francisco

New York, Cambridge, Philadelphia, St. Louis
London, Singapore, Sydney, Tokyo

To the women of the
Women and Religion Section
of the American Academy of Religion,
with whom we began
weaving new visions

Permission credits to appear on p. 357.

WEAVING THE VISIONS. Copyright © 1989 by Judith Plaskow and Carol P. Christ.
All rights reserved. Printed in the United States of America. No part of this
book may be used or reproduced in any manner whatsoever without written
permission except in the case of brief quotations embodied in critical articles
and reviews. For information address Harper & Row, Publishers, Inc., 10 East
53rd Street, New York, NY 10022. Published simultaneously in Canada by
Fitzhenry & Whiteside Limited, Toronto.

Library of Congress Cataloging-in-Publication Data

Weaving the visions.

Includes index.
1. Women—Religious life.   2. Feminism—Religious aspects.   3. Woman
(Theology) I. Christ, Carol P.   II. Plaskow, Judith.
BL625.7.W43 1989   291'.088042 88-45697
ISBN 0-06-061382-3
ISBN 0-06-061383-1 (pbk.)

89 90 91 92 93 HC 10 9 8 7 6 5 4 3 2 1

Contents

Preface

In the course of the past decade, a number of women have told us that the part of *Womanspirit Rising* they found most helpful and meaningful was the preface. In reading about the trials and tribulations we went through as women graduate students, they felt themselves less crazy and alone, and began to see their own painful experiences in a wider social and political context. It seemed to us, therefore, that it was important to write a preface for this sequel to *Womanspirit Rising* that would touch on some of the issues that have emerged for us as we have left behind the difficult days of graduate school and become established in our careers.

Anyone who reads our essays in this volume will perceive immediately that our intellectual and religious commitments have drawn us away from each other in the last ten years. In *Womanspirit Rising*, Judith had one foot in the "reformist," the other in the "revolutionary" camp, while Carol was just beginning to explore Goddess spirituality alongside her work on feminist theology and spiritual quest in women's literature. In the last decade, Carol has more deeply embraced Goddess and nature spirituality, while Judith has clearly committed herself to the transformation of Judaism.

We would be less than honest if we did not acknowledge that our differences have tested our abilities to communicate with and hear each other. There have been times when each of us has reduced the other to tears and when our sensitivity to each other's criticism has strained our friendship. Jealousy and competitiveness have intruded themselves into our relationship, as each of us has envied perquisites she perceived as attending the other's choices. Yet we have gradually learned to express our anger at each other (sometimes across the distances of the American continent or the Atlantic Ocean), while affirming a friendship and a mutual commitment to feminism and the feminist transformation of religion that now spans almost twenty years. Our personal struggles have taught us the importance of working with and learning from differences in feminist theologies and thealogies, and we believe they make this a stronger book. But it is also true that we sometimes nostalgically recall the days when, united in our critiques of patriarchy and Christian anti-Judaism, it seemed almost as if we were seeing the world through the same eyes and speaking in one voice.

It is not only in the content of our commitments that we have diverged from each other, but also in our methods and styles. Carol's work has come to integrate personal reflection with scholarly analysis, as she has become convinced that naming the sources of our understandings of women's experience makes our work richer and more interesting, keeps us from false and inappropriate generalizations, and challenges the myth of scholarly objectivity that still holds the academy in its thrall. Judith's work has become more committed without becoming more autobiographical, reflecting both her sense of privacy and her conviction that experience can inform and enliven feminist theology without needing to be explicitly named.

One statement about our personal experiences of the past decade we agree belongs in this preface, however, for it is central to our perspectives as feminists in religion. Over the years, as each of us has given lectures at academic institutions and at women's conferences, we have heard repeatedly from women graduate students that they are advised not to do any feminist writing until they have tenure or are well established in their careers. Obviously, this is a path we did not take, and it is a piece of advice we find disturbing and contradictory. (If we put away our most pressing concerns until we are established, will we ever be established enough, and will those concerns still be there when we are?) We cannot say that we have not paid for our choices. Both of us have received tenure at primarily undergraduate teaching institutions where the course loads are heavy and largely at the introductory level, and where we have had little opportunity to share our best thinking with our students and little time during the academic year to pursue our own research and writing. Nevertheless, our decision to write as feminists about feminist theology and thealogy has meant that our intellectual journeys have also always been journeys to the center of ourselves. Pursuing our work and writing has been a matter of finding our own voices and our own power, discoveries that have often brought changes in our lives. We have had the privilege of participating in and helping to create a new area of study within religious studies, an area we believe has the power to transform the discipline, and that is tied to a broader movement for religious and social change that reaches out beyond the walls of the academy. And we have had the pleasure of knowing that our work has spoken to and touched the lives of a great number of women, many of whom have struggled with the same issues we have, but who have lacked the privilege, tools, or leisure to bring their deepest concerns to speech. These are satisfactions we would not readily surrender.

We have worked together on *Weaving the Visions* in much the same way as on *Womanspirit Rising*, with one significant exception. Two major kinds of work that go into an anthology are letter writing and cutting and pasting—work that for *Womanspirit Rising*, we did ourselves. This time, we were able to negotiate an advance that covered the costs of a student assistant. Stacey Kabat, who worked with Carol when Carol taught at Harvard Divinity School, joined us in our project, devoting over a hundred hours to the details of bookmaking. She has therefore been an important participant in the process by which this book came to be. Otherwise, aside from the fact that the task of choosing selections was far more drawn out and agonizing than for *Womanspirit Rising*, we used our time-tried editorial methods. We outlined the introductions together on one of Carol's trips to the United States from Greece, divided up the writing, and made suggestions for revision of each other's work. Judith's name appears first on the title page of this book because Carol's was listed first in *Womanspirit Rising*. In neither case does order represent precedence; both books are fully joint projects. The process of editing *Weaving the Visions* has been prolonged by the difficulties of intercontinental communication, but otherwise has proceeded sufficiently smoothly to enable us to maintain our faith in the possibility of working across religious boundaries.

Stacey Kabat has not been our only helper. We also want to thank our editor Marie Cantlon, whose judgment we have come to respect and trust, Janice Johnson at Harper & Row in San Francisco, who was an enthusiastic advocate of this anthology, and John Loudon, also of Harper & Row, who originally encouraged us to undertake a sequel to *Womanspirit Rising*.

Judith Plaskow
Queens, New York

Carol P. Christ
Míthimna, Lesbos, Greece

Introduction

In the ten years since we wrote the introduction to *Womanspirit Rising*, feminist theology and thealogy have grown by leaps and bounds. Putting together our first anthology did not seem a particularly daunting task. To be sure, there were articles we would have liked to include that we had to leave out for lack of space, and we briefly debated how to organize our materials. But in 1978, there were only a small number of books and essays from which to choose chapters for our collection, and, rightly or wrongly, principles of organization seemed to leap out at us. This time, by way of contrast, we found ourselves confronted with hundreds of books and articles having strong claims on us, and with numerous possible structures into which they might fit. In weighing what to use, we found ourselves searching for balance on many different scales, and—despite the larger size of this book—feeling a much sharper sense of regret about what was excluded.

The challenge and excitement of this enormous growth is that it has represented not simply more writing on familiar subjects but a dramatic broadening and diversification of feminist thealogy and theology. The issues and tensions we described in *Womanspirit Rising* are all still here in *Weaving the Visions*: the criticisms of patriarchal religion, the centrality of women's experience to feminist work, the emphasis on nature and the body, the conflict between reforming established traditions and creating new ones. But these themes are now taken up by such an expanded range of voices that they take on a new character, and many fresh questions come to the fore. The fact that it is now necessary to speak of both theology and thealogy, for example, signals a great blossoming of feminist interest in Goddesses, an interest that has generated so much creative thinking and writing that it is no longer adequate to refer to literature on Goddesses using old terms. At the same time, the emergence of voices of women of color and other minority women has transformed feminist thinking, raising the question of standpoint on every feminist issue. Indeed, the increasing chorus of minority voices has been the single most important development in feminist work in religion in the last ten years. This development necessitates reconceptualizing much early feminist reflection and practice as surely as the appearance of feminism made and continues to make necessary important changes in religion.

BROADENING THE CRITIQUE OF PATRIARCHY

In the introduction to and first section of *Womanspirit Rising*, we presented the essential feminist critique of patriarchal religion as the foundation and impetus for constructive work. Beginning with Valerie Saiving's insight that much theology has been formulated from the perspective of male—rather than universal—experience, we argued that exclusion of women from religious leadership, and explicit teachings on women's subordination in marriage and family are "systematically related to the theological world view of the biblical faith."[1] Rosemary Radford Ruether, in her essay "Motherearth and the Megamachine," elaborated this claim by describing the mind/body, spirit/nature, and male/female dualisms that have deeply shaped Western religious thinking. Mary Daly, in "After the Death of God the Father," examined the ways in which the fundamental Christian symbols of Father God and His Son emerge out of and support sexual hierarchy.

This basic critique and the large amount of further work that has developed and specified it are taken as givens by the authors in this volume. While many of the essays included here allude to or discuss the patriarchal character of Judaism or Christianity, criticisms of patriarchal religion serve largely to highlight or set the stage for the constructive proposals that are at the heart of each essay. The critical edge of this anthology lies not in further elaboration of the sexism of traditional religion, but in the insistence on connecting patriarchy with other types of oppression. For many of the articles in *Weaving the Visions*, Western religion is not simply sexist but racist, imperialist, ethnocentric, and heterosexist as well. These distinct forms of oppression are not separate from or incidental to sexism, but are thoroughly interstructured with it as different aspects of a dualistic and hierarchical religious worldview. As Alice Walker points out, the tall, old, grey-bearded man in the sky who needs to be dethroned is a *white* man, who, like human whites, "never listen[s] to colored." Gloria Anzaldúa and Carol Lee Sanchez argue that patriarchal Christianity destroyed the cultures and religious beliefs of the indigenous peoples of the Americas, and Marija Gimbutas makes an analogous argument for the cultures of Old Europe. E. Ann Matter and Carter Heyward show that the erasure of women's experience that is part of the legacy of patriarchy applies doubly to lesbians, whose experience is rendered invisible by hostility to sexuality as well as hostility to women. Because of the intertwining of these oppressions, and also because women are half of every oppressed group, it is impossible to empower women without addressing and eradicating all forms of oppression.

REDEFINING WOMEN'S EXPERIENCE

The insight that different forms of oppression are interlocking has its constructive analogue in a new and complex understanding of women's experience. In *Womanspirit Rising*, we presented women's experience as an important norm for feminist theology. Recognizing that women's perspectives had not been included in the Jewish or Christian naming of God, human beings, or the world, feminist theology began with women claiming and naming our own experiences and exploring the ways in which incorporating women's experience might transform traditional religion or lead to the creation of new traditions. While women's experience as a starting point and norm remains central to feminist work in religion and to the essays in this volume, our understanding of the meaning and scope of women's experience has expanded and changed.

In the introduction to *Womanspirit Rising*, we delineated two poles within the feminist understanding of women's experience—women's feminist experience and women's traditional experience—and in doing so passed over in silence the enormous variety subsumed under each pole. Although Judith had written elsewhere that "women's experience is as diverse and complex as the experience of the human race," and that "the real impact of our criticism of the universalizing tendency of much theology should be to send us delving more and more deeply into the experiences of all kinds of women,"[2] we did not apply this insight in *Womanspirit Rising*, but often wrote of women's experience in universalizing terms. Ten years later, we recognize that the term "women's experience" too often means "white, middle-class women's experience," in just the way that "human" too often means "male." The work of women of color and other minority women that both criticizes the dominant feminist discourse and names their own experience has made facile generalizations impossible, and we can no longer speak of women's experience as if it were a "Platonic form."[3] To continue using the concept of women's experience under these circumstances obligates us to uncover and describe the diversity it encompasses. The notion of women's experience must be taken as an invitation to explore particularity rather than to homogenize significant differences.

The diversity that constitutes women's experience comprises different experiences of oppression, and also a diversity of positive religious, racial, ethnic, national, and cultural identities that shape our lives as women—identities that come together in holistic and interactive ways. Women's experience and sexism are not constants for every woman to which are added other dimensions of self-definition and oppression. The experience of being a woman is inseparable from being the kind of woman one is.[4] Thus a Native American woman living on a reservation grows into a very different understanding of womanhood from that of a working-class white woman, a rural black woman, or a West Coast Asian American woman. Again and again in the course of this volume, contributors turn to such particularities as a source of knowledge, strength, and possible vision for social change. Katie Geneva Cannon talks about the "moral wisdom" that emerges from the literature of black women, women at the bottom of every hierarchy of oppression. Paula Gunn Allen, Dhyani Ywahoo, and Carol Lee Sanchez discuss the deep respect and love for the earth that they learned through their tribal traditions, attitudes that contain an important message for our ecologically destructive times. Elisabeth Schüssler Fiorenza reclaims early Christian history as women's history in order to empower Christian women in their struggle against oppression, and Rosemary Radford Ruether speaks of critical elements in biblical religion that contradict patriarchy. Audre Lorde describes the power of the erotic in women's lives, a power she came to recognize when she learned to value her experience as a black, lesbian, feminist "in the face of a racist, patriarchal, and anti-erotic society." As Lorde argues in another context, feminists too often have avoided and denied such differences, fearful that difference always entails hierarchy; but difference is also the source of our creativity, the "raw and powerful connection from which our personal power is forged."[5]

When we learn to claim the diversity of women's lives as an important resource and to appreciate the various strategies for survival and resistance that come out of our particular histories, the concept of women's experience takes on new richness and meaning. While this diversity of experience can be disturbing because it threatens to disrupt the sense of sisterhood so newly discovered, sisterhood is not a reality when it is predicated on the experience of only a small group of women. If we wish to speak of and act on the commonalities that link women together, to discover where our joint interests lie in vision and in struggle, we must do so on the basis of long and careful listening to the pains and satisfactions of many women's lives. The full reality of "women's experience" is contained not in any one voice but in the rising chorus that speaks from many standpoints, pressing toward the creation of a society in which all can be heard.[6]

METHODOLOGICAL DIVERSITY

Not only is the range of women's experiences more diverse in this volume than in *Womanspirit Rising*, but also the methodologies, voices, and forms of expression are far more varied. In our earlier book, there were essays, and then there were rituals. In this volume, there is no simple distinction between discursive or linear writing, and writing that is nondiscursive, meditative, or poetic. Meditations and rituals are inspired by or become occasions for reflection, and midrash bursts out from theology. More writing contains autobiographical elements. More nonlinear modes of discourse are represented. While in part, this diversity reflects our decision to include material by nonacademics, use of autobiographical or nonlinear forms of expression does not break down neatly along academic/nonacademic lines. Moreover, our decision to include material by writers and activists itself reflects the fact that what counts as resources for feminist spirituality is very broad. That Shug and Celie's dialogue on God in Alice Walker's *The Color Purple* is one of the most widely quoted feminist theological texts indicates that feminist theology is not defined by what happens in the academy but draws on a wide range of sources that allow women's experiences to emerge.

This diversity presents a *formal* challenge to the canons of scholarly objectivity that have controlled academic writing. Elisabeth Schüssler Fiorenza, in her essay, criticizes the traditional assumption that the content of historical work can be free from ideological and societal interests. Since historiography, she says, is always a selective view of the past based on some framing perspective and values, historians who claim to be recording pure facts "succeed only in concealing from themselves the ideologies upon which their historiography is based." The plurality of styles and methods that characterizes this book extends her criticism to the forms of academic work. If, as Beverly Harrison and Audre Lorde so brilliantly argue, we recognize that all knowledge is mediated through the body and that feeling is a profound source of information about our lives, then feminist scholarship may have to challenge the boundaries not just between "objective," and "committed" scholarship but "impersonal" and "personal" scholarship as well. Writing addressed to embodied selves may call for different forms and strategies than writing addressed to dispassionate intellects.

The inclusion of personal experience in feminist work is also a way of addressing the critique of false universalism, and as such is closely allied with the emphasis on diversity and particularity in women's experience. Acknowledging the personal sources of our work, rather than writing about women's experience abstractly and in the third person, may save us from false generalizations, from defining women's experience in a univocal way. As Carol says in another context, "If we are more clear about why we each think the way we do, we may be less likely to label or dismiss or misunderstand the work of other feminists whose work comes from different histories."[7] Moreover, although this may seem paradoxical, it is often through the personal, through the articulation of particularity and what seems to be difference, that connection and universality are suddenly revealed. Indeed, one of the early insights of feminist theology was that, like a good novel, poem, or play, theology best illumines the universal in human experience through attention to the details of human life.[8] Just as feminists criticized the universalizing tendencies of dominant (male) theologies, so we have turned the critique on ourselves and are struggling to acknowledge the particularity of our experience through the forms as well as the content of our writing.

There are dangers, of course, in the personal and nonlinear modes of expression included in this volume. To acknowledge our personal standpoints and experience is to risk being misunderstood about things we hold dear and feel vulnerable about. To choose to violate standards of scholarly objectivity by writing in a way that speaks to the whole self rather than the head is to run the often costly risks of scholarly depreciation or academic dismissal. This book, in choosing to affirm these risks, in including a diversity of voices and methods, poses a stronger challenge to the academy than did *Womanspirit Rising*. It questions not only the content of much religious thought, but asks who is doing that thinking, what counts as theology, and how theology is being done. In doing so, it joins a growing insistence among feminists that feminism entails the transformation of traditional processes of writing, teaching, learning, and thinking; and that this transformation is inextricably connected to the subversion of the substance of patriarchal thought.[9]

DIVERSITY AND DIVISION

While the new diversity of voice and method has been a creative and exciting development in feminist work in religion, there is no question but that it has also brought with it anger and division. In the introduction to *Womanspirit Rising*, we talked about "tensions" in feminist theology: tensions between different views of women's experience, tensions between those who would reconstruct traditional religion and those who would create new religious forms, tensions between those who would name and celebrate women's body experience and those who would emphasize women's transcendence and freedom. These and other tensions have not only survived the decade but have festered and sometimes erupted into conflict as feminists have questioned each other's allegiances and choices, and as institutional resources have increasingly aligned themselves behind certain alternatives and not others.

We recognize now that we contributed to these tensions by using the categories "reformist" and "revolutionary" to structure our previous book. Although we acknowledged the difficulties of drawing clear boundaries between those engaged in trying to transform established traditions and those who see Judaism and Christianity as irreformably sexist, the terms seemed to some feminists to reify the separation between the two groups and to endow the separation with a centrality that it does not deserve. Moreover, despite our explicit protestations to the contrary, some women experienced the distinction as a hierarchical one. Revolutionaries, the word seemed to imply, are more radical and therefore "better" than reformists.

With hindsight, some of the problems with the reformist/revolutionary dichotomy are clearer to us. Aside from the issues just mentioned, the range of views within the so-called reformist camp is itself so large that the term disguises as much as it reveals. In *Womanspirit Rising*, we described a reformist as one who sees a liberating core within Judaism or Christianity and who is calling her tradition back to that essential truth. But even in *Womanspirit Rising*, and certainly in this volume, there are "reformists" who strongly reject this position, sharing the "revolutionary" view that many ideas and symbols of Western religions are profoundly patriarchal. These feminists are interested not in reforming tradition but in transforming it, in fundamentally rethinking and restructuring traditional institutions, symbols, and ideas. The diversity of views among "reformists" suggests that a continuum model of feminist positions in religion might be more appropriate than the dichotomous one we proposed.

At the same time that we recognize that the distinction between reformists and revolutionaries needs to be made far more subtle, we are also increasingly aware that loyalty to or rejection of tradition is not the only way to categorize differences among feminists in religion. Carter Heyward, for example, has suggested that an important dividing line between feminists is whether one recognizes the structural character of oppression and sees the world as changing through action or ideas. While some feminists see sexism as rooted in attitudes and opinions that can be changed through education and consciousness raising, others would argue that social change happens only through restructuring social institutions and redistributing power.[10] Sheila Greeve Davaney has argued that the reformist/revolutionary dichotomy obscures the similarity between many members of both groups who assume that feminist aspirations reflect divine purpose or universal truth. The key issue for her is whether feminists are willing to relativize their own truths claims even as they unmask the pretensions of patriarchal claims to truth.[11]

These different possible ways of looking at feminist theology and thealogy suggest the limitations of categorization—but also the usefulness of categorization if it is carefully applied. Any particular set of categories will obscure some differences even as it illuminates others, will bring certain issues to the fore for exploration and discussion, but subordinate others that might be equally important and fruitful. Categories are helpful if they are taken as one angle of vision on a particular subject. Thus, while we would no longer use the terms reformist and revolutionary, we would still insist that the distinction names a real division between and within women. The question of whether to struggle in relation to Judaism or Christianity or to focus on alternative resources for women's spirituality both divides us ideologically and institutionally and remains a deeply-felt personal issue for many women.

While significant differences in perspective and method may themselves be sufficient reason for division among feminists, it must also be said that the institutions that employ feminists in religion have contributed to the discord within feminist thealogy and theology by playing "patriarchal policeman"—rewarding certain kinds of scholarship and certain decisions about religious commitment, even as they punish others. Often women who do "objective" scholarly work on women's issues have an easier time finding jobs and keeping them than do woman who do committed feminist work. Feminists who remain within the Christian tradition have seminary jobs available to them that are closed to similarly trained women who choose to leave the church. Jewish feminists who use the term Goddess immediately cut themselves off from legitimacy and job opportunities in the Jewish community. Feminists who come out as lesbians or do work in lesbian theory have had speaking engagements canceled and job interviews withheld. The list could go on and on. We would simply mention that it is no coincidence that the women's spirituality movement and neopagan thealogy have developed largely outside any institutional context. Not only church- and synagogue-supported institutions, but also academic ones, have been largely unwilling to expand their canons to include areas of research and teaching inspired by the women's spirituality movement.

Especially given the very real economic and institutional rewards and punishments that attend different kinds of feminist work, the way we view and treat each other as feminists becomes a significant ethical issue. In a structural context in which it is possible to secure one's own position by attacking women whose work is perceived as more radical or threatening, we need to find ways of disagreeing and calling each other to account that do not feed into patriarchal boundary making and methods of control.[12] For example, before criticizing or even characterizing another feminist's position publicly, we ought to do everything we can to insure that we have understood that position clearly and are describing it accurately. Instead of reading each other's work in the worst possible light, we should assume that we are engaged in a common project of working toward more just and human religious and social institutions, and we should speak to that in each other which shares this common goal. Perhaps most important, we need to be aware of our own writing and commitments as small pieces in a larger mosaic of struggle that will require many different kinds of contributions for a just society to emerge. As Sharon Welch argues in her article, we ought to theorize boldly but hold our theory lightly, because we will need more than ideological correctness to defeat the forces of sexism, racism, imperialism, and class domination at work in our world.

THEOLOGY IN A DIFFERENT VOICE

Because of these institutionally reinforced separations among feminists, we have chosen to organize this book thematically rather than to emphasize particular religious, sexual, racial, or ethnic divisions that characterize feminist thought. The purpose of this structure is not to homogenize the differences among feminists or come up with some universal feminist perspective on central religious questions. On the contrary, we want precisely to communicate the diversity of voice, content, method, and perspective that marks feminist consideration of a number of significant themes. It is true, however, that the commonality of concerns among feminists in religion impresses us as deeply as the different ways of addressing these concerns. Setting side by side varied approaches to the same question provides an opportunity to learn through difference, to see the fullness of an issue emerge from the range of ways in which feminists interpret and tease it out. Placing E. Ann Matter and Luisah Teish together on reclaiming women's history suggests something of the wide range of meaning that reclaiming a heritage can have. Juxtaposing Delores Williams, Ellen Umansky, and Rita Nakashima Brock on community clarifies the ways in which different communities both nurture and limit their members, providing resources for survival and change and also erecting boundaries within which change must occur. Seeing "the other" grappling with familiar issues, we find unexpected insights into ourselves.

The themes we have chosen as our organizing framework are based on the traditional theological categories of history, God, man, and world, but we significantly transform these categories. We begin with an initial section called "Our Heritage Is Our Power" (history), followed by "Naming the Sacred" ("God"), "Self in Relation" ("man"), and "Transforming the World" (world). Thus it is clear that this volume deals not with "women's issues" that can be safely tucked away on the margins of theological or thealogical discourse, but with the fundamental naming of ourselves, the universe, and the sacred powers that sustain us. It addresses basic theological questions "in a different voice," bringing to articulation the insights and passions of women's experience as it intersects with the particularities of religion, race, ethnicity, and sexual orientation.

Many of the issues central to this volume were present already in *Womanspirit Rising*—the need for a positive past with which feminists can identify, the search for new ways to image and speak about the sacred, the effort to redefine the self and to transform a patriarchal world. But as befits the passage of ten years filled with lively experimentation, these issues are now addressed with greater sophistication and precision by a wider range of voices, so that continuing themes take on new aspects and new developments emerge. Thus in *Woman-spirit Rising*, explorations of the past focused on the Christian past, with brief forays into Gnosticism and Goddess religion. In this book, the Christian past is relativized as the concept of women's heritage is expanded. The essays in the first section deal with Christianity, but also with Native American and African traditions, Goddess religion, and Judaism. Not only is the past defined more broadly, but also the methods for reclaiming women's heritages are more diverse. While feminist historiography remains an important tool for recovering the lost stories of women, oral traditions passed on from grandmother to granddaughter, creation of feminist myth and midrash, ritual invocation of and connection with the ancestors take their place alongside historiography as significant and empowering modes of remembering.

In *Womanspirit Rising*, articles on naming the sacred focused largely on the problem of male imagery and on the need for a new female language to replace or balance traditional forms. Two chapters argued for female God-language in a Jewish context, and another explored "Why Women Need the Goddess." In this book, authors who write on female language are concerned not so much to defend its necessity or legitimacy as to explore its implications and meaning. When even the relatively traditional *Inclusive Language Lectionary* addresses God as Father and Mother, a theologian like Sallie McFague is freer to describe and refine the many dimensions of the mother image. When post-traditional thealogians like Nelle Morton and Christine Downing examine the many different levels on which Goddess symbols function, a Christian thinker like Rosemary Radford Ruether can name the sacred as God/ess, knowing she speaks to a broad group of women. The articles in this book also move beyond the issue of female language to the question of how God or Goddess is conceptualized. Recognizing that female as well as male images can perpetuate models of domination and power-over, feminists both in and outside traditional religions are seeking ways to imagine sacred power as present in the whole complex web of life, not as power-taker but as empowerer. Indeed, the issue of the *nature* of Goddess or God has really come to take precedence over the issue of gender—a development made possible because ten year's use of female imagery in liturgy and ritual has pointed the way to deeper questions.

The section on self is the most unwieldy part of this volume, indicating the tremendous burgeoning of interest in feminist perspectives on the nature of human selfhood. Familiar issues are developed in new directions, and a number of new emphases are sounded. The traditional association of women with nature and the body—an issue central in *Womanspirit Rising*—remains important in this book, but contributors have more clearly moved beyond simple reclaiming of the neglected side of the traditional mind/body dualism to articulate a fuller view of the embodied character of human existence. Audre Lorde, Beverly Wildung Harrison, and Naomi R. Goldenberg all, in different ways, set forth conceptions of selfhood that root consciousness in bodily feeling and passion without reducing consciousness to the body or neglecting the connection of body to spiritual and intellectual life. Moreover, since embodied experience is always spatially located, the emphasis on embodiment connects with a new issue that comes to the fore in this volume—the importance of relationship in women's experience. Feminist writers in a variety of disciplines have been examining the "pull to relation" among women—relation to particular others, to communities of origin and choice, and to a wider web of connectedness that encompasses the earth. It is in the context of this theme of relation that the significance of particularity—an implicit issue throughout the book— receives sustained attention as several authors discuss their relation to distinct communities that have shaped their identity, challenging and providing resources for feminist thealogical work. A number of essays in this section also develop theologies of connection in both communal and cosmic contexts, arguing, in Beverly Harrison's words, that "relationality is at the heart of all things."

Many of the essays in *Weaving the Visions* could easily have fit into a number of sections, but we were seeking a balance of themes and types of diversity within each quarter of the book. Nowhere is the arbitrariness of our boundaries clearer, however, than in the last section, "Transforming the World," which might well serve as the title for the whole volume. While all the authors in this book see their work as contributing to the creation of new ways of seeing and acting in the world, certain essays focus on particular issues or strategies for individual and social transformation in a way that helps to highlight this dimension of all feminist work. In relation to this subject, as with all the others, the extent to which feminist spirituality has developed in the last ten years is striking. Feminist ritual making and literary and biblical textual analysis are applied to specific issues of racism, nuclearism, violence against women, and ecological crisis, clarifying the relation between feminist spiritual transformation and the transformation of the social order. The insistence on connecting sexism with other sorts of oppression that characterizes this last section ties the broader emphasis on diversity to the many specific areas of social change that claim feminist attention—areas that finally come together in the project to end all forms of domination and create a society in which diversity is nourished and respected across sex, race, class, national, and species lines.

DIVERSITY AND UNITY

The idea of a society that honors difference at the same time it recognizes the fundamental character of relation brings us to the vision with which we want to end. In *Womanspirit Rising*, we argued that the tensions within feminist theology are creative and exhilarating and that "the fundamental commitment that feminists in religion share to end male ascendency in society and religion is more important than [our] differences." Today, we are more aware of the element of naïveté in that optimism and of the very real divisions—rather than "tensions"— that seem to undermine a feminist alliance. The work of women of color and other minority women has made very clear that the continuing existence of racism, heterosexism, class oppression, imperialism, and anti-Semitism *within* feminist theory and practice raises serious questions about whether all feminists share a common vision. If the struggle to end male ascendency is just one dimension of the struggle to end all forms of social and political domination, feminists as a group do not clearly share an analysis of the interconnections between patriarchy and other forms of oppression. Black feminist Renita Weems has asked whether feminists mean the same things when we talk about evil, sin, accountability, love, and justice.[13] We recognize the importance of this searching question, and we know that in the past, the answer has often been "no."

Despite the deep-seated nature of the divisions among feminists, we are unwilling to relinquish either our affirmation of diversity or our belief in the importance of solidarity among those working to transform ourselves, religion, and our world. In this time of both crisis and rising social and religious conservatism in the United States and other parts of the globe, it is urgent that those committed to religious and social change find ways to build bridges to each other as we work on the particular projects that claim our primary energy and attention. As feminists affirming embodiment, we must recognize that we cannot each make all issues our priority, and those that seem most urgent to us will likely be connected to our own histories and identities. We can, however, cultivate and act on awareness of the connection between our own oppression and that of others, so that feminist work for social transformation does not entail any group's domination or rest on ignorance and neglect of others' experience. In this sense, the increasing diversity of feminist religious discourse calls us to responsibility and to deeper listening, to a commitment to inclusiveness that at the same time allows individual and communal differences to emerge. We believe that this commitment, present now and again in reality and always as a hope, remains a base point for feminist theological and thealogical reflection, animating our sometimes tear-filled, angry, joyful, always lively conversations, and pointing us to a vision of transformation that includes each one of us and the entire web of life.

NOTES

1. Carol P. Christ and Judith Plaskow, "Introduction: Womanspirit Rising," in *Womanspirit Rising: A Feminist Reader in Religion* (San Francisco: Harper & Row, 1979), 4.

2. Judith Plaskow, "The Feminist Transformation of Theology," in *Beyond Androcentrism: New Essays on Women and Religion*, ed. Rita M. Gross (Missoula, MT: Scholars Press, 1977), 26, 27.

3. Carol P. Christ, *Laughter of Aphrodite: Reflections on a Journey to the Goddess* (San Francisco: Harper & Row, 1987), xv.

4. Elizabeth V. Spelman, "Theories of Race and Gender: The Erasure of Black Women," *Quest: A Feminist Quarterly* 5 (1982): 42–46; and *Inessential Woman: Problems of Exclusion in Feminist Theory* (Boston: Beacon Press, 1988).

5. Audre Lorde, "Age, Race, Class, and Sex: Women Redefining Difference" and "The Master's Tools Will Never Dismantle the Master's House," in *Sister Outsider* (Trumansburg, NY: The Crossing Press, 1984), 118, 112.

6. Obviously this anthology takes just a first step in recording this diversity, even in the context of the United States. Issues of class, for example, have not yet been widely addressed as a distinct subject by feminist theologians, and there is therefore no essay on class in this volume. The same is true of many other forms of oppression and other particular identities.

7. Christ, *Laughter of Aphrodite*, xv.

8. Sheila Collins, *A Different Heaven and Earth* (Valley Forge, PA: Judson Press, 1974), 44.

9. See, for example, The Mud Flower Collective, *God's Fierce Whimsey: Christian Feminism and Theological Education* (New York: Pilgrim Press, 1985); Patricia Shechter and respondents, "A Vision of Feminist Religious Scholarship," *Journal of Feminist Studies in Religion* 3 (Spring 1987): 91–111; Emily Culpepper, "Philosophia: Feminist Methodology for Constructing a Female Train of Thought," *Journal of Feminist Studies in Religion* 3 (Fall 1987): 7–16. The fact that the first two references are collective efforts is itself an important indication of new method.

10. Carter Heyward, "Introduction to Feminist Theology: A Christian Feminist Perspective" and "Ruether and Daly: Speaking and Sparking/Building and Burning," in *Our Passion for Justice: Images of Power, Sexuality and Liberation* (New York: Pilgrim Press, 1984), 55–68, 222–29.

11. Sheila Greeve Davaney, "Problems with Feminist Theory: Historicity and the Search for Sure Foundations," in *Embodied Love: Sensuality and Relationship as Feminist Values*, ed. Paula Cooey, Sharon Farmer, and Mary Ellen Ross (San Francisco: Harper & Row, 1987), 79–95.

12. Emily Culpepper addresses this issue in "Contemporary Goddess Thealogy: A Sympathetic Critique," in *Shaping New Vision: Gender and Values in American Culture*, ed. Clarissa Atkinson, Constance Buchanan, Margaret Miles (Ann Arbor, MI: UMI Research Press, 1987), 53, 56.

13. Roundtable discussion on "Racism in the Women's Movement," *Journal of Feminist Studies in Religion* 4 (Spring 1988): 108.

Part 1

OUR HERITAGE IS OUR POWER

Our Heritage Is Our Power

This section opens with Paula Gunn Allen's evocation of the Grandmothers of the North American land and closes with Luisah Teish's eloquent and practical assertion that our wholeness depends on honoring our spiritual connections with our personal ancestors. In between we are given glimpses of empowering history in more distant pasts. The authors in this section agree that our heritage is our power, but they hold different views of what heritage is "ours." Some argue that authenticity is to be found in allegiance to the biblical pasts, while others reject biblical religions and seek heritages both nearer and more distant. Recovering the history of women is no simple task because so many resources have been lost or destroyed. The histories of women and female leadership have for the most part been excluded from the Jewish and Christian Bibles. The history of lesbians has been further obscured by biases against sexuality and homosexuality. Those attempting to recreate the histories of women and female power within traditions conquered by Christianity face an even more difficult task: the resources they need have often been destroyed not only by Christians, but also by pre-Christian patriarchal groups, such as, for example, the Indo-Europeans and the Aztecs.

Perhaps in part because of the scarcity of resources for recovering women's heritages, the authors in this section employ a variety of methods. Some rely on written or archaeological evidence, while others freely invoke personal memory or imagination to fill gaps in the androcentric record. While these differences in method are significant, they should not be taken as absolute. All agree that the history we have inherited is not objective, that it contains gaps and distortions created by the androcentric and other biases of those who have had the power to write history. Judith Plaskow speaks for many others when she writes that historiographical reconstruction of the past must be complemented by storytelling and by ritual celebration. The diversity found in these feminist constructions of empowering history is both exciting and potentially divisive. While the dream of a common history remains elusive, the resources and methods for claiming our heritage as our power are astonishing and stimulating in their richness.

This section begins with Paula Gunn Allen's "Grandmother of the Sun" because we agree with Allen and her sister Carol Lee Sanchez that healing the North American people and our land requires that we learn to honor the spirits of the American land, the Native American Grandmothers, to whom "we owe our very breath." We who live on the North American land are all heirs to an educational and cultural system that has taught us that the original human inhabitants of our land were ignorant savages and that the land and the beings who live upon it are material to conquer and exploit. Many Indians and non-Indians are discovering resources in Native American traditions that can help us learn again to live in harmony with the earth and its creatures.

Paula Gunn Allen uncovers a rich heritage in Native American religion, reminding us that for many Native Americans all things proceed from Thought Woman, the "power of intelligence," whose other names include Old Spider Woman, Serpent Woman, Corn Woman, and Earth Woman (note the similarities to Arachne, the Cretan Snake Goddess, Demeter and Persephone, Gaia). Allen states that tribal women valued their roles as "vitalizers," whose power was not only to give birth, but to "make, to create, to transform." Her view of the role of women and female imagery in Native American religion contrasts sharply with racist and androcentric popular images and differs from much contemporary scholarship about Native Americans. Allen notes that Native American myths were distorted by those who first wrote them down, in order to make them conform more closely to European and Christian patrifocal conventions. In reconstructing the myths and history of Native Americans, Allen often relies on information she has gained through oral tradition, from her mother and grandmother.

Elisabeth Schüssler Fiorenza clearly sets forth the argument for a "feminist critical" approach to the past: androcentric or male-centered traditions and sources cannot be trusted as providing a reliable—factual or true—history. Her approach is feminist in that it begins with the assumption that women have been active agents—not merely passive victims—in the historical process. Her approach is critical because it unmasks the male-centered biases of so-called "value neutral," "scientific," "objective" scholarship. Though feminists have been accused of being "biased towards women" and "having a point to prove," the feminist critical approach reminds us that all history is written from a particular perspective with certain goals in mind. Feminist scholarship becomes a model urging all scholars forthrightly to acknowledge the perspectives or biases that shape their work. Schüssler Fiorenza also criticizes the biases found in the texts that provide so-called "primary" data for the historian. The Greek Bible or Christian New Testament is, she claims, the product of androcentric imagination. We will discover the history of women in the early Christian movement, she argues, not by accepting the Bible as it stands, but by reading between the lines of the texts to uncover a history of women that the biblical writers themselves attempted to suppress. Schüssler Fiorenza's interpretation of the anointing of Jesus' feet by a woman as a "prophetic sign-action" that was originally an anointing of Jesus' head, is a tantalizing example of her contention that the biblical writers distorted the history they had inherited.

Judith Plaskow applies Schüssler Fiorenza's feminist critical approach to the history of Jewish women. Appalled by the invisibility of women "at the central moment of Jewish history," the founding of the covenant, she maintains that the words of the biblical text contradict women's experience of "the certainty of our membership in our own people." Plaskow expands the notion of feminist history through a consideration of the process of remembering in the Jewish tradition. Jewish memory, Plaskow argues, has always been dynamic: the past is imaginatively reinterpreted and embellished in response to the questions of different historical periods. Seeking to recover living memory, Jewish storytellers have not been bound by the conventions of modern historiography. While modern historical method may restore pieces of history to Jewish women, even these must be filtered through contemporary consciousness for their significance as living memory to be understood. Where historical method produces gaps, Plaskow suggests that "midrashic" or storytelling methods and experiments in ritual and liturgy may allow the recovery of memories that would otherwise be lost.

Such an approach might be dismissed as subjective, allowing each woman to imaginatively recreate her own view of the past. But other essays in this volume suggest that inspiration and community provide limits to personal whim. Sarah's version of the sacrifice of Isaac told by Ellen M. Umansky in "Creating a Jewish Feminist Theology" was "received" in the context of communal prayer and meditation. Plaskow's well-known retelling of "The Coming of Lilith" reprinted in *Womanspirit Rising* was created in a communal setting and has been widely used in feminist liturgies. Charlene Spretnak's retellings of the myths of the lost Goddesses of early Greece have been embraced by communities who tell and enact them in feminist rituals.

E. Ann Matter is one of the first scholars to ask a question that has remained shrouded in silence: were there lesbians in the female religious communities of Christian Europe? Because many medieval women were illiterate, and because the church was hostile to sexuality, this question is difficult to answer. Nonetheless, Matter uncovers several poems and letters expressing passionate feelings between women. Whether these women were physically as well as emotionally intimate remains an open question, though Matter notes that even today many feminists do not limit the word "lesbian" to women who engage in genital sexuality with other women. In the penitential literature of the period, Matter finds lesbian sexuality given less frequent attention than male homosexuality, with the strongest condemnations of female homosexuals reserved for "sex between women involving imitation of male genitalia." The data Matter considers is sparse, but suggestive of love and longing between women in the convents. The recent volume *Lesbian Nuns: Breaking the Silence* documents the existence of lesbian sexuality in religious communities in the twentieth century, and Matter's research suggests that love between religiously committed women may have a long history.

Marija Gimbutas, an archaeologist who has directed numerous digs, coined the term Old Europe to define the cultures of the Neolithic, or New Stone Age, and Chalcolithic, or Copper Age, in the settled agricultural villages and towns of eastern and southern Europe c. 6500–3500 B.C.E. The inhabitants of Old Europe left no written records, and therefore the culture can only be understood through analysis of physical evidence. Though Western scholars often confine historical knowledge to the written word, the remains of houses, temples, graves, and the rich and highly stylized artistic and symbolic legacy of Old Europe speak eloquently to the trained eye. Limiting history to the written word serves patriarchal interests because societies for which there are substantial and decipherable written records were and are patriarchal: some feminists have even suggested that writing developed as a mode of social control in hierarchical societies.

According to Gimbutas, Old Europe was prosperous, settled, artistic, peaceful, and dominated by the symbol of the great Goddess in her dual aspect as Creatress, or Giver and Taker of All, and as the principle of Regeneration and Renewal. In Old Europe, there is no evidence of military organization, one of the hallmarks of patriarchal cultures, and there is no other evidence that women were in any way subordinate. Gimbutas's description of Old Europe is strikingly similar to Paula Gunn Allen's view of Native American society, to Gloria Anzaldúa's depiction of prepatriarchal Mesoamerica, and to Rita Nakashima Brock's suggestions about ancient Japan. Gimbutas states that the cultures of Old Europe were overthrown by pre–Indo-European and Indo-European patriarchal warrior groups who began their invasions about 4400 B.C.E. Though Gimbutas's methodology is implicitly rather that explicitly feminist, her conclusion that patriarchy is not a universal social structure and that the female images of Old Europe are more than mute fertility figurines or idols has provoked the ire of more androcentrically inclined archaeologists and historians of religion.

Building on the work of Gimbutas and other scholars, Charlene Spretnak imaginatively re-creates the pre-Hellenic (pre–Indo-European) myths of Greece. According to Spretnak, the major sources for popular and scholarly views of the Greek Goddesses—Homer, Hesiod, and the *Homeric Hymns*—are patriarchal reworkings of earlier female-centered myths. In retelling the myth of Demeter and Persephone, Spretnak rejects the familiar "rape of Persephone" by the God of the Underworld, viewing the story of the Mother and Daughter Goddesses who rule over the Upper and Underworlds as authentic legacies of earlier matrifocal cultures. Persephone's concern for the dead expresses the sense of connection with ancestors found in many traditional cultures, including the African traditions discussed by Luisah Teish.

For Gloria Anzaldúa, an empowering heritage is found in the pre-Christian and prepatriarchal elements of the Mesoamerican past she inherited through the "folk Catholicism with many pagan elements" of her grandmother and the Chicano community of South Texas. Anzaldúa's experiences of serpents led her to study the histories of the Mesoamerican Goddess Coatlicue, or Serpent Skirt, whose name is similar to the Indian name for the Virgin of Guadalupe. Like other authors in this section, Anzaldúa finds the history of the Goddess suppressed not only by (Spanish) Christianity, but also by the earlier Mesoamerican conquerors, the militaristic and patriarchal Aztecs. "Entering into the serpent" for Anzaldúa not only means recovering an ancient image of female power, but also, learning to trust the messages of her body and spirit, her psychic powers and her dreams, which the Christian and rational culture of her education had taught her to despise.

Luisah Teish, a priestess of Oshun in the Yoruba Lucumi tradition, re-creates rituals of African and Afro-American ancestor reverence. She suggests that an empowering history may be found in the recent past of our immediate ancestors, great-grandparents, grandparents, and parents, without whom we would not be. The sense of connection to ancestors is implicit in all attempts to find an empowering history. Several of the authors in this section speak of the spirituality of their mothers and grandmothers. Even the God of Israel is known as "our fathers' God" and Christians sing "Faith of our Fathers." Yet the biblically based religions have taught us to worship "God, not man," and have often interpreted veneration of ancestors as pagan superstition. North American culture's enchantment with so-called progress has led many to view their immediate ancestors as "old-fashioned." Thus the notion of building an altar to honor the ancestors may seem odd to many. Yet for African-based, as well as many other religions, the dead and living are bound in an ongoing relation more vital and personal than that commonly understood by the Jewish notion of "all Israel" and the Christian notion of "the community of saints." Teish's instructions for creating ancestor rituals provide the opportunity for others to learn that reclaiming an empowering history begins at home.

Grandmother of the Sun

The Power of Woman in Native America

PAULA GUNN ALLEN

There is a spirit that pervades everything, that is capable of powerful song and radiant movement, and that moves in and out of the mind. The colors of this spirit are multitudinous, a glowing, pulsing rainbow. Old Spider Woman is one name for this quintessential spirit, and Serpent Woman is another. Corn Woman is one aspect of her, and Earth Woman is another, and what they together have made is called Creation, Earth, creatures, plants, and light.

At the center of all is Woman, and no thing is sacred (cooked, ripe, as the Keres Indians of Laguna Pueblo say it) without her blessing, her thinking.

... In the beginning Tse che nako, Thought Woman finished everything, thoughts, and the names of all things. She finished also all the languages. And then our mothers, Uretsete and Naotsete said they would make names and they would make thoughts. Thus they said. Thus they did.[1]

This spirit, this power of intelligence, has many names and many emblems. She appears on the plains, in the forests, in the great canyons, on the mesas, beneath the seas. To her we owe our very breath, and to her our prayers are sent blown on pollen, on corn meal, planted into the earth on feather-sticks, spit onto the water, burned and sent to her on the wind. Her variety and multiplicity testify to her complexity: she is the true Creatrix for she is thought itself, from which all else is born. She is the necessary precondition for material creation, and she, like all of her creation, is fundamentally female—potential and primary.

She is also the spirit that informs right balance, right harmony, and these in turn order all relationships in conformity with her law.

To assign to this great being the position of "fertility goddess" is exceedingly demeaning: it trivializes the tribes and it trivializes the power of woman. Woman bears, that is true. She also destroys. That

---

Paula Gunn Allen, a Laguna Pueblo/Sioux Indian, teaches Native American Studies at the University of California, Berkeley. She is author of several books of poetry, the novel *The Woman Who Owned the Shadows*, and *The Sacred Hoop: Recovering the Feminine in American Indian Traditions*.

is true. She also wars and hexes and mends and breaks. She creates the power of the seeds, and she plants them. As Anthony Purley, a Laguna writer, has translated a Keres ceremonial prayer, "She is mother of us all, after Her, mother earth follows, in fertility, in holding, and taking again us back to her breast."[2]

The Hopi account of their genatrix, Hard Beings Woman, gives the most articulate rendering of the difference between simple fertility cultism and the creative prowess of the Creatrix. Hard Beings Woman (Huruing Wuhti) is of the earth. But she lives in the worlds above where she "owns" (empowers) the moon and stars. Hard Beings Woman has solidity and hardness as her major aspects. She, like Thought Woman, does not give birth to creation or to human beings but breathes life into male and female effigies that become the parents of the Hopi—in this way she "creates" them. The male is Muingwu, the god of crops, and his sister-consort is Sand Altar Woman who is also known as Childbirth Water Woman. In Sand Altar Woman the mystical relationship between water, worship, and woman is established; she is also said to be the mother of the katsinas, those powerful messengers who relate the spirit world to the world of humankind and vice versa.[3]

Like Thought Woman, Hard Beings Woman lived in the beginning on an island which was the only land there was. In this regard she resembles a number of Spirit Woman Beings; the Spirit genatrix of the Iroquois, Sky Woman, also lived on an island in the void which only later became the earth. On this island, Hard Beings Woman is identified with or, as they say, "owns" all hard substances—moon, stars, beads, coral, shell, and so forth. She is a sea goddess as well, the single inhabitant of the earth, that island that floats alone in the waters of space. From this meeting of woman and water, earth and her creatures were born.[4] . . .

Contemporary Indian tales suggest that the creatures are born from the mating of sky father and earth mother, but that seems to be a recent interpolation of the original sacred texts. The revision may have occurred since the Christianizing influence on even the arcane traditions, or it may have predated Christianity. But the older, more secret texts suggest that it is a revision. It may be that the revision appears only in popular versions of the old mythic cycles on which ceremony and ritual are based; this would accord with the penchant in the old oral tradition for shaping tales to reflect present social realities, making the rearing and education of children possible even within the divergent worlds of the United States of America and the tribes.

According to the older texts (which are sacred, that is, power-engendering), Thought Woman is not a passive personage: her potentiality is dynamic and unimaginably powerful. She brought corn and agriculture, potting, weaving, social systems, religion, ceremony, ritual, building, memory, intuition, and their expressions in language, creativity, dance, human-to-animal relations, and she gave these offerings power and authority and blessed the people with the ability to provide for themselves and their progeny.

Thought Woman is not limited to a female role in the total theology of the Keres people. Since she is the supreme Spirit, she is both Mother and Father to all people and to all creatures. She is the only creator of thought, and thought precedes creation.[5]

Central to Keres theology is the basic idea of the Creatrix as She Who Thinks rather than She Who Bears, of woman as creation thinker and female thought as origin of material and nonmaterial reality. In this epistemology, the perception of female power as confined to maternity is a limit on the power inherent in femininity. But "she is the supreme Spirit, . . . both Mother and Father to all people and to all creatures."[6] . . .

In Keres theology the creation does not take place through copulation. In the beginning existed Thought Woman and her dormant sisters, and Thought Woman thinks creation and sings her two sisters into life. After they are vital she instructs them to sing over the items in their baskets (medicine bundles) in such a way that those items will have life. After that crucial task is accomplished, the creatures thus vitalized take on the power to regenerate themselves—that is, they can reproduce others of their kind. But they are not in and of themselves self-sufficient; they depend for their being on the medicine power of the three great Witch creatrixes, Thought Woman, Uretsete, and Naotsete. The sisters are not related by virtue of having parents in common; that is, they are not alive because anyone bore them. Thought Woman turns up, so to speak, first as Creatrix and then as a personage who is acting out someone else's "dream." But there is no time when she did not exist. She has two bundles in her power, and these bundles contain Uretsete and Naotsete, who are not viewed as her daughters but as her sisters, her coequals who possess the medicine power to vitalize the creatures that will inhabit the earth. They also have the power to create the firmament, the skies, the galaxies, and the seas, which they do through the use of ritual magic.

The idea that Woman is possessed of great medicine power is elaborated in the Lakota myth of White Buffalo Woman. She brought the Sacred Pipe to the Lakota, and it is through the agency of this pipe that the ceremonies and rituals of the Lakota are empowered.[7] Without the pipe, no ritual magic can occur. According to one story about White Buffalo Woman, she lives in a cave where she presides over the Four Winds.[8] In Lakota ceremonies, the four wind directions are always acknowledged, usually by offering a pipe to them. The pipe is ceremonial, modeled after the Sacred Pipe given the people by the Sacred Woman. The Four Winds are very powerful beings themselves, but they can function only at the bidding of White Buffalo Woman. The Lakota are connected to her still, partly because some still keep to the ways she taught them and partly because her pipe still resides with them.

The pipe of the Sacred Woman is analogous in function to the ear of corn left with the people by Iyatiku, Corn Woman, the mother goddess of the Keres. Iyatiku, who is called the mother of the people, is in a ceremonial sense another aspect of Thought Woman. She presently resides in Shipap from whence she sends counsel to the people and greets them when they enter the spirit world of the dead. Her representative, Irriaku (Corn Mother), maintains the connection between individuals in the tribe as well as the connection between the nonhuman supernaturals and the tribe. It is through the agency of the Irriaku that the religious leaders of the tribe, called Yaya and Hotchin, or hochin in some spellings of the word, (Mother and leader or chief), are empowered to govern.

The Irriaku, like the Sacred Pipe, is the heart of the people as it is the heart of Iyatiku. In the form of the perfect ear of corn, Naiya Iyatiku (Mother, Chief) is present at every ceremony. Without the presence of her power, no ceremony can produce the power it is designed to create or release.[9] These uses of the feminine testify that primary power—the power to make and to relate—belongs to the preponderantly feminine powers of the universe. . . .

THE HEART OF POWER

As the power of woman is the center of the universe and is both heart (womb) and thought (creativity), the power of the Keres people is the corn that holds the thought of the All Power (deity) and connects the people to that power through the heart of Earth Woman, Iyatiku. She is the breath of life to the Keres because for them corn holds the essence of earth and conveys the power of earth to the people. Corn connects us to the heart of power, and that heart is Iyatiku, who under the guidance of Thought Woman directs the people in their affairs.

It is likely that the power embodied in the Irriaku (Corn Mother) is the power of dream, for dream connections play an important part in the ritual of life of the Pueblos as in other tribes of the Americas. As the frightening katsina, K'oo'ko, can haunt the dreams of uncleansed warriors and thus endanger everything, the power that moves between the material and nonmaterial worlds often does so in dreams. The place when certain dreams or ceremonies occur is said to be in "time immemorial." And the point where the two meet is Shipap, where Earth Woman lives. Corn, like many of its power counterparts, is responsible for maintaining linkage between the worlds, and Corn Mother, Irriaku, is the most powerful element in that link. John Gunn describes the

Irriaku as "an ear of corn perfect in every grain, the plume is a feather from every known bird."[10]

This representative of Iyatiku is an individual's link and the ceremonial link to medicine power. Of similar power is the Sacred Pipe that White Buffalo Woman brought to the Lakota. This pipe is called *wakan*, which means "sacred" or possessing power.

The concept of power among tribal people is related to their understanding of the relationships that occur between the human and nonhuman worlds. They believe that all are linked within one vast, living sphere, that the linkage is not material but spiritual, and that its essence is the power that enables magical things to happen. Among these magical things are transformation of objects from one form to another, the movement of objects from one place to another by teleportation, the curing of the sick (and conversely creating sickness in people, animals, or plants), communication with animals, plants, and nonphysical beings (spirits, katsinas, goddesses, and gods), the compelling of the will of another, and the stealing or storing of souls. Mythical accounts from a number of sources illustrate the variety of forms the uses of ritual power can take. . . .

Certainly, there is reason to believe that many American Indian tribes thought that the primary potency in the universe was female, and that understanding authorizes all tribal activities, religious or social. That power inevitably carries with it the requirement that the people live in cooperative harmony with each other and with the beings and powers that surround them. For without peacefulness and harmony, which are the powers of a woman's heart, the power of the light and of the corn, of generativity and of ritual magic, cannot function. Thus, when Corn Woman, Iyatiku, was about to leave the people and return to Shipap, she told the chief, or cacique, how to guide and counsel the people:

I will soon leave you. I will return to the home whence I came. You will be to my people as myself; you will pass with them over the straight road; I will remain in my house below and will hear all that you say to me. I give you all my wisdom, my thoughts, my heart, and all. I fill your head with my mind.[11] . . .

Pre-Conquest American Indian women valued their role as vitalizers. Through their own bodies they could bring vital beings into the world—a miraculous power whose potency does not diminish with industrial sophistication or time. They were mothers, and that word did not imply slaves, drudges, drones who are required to live only for others rather than for themselves as it does so tragically for many modern women. The ancient ones were empowered by their certain knowledge that the power to make life is the source of all power and that no other power can gainsay it. Nor is that power simply of biology, as modernists tendentiously believe. When Thought Woman brought to life the twin sisters, she did not give birth to them in the biological sense. She sang over the medicine bundles that contained their potentials. With her singing and shaking she infused them with vitality. She gathered the power that she controlled and focused it on those bundles, and thus they were "born." Similarly, when the sister goddesses Naotsete and Uretsete wished to bring forth some plant or creature they reached into the basket (bundle) that Thought Woman had given them, took out the effigy of the creature, and thought it into life. Usually they then instructed it in its proper role. They also meted out consequences to creatures (this included plants, spirits, and katsinas) who disobeyed them.

The water of life, menstrual or postpartum blood, was held sacred. Sacred often means taboo; that is, what is empowered in a ritual sense is not to be touched or approached by any who are weaker than the power itself, lest they suffer negative consequences from contact. The blood of woman was in and of itself infused with the power of Supreme Mind, and so women were held in awe and respect. The term *sacred*, which is connected with power, is similar in meaning to the term *sacrifice*, which means "to make sacred." What is made sacred is empowered. Thus, in the old way, sacrificing meant empowering, which is exactly what it still means to American Indians who adhere to traditional practice. Blood was and is used in sacrifice because it possesses the power to make something else powerful or, conversely, to weaken or kill it.

Pre-contact American Indian women valued their role as vitalizers because they understood that bearing, like bleeding, was a transformative ritual act. Through their own bodies they could bring vital beings into the world—a miraculous power unrivaled by mere shamanic displays. They were mothers, and that word implied the highest degree of status in ritual cultures. The status of mother was so high, in fact, that in some cultures Mother or its analogue, Matron, was the highest office to which a man or woman could aspire.

The old ones were empowered by their certain knowledge that the power to make life is the source and model for all ritual magic and that no other power can gainsay it. Nor is that power really biological at base; it is the power of ritual magic, the power of Thought, of Mind, that gives rise to biological organisms as it gives rise to social organizations, material culture, and transformations of all kinds—including hunting, war, healing, spirit communication, rain-making, and all the rest. . . .

A strong attitude integrally connects the power of Original Thinking or Creation Thinking to the power of mothering. That power is not so much the power to give birth, as we have noted, but the power to make, to create, to transform. Ritual means transforming something from one state or condition to another, and that ability is inherent in the action of mothering. It is the ability that is sought and treasured by adepts, and it is the ability that male seekers devote years of study and discipline to acquire. Without it, no practice of the sacred is possible, at least not within the Great Mother societies.

And as the cultures that are woman-centered and Mother-ritual based are also cultures that value peacefulness, harmony, cooperation, health, and general prosperity, they are systems of thought and practice that would bear deeper study in our troubled, conflict-ridden time.

NOTES

1. Anthony Purley, "Keres Pueblo Concepts of Deity," *American Indian Culture and Research Journal* 1 (Fall 1974): 29. The passage cited is Purley's literal translation from the Keres Indian language of a portion of the Thought Woman story. Purley is a native-speaker Laguna Pueblo Keres.
2. Ibid., 30–31.
3. Hamilton A. Tyler, *Pueblo Gods and Myths*, Civilization of the American Indian Series (Norman, OK: University of Oklahoma Press, 1964), 37. Evidently, Huruing Wuhti has other transformative abilities as well. Under pressure from patriarchal politics, she can change her gender, her name, and even her spiritual nature.
4. Ibid., 93.
5. Purley, "Keres Pueblo Concepts," 31.
6. Ibid.
7. John G. Neihardt, *Black Elk Speaks* (Lincoln, NE: University of Nebraska Press, 1961), and Joseph Epes Brown, *The Sacred Pipe* (Baltimore: Penguin, 1971), 44.
8. Alice Baldeagle, personal correspondence, May 8, 1978.
9. See Franz Boas, *Keresan Texts* (New York: American Ethnological Society, 1928), especially "P'acaya'Nyi," vol. 8, pt. 1, 13–16.
10. John M. Gunn, *Schat Chen* (Albuquerque, NM: Albright and Anderson, 1917), 218.
11. Matilda Coxe Stevenson, "The Sia," in *Eleventh Annual Report, 1889–90*, Bureau of American Ethnology (Washington, DC, 1894), 40–41.

In Search of Women's Heritage

ELISABETH SCHÜSSLER FIORENZA

In the passion account of Mark's Gospel, three disciples figure prominently: on the one hand, two of the twelve—Judas who betrays Jesus and Peter who denies him—and on the other, the unnamed woman who anoints Jesus. But while the stories of Judas and Peter are engraved in the memory of Christians, the story of the woman is virtually forgotten. Although Jesus pronounces in Mark: "And truly I say to you, wherever the gospel is preached in the whole world, what she has done will be told in memory of her" (14:9), the woman's prophetic sign-action did not become a part of the gospel knowledge of Christians. Even her name is lost to us. Wherever the gospel is proclaimed and the eucharist celebrated another story is told: the story of the apostle who betrayed Jesus. The name of the betrayer is remembered, but the name of the faithful disciple is forgotten because she was a woman.

Although the story of the anointing is told in all four Gospels,[1] it is obvious that the redactional retelling of the story seeks to make the story more palatable to a patriarchal Greco-Roman audience. Whereas the Fourth Gospel identifies the woman as Mary of Bethany who as faithful friend of Jesus shows her love by anointing him, Luke shifts the focus of the story from woman as disciple to woman as sinner. Whether Luke used Mark's text or transmits a different tradition is disputed. But this exegetical dispute does not matter much since we are used to reading the Markan story in the light of Luke. In the process the woman becomes a great sinner who is forgiven by Jesus.

Despite their differences, all four Gospels reflect the same basic story: a woman anoints Jesus. This incident causes objections that Jesus rejects by approving of the woman's action. If the original story had been just a story about the anointing of a guest's feet, it is unlikely that such a commonplace gesture would have been remembered and retold as the proclamation of the gospel. Therefore, it is much more likely that in

Elisabeth Schüssler Fiorenza is Krister Stendahl Professor of Divinity at Harvard Divinity School. She is cofounder and coeditor of the *Journal of Feminist Studies in Religion* (with Judith Plaskow) and coeditor of the feminist issue of *Concilium* (with Anne Carr). She is author of many books including *In Memory of Her* and *Bread Not Stone*.

the original story the woman anointed Jesus' head. Since the prophet in the Old Testament anointed the head of the Jewish king, the anointing of Jesus' head must have been understood immediately as the prophetic recognition of Jesus, the Anointed, the Messiah, the Christ. According to the tradition it was a woman who named Jesus by and through her prophetic sign-action. It was a politically dangerous story.[2]

In Mark's Gospel the story is sandwiched between the statement that the leaders of Jesus' people wanted to arrest him and the announcement of Jesus' betrayal by Judas for money. Mark thus depoliticizes the story of Jesus' passion: first, by shifting the blame for his death from the Romans to the Jewish establishment; and second, by theologically defining Jesus' messiahship as one of suffering and death. Whereas according to Mark the leading male disciples do not understand this suffering messiahship of Jesus, reject it, and finally abandon him, the women disciples who have followed Jesus from Galilee to Jerusalem suddenly emerge as the true disciples in the passion narrative. They are Jesus' true followers (*akolouthein*) who have understood that his ministry was not rule and kingly glory but *diakonia*, "service" (Mark 15:41). Thus the women emerge as the true Christian ministers and witnesses. The unnamed woman who names Jesus with a prophetic sign-action in Mark's Gospel is the paradigm for the true disciple. While Peter had confessed, without truly understanding it, "you are the anointed one," the woman anointing Jesus recognizes clearly that Jesus' messiahship means suffering and death.

Both Christian feminist theology and biblical interpretation are in the process of rediscovering that the Christian gospel cannot be proclaimed if the women disciples and what they have done are not remembered. They are in the process of reclaiming the supper at Bethany as women's Christian heritage in order to correct symbols and ritualizations of an all-male Last Supper that is a betrayal of true Christian discipleship and ministry.[3] Or, in the words of the artist Judy Chicago: "All the institutions of our culture tell us through words, deeds, and even worse silence that we are insignificant. But our heritage is our power."[4]

I attempt to reconstruct early Christian history as women's history in order not only to restore women's stories to early Christian history but also to reclaim this history as the history of women and men. I do this not only as a feminist historian but also as a feminist theologian. The Bible is not just a historical collection of writings but also Holy Scripture, gospel, for Christians today. As such it informs not only theology but also the commitment of many women today. Yet as long as the stories and history of women in the beginnings of early Christianity are not theologically conceptualized as an integral part of the proclamation of the gospel, biblical texts and traditions formulated and codified by men will remain oppressive to women.

Such a reconstruction of early Christian history as women's history and of biblical-historical theology as feminist theology presupposes historical and theological critical analysis as well as the development of a feminist biblical-historical hermeneutics. . . . Methodologically, however, it will be necessary to go beyond the limits of the New Testament canon since it is a product of the patristic church, that is, a theological document of the "historical winners." To forego such an undertaking because historical-critical scholarship and hermeneutics are "male" but not feminist does an intellectual disservice to women. Since it reinforces male-female role stereotypes, such an assumption is not capable of naming the particular oppressive assumptions and androcentric components of such scholarship.

Reconstruction of early Christian history in a feminist perspective raises difficult hermeneutical, textual, and historical problems. Since feminism has developed different theoretical perspectives and models, this reconstruction must also include the formulation of a feminist heuristic framework or model that allows for the oppression as well as for the historical agency of women in early Christianity.

1. A fundamental methodological insight of historical criticism of the Bible was the realization that the *Sitz im Leben* or life setting of a text is as important for its understanding as its actual formulation. Biblical texts are not verbally inspired revelation nor doctrinal principles but historical formulations within the context of a religious community. Although this insight is challenged today by literary formalism as well as textual biblicism, it nevertheless remains basic to any historical reconstruction. Studies of the social world of Israel and early Christianity are in the process of developing heuristic models [models used for understanding] that comprehend more fully the social-historical context of the biblical texts.

Similarly, feminist theory insists that all texts are products of an androcentric patriarchal culture and history. The current feminist movement has therefore engendered an explosion of scholarly works in all areas of scientific inquiry and research.[5] Historians, philosophers, and anthropologists have emphasized that current scholarly theory and research are deficient because they neglect women's lives and contributions and construe humanity and human history as male. Feminist scholarship in all areas, therefore, seeks to construct heuristic models and concepts that allow us to perceive the human reality articulated insufficiently in androcentric texts and research.

My purpose is to move away from the pervasive apologetic that characterizes most treatments of women in the Bible, to a historical-critical reconstruction of women's history and women's contributions to early Christian beginnings. Moreover, I assume that the new questions raised by feminist scholarship will enhance our understanding of early Christian history. The attempt to "write women back into early Christian history" should not only restore early Christian history to women but also lead to a richer and more accurate perception of early Christian beginnings. If scholars employ philosophical, sociological, or psychological analyses for constructing new interpretative models of early Christian development, nothing should prevent us from utilizing feminist heuristic analyses as well, in order to reconstruct an early Christian history in which women are not hidden and invisible. While an androcentric model cannot do justice to those texts that positively mention women's leadership in early Christianity, a feminist model can positively integrate them.

Biblical scholars, however, do not perceive the question as a serious historical problem of great significance for the reconstruction of early Christian history and theology. As a "woman's issue" it is trivial or marginal to the academic enterprise. Seen as a "woman's problem" the issue belongs to books and symposia on "woman" but not in the program of exegetical conferences or in the pages of an exegetical *Festschrift*. Usually, anyone identified with the "feminist cause" is ideologically suspect and professionally discredited. As one of my colleagues remarked about a professor who had written a moderate article on women in the Old Testament: "It is a shame, she may have ruined her scholarly career."

The tacit assumption underlying such expressed or unexpressed reservations is that scholars who do not reflect or articulate their political allegiances are "objective," free from bias, nonpartisan, and scientific. Yet, anyone even slightly familiar with problems raised by the sociology of knowledge or by critical theory will have difficulty asserting such scholarly objectivity on scientific grounds. In a brilliant analysis of slavery in antiquity, the eminent scholar Moses Finley has explored the ways in which current ideological and societal interests have deeply affected the historiography of ancient slavery. He sums up his explorations:

Nevertheless, other contemporary ideological considerations are active in that seemingly remote field of historical study—active in the sense that they underlie, and even direct, what often appears to be a purely "factual," "objective" presentation. . . . I believe that a full, open account of how modern interest in ancient slavery has manifested itself is a necessary prerequisite to the substantive analysis of the institution itself, and I have therefore begun with that theme.[6]

Since historical knowledge is inferential (Collingwood), historians have to construct some frame of reference within which to discuss the available historical evidence. Such a frame of reference is always determined by their own philosophical perspective and values. Historians who pretend to record nothing but pure facts while refusing to acknowledge their own presuppositions and theoretical perspectives succeed only in concealing from themselves the ideologies upon which their historiography is based. All historiography is a selective view of the past. Historical interpretation is defined by contemporary questions and horizons of reality and conditioned by contemporary political interests and structures of domination. Historical "objectivity" can only be approached by reflecting critically on and naming one's theoretical presuppositions and political allegiances.

Interest in legitimization, as well as in opening up future possibilities, is a major motif in biblical interpretation. As James Robinson states:

New Testament scholarship as an intellectual activity is a modern science reflecting as well as molding the modern understanding of reality, a reciprocity it shares with the humanities in general. . . . Every scholar or scientist who deals with a subject matter from the past does so in terms of his present grasp of reality and the results of his research in turn flow into the current body of knowledge from which the continual modification of our understanding of reality emerges.[7]

If this is the case—and I believe it is—then it must be asked whether the reluctance of scholars to investigate the present topic might be sustained by an unconscious or conscious refusal to modify our androcentric grasp of reality and religion rather than by a legitimate concern for the integrity of biblical-historical scholarship. The dictum of Simone de Beauvoir about scholarship on women in general applies also to studies of women in the Bible: "If the 'woman's question' seems trivial it is because masculine arrogance has made it a 'quarrel' and when quarrelling one no longer reasons well."[8]

2. While it is hard to dislodge the intellectual misgivings of my colleagues in the academy, I have found it even more difficult to sustain my biblical interests in the face of feminist objections. Questions and misgivings expressed by women in response to my lectures and publications have taught me how to phrase problems more clearly and how to keep in mind the structural obstacles to a feminist historiography or theology. Such exchanges have also compelled me to explore more deeply how a "feminist hermeneutics" can be formulated. . . .

When I attempt to explore the history of women who became Christians in the beginnings of Christianity this should not be misunderstood as an attempt to save the Bible from its feminist critics. I simply mean to raise the question: How can early Christian origins be reconstructed in such a way as to be understood as "women's affairs"? In other words, is early Christian history "our own" history or heritage? Were women as well as men the initiators of the Christian movement?

While theologians in the academy refuse to discuss publicly their own political allegiance and preconceived bias and function, many post-biblical feminists are prepared to relinquish their historical roots and their solidarity with women in biblical religion. Recognizing that androcentric Western language and patriarchal religion have "erased" women from history and made them "non-beings," such feminists argue that biblical religion (and theology) is sexist to the core. It is not retrievable for women, since it ignores women's experience, speaks of the godhead in male terms, legitimizes women's subordinate positions of powerlessness, and promotes male dominance and violence against women. Therefore, feminists must move beyond the boundaries of biblical religion and reject the patriarchal authority of biblical revelation. Revisionist interpretations of the Bible are at best a waste of time and at worst a legitimization of the prevailing sexism of biblical religion— therefore, a cooptation of women and the feminist movement. Feminist praxis is rooted in the religious experience of contemporary women but does not derive its inspiration from the Christian past.

Yet such a postbiblical feminist stance is in danger of becoming ahistorical and apolitical. It too quickly concedes that women have no authentic history within biblical religion and too easily relinquishes women's feminist biblical heritage. Nor can such a stance do justice to the positive experiences of contemporary women within biblical religion. It must either neglect the influence of biblical religion on women today or declare women's adherence to biblical religion as "false consciousness." Insofar as biblical religion is still influential today, a cultural and social feminist transformation of Western society must take into account the biblical story and the historical impact of the biblical tradition. Western women are not able to discard completely and forget our personal, cultural, or religious Christian history. We will either transform it into a new liberating future or continue to be subject to its tyranny whether we recognize its power or not.

Feminists cannot afford such an ahistorical or antihistorical stance because it is precisely the power of oppression that deprives people of their history. This is perceived by both black and Latin American theologians. In his book *Roots*, Alex Haley traces the history of his people from its slave days. He does so in the hope "that this story of our people can alleviate the legacies of the fact that preponderantly the histories are written by the winners."[9] In a similar mode Gustavo Gutierrez states:

Human history has been written by a white hand, a male hand, from the dominating social class. The perspective of the defeated in history is different. Attempts have been made to wipe from their minds the memories of their struggles. This is to deprive them of a source of energy, of an historical will to rebellion.[10]

Among feminists, artist Judy Chicago has underlined the importance of women's heritage as a source for women's power. She created the *Dinner Party* as a symbolic history of women's past "pieced together" from the scanty information gleaned from cultural-religious channels. She observes:

Sadly most of the 1038 women included in the Dinner Party are unfamiliar, their lives and achievements unknown to most of us. To make people feel worthless, society robs them of their pride: this has happened to women. All the institutions of our culture tell us—through words, deeds and even worse silence—that we are insignificant. But our heritage is our power.[11]

Thus to reclaim early Christian history as women's own past and to insist that women's history is an integral part of early Christian historiography imply the search for roots, for solidarity with our foresisters, and finally for the memory of their sufferings, struggles, and powers as women.

If history in general, and early Christian history in particular, is one way in which androcentric culture and religion have defined women, then it must become a major object for feminist analysis. Such an analysis of history and the Bible must critically reveal patriarchal history for what it is and, at the same time, reconstruct the history of women in early Christianity as a challenge to historical-religious patriarchy. Therefore, a feminist reconstruction of early Christian history has not only a theoretical but also a practical goal: it aims at both cultural-religious critique and at reconstruction of women's history as women's story within Christianity. It seeks not just to undermine the legitimization of patriarchal religious structures but also to empower women in their struggle against such oppressive structures. In other words, a feminist reconstruction of early Christian beginnings seeks to recover the Christian heritage of women because, in the words of Judy Chicago, "our heritage is our power."

Yet such a recovery of women's history in early Christianity must not only restore women to history, it must also restore the history of Christian beginnings to women. It claims the Christian past as women's own past, not just as a male past in which women participated only on the fringes or were not active at all. The New Testament sources provide sufficient indicators for such a history of early Christian beginnings, since they mention that women are both followers of Jesus and leading members of the early Christian communities. Moreover, in the second and third centuries Christianity was still defending itself against the accusation that it was a religion of women and uncultured people. The task, therefore, involves not so much rediscovering new sources as re-reading the available sources in a different key. The goal is an increase in "historical imagination."

3. The debate between feminist "engaged" and androcentric academic "neutral" scholarship indicates a shift in interpretative paradigms.[12] Whereas traditional academic scholarship has identified humanness with maleness and understood women only as a peripheral category in the "human" interpretation of reality, the new field of women's studies not only attempts to make "women's" agency a key interpretative category but also seeks to transform androcentric schol-

arship and knowledge into truly human scholarship and knowledge, that is, inclusive of *all* people, men and women, upper and lower classes, aristocracy and "common people," different cultures and races, the powerful and the weak.

Thomas Kuhn's notion of scientific paradigms and heuristic interpretative models[13] can help us to understand this shift in interpretation and to map out a new feminist paradigm that has as its scientific goal an inclusive "human" reconstruction of early Christian history. According to Kuhn, a paradigm represents a coherent research tradition created and sustained by a scientific community. A paradigm defines the type of problems to be researched, interpretations to be given, and interpretative systems to be constructed. Thus a scientific paradigm determines all aspects of scientific research: observations, theories and interpretative models, research traditions and exemplars, as well as the philosophical-theoretical assumptions about the nature of the world and its total worldview. All data and recorded observations are theory laden, no bare uninterpreted data and sources exist. Equally there are no criteria and research models that are not dependent on the scientific paradigm in which they were developed.

The shift from an androcentric to a feminist interpretation of the world implies a revolutionary shift in scientific paradigm, a shift with far-reaching ramifications not only for the interpretation of the world but also for its change. Since paradigms determine how scholars see the world and how they conceive of theoretical problems, a shift from an androcentric to a feminist paradigm implies a transformation of the scientific imagination. It demands an intellectual conversion that cannot be logically deduced but is rooted in a change of patriarchal-social relationships. Such an intellectual conversion engenders a shift in commitment that allows the community of scholars to see old "data" in a completely new perspective. The debate between androcentric scholarship and feminist scholarship does more than indicate the intellectual limitations of the scholars involved in the argument. In fact, it shows a competition between rival paradigms that may exist alongside each other in the phase of transition, but ultimately are exclusive of each other.

According to Kuhn, such a transition can only be accomplished when the emerging paradigm has produced its own institutional structures and support-systems. While the androcentric paradigm of scholarship is rooted in the patriarchal institutions of the academy, the feminist paradigm has created its own institutional basis in the alternative institutions of women's centers, academic institutes, and study programs. Yet the patriarchal dependencies and hierarchical institutions of the academy guarantee structural perpetuation of the androcentric scientific paradigm. The issue is not just a problem of feminist reconstruction of history and of a renaming of the world, but a fundamental change of both scholarship and the academy. Feminist studies are therefore primarily accountable to the women's movement for societal-ecclesial change rather than to the academy. Or in the words of Michelle Russell:

The question is this: How will you refuse to let the academy separate the dead from the living, and then yourself declare allegiance to life? As teachers, scholars, and students, how available will you make your knowledge to others as tools for their own liberation? This is not a call for mindless activism, but rather for engaged scholarship.[14]

While a critical feminist reconstruction of women's early Christian history is in the interest of all women who are affected by the influence of biblical religion in Western societies, it nevertheless owes its special allegiance to Christian women of the present and of the past. In my opinion, feminist biblical scholarship and historical biblical scholarship share as their common hermeneutical perspective a critical commitment to the Christian community and its traditions. Although historical-critical analysis of the Bible has developed over and against a doctrinal understanding of Scripture and has challenged clerical control of theology, it nevertheless has as its hermeneutical presupposition a theological engagement insofar as it operates theoretically within the boundaries of the canon as well as institutionally within Christian schools of theology. The Bible is not just a document of past history but functions as Scripture in present day religious communities. Therefore, like women's studies, exegetical-biblical studies are by definition already "engaged." Insofar as biblical studies are canonical studies they are conditioned by and related to their *Sitz im Leben* in the Christian past and present. Like feminist studies, historical-critical interpretations of the Bible cannot abstract from the presuppositions, commitments, beliefs, or cultural and institutional structures influencing the questions they raise and the models they choose for interpreting their data. Historical biblical studies, like historical studies in general, are a selective view of the past whose scope and meaning is limited not only by the extant sources and materials but also by the interests and perspectives of the present.

Similarly feminist theology as a critical theology of liberation[15] has developed over and against symbolic androcentrism and patriarchal domination within biblical religion, while at the same time seeking to recover the biblical heritage of women for the sake of empowering women in the struggle for liberation. Feminist historical analyses, therefore, share both the impetus of historical biblical studies and an explicit commitment to a contemporary group of people, women, who, either religiously or culturally, are impacted by the traditions of the Bible. Critical-historical analysis and a clearly specified commitment serve as the common ground between academic biblical scholarship and a feminist critical theology of liberation. My explorations, therefore, begin with the hope that this common ground might engender a hermeneutical perspective and method for reconstructing early Christian history in such a way that it overcomes the chasm between historical-critical studies and the contemporary church of women. . . .

Feminist analysis and consciousness raising enables one to see the world and human lives, as well as the Bible and tradition, in a different light and with different "glasses." It has as its goal a new feminist engagement and way of life, a process traditionally called conversion. . . . I hope to provide new lenses that enable one to read the biblical sources in a new feminist light, in order to engage in the struggle for women's liberation inspired by the Christian feminist vision of the discipleship of equals.

NOTES

1. For an extensive discussion of the exegetical literature, see Robert Holst, "The Anointing of Jesus: Another Application of the Form-Critical Method," *Journal of Biblical Literature* 95 (1976): 435–46.
2. Cf. J. K. Elliott, "The Anointing of Jesus," *Expository Times* 85 (1974): 105–7.
3. Cf. also Elizabeth E. Platt, "The Ministry of Mary of Bethany," *Theology Today* 34 (1977): 29–39.
4. Judy Chicago, *The Dinner Party: A Symbol of Our Heritage* (New York: Doubleday, Anchor Books, 1979): 246–49.
5. *Signs: Journal of Women in Culture and Society*, which was founded in 1975, has regular reviews of scholarship in various areas. Of equal importance are the *Women's Studies International Quarterly* and *Feminist Studies*. See also Dale Spender, ed., *Men's Studies Modified: The Impact of Feminism on the Academic Disciplines* (Oxford/New York: Pergamon Press, 1981).
6. Moses I. Finley, *Ancient Slavery and Modern Ideology* (New York: Viking Press, 1980), 9–10.
7. James M. Robinson and Helmut Koester, *Trajectories through Early Christianity* (Philadelphia: Fortress Press, 1971), 1–2.
8. See the introduction in Simone de Beauvoir, *The Second Sex* (New York: Knopf, 1953), 18ff.
9. Alex Haley, *Roots: The Saga of An American Family* (New York: Doubleday, 1976), 687–88.
10. Gustavo Gutierrez, "Where Hunger Is, God Is Not," *The Witness* (April 1976): 6.
11. Chicago, *The Dinner Party*, 241–51.
12. For a discussion of this shift, cf. Elizabeth Janeway, "Who Is Sylvia? On the Loss of Sexual Paradigms," *Signs* 5 (1980): 573–89.
13. See Thomas S. Kuhn, *The Structure of Scientific Revolutions* (Chicago: University of Chicago Press, 1962); Ian G. Barbour, *Myths, Models, and Paradigms* (New York: Harper & Row, 1974).
14. Michelle Russell, "An Open Letter to the Academy," *Quest* 3 (1977): 77f.
15. See my articles "Feminist Theology as a Critical Theology of Liberation," *Theological Studies* 36 (1975): 605–26; "Towards a Liberating and Liberated Theology," *Concilium* 15 (1979): 22–32; "To Comfort or to Challenge: Theological Reflections," in *New Woman, New Church, New Priestly Ministry*, ed. M. Dwyer (Rochester, NY: Women's Ordination Conference, 1980), 43–60.

Jewish Memory from a Feminist Perspective

JUDITH PLASKOW

There is perhaps no verse in the Torah more disturbing to the feminist than Moses' warning to his people in Exodus 19:15, "Be ready for the third day; do not go near a woman." For here, at the very moment that the Jewish people stand at Mount Sinai ready to enter into the covenant—not now the covenant with the individual patriarchs but presumably with the people as a whole—Moses addresses the community only as men. The specific issue is ritual impurity: an emission of semen renders both a man and his female partner temporarily unfit to approach the sacred (Leviticus 15:16–18). But Moses does not say, "Men and women do not go near each other." At the central moment of Jewish history, women are invisible. It was not their experience that interested the chronicler or that informed and shaped the text.

This verse sets forth a pattern recapitulated again and again in Jewish sources. Women's invisibility at the moment of entry into the covenant is reflected in the content of the covenant which, in both grammar and substance, addresses the community as male heads of household. It is perpetuated by the later tradition that in its comments and codifications takes women as objects of concern or legislation but rarely sees them as shapers of tradition and actors in their own right.

It is not just a historical injustice that is at stake in this verse, however. There is another dimension to the problem of the Sinai passage essential for understanding the task of Jewish feminism today. Were this passage simply the record of a historical event long in the past, the exclusion of women at this critical juncture would be troubling, but also comprehensible for its time. The Torah is not just history, however, but also living memory. The Torah reading, as a central part of the Sabbath and holiday liturgy, calls to mind and recreates the past for succeeding generations. When the story of Sinai is recited as part of the annual cycle of Torah readings or as a special reading for Sha-

Judith Plaskow is Associate Professor of Religious Studies at Manhattan College. Cofounder and coeditor of the *Journal of Feminist Studies in Religion* (with Elisabeth Schüssler Fiorenza), she is currently completing a Jewish feminist theology entitled *Standing Again at Sinai: Rethinking Judaism From a Feminist Perspective*.

vuot, women each time hear ourselves thrust aside anew, eavesdropping on a conversation among men and between man and God.[1]

Significant and disturbing as this passage is, however, equally significant is the tension between it and the reality of the Jewish woman who hears or reads it. The passage affronts because of a contradiction between the holes in the text and many women's felt experience. If Moses' words shock and anger, it is because women have always known or assumed our presence at Sinai; the passage is painful because it seems to deny what we have always taken for granted. On the one hand, of course we were there; on the other, how is it then that the text could imply we were not there?

This contradiction seems to me crucial, for construed a certain way, it is a potential bridge to a new relationship with the tradition. On the one hand, women can choose to accept our absence from Sinai, in which case we allow the male text to define us and our relationship to the tradition. On the other hand, we can stand on the ground of our experience, on the certainty of our membership in our own people. To do this, however, is to be forced to re-member and recreate its history. It is to move from anger at the tradition, through anger to empowerment. It is to begin the journey toward the creation of a feminist Judaism.

GIVE US OUR HISTORY

The notion that a feminist Judaism must reclaim Jewish history requires some explication, for it is by no means generally accepted. There are many Jewish feminists who feel that women can take on positions of authority, create new liturgy, and do what we need to do to create a community responsive to our needs in the present without dredging around in a history that can only cause us pain. What we need to do, according to this view, is to acknowledge and accept the patriarchal nature of the Jewish past and then get on with issues of contemporary change.

But while the notion of accepting women's past subordination and attending to the present has some attractiveness, it strikes me as in the end untenable. If it is possible within any historical, textual tradition to create a present in dramatic discontinuity with the past—and I doubt that it is—it certainly seems impossible within Judaism. For as I have already suggested, the central events of the Jewish past are not simply history but living, active memory that continues to shape Jewish identity and self-understanding. In Judaism, memory is not simply a given but a religious obligation.[2] "We Jews are a community based on memory," says Martin Buber. "The spiritual life of the Jews is part and parcel of their memory."[3] It is in retelling the story of our past as Jews that we learn who we truly are in the present.

While the Passover Seder is perhaps the most vivid example of the importance of memory in Judaism, the rabbinic reconstruction of Jewish history after the destruction of the second Temple provides an example of remembrance that is also recreation. So deeply is the Jewish present rooted in Jewish history that, after 70 C.E., when the rabbis profoundly transformed Jewish life, the changes they wrought in Jewish reality were also read back into the past so that they could be read out of the past as a foundation for the present. Again and again in rabbinic interpretations, we find contemporary practice projected back into earlier periods so that the chain of tradition can remain unbroken. In Genesis, for example, Abraham greets his three angelic visitors by killing a calf and serving it to them with milk (18:7–8), clearly a violation of the laws of kashrut which forbid eating milk and meat together. As later rabbinic sources read the passage, however, Abraham first served his visitors milk and only then meat, a practice permitted by rabbinic law.[4] The links between past and present were felt so passionately that any important change in the present had to entail a new understanding of history.

This has an important moral for Jewish feminists. We too cannot redefine Judaism in the present without redefining our past because our present grows out of our history. The Jewish need to reconstruct the past in light of the present converges with the feminist need to recover women's history within Judaism. Knowing that women are active members of the Jewish community in the present, we know that we were always part of the community, not simply as objects of male purposes but as subjects and shapers of tradition. To accept androcentric texts and contemporary androcentric histories as the whole of Jewish history is to enter into a secret collusion with those who would exclude us from full membership in the Jewish community. It is to accept the idea that men were the only significant agents in Jewish history when we would never accept this (still current) account of contemporary Jewish life. The Jewish community today is a community of women and men, and it has never been otherwise. It is time, therefore, to recover our history as the history of women and men, a task that will both restore our own history to women and provide a fuller Jewish history for the Jewish community as a whole.[5]

HISTORY, HISTORIOGRAPHY, AND TORAH

It is one thing to see the importance of recovering women's history, however, and another to accomplish this task in a meaningful way. First of all, as historian, the Jewish feminist faces all the same problems as any feminist historian trying to recover women's experience: both her sources and the historians who have gone before her record male activities and male deeds in accounts ordered by male values. What we know of women's past are those things men considered significant to remember, seen and interpreted through a value system that places men at the center.[6] But, as if this were not enough, the Jewish feminist faces additional problems raised by working with religious sources. The primary Jewish sources available to her for historical reconstruction are not simply collections of historical materials but also Torah. As Torah, as Jewish teaching, they are understood by the tradition to represent divine revelation, patterns of living adequate for all time. In seeking to restore the history of Jewish women, the Jewish feminist historian is not "simply" trying to revolutionize the writing of history but is also implicitly or explicitly acting as theologian, claiming to amplify Torah, and thus questioning the finality of the Torah we have. It is important, therefore, in placing the recovery of women's history in the context of a feminist Judaism to confront the view of Torah that this implies.

I understand Torah, both in the narrow sense of the five books of Moses and in the broader sense of Jewish teaching, to be the partial record of the "Godwrestling" of part of the Jewish people.[7] Again and again in the course of its existence, the Jewish people has felt itself called by and held accountable to a power not of its own making, a power that seemed to direct its destiny and give meaning to its life. In both ordinary and extraordinary moments, it has found itself guided by a reality that both propelled and sustained it and to which gratitude and obedience seemed the only fitting response.

The term "Godwrestling" seems appropriate to me to describe the written residue of these experiences, for I do not imagine them à la Cecil B. DeMille as the booming of a clear (male) voice or the flashing of tongues of flame, publicly visible, publicly verifiable, needing only to be transcribed. Rather, they were moments of profound experience, sometimes of illumination but also of mystery, moments when some who had eyes to see understood the meaning of events that all had undergone. Such illumination might be hard-won, or sudden experiences of clarity or presence that come unexpected as precious gifts. But they would need to be interpreted and applied, struggled with and puzzled over, passed down and lived out before they came to us as the Torah of God.

I call this record partial, for moments of intense religious experience cannot be pinned down and reproduced; they can only be suggested and pointed to so that readers or listeners may, from time to time, catch for themselves the deeper reality vibrating behind the text. Moreover, while moments of revelation may lead to abandonment of important presuppositions and openness to ideas and experiences that are genuinely new, they also occur within cultural frameworks that can never be escaped entirely, so that the more radical implications of a new understanding may not even be seen. I call Torah the record of part of the Jewish people because the experience and wrestling found there are for the most part those of men. The experience of being summoned and saved by a single power, the experience of human likeness to the creator God, the experiences of liberation and God's passion for justice were sustained within a patriarchal framework that the interpretation of divine revelation served to consolidate rather than shatter.[8]

There is a strand in the tradition that acknowledges this partiality of Torah and thus indirectly allows us to see what is at stake in the recovery of women's past. According to many ancient Jewish sources, the Torah pre-existed the creation of the world. It was the first of God's works, identified with the divine wisdom in Proverbs 8. It was written with black fire on white fire and rested on the knee of God. It was the architectural plan God consulted in creating the universe.[9] For the Kabbalists, this pre-existent or primordial Torah is God's wisdom and essence; it expresses the immensity of God's being and power. The written Torah of ink and parchment is only the "outer garments," a limited interpretation of what lies hidden, a document that the initiate must penetrate more and more deeply to gain momentary glimpses of what lies behind. A later development of the idea of a secret Torah asserted that each of the 600,000 souls that stood at Sinai had its own special portion of Torah that only that soul could understand.[10] Obviously, no account of revelatory experience by men or women can describe or exhaust the depths of divine reality. But this image of the relation between hidden and manifest Torah reminds us that half the souls of Israel have not left for us the Torah they have seen. Insofar as we can begin to recover the God-wrestling of women, insofar as we can restore a part of their vision and experience, we have more of the primordial Torah, the divine fullness, of which the present Torah of Israel is only a fragment and a sign.

The recovery of primordial Torah is a large task, however, to ask "history" to perform. And in fact, in the foregoing discussion, I have been slipping back and forth between different meanings and levels of the term "history." The rabbinic reconstruction of history, which I used as an example of rewriting Jewish history, by no means involved "doing history" in our modern sense. On the contrary, it was anachronistic and ahistorical. Taking for granted the historical factuality of the momentous events at Sinai, the rabbis turned their attention to mining their eternal significance. Reshaping Jewish memory did not involve discovering what "really happened," but projecting later developments back onto the eternal present of Sinai.[11]

Recovering women's history through modern historiography, a second meaning of history that I have used implicitly, is not just different from rabbinic modes of thinking, it is in conflict with them. It assumes precisely that the original revelation, at least as we have it, is not sufficient, that there are enormous gaps both in tradition and in the scriptural record, that to recapture women's experiences we need to go behind our records and *add* to Torah, acknowledging that that is what we are doing.[12]

But while the tensions between feminist and traditional approaches to Jewish history are significant and real, there is one important thing they have in common. The feminist too is not simply interested in acquiring more knowledge about the past but in incorporating women's history as part of the living memory of the Jewish people. Information about women's past may be instructive and even stirring, but it is not transformative until it becomes part of the community's collective memory, part of what Jews call to mind in remembering Jewish history. While historiographical research may be crucial to recovering women's history, it is not sufficient to make that history live. The Jewish feminist reshaping of Jewish history must therefore proceed on several levels at once. Feminist historiography can open up new questions to be brought to the past and new perspectives to be gleaned from it. It must be combined, however, with feminist midrash, or storytelling, and feminist liturgy before it becomes part of a living feminist Judaism.

RESHAPING JEWISH MEMORY

Feminist historiography as a starting point for the feminist reconstruction of Jewish memory challenges the traditional androcentric view of Jewish history and opens up our understanding of the Jewish past. In the last two decades, feminist historians have demanded and effected a far-reaching reorientation of the presuppositions and methods of historical writing. Questioning the assumption that men have made history while women have stayed home and had babies, they have insisted that women and men have lived and shaped history together. Any account of a period or civilization that does not look at the roles of both women and men, their relation and interaction, is "men's history" rather than the universal history it generally claims to be.[13]

Any number of examples might show how the insights and methods of feminist historians have been applied to Jewish women's history. Archeologist Carol Meyers, for instance, has begun to reconstruct the roles of women in ancient Israel through a combination of biblical and archeological evidence. She asks important new questions about the changing roles of women in biblical society, questions that point to the social construction of gender in biblical culture. In the period of early settlement, she argues, when women's biological and agricultural contributions would have been crucial, their status was likely higher than in the different cultural context of the monarchy. Restrictions on women's roles that were initially practical only later became the basis for "ideologies of female inferiority and subordination."[14] New Testament scholar Bernadette Brooten, working on the inscriptional evidence for women's leadership in the ancient synagogue, shows that during the Roman and Byzantine periods, women took on important synagogue functions in a number of corners of the Jewish world.[15] Her research on the inscriptions, and also on Jewish women's exercise of the right to divorce,[16] sheds light on the wider social world in which the Mishnah (a second century code of Jewish law) emerged, clarifying and questioning the extent of its authority. Chava Weissler's work on the *tekhines*, the petitionary prayers of Eastern European Jewish women, provides us with sources that come in part from women's hands, giving us an intimate view of women's perceptions. While these sources have often been dismissed as "women's literature" or relegated to casual reading, they give us important glimpses of women's religious experiences. They also make us aware of the subtle interplay between the ways women have found to express themselves and the influence of patriarchal religion.[17]

While none of this women's history alters the fundamentally androcentric perspective of "normative" texts or proves that Judaism is really egalitarian, it does reveal another world around and underneath the textual tradition, a world in which women are historical agents struggling within and against a patriarchal culture. In the light of women's history, we cannot see the Tanakh (the Bible) or the Mishnah or any Jewish text simply as given, as having emerged organically from an eternal, unambiguous, uncontested religious vision. Indeed, feminist historians have come to recognize that religious, literary, and philosophical works setting forth women's nature or tasks are often prescriptive rather than descriptive of reality. So far from giving us the world "as it is," "normative" texts may reflect the tensions within patriarchal culture, seeking to maintain a particular view of the world over against social, political, or religious change.[18] "Normative" texts reflect the views of the historical winners, winners whose victories were often achieved at the expense of women and of religious forms that allowed women some power and scope.[19] Insofar as women's religious and social self-expression and empowerment are values we bring to these texts, the texts are relativized, their normative status shaken. We see them against the background of alternative religious possibilities, alternatives that must now be taken seriously because without them, we have only the Judaism of a male elite and not the Judaism of all Jews.

Recovering Jewish women's history, then, extends the realm of the potentially usable Jewish past. Women's experiences expand the domain of Jewish resources on which we can draw in recreating Judaism in the present. In writing women into Jewish history, we ground a contemporary Jewish community that can be a community of women and men. But historiography by itself cannot reshape Jewish memory. The gaps in the historical record alone would prompt us to seek other ways of remembering. However sensitively we read between the lines of mainstream texts seeking to recapture the reality of women's lives, however carefully we mine non-literary and non-Jewish materials using them to challenge "normative" sources, many of our constructions will remain speculations and many of our questions will go unanswered.

Moreover, even if it were not the case that the sources are sparse and unconcerned with our most urgent questions, feminist historiography would still provide only a fragile grounding for Jewish feminist memory. For historiography recalls events that memory does not recognize.[20] It challenges memory, tries to dethrone it; it calls it partial and distorted. History provides a more and more complex and nuanced picture of the past; memory is selective. How do we recover the parts of Jewish women's history that are forgotten, and how do we then ensure that they will be *remembered*—incorporated into our communal sense of self?

The answer to these questions is partly connected to the wider reconstruction of Jewish life. We turn to the past with new questions because of present commitments, but we also remember more deeply what a changed present requires us to know. Yet Jewish feminists are already entering into a new relationship with history based not simply on historiography but also on more traditional strategies for Jewish remembrance. The rabbinic reconstruction of Jewish history, after all, was not historiographical but midrashic. Assuming the infinite meaningfulness of biblical texts, the rabbis took passages that were sketchy or troubling and wrote them forward. They brought to the Bible their own questions and found answers that showed the eternal relevance of biblical truth. Why was Abraham chosen to be the father of a people? What was the status of the law before the Torah was given? Who was Adam's first wife? Why was Dinah raped? These were not questions for historical investigation but imaginative exegesis and literary amplification.

The open-ended process of writing midrash, simultaneously serious and playful, imaginative, metaphoric, has easily lent itself to feminist use. While feminist midrash—like all midrash—is a reflection of contemporary beliefs and experiences, its root conviction is utterly traditional. It stands on the rabbinic insistence that the Bible can be made to speak to the present day. If the Torah is our text, it can and must answer our questions and share our values; if we wrestle with it, it will yield meaning.

Together and individually then, orally and in writing, women are exploring and telling stories that connect our history with present experience. Ellen Umansky, for example, retelling the story of the sacrifice of Isaac from Sarah's perspective, explores the dilemma of a woman in patriarchal culture trying to hold onto her sense of self. Isaac was God's gift to Sarah in her old age. She has no power to prevent Abraham's journey to Moriah; she can only wait wailing and trembling for him to return. But she is angry; she knows that God does not require such sacrifices. Abraham cannot deprive her of her own religious understanding, whatever demands he may make upon her as his wife.[21]

While midrash can float entirely free from historiography, as it does in this example, the latter can also feed the former so that midrash plays with historical clues but extends them beyond the boundaries of the fragmentary evidence. In her midrash on the verse, "And Dinah . . . went out to see the daughters of the land" (Genesis 34:1), Lynn Gottlieb explores the possible relations between Dinah and Canaanite women based on the presumption of Israelite women's historical attachment to many gods and goddesses.[22] A group of my students once used the same historical theme to write their own midrash on the sacrifice of Isaac as experienced by Sarah. In their version, Sarah, finding Abraham and Isaac absent, calls to Yahweh all day without avail. Finally, almost in despair, she takes out her Asherah and prays to it, only to see her husband and son over the horizon wending their way home.

Moving from history into midrash, Jewish feminists cross a boundary to be both honored and ignored. Certainly, there is a difference between an ancient Aramaic divorce document written by a woman and a modern midrash on Miriam or Sarah. The former confronts and challenges; it invites us to find a framework for understanding the past broad enough to include data at odds with selective memory. The latter is more fully an expression of our own convictions, a creative imagining based on our own experience. Yet in the realm of Jewish religious expression, imagination is permitted and even encouraged. Midrash is not a violation of historical canons but an enactment of commitment to the fruitfulness and relevance of biblical texts. It is partly through midrash that the figurine or document, potentially integrable into memory but still on the periphery, is transformed into narrative the religious ear can hear. The discovery of women in our history can feed the impulse to create midrash; midrash can seize on history and make it religiously meaningful. Remembering and inventing together help recover the hidden half of Torah, reshaping Jewish memory to let women speak.

There is also a third mode of recovery: speaking/acting. Historically, the primary vehicle for transmission of Jewish memory has been prayer and ritual, the liturgical reenactment and celebration of formative events. Midrash can instruct, amuse, edify, but the cycles of the week and year have been the most potent reminders of central Jewish experience and values. The entry of the High Priest into the Holy of Holies on the Day of Atonement, the Exodus of Israel from Egypt every Passover: these are remembered not just verbally but through the body and thus doubly imprinted on Jewish consciousness.

Liturgy and ritual, therefore, have been particularly important areas for Jewish feminist inventiveness. Feminists have been writing liturgy and ritual that flow from and incorporate women's experience, in the process drawing on history and midrash but also allowing them to emerge from concrete forms. One of the earliest and most tenacious feminist rituals, for example, is the celebration of Rosh Hodesh, the new moon, as a woman's holiday. The numerous Rosh Hodesh groups that have sprung up around the country in the last decade have experimented with new spiritual forms within the framework of a traditional women's observance that had been largely forgotten. The association of women with the moon at the heart of the original ceremony provides a starting point for exploration of women's symbols within Judaism and cross-culturally. At the same time, the simplicity of the traditional ritual leaves ample space for invention.[23] Feminist haggadot, on the other hand, seek to inject women's presence into an already established ritual, building on the theme of liberation to make women's experience and struggle an issue for the Seder. Drawing on history, poetry, and midrash, they seek to integrate women's experiences into the central Jewish story and central ritual enactment of the Jewish year.[24]

These two areas have provided basic structures around which a great deal of varied experimentation has taken place. But from reinterpretations of mikveh, to a major reworking of Sabbath blessings, to simple inclusion of the *imahot* (matriarchs) in daily and Sabbath liturgies—which, however minimally, says, "We too had a covenant; we too were there"—women are seeking to transform Jewish ritual so that it acknowledges our existence and experience.[25] In the ritual moment, women's history is made present.

We have then an interweaving of forms that borrow from and give life to each other. Women's history challenges us to confront the incompleteness of what has been called "Jewish history," to attend to the hidden and hitherto marginal, to attempt a true Jewish history which is a history of women and men. It restores to us some of women's voices in and out of the "normative" tradition, sometimes in accommodation and sometimes in struggle, but the voices of Jews defining their own Jewishness as they participate in the communal life. Midrash expands and burrows, invents the forgotten and prods the memory, takes from history and asks for more. It gives us the inner life history cannot follow, building links between the stories of our foremothers and our own joy and pain. Ritual asserts women's presence in the present. Borrowing from history and midrash, it transforms them into living memory. Creating new forms, it offers them to be remembered.

Thus, through diverse paths, we re-member ourselves. Moses' injunction at Sinai—"Do not go near a woman"—though no less painful, is only part of a story expanded and reinvigorated as women enter into the shaping of Torah. If in Jewish terms history provides a basis for identity, then out of our new sense of identity we are also claiming our past. Beginning with the conviction of our presence both at Sinai and now, we rediscover and invent ourselves in the Jewish communal past and present, continuing the age-old process of reshaping Jewish memory as we reshape the community today.

NOTES

1. Rachel Adler, " 'I've Had Nothing Yet So I Can't Take More,' " *Moment* 8 (Sept. 1983): 22–23.
2. Yosef Hayim Yerushalmi, *Zakhor: Jewish History and Jewish Memory* (Seattle, WA: University of Washington Press, 1982), 9.
3. Martin Buber, *Israel and the World: Essays in a Time of Crisis* (New York: Schocken Books, 1963), 146.
4. Louis Ginsberg, *The Legends of the Jews*, 7 vols. (Philadelphia: Jewish Publication Society, 1909), 5:235, n. 140.
5. Elisabeth Schüssler Fiorenza, *In Memory of Her: A Feminist Theological Reconstruction of Christian Origins* (New York: Crossroad, 1983), 14–20. I am indebted to Schüssler Fiorenza for this whole paragraph and, indeed, much of my approach to the recovery of Jewish women's history.
6. Gerda Lerner, *The Majority Finds Its Past: Placing Women in History* (New York: Oxford University Press, 1979), 160, 168–169.
7. The term "Godwrestling" comes from Arthur Waskow, *Godwrestling* (New York: Schocken Books, 1978).
8. See Norman K. Gottwald, *The Tribes of Yahweh* (Maryknoll, NY: Orbis Books, 1979), 685.
9. Ginsberg, *The Legends of the Jews*, 1:3–4.
10. Gershom G. Scholem, *On the Kabbalah and Its Symbolism* (New York: Schocken Books, 1965), 37–65.
11. Gershom G. Scholem, "Tradition and Commentary as Religious Categories in Judaism," *Judaism* 15 (Winter 1966): 26.
12. See Yerushalmi, *Zakhor*, 94.
13. Lerner, *The Majority Finds Its Past*, chaps. 10–12, especially pp. 168, 180.
14. Carol Meyers, "The Roots of Restriction: Women in Early Israel," *Biblical Archeologist* 41 (Sept. 1978): 101. See the whole article (pp. 91–103) and also her "Procreation, Production, and Protection: Male-Female Balance in Early Israel," *Journal of the American Academy of Religion* 51 (December 1983): 569–93.
15. Bernadette J. Brooten, *Women Leaders in the Ancient Synagogue: Inscriptional Evidence and Background Issues* (Chico, CA: Scholars Press, 1982).
16. Bernadette J. Brooten, "Could Women Initiate Divorce in Ancient Judaism? The Implications for Mark 10:11–12 and I Corinthians 7:10–11" (The Ernest Cadman Colwell Lecture, School of Theology at Claremont, CA, April 14, 1981).
17. Chava Weissler, "Voices From the Heart: Women's Devotional Prayers," in *The Jewish Almanac*, ed. Richard Siegel and Carl Rheins (New York: Bantam Books, 1980), 541–45.
18. Lerner, *The Majority Finds Its Past*, 149. Schüssler Fiorenza makes this point repeatedly. See, for example, *In Memory of Her*, 60.
19. Sheila Collins, *A Different Heaven and Earth* (Valley Forge, PA: Judson Press), chap. 4; Carol P. Christ, "Heretics and Outsiders: The Struggle Over Female Power in Western Religion," *Soundings* 61 (Fall 1978): 260–80.
20. Yerushalmi, *Zakhor*, 94.
21. Ellen M. Umansky, "Creating a Jewish Feminist Theology: Possibilities and Problems," *Anima* 10 (Spring Equinox 1984): 133–34.
22. Presentation at the First National Havurah Summer Institute, West Hartford, CT, in 1980.

23. Arlene Agus, "This Month is for You: Observing Rosh Hodesh as a Woman's Holiday," in *The Jewish Woman: New Perspectives*, ed. Elizabeth Koltun (New York: Schocken Books, 1976), 84–93; Penina Adelman, *Miriam's Well: Rituals for Jewish Women Around the Year* (Fresh Meadows, NY: Biblio Press, 1986).
24. See, for example, Esther Broner, "Honor and Ceremony in Women's Rituals," in *The Politics of Women's Spirituality: Essays on the Rise of Spiritual Power Within the Feminist Movement*, ed. Charlene Spretnak (Garden City, NY: Doubleday, Anchor Press, 1982), 237–41; Aviva Cantor Zuckoff (now Cantor), "Jewish Women's Haggadah," in *The Jewish Woman*, ed. Koltun, 94–102. There are numerous *haggadot* circulating privately.
25. Rachel Adler, "Tumah and Taharah; Ends and Beginnings," in *The Jewish Woman*, ed. Koltun, 63–71; Marcia Falk, "What About God?" *Moment* 10 (March 1985): 32–36, and her essay in this volume.

My Sister, My Spouse

Woman-Identified Women in Medieval Christianity

E. ANN MATTER

An inquiry into the history of lesbians in medieval Christian Europe faces double jeopardy. First, there is the difficulty of speaking about women's lives in a society that was solidly patriarchal in both its Roman and Teutonic roots, and which made very little provision for women except as objects for or possessions of men. Secondly, the inquiry must confront the problem of speaking about sexual mores in a culture essentially hostile to sexuality, particularly nonprocreative sexuality. These realities have necessarily limited my research and shaped my interpretations. This is, then, by no means a statistically valid study; it is rather a venture into a realm of silence and contradiction.

Scholars have by now reached accord about the great contributions of women to Christian monastic culture. Similarly, we are increasingly aware of the advantages offered to women by life in the cloister, and of the ways in which women's life in religion was changed by and helped to change medieval Christian society. No other group of medieval women, not even queens and other aristocrats, enjoyed the economic, political, and intellectual autonomy of nuns. It is no wonder that so many women who achieved power in secular life (Eleanor of Aquitaine is the obvious example) chose to retire to monasteries. Nuns also had the great advantage of literacy; only in the cloister could a medieval woman attend a school or live in an intellectual environment. One consequence of this, from a modern perspective, is that we know very little about the lives of medieval lay women. It is not clear whether generalizations from sources about women in monastic life might also suggest patterns for women's lives in the secular world. It is, nevertheless, striking that many of the women mystics, and most of the female literary figures of the Middle Ages were in religious life. The three most famous, Hroswitha, Hildegard, and Heloise, were all nuns;

E. Ann Matter is Associate Professor of Religious Studies at the University of Pennsylvania. A historian of medieval Christian culture, she is currently exploring the impact of spiritual traditions on women's lives through a study of the monastery of Santa Maria alle Pertiche in Pavia, Italy.

although, of course, it is not for her vow of chastity that Heloise is primarily remembered.

Men, even priests, were limited in their contacts with nuns, but many close intellectual and emotional relationships developed between men and women in religious life—and, of course, sexuality could not be summarily dismissed. Cloistered women expressed their longings for (and knowledge of) physical intimacy in outbursts such as the entry of a nun of Auxerre on the mortuary role of Matilda, daughter of William the Conquerer:

> All Abbesses deserve to die
> Who order subject nuns to lie
> In dire distress and lonely bed
> Only for giving love its head.
> I speak who know, for I've been fed,
> For loving, long on stony bread.[1]

Several monastic manuscripts from south Germany record what has been called a "magnificent chaos" of literary fragments, including a number of love-lyrics and epistolatory poems from lover to beloved. Many of these poems speak in the voice of a woman; as Peter Dronke says, they "show us beyond any doubt that a number of cultivated, witty, and tender young women in an eleventh-century convent in south Germany imposed on the clerics who frequented their society the values of *amour courtois* [courtly love]."[2]

In a series of remarkable poems found in a twelfth-century manuscript from the monastery of Tegernsee, this courtly amorousness is directed by a woman poet to a woman beloved. Tegernsee, a men's community, was in the thick of the poetic flowering of twelfth-century Bavaria, being the motherhouse of Benediktbeuern, the home of the famous *Carmina Burana* manuscript. These poems were probably written at a women's monastery in the region. One has received particular attention from John Boswell, who considers it "perhaps the most outstanding example of medieval lesbian literature." Boswell translates it in this way:

> To G.; her singular rose
> From A. the bonds of precious love.
> What is my strength, that I may bear it,
> That I should have patience in your absence?
> Is my strength the strength of stones,
> That I should await your return?
> I, who grieve ceaselessly day and night
> Like someone who has lost a hand or a foot?
> Everything pleasant and delightful
> Without you seems like mud underfoot
> I shed tears as I used to smile,
> And my heart is never glad.
> When I recall the kisses you gave me,

And how with tender word you caressed my little breasts,
I want to die
Because I cannot see you.
What can I, so wretched, do?
Where can I, so miserable, turn?
If only my body could be entrusted to the earth
Until your longed-for return
Or if passage could be granted to me as it was to Habakkuk
So that I might come there just once
To gaze on my beloved's face—
Then I should not care if it were the hour of death itself.
For no one has been born into the world
So lovely and full of grace,
Or who so honestly
And with such deep affection loves me.
I shall therefore not cease to grieve
Until I deserve to see you again.
Well has a wise man said that it is a great sorrow for [one] to
    be without that
Without which [one] cannot live.
As long as the world stands
You shall never be removed from the core of my being.
What more can I say?
Come home, sweet love!
Prolong your trip no longer;
Know that I can bear your absence no longer.
Farewell,
Remember me.[3]

This poem elicited from Dronke the observation that it "seems to presuppose a passionate physical relationship."[4] Yet it is stylistically quite traditional. The poem is made up of rhymed couplets (untranslatable), but with no discernible rhyme scheme or meter. It echoes the spirituality of medieval Christian readings of the Song of Songs, and the passionate friendships of Jerome and Alcuin.[5] Both Boswell and Dronke are careful to set it within the sophisticated and venerable tradition of spiritual friendship—the *amicitia* discussed so tenderly by Aelred of Rievaulx.[6] Whether the poet thought of herself in any way we would recognize as a "lesbian identity," she certainly celebrated a deep homoerotic orientation.

The poem that precedes this one in the Tegernsee manuscript is more elliptical, but just as erotic. Here the poet says to her beloved:

> You are sweeter than milk and honey
> You are peerless among thousands.
> I love you more than any.
> You alone are my love and longing,
> You the sweet cooling of my mind,
> No joy for me anywhere without you.[7]

This theme of longing for the absent beloved, sometimes expressed in courtly love language, is a recurrent theme of medieval monastic authors, male and female. It is poignantly found in the letters of Hadewijch, a thirteenth-century Flemish Beguine whose works have only recently appeared in English translation.[8] We know very little of the life of Hadewijch. It is debated, for example, whether she lived in Brussels or Antwerp, what sort of family she came from, or where she was educated. What we do know about Hadewijch is gleaned from the poems, letters, and visions that make up her collected works. She was not a nun, but a Beguine, one of the many women in the thirteenth century who chose to live in piety and apostolic poverty without making monastic vows. Beguine communities were especially popular in the low countries and the Rhineland, so popular, in fact, as to arouse ecclesiastical fear and restrictions.[9]

Hadewijch gained a reputation for spiritual authority among the Beguines of Flanders both because of her remarkable series of visions and the elegant prose and poetry in which she recorded them. She certainly ranks as one of the leading figures of medieval Dutch literature. Her consistent theme was love—*Minne*—the same word celebrated in the secular poetry of medieval Germany and Flanders. God is experienced by Hadewijch as *Minne*, in a love relationship with parallels to human love. The passion of Hadewijch for her spiritual spouse, Christ, is expressed in ravishingly sensual language. And yet, these writings stress that only through the imperfect experience of earthly love can union with the heavenly lover be glimpsed.[10] The letters of Hadewijch urge her fellow Beguines to strive for this mystical love, while giving us glimpses of her very human love relationships, and of the pain of a prolonged separation from her sisters.

Letter 25 is an excellent example of the power of *Minne*, at once divine and intimately human:

Greet Sara also in my behalf, whether I am anything to her or nothing.

Could I be fully all that in my love I wish to be for her, I would gladly do so; and I shall do so fully, however she may treat me. She has very largely forgotten my affliction, but I do not wish to blame or reproach her, seeing that Love [*Minne*] leaves her at rest, and does not reproach her, although Love ought ever anew to urge her to be busy with her noble Beloved. Now that she has other occupations and can look on quietly and tolerate my heart's affliction, she lets me suffer. She is well aware, however, that she should be a comfort to me, both in this life of exile and in the other life in bliss. There she will indeed be my comfort, although she now leaves me in the lurch.

And you, Emma and yourself—who can obtain more from me than any other person now living can, except Sara—are equally dear to me. But both of you turn too little to Love, who has so fearfully subdued me in the commotion of unappeased love. My heart, soul, and senses have not a moment's rest, day or night; the flame burns constantly in the very marrow of my soul.

Tell Margriet to be on her guard against haughtiness, and to be sensible, and to attend to God each day; and that she may apply herself to the attainment of perfection and prepare herself to live with us, where we shall one day be together, and that she should neither live nor remain with aliens. It would be a great disloyalty if she deserted us, since she so much desires to satisfy us, and she is now close to us—indeed, very close—and we also so much desire her to be with us.

Once I heard a sermon in which Saint Augustine was spoken of. No sooner had I heard it than I became inwardly so on fire that it seemed to me everything on earth must be set ablaze by the flame I felt within me. Love is all![11]

The love that Hadewijch bears for Sara is particularly interesting. Sara, the best beloved, returns Hadewijch's fervor with indifference; yet Hadewijch urges her on to new heights of *Minne* for "her noble beloved," that is, the heavenly bridegroom, Christ. Yet, the author's mourning for Sara's *human* love spills out between the lines: "whether I am anything to her or nothing . . . however she may treat me" Hadewijch will "fully be all that in my love I wish to be for her," without "blame or reproach." The intensity, awkwardness, and sublimation of this love should be recognized by all who have read the recent collection of memoirs, *Lesbian Nuns: Breaking Silence.*[12] Certainly, Hadewijch did not see herself as "lesbian" in any modern understanding of the term. And yet, whether or not their relationship was explicitly sexual, it seems a possible interpretation that Hadewijch and Sara were "Particular Friends."

From the same period as Hadewijch, but another corner of Europe, the courts of Provence, comes the only medieval lesbian voice I have found outside of the religious life: the poem attributed to Bieris de Romans, addressed to the Lady Maria.[13] We know nothing at all about either the poet or the object of her poem. But in the worldly tradition of Provence, where the ladies at court sang alongside the more famous male troubadours, at least one *trobairitz*, as the women poets were called, addressed her praises to another woman.

The poem begins with a catalogue of Lady Maria's finer points; then, in the second stanza, the lover pleads more directly:

> Thus I pray you, if it please you that true love
> and celebration and sweet humility
> should bring me such relief with you,
> if it please you, lovely woman, then give me
> that which most hope and joy promises
> for in you lie my desire and my heart
> and from you stems all my happiness,
> and because of you I'm often sighing.[14]

We've heard these sighs already, in the poems of an anonymous nun of south Germany, and in a letter of a Flemish Beguine. The relative sophistication and freedom of courtly Provençal society allows the love message to be expressed more directly, without the monastic habit of spiritual *amicitia*. Yet, all of these medieval lesbian voices speak within the courtly tradition of longing, separation, and hope for union with the object of love.

These voices assure us that there was passionate love between women in medieval Europe, love that could sometimes be expressed in the elite, discreet, and rarified air of the cloister, community, or court. This brings us to the second consideration of my paper: the interpretation and reception of this love in the context of medieval Christian social mores. For this inquiry, it is necessary to consider far less pleasing material: penitential and juridical attention to love between women.

A good deal of the scholarship on homosexuality in the Middle Ages is concerned with the writings known as "penitentials," handbooks for confessors which catalogue sins and their respective penances. Penitentials originated in the British Isles in the sixth century; until the twelfth century, they were increasingly found in continental Europe as well.[15] John Boswell has rightly cautioned against the use of penitential literature as an index to popular attitudes towards sinful acts. Medieval penitentials are anything but standardized, and their credibility is further brought into question by the scorn with which they were regarded by some well-known ecclesiastics.[16] Yet, it is worth noting that disapproval of the penitentials was usually on account of their *laxity*; this is certainly the case in Peter Damian's *Liber Gomorrhianus*, a vituperative denunciation of homosexuality among the clergy of the mid-eleventh century.[17]

The penitentials were a product of the missionary activity of early medieval Europe. As Vern Bullough has put it, they "give us a picture of the attempts of the Christian Church to impose its will upon a society that, though nominally Christian, had not yet accepted Christian morality."[18] The burden of this missionizing was carried out by monks and nuns; many medieval monasteries, especially in Germany, were outposts of Christianity in essentially pagan rural areas. The penitentials, then, belong to the same monastic culture as the poems of the Tegernsee manuscript. As such, they deserve some consideration as evidence of lesbian activities, at least in the cloister.

In the penitentials, sins are roughly categorized by type and seriousness; often the status and spiritual record of the sinner are brought into account in assigning a penance. The penances listed are units of time—so many days, months, or years for a given act of theft, irreverence, or fornication, for example. The punishment consisted of fasting (on bread and water, with normal food on Sunday and feast days); but provision was made to work off the penance more quickly by means of prayers, vigils, or giving of alms.[19]

Except as objects of male lust, women are of little interest to the authors of the penitentials. Sections on heterosexual fornication typically go into great detail about the status of the woman as part of assigning a penance to a man. Was she a virgin? A nun? Someone's wife? (Whose wife?) Was she related by blood? Did she resist? Was there conception? What happened to the child? The greatest detail on women's sexual penances has, in fact, to do with abortion and infanticide.[20]

The details of penances for sexual acts between men are given in almost obsessive detail. In the penitential attributed to Bede, an eighth-century document from England, male sodomy is adjudicated according to the age of the participants, the clerical status (lay, monk, priest, deacon—other texts add bishop), and the nature of the intimacy. There is a certain fascination in these discussions. A penitential ascribed to Irish abbot Cummean, in circulation in seventh-century Frankland, even goes into prurient detail on the subject of kisses between boys:

> Those who kiss simply shall be corrected with six special fasts; those who kiss licentiously without pollution, with eight special fasts; if with pollution or embrace, with ten special fasts.
>
> But after the twentieth year (that is, adults) they shall live at a separate table (that is, in continence) and excluded from the church, on bread and water.[21]

Amid this profusion of pastoral concern for the sexual practices of men are only a few comments about lesbian acts. The earliest is found in the Penitential of Theodore (ascribed to Theodore of Tarsus, Archbishop of Canterbury) and it is relatively simple:

> If a woman practices vice with a woman, she shall do penance for three years.
>
> And if she practices solitary vice, she shall do penance for the same period.[22]

The penance is actually quite light; the same document prescribes a penance of ten years for male homosexual acts.[23]

Homosexual men suffer heavier punishments than lesbians in other Anglo-Saxon penitentials as well. The document ascribed to Bede lists a four-year penance for male sodomites, but only three years for "fornication" between women.[24] A Carolingian conflation of this text with the Penitential of Egbert returns to the old formula: ten years for a man, only three for a woman who "fornicates with herself or another by whatever means possible."[25] But this Bede-Egbert text adds another consideration: women (nuns are specified) who fornicate "per machina," by means of some device, must do penance for seven years rather than three.[26]

Sex between women by means of "machines" is also mentioned by Hincmar, the ninth-century Archbishop of Rheims. His treatise on the divorce of the Emperor Lothar defends the decision of a Carolingian monarch to put aside his wife in order to marry his concubine.[27] Hincmar's argument is dependent on the belief that women practicing witchcraft (*maleficio*) can render men impotent.[28] This subject gives Hincmar, one of the most flamboyant of Carolingian authors, an excellent opportunity to hold forth about sexual deviance of all kinds. It is a diabolical force, he says, that controls human sexual desires. Therefore:

> Even females have this sordid appetite, as Ambrose says in expounding the Apostle (Romans 1:26) on the subject of females engaging in filthy acts. They do not put flesh to flesh in the sense of the genital organ of the one in the body of the other, since nature precludes this, but they do transform the use of the member in question into an unnatural one, in that they are reported to use certain instruments (*machinas*) of diabolical operation to excite desire. Thus they sin nonetheless by committing fornication against their own bodies.[29]

Boswell has taken this as a comment "specifically on lesbianism."[30] This may be so, but there is a derivative quality about the passage, in Hincmar's testimony that such acts "are reported" and in the echoes of the penitentials, which may bring any real knowledge of lesbianism into question. About Hincmar's attitude towards the possibility, though, there can be no doubt. We will again see the charge of diabolical intervention in the case of a seventeenth-century nun, Benedetta Carlini. It should also be noticed that Hincmar's denunciation of women who use such *machinas* evokes the only reference we have seen so far to Paul's supposed denunciation of lesbians in Romans 1:26.[31]

In any case, sex between women involving imitation of male genitalia was considered a far more serious sin than simple "fornication" between women. This gives us a different glimpse of the attitude of medieval ecclesiastics towards lesbians: the condemnation of women perceived to be conducting themselves, especially sexually, in ways reserved "by nature" for men. A remarkable number of references to lesbians before the modern era list instances of women acting like, even posing as, men. Just as remarkable is the fact that scholars have neglected this nuance in evaluating lesbian history.

A poem from sixth-century France serves as an excellent example:

> You, strange mixture of the female gender,
> Whom driving lust makes a male,
> Who love to fuck with your crazed cunt.
> Why has pointless desire seized you?
> You do not give what you get, though you service a cunt.
> When you have given that part by which you are judged a woman,
> Then you will be a girl.[32]

To contrast this bit of misogynist verse with the poems of the gay clerical underground which flourished in the same culture, or the celebratory "Ganymede" literature of the twelfth century, is to be brought face to face with the unpleasant possibility that intimate relations between women were most despised—and perhaps only noticed—when they challenged male cultural prerogatives. Nor was this zeal for safe-guarding male privilege limited to the realm of sexuality. The tenth-century *Decretals* of Burchard of Worms, which does not mention sexual acts between women, nonetheless stipulates:

> If any woman because of continence (as she may think) changes her habit, and for that customary to women puts on a male garment, let her be anathema.[33]

This prohibition seems oddly harsh in view of such Christian ascetic heroines as Mary of Egypt and Pelagia the Harlot, although it does add to our understanding of the harsh condemnation of Joan of Arc.[34]

I would like to conclude by considering two documented trials that bear out my hypothesis. Both date from the early modern period, but they are so unusually detailed as to provide important evidence about magisterial attitudes towards lesbians.

The 1721 trial and execution of Catherina Margaretha Linck in Hal-berstadt, Germany, involves action against a woman who posed suc-cessfully as a man, in military and private life, for many years. The accused married another Catherina Margaretha, surnamed Mühlhahn, in 1717. Catherina Linck escaped detection by her fellow soldiers, even by her wife, by the skillful use of "a penis of stuffed leather with two stuffed testicles made from pig's bladder attached to it."[35] The death sentence was deemed appropriate as much for her religious apostasy as for sexual crimes. Linck was in the habit of affiliating with the re-ligious sect of each town in which she lived, professing by turn Lu-theranism and Catholicism; she and Mühlhahn were actually married twice, in Lutheran and Catholic ceremonies. So, the trial document states:

> ... Since the outrages perpetrated by the Linck woman were hideous and nasty, and it can furthermore not be denied that she engaged in repeated baptism for which she should be punished, the jurists are also of the opinion that a woman who commits sodomy with another woman with such an instru-ment could therefore be given *poena ordinaria* [that is, capital punishment].[36]

There was some question, however, as to how the sentence should be carried out. The penalty for sodomy, the magistrates note, is or-dinarily burning, "since because of them [sodomites] God let fire and brimstone rain from the sky and whole cities be destroyed." But this case presented special difficulties, since "it might appear that no gen-uine sodomy could be committed with a lifeless leather device, in which case capital punishment would not apply." The magistrates settled on a compromise: death by the sword. Catherina Mühlhahn, "who let her-self be seduced into depravity," was sentenced to three years in the penitentiary or spinning room, followed by banishment.[37]

Equally striking is the case of the Italian nun, Benedetta Carlini,

Abbess of the Convent of the Mother of God in Pescia. Ecclesiastical records from 1619–23 document (in explicit detail) her sexual relations with another nun, Bartolomea Crivelli. Benedetta defended herself by claiming that she had been repeatedly possessed by an angel. "She always appeared to be in a trance while doing this. Her Angel, Splenditello, did these things, appearing as a boy of eight or nine years of age."[38] In commenting on this account, Judith Brown has noted: "In this double role, as male and as angel, Benedetta absolved herself from any possible wrongdoing."[39] This brings to mind the fourteenth-century French romance of Princess Ide, where the heroine, disguised as a man, marries the daughter of the Emperor, but is exposed. On the brink of being burned by her furious father-in-law, Princess Ide is saved by the miraculous intervention of the Virgin Mary, who turns her into a man.[40]

Brown's study of Benedetta Carlini raises very pertinent questions about the applicability of the term "lesbian" to any case before the late nineteenth century. Brown acknowledges the imprecision of the term for Benedetta Carlini, but uses it nonetheless in the subtitle of her book.[41] The difficulty lies in the paucity of information about women's sexuality in general:

Although medieval theologians and other learned men were not totally unaware of sexual relations between women, they for the most part ignored them. The world of the Middle Ages and Renaissance was not prudish. It was a world that was fully cognizant of human sexuality, but it was also phallocentric. The thought that women could bring sexual pleasure to each other without the aid of a man occurred to very few theologians and physicians.[42]

These observations are certainly reinforced by the medieval ecclesiastical material examined in this paper. I further suggest that sexual activities between women primarily came to the notice of medieval ecclesiastics when the women implicated seemed to be appropriating recognized male sexual roles. In those cases, the response could be, literally, deadly. But it must be noted that this was the penalty for male posturing, not for what we recognize today as "a lesbian relationship."

And yet, turning away from the penitentials, trials, inquisitors, and executions, we have still the charm of the poems and letters with which this essay began. We have the first-person testimony of "a number of cultivated, witty and tender young women" who wrote to each other of their love and longing. Perhaps it is not anachronistic to consider here Adrienne Rich's thesis of a "lesbian continuum" marked primarily by emotional orientation.[43] Perhaps Hadewijch and the twelfth-century German poets would echo the twentieth-century provincial quoted in *Lesbian Nuns* on the thorny subject of Particular Friendships: "Let them go to it! Thank God somebody loves somebody!"[44]

NOTES

1. Quoted by R. W. Southern, *The Making of the Middle Ages* (New Haven, CT: Yale University Press, 1953), 24.
2. Peter Dronke, *Medieval Latin and the Rise of European Love-Lyric*, 2 vols. (Oxford: Clarendon Press, 1968), 1:225–26.
3. John Boswell, *Christianity, Social Tolerance, and Homosexuality: Gay People in Western Europe from the Beginning of the Christian Era to the Fourteenth Century* (Chicago: University of Chicago Press, 1980), 220–21; Dronke, *Medieval Latin*, 2:480–81. Lines 31, 32, my emendations.
4. Dronke, *Medieval Latin*, 2:482.
5. Compare line 17, "Quid faciam, miserrima" to the eleventh-century poem "Quis est hic?" in *The Oxford Book of Medieval Latin Verse*, ed. F. J. E. Raby (Oxford: Clarendon Press, 1959), 158.
6. Boswell, *Christianity, Social Tolerance, and Homosexuality*, 221–26; Dronke, *Medieval Latin*, 1:192–221.
7. Dronke, *Medieval Latin*, 2:478–79.
8. Mother Columba Hart, ed. and trans., *Hadewijch: The Complete Works* (New York: Paulist Press, 1980).
9. See E. McDonnell, *The Beguines and the Beghards in Medieval Culture: With Special Emphasis on the Belgian Scene* (New Brunswick, NJ: Rutgers University Press, 1954).
10. See the preface of Paul Mommaers in Hart, *Hadewijch*, xiii–xxiv; for the Latin tradition behind it, see Dronke, *Medieval Latin*, 1:192–221.
11. Hart, *Hadewijch*, 105–6.
12. Rosemary Curb and Nancy Manahan, eds., *Lesbian Nuns: Breaking Silence* (Tallahassee, FL: Naiad Press, 1985).
13. Meg Bogin, ed. and trans., *The Women Troubadours* (New York: Norton, 1976), 132–33; note on the text, pp. 176–77. Bogin describes the lengths to which scholars have gone to interpret this as anything *but* a poem by a woman to a woman.
14. Ibid., 133.
15. See John T. McNeill and Helena Gamer, *Medieval Handbooks of Penance* (New York: Columbia University Press, 1938); also John T. McNeill, *The Celtic Penitentials* (Paris: Champion, 1923). Many of the texts are found in A. W. Haddan and W. Stubbs, *Councils and Ecclesiastical Documents Relating to Great Britain and Ireland*, vol. 3 (Oxford: Clarendon Press, 1871), and Herm. Jos. Schmitz, *Die Bussbücher und die Bussdisciplin der Kirche*, 2 vols. (Mainz: Verlag von Franz Kirchheim, 1883). A recent discussion of this literature is Pierre J. Payer, *Prayer, Sex and the Penitentials: The Development of a Sexual Code 500–1150* (Toronto: University of Toronto Press, 1984).
16. Boswell, *Christianity, Social Tolerance, and Homosexuality*, 180–85.
17. PL 145:172, translated by McNeill and Gamer in *Medieval Handbooks*, 411. See Boswell, *Christianity, Social Tolerance, and Homosexuality*, 210–13, Derrick Sherwin Bailey, *Homosexuality and the Western Christian Tradition* (London: Longmans, Green, and Co., 1955), 111–17; and Vern Bullough, *Sexual Variance in Society and History* (New York: John Wiley and Sons, 1976), 363–64. Peter Damian's treatise does not mention lesbianism.
18. Bullough, *Sexual Variance*, 357.
19. See especially the so-called *Roman Penitential of Halitgar of Cambrai* (ca. 830), preface and directions to confessors, in Schmitz, *Die Bussbücher*, 1:471–74; Eng. trans. in McNeill and Gamer, *Medieval Handbooks*, 297–301.
20. Cf. the so-called *Penitential of Bede*, "De fornicatione," in Haddan and Stubbs, *Councils and Ecclesiastical Documents*, 327–29; *Egbert's Penitential*, "De machina mulierum," in Schmitz, *Die Bussbücher*, 1:535–37; Eng. trans. in McNeill and Gamer, *Medieval Handbooks*, 196–97.
21. Schmitz, *Die Bussbücher*, 1:661; Eng. trans. in McNeill and Gamer, *Medieval Handbooks*, 112–13. See also the tenth-century *Decretals* of Burchard of Worms, 17, lvi, PL 140:931–33.
22. Schmitz, *Die Bussbücher*, 1:526; Eng. trans. in McNeill and Gamer, *Medieval Handbooks*,

185. The Latin verb "fornicare" is used in canon 12; "solitary vice" is in the Latin "sola cum se ipsa coitum habet."

23. Schmitz, *Die Bussbücher*, 1:526; Eng. trans. in McNeill and Gamer, *Medieval Handbooks*, 185.

24. Haddan and Stubbs, *Councils and Ecclesiastical Documents*, 328.

25. Schmitz, *Die Bussbücher*, 2:688.

26. Haddan and Stubbs, *Councils and Ecclesiastical Documents*, 328.

27. PL 123:619–722. I am indebted to an unpublished study of this text by Burton Van Name Edwards of the University of Pennsylvania, "Hincmar of Rheims and the Relationship Between Women and Witchcraft in Medieval Culture," 1974.

28. PL 125:707.

29. PL 125:692–93; Eng. trans. from "they do not" to end, in Boswell, *Christianity, Social Tolerance, and Homosexuality*, 204.

30. Boswell, *Christianity, Social Tolerance, and Homosexuality*, 204.

31. The ninth-century commentary on Romans by Hrabanus Maurus also glosses 1:26 with a reference to Satan, PL 111:1301.

32. Boswell's translation, *Christianity, Social Tolerance, and Homosexuality*, 185, with notes on the textual difficulties.

33. Liber Octavus, lx PL 140:805.

34. Joan's androgyny and the impact of her masculine attire are considered by Anne Llewellyn Barstow in her article, "Joan of Arc and Female Mysticism," *Journal of Feminist Studies in Religion* 1 (Fall 1985): 29–42, esp. 40–42.

35. Brigitte Eriksson, "A Lesbian Execution in Germany, 1721: The Trial Records," in *Historical Perspectives on Homosexuality*, ed. S. J. Licata and R. P. Petersen, *Journal of Homosexuality* (1980/81): 27–40. The quotation is from the trial record, dated 13 October 1721, p. 31.

36. Eng. trans. in Eriksson, "A Lesbian Execution," 31.

37. Ibid., 38, 40.

38. Judith C. Brown, "Lesbian Sexuality in Renaissance Italy: The Case of Sister Benedetta Carlini," *Signs: Journal of Women in Culture and Society* (The Lesbian Issue) 9 (Summer 1984): 757.

39. Ibid., 756.

40. Related by Louis Crompton, "The Myth of Lesbian Impunity: Capital Laws from 1270 to 1791," in Licata and Petersen, *Historical Perspectives on Homosexuality*, 13. Crompton does not consider the significance of Ide's male disguise.

41. Judith C. Brown, *Immodest Acts: The Life of a Lesbian Nun in Renaissance Italy* (New York: Oxford University Press, 1986), see pp. 17–20. The book relates the outcome of the Carlini case, life imprisonment. The book gives a much broader context for the visionary career of Benedetta Carlini. It should be noted that the angel's name, "Splenditello," was transcribed as "Splendidiello" in "Lesbian Sexuality," and changed here without explanation.

42. Brown, "Lesbian Sexuality," 754.

43. Adrienne Rich, "Compulsory Heterosexuality and Lesbian Existence," *Signs* 5 (Summer 1980): 631–60; critiqued as anachronistic for historical inquiry by Brown, "Lesbian Sexuality," 756.

44. Curb and Manahan, *Lesbian Nuns*, 92. *Lesbian Nuns* has been especially illuminating in providing firsthand documentation of theories and interpretations for which medieval evidence is sparse: for example, that nuns entered convents in search of social mobility, education, and to avoid contact with men; and that confessors and spiritual guides often considered the emotional attachments between nuns as unthreatening and inconsequential.

Women and Culture in Goddess-Oriented Old Europe

MARIJA GIMBUTAS

With the growing realization of the necessity to distinguish the Neolithic and Copper Age pre–Indo-European civilization from the Indo-Europeanized Europe of the Bronze Age, I coined, ten years ago, the new term "Old Europe." This term covers, in a broad sense, all Europe west of the Pontic steppe before the series of incursions of the steppe (or "Kurgan") pastoralists in the second half of the fifth, the fourth, and the beginning of the third millennium B.C.E., for in my view Europe is not the homeland of the Indo-European speakers. In a narrower sense, the term Old Europe applies to Europe's first civilization, i.e., the highest Neolithic and Copper Age culture, which was focused in the southeast and the Danubian basin and was gradually destroyed by repeated Kurgan infiltrations.

The two cultural systems were very different: The first was matrifocal, sedentary, peaceful, art-loving, earth- and sea-bound; the second was patrifocal, mobile, warlike, ideologically sky oriented, and indifferent to art. The two systems can best be understood if studied before the period of their clash and melange, i.e., before c. 4500–4000 B.C.E.

SOCIAL ORGANIZATION

Old European societies were unstratified. There were no contrasting classes of rulers and laborers, but there was a rich middle class that arose as a consequence of metallurgy and expansion of trade. Neither royal tombs, distinct in burial rites from those of the rest of the population, nor royal quarters, distinguished by extravagance, have been discovered. I see no evidence of the existence of a patriarchal chieftain system with pronounced ranking of the Indo-European type. Instead, there were in Old Europe a multitude of temples with accumulations of wealth—gold, copper, marble, shells, and exquisite ceramics. The goods of highest quality, produced by the best craftspeople, belonged

Marija Gimbutas is Professor of European Archeology at UCLA. She is the author of two hundred articles and seventeen books on the pre–Indo-European and Indo-European prehistory of Europe. Among her books are *Goddesses and Gods of Old Europe* and *The Language of the Goddess*.

not to the chief, as is customary in chiefdoms, but to the Goddess and to Her representative, the queen-priestess. The social organization represented by the rise of temples was a primary centrifugal social force.

The question of governmental organization is, as yet, difficult to answer. Central areas and secondary provinces can be observed in each culture group. Some of the foci were clearly more influential than others, but whether centralized government existed we do not know. I favor the theory of small theocratic kingdoms, or city-states, analogous to Etruscan *lucomonies* and Minoan palaces, with a queen-priestess as ruler, and her brother or husband as supervisor of agriculture and trade. The basis of such structure was more social and religious in character than civil, political, or military.

There is absolutely no indication that Old European society was patrilinear or patriarchal. Evidence from the cemeteries does not indicate a subordinate position of women. There was no ranking along a patriarchal masculine-feminine value scale as there was in Europe after the infiltration of steppe pastoralists, who introduced the patriarchal and the patrilinear system. The study of grave equipment in each culture group suggests an egalitarian society. A division of labor between the sexes is demonstrated by grave goods, but not a superiority of either. The richest graves belong to both men and women. Age was a determining factor; children had the lowest number of objects.

A strong support for the existence of matrilinearity in Old Europe is the historic continuity of matrilinear succession in the non–Indo-European societies of Europe and Asia Minor, such as the Etruscan, Pelasgian, Lydian, Carian, and Basque. Even in Rome during the monarchy, royal office passed regularly through the female line—clearly a non–Indo-European tradition, most probably inherited from Old Europe. Polybius, in the second century B.C.E., speaking of the Greek colony Lokroi on the toe of Italy, observed, "All their ancestral honors are traced through women." Furthermore, we hear from Greek historians that the Etruscans and prehistoric Athenians had "wives in common" and "their children did not know their own fathers." The woman in such a system was free to marry the man of her choice, and as many as she pleased (there was no question of adultery; that was a male invention). Children's lineage was traced through the mother only. This evidence led George Thomson to the assumption that group marriage was combined with common ownership in prehistoric Aegean societies.[1] Matrilinear succession on some Aegean islands, e.g., Lesbos, Skyros, is reported by written records in the eighteenth century C.E. and continues in partial form to this very day. Matrilinear succession to real property and prenuptial promiscuity were practiced in isolated mountainous regions of southwestern Yugoslavia up to the twentieth century.[2] Such customs are certainly unthinkable in present patriarchal society; only a very deeply rooted tradition could have survived for millennia the counterinfluence of the patrilinearity of surrounding tribes.

A matrifocal society is reflected by the Old European manifestations of the Goddess and Her worship. It is obvious that the Goddess, not gods, dominated the Old European pantheon; the Goddess ruled absolutely over human, animal, and plant life. The Goddess, not gods, spontaneously generated the life-force and created the universe. As demonstrated by the thousands of figurines and temples from the Neolithic through the Copper Ages, the male god was an adjunct of the female Goddess, as consort or son.[3] In the models of temples and household shrines, and in actual temple remains, females are shown supervising the preparation and performance of rituals dedicated to the various aspects and functions of the Goddess.[4] Enormous energy was expended in the production of religious equipment and votive gifts. Some temple models show the grinding of grain and the baking of sacred bread. The routine acts of daily existence were religious rituals by virtue of replicating the sacred models. In the temple workshops, which usually constituted half the building or occupied the floor below the temple proper, females made and decorated quantities of the various pots appropriate to different rites. Next to the altar of the temple stood a vertical loom on which were probably woven the sacred garments and temple appurtenances. The most sophisticated creations of Old Europe—the most exquisite vases, sculptures, etc., now extant— were women's work (the equipment for decoration of vases so far is known only from female graves). Since the requirements of the temple were of primary importance, production for the temple must have doubled or tripled the general level of productivity, both stimulating and maintaining the level of female craftsmanship.

RELIGION

TEMPLES

The tradition of temple building began in the seventh millennium B.C.E. A remarkable series of temple models and actual rectangular temples from the sixth and fifth millennia B.C.E. bear witness to a great architectural tradition.

At present about fifty models from various culture groups and phases are known. They are more informative than the actual temple remains, since they present details of architecture, decoration, and furnishings otherwise unavailable to prehistoric archaeology. Actual remains of sanctuaries suggest that miniature models in clay were replicas of the real temples. They almost always were found at the altars, probably as gifts to the Goddess. The seventh- and sixth-millennia temple models seemed to have conceived of the temple literally as the body or the house of the deity.

The figurines portrayed (in clay models) and found in actual shrines are shown to perform various religious activities—ritual grinding, baking of sacred bread, attending offerings—or are seated on the altar, apparently used for the reenactment of a particular religious ceremony. In the mid-fifth-millennium Cucuteni (Early Tripolyte) shrine at Sabatinivka in the valley of Southern Bug in the Ukraine, sixteen female figurines were sitting on chairs on the altar, all with snake-shaped heads and massive thighs. One held a baby snake. Another group of sixteen were in action—baking, grinding, or standing at the dish containing remains of a bull sacrifice. In the corner next to the altar stood a life-size clay throne with a horned back support, perhaps for a priestess to supervise the ceremony.[5] At Ovčarovo near Trgovište in northeastern Bulgaria, twenty-six miniature religious objects were found within the remains of a burnt shrine. They included four female figurines with upraised arms, three altar screens (or temple facades) decorated with symbols, nine chairs, three tables, three lidded vessels, three drums, and several dishes larger than figurines. Such objects vividly suggest ceremonies with music and dances, lustrations, and offerings.[6]

The production of an enormous variety of religious paraphernalia—exquisite anthropomorphic, zoomorphic, and ornithomorphic vases, sacrificial containers, lamps, ladles, etc.—is one of the very characteristic features of this culture and may be viewed as a response to the demands of a theocentric culture where most production centered around the temple. The consideration of these creations is unfortunately beyond the scope of this article. Regarding the technological and aesthetic skills, nothing similar was created in the millennia that immediately followed the demise of Old Europe.

CEREMONIAL COSTUMES AND MASKS

A wealth of costume details is preserved on the clay figurines. Deep incisions encrusted with white paste or red ocher affirm the presence of hip-belts, fringe, aprons, narrow skirts, blouses, stoles; a variety of hairstyles, and the use of caps, necklaces, bracelets, and medallions. Whether these fashions were worn commonly or were traditional garb for priestesses or other participants in ritual celebrations can only be conjectured. The latter was probably the case; most of the figurines seem to have been characters in tableaux of ritual. But ritual or not, the costumes reflect stylistic conventions of dress and taste characteristic of the period.

In the female costume several dress combinations recur persistently: Partly dressed figures wear only a hip-belt, or a hip-belt from which hangs an apron or panels of an entire skirt of fringe; others wear a tight skirt with shoulder straps or a blouse. A number of figurines show incised or painted stoles over the shoulders and in front and back. The skirt, which generally begins below the waist and hugs the hips, has a decorative texture of white encrusted incisions, showing net-pattern, zigzags, checkerboard, or dots. The skirt narrows below the knees, and on some figurines wrappings around the legs are indicated. It may be that the skirt was slit in front below the knees and fastened between the legs with woven bands. This type of skirt gives the impression of constraining movement and very likely had a ritualistic purpose.

The figurines tell little about male attire. Males are usually portrayed nude, except for a large V-shaped collar and a belt. In the last phase of the Cucuteni culture, male figures wear a hip-belt and a strap passing diagonally across the chest and back over one of the shoulders.

Special attention to coiffure and headgear is evidenced. The Bird and Snake Goddesses in particular, or devotees associated with their images, had beautiful coiffures, a crown, or decorative headbands. Vinča and Butmir female figurines have hair neatly combed and divided symmetrically in the center, the two panels perhaps separated by a central ribbon. Late Cucutenian female figurines, primarily nude, but some wearing hip-belt and necklace, have a long, thick coil of hair hanging down the back and ending in a large, circular bun or with an attached disc, reminiscent of the style favored by Egyptian ritual dancers of the third millennium B.C.E. A typical item of dress is a conical cap on which radial or horizontal parallel incisions perhaps represent its construction of narrow ribbonlike bands.

Figurines were portrayed wearing masks representing certain aspects of the Goddess, gods, or their sacred animals, or else they were simply shown as bird-headed (with beaked faces on a cylindrical neck), snake-headed (with a long mouth, round eyes, and no nose), ram- or other animal-headed. Frequently occurring perforations of the mask were obviously intended to carry some sort of organic attachment. Plumes, flowers, fruits, and other materials could have been employed in this way.

DEITIES

In the literature on prehistoric religion the female figures of clay, bone, and stone are usually considered to be the "Mother-Goddess." Is She indeed nothing more than an image of motherhood? The term is not entirely a misnomer if we understand Her as a creator or as a cosmogenic woman. It must be emphasized that from the Upper Paleolithic onward the persona of the Goddess splintered in response to the developing economy, and the images of deities portray far more than the single maternal metaphor. Study of the several stereotypical shapes and postures of the figurines and of the associated symbolism of the signs incised upon them clearly shows that the figurines were intended to project a multiplicity of divine aspects and a variety of divine functions.

There were, in my opinion, two primary aspects of the Goddess (not necessarily two Goddesses) presented by the effigies. The first is "She Who Is the Giver of All"—giver of life, of moisture, of food, of happiness—and "Taker of All," i.e., death. The second aspect of the Goddess is Her association with the periodic awakening of nature: She is springtime, the new moon, rebirth, regeneration, and metamorphosis. Both go back to the Upper Paleolithic. The significance of each aspect is visually supported on the figurines by appropriate symbols and signs. The first aspect of the Goddess as Giver and Taker of All, that is, as both beginning and end of life, is accompanied by aquatic symbols—water birds, snakes, fish, frogs, and animals associated with water—and by representations of water itself in the form of zigzag bands, groups of parallel lines, meanders, nets, checkerboards, and running spirals. The second aspect of the Goddess as rebirth, renewal, and transcendence is accompanied by the symbols of "becoming": eggs, uteri, phalluses, whirls, crescents, and horns that resemble cornucopias. The Goddess often appears in the form of a bee, butterfly, or caterpillar. This second group involves male animals, such as bulls and dogs.

Hybrids of the human female with a bird or snake dominated mythical imagery throughout the Upper Paleolithic, Neolithic, Chalcolithic, and Copper Age from c. 26,000 to the end of Old Europe at c. 3000 B.C.E., but lingered in the Aegean and Mediterranean region through the Bronze Age and later; at least forty percent of the total number of figurines belong to this type. The Fish, Bird, and Snake Goddesses were interrelated in meaning and function. Each is Creator and Giver. They are, therefore, inseparable from cosmogonic and cosmogenic myths, such as water birds carrying cosmic eggs. She, as the Mother or *Source*, is the giver of rain, water, milk, and meat (plus hides and wool). Her portrayals usually show exaggerated breasts marked with parallel lines, or a wide-open beak or round hole for a mouth. Her large eyes are a magical source and are surrounded by aquatic symbolism (usually groups of parallel lines). Beginning in the Neolithic, the ram (the earliest domesticated animal, a vital source of food and clothing) became Her sacred animal. The symbols of this aspect of the Goddess on spindle whorls and loom weights suggest She was the originator or guardian of the crafts of spinning and weaving. Metaphorically, as "the spinner and weaver of human life," She became the Goddess of Fate.

Along with the life-giving aspect of the Goddess, Her life-taking or death-giving aspect must have developed in preagricultural times. The images of vultures and owls are known from the Upper Paleolithic and from the earliest Neolithic (in the frescoes of Çatal Hüyük, in central Anatolia, vultures appear above headless human beings). The figurines of the nude Goddess with large pubic triangle, folded arms, and face of an owl, well known from Old European graves, may be representations of the Goddess in the aspect of night and death.

In early agricultural times, the Giver of All developed another function, a function vital to tillers of the soil: Giver of Bread. Her images were deposited in grain silos or in egg-shaped vases, where they were indispensable insurance for the resurgence of plant life. She also appears as a pregnant woman, Her ripe body a metaphor of the fertile field. She was worshipped with Her sacred animal, the pig. The fattening of the pig was associated with the growth and ripening of crops and fertility in general.

Richly represented throughout the Neolithic, Chalcolithic, and Copper Age is still another aspect of the Goddess: Birth-giving Goddess. She is portrayed with outstretched legs and upraised arms in a naturalistic birth-giving posture. This stereotypic image appears in relief on large vases and on temple walls; carved in black and green stone or alabaster, it was worn as an amulet.

The "periodic regeneration" aspect of the Goddess may be as ancient as the Giver of All aspect, since symbols of "becoming" are present in the Upper Paleolithic: crescents and horns appear in association with Paleolithic nudes. Because regenerating the life-force was Her main function, the Goddess was flanked by male animals noted for physical strength—bulls, he-goats, dogs. In Her incarnation as a crescent, caterpillar, bee, or butterfly, She was a symbol of new life; She emerged from the body or horns of the bull as a bee or butterfly.

The female principle was conceived as creative and eternal, the male as spontaneous and ephemeral. The male principle was represented symbolically by male animals and by phalluses and ithyphallic animal-masked men—goat-man or bull-man. They appear as adjuncts of the Goddess. The figurines of ecstatic dancers, goat- or bull-masked, may represent worshippers of the Goddess in rituals enacting the dance of life.

THE PATRIARCHAL INVASIONS

Old Europe was rapidly developing into an urban culture, but its growth was interrupted and eventually stopped by destructive forces from the East: the steadily increasing infiltration of the seminomadic, horse-riding ("Kurgan") pastoralists from the Pontic steppe. Periodic waves of infiltration into civilized Europe effected the disintegration of the first European civilization. Only on the islands, such as Crete, Thera, and Malta, did the traditions, symbols, and syllabic script of Old Europe survive for almost two millennia. The Bronze Age culture that followed north of the Aegean, however, was an amalgam of the Old European substrate plus totally different elements of an Eastern culture.

Thanks to a growing number of radiocarbon dates, archaeologists can ascertain the periods of Kurgan penetration into Europe. There was no single massive invasion, but a series of repeated incursions concentrated into three major thrusts: c. 4400–4300 B.C.E.; c. 3400–3200 B.C.E.; and c. 3000–2900 B.C.E.[7]

The steppe people were, above all, pastoralists. As such, their social system was composed of small patrilinear units that were socially stratified according to the strategic services performed by its male members. The grazing of large herds over vast expanses of land necessitated a living pattern of seasonal settlements or small villages affording sufficient pasturage for animals. The chief tasks of a pastoral economy were executed by men, not by women, as was characteristic of the indigenous agricultural system.

It was inevitable that an economy based on farming and another which relied on stock-breeding would produce unrelated ideologies. The upheaval of the Old European civilization is registered in the abrupt cessation of painted pottery and figurines, the disappearance of shrines, the termination of symbols and signs, the abolition of matrifocal culture, and the annihilation or co-optation of the Goddess religion.

Old European ceramics are readily identified with the rich symbolic signs and decorative motifs that reflect an ideology concerned with cosmogony, generation, birth, and regeneration. Symbols were compartmentalized or interwoven in myriad combinations—meanders and spirals, chevrons and zigzags, circles, eggs, horns, etc. There were a multitude of pictorial and sculptural representations of the Goddess and subordinate gods, of worshippers, and sacred animals. In contrast, Kurgan pottery is devoid of symbolic language and of aesthetic treatment in general because it obviously did not serve the same ceremonial purposes as that of Old Europe. The Kurgan stabbing and impressing technique is quite primitive and seems to focus on only one symbol, the sun. Occasionally, a schematized fir tree occurs, which may symbolize a "tree of life."

Mythical images that were in existence on the Eurasian steppe dispersed now over a large part of Europe and continued to the beginning of Christianity and beyond. The new ideology was an apotheosis of the horseman and warrior. The principal gods carried weapons and rode horses or chariots; they were figures of inexhaustible energy, physical power, and fecundity. In contrast to the sacred myths of pre–Indo-European peoples which centered around the moon, water, and the female, the religion of pastoral, semisedentary Indo-European peoples was oriented toward the rotating sky, the sun, stars, planets, and other sky phenomena, such as thunder and lightning. Their sky and sun gods shone "bright as the sky"; they wore starry cloaks adorned with glittering gold, copper, or amber pendants, torques, chest plates, and belts.

They carried shining daggers, swords, and shields. The Indo-Europeans glorified the magical swiftness of arrow and javelin and the sharpness of the blade. Throughout the millennia, the Indo-Europeans exulted in the making of weapons, not pottery or sculpture. They believed that the touch of the axe blade awakened the powers of nature and transmitted the fecundity of the Thunder God; by the touch of His spear tip, the God of War and the Underworld marked the hero for glorious death.

NOTES

1. George Thomson, *The Prehistoric Aegean: Studies in Ancient Greek Society* (London: Lawrence and Wishart, 1978 edition), 97 ff.
2. Conversation with Djuro Basler, Sarajevo, 1968.
3. Marija Gimbutas, *The Gods and Goddesses of Old Europe, 7000–3500 B.C.: Myths, Legends and Cult Images* (London: Thames and Hudson, 1974; Berkeley: University of California Press, 1974).
4. Marija Gimbutas, "Temples of Old Europe," *Archaeology* (November/December 1980): 41–50.
5. M. L. Makarevich, "Ob Ideologicheskikh Predstavleniyakh u Tripol'skikh Plemen'," *Zapiski Odesskogo Arkheol. Obshchestva*, Odessa, 1960.
6. Henrieta Todorova, *Ovčharovo*, Izdatelstvo "Septemvri," Sofia, 1976.
7. Marija Gimbutas, "The Three Waves of the Steppe People into East Central Europe," *Arch. suisses d'anthrop. gén.*, Geneva, 43, 2 (1980). Also consult "Proceedings of the International Conference on the Transformation of European Culture at 4500–2500 B.C.," Dubrovnik, 12–17 Sept. 1979, ed. by Marija Gimbutas, *Journal of Indo-European Studies* 8 (1980).

The Myth of Demeter and Persephone

CHARLENE SPRETNAK

Demeter is the Grain-Mother, the giver of crops. Her origins are Cretan, and she has been strongly connected to Gaia[1] and to Isis.[2] Demeter's daughter, Persephone, or Kore, is the Grain-Maiden, who embodies the new crop. Every autumn the women of early Greece observed a three-day, agricultural fertility ritual, the Thesmophoria, in honor of Demeter. The three days were called the *Kathodos* and *Anodos* (Downgoing and Uprising), the *Nesteia* (Fasting), and the *Kalligeneia* (Fair-Born or Fair Birth).[3] The Thesmophoria, the Arrephoria, the Skirophoria, the Stenia, and the Haloa were rites practiced by women only and were of extremely early origin. They were preserved "in pristine purity down to the late days and were left almost uncontaminated by Olympian usage"; they emerged later in the most widely influential of all Greek rituals, the Eleusinian Mysteries.[4] Isocrates wrote that Demeter brought to Attica "twofold gifts": "crops" and the "Rite of Initiation"; "those who partake of the rite have fairer hopes concerning the end of life."[5]

The Homeric *Hymn to Demeter*, assigned to the seventh century B.C.E., is a story written to explain the Eleusinian Mysteries, which honored Demeter.[6] The tale became famous as "The Rape of Persephone," who was carried off to the underworld and forced to become the bride of Hades. However, prior to the Olympian version of the myth at a rather late date, there was no mention of rape in the ancient cult of Demeter and her daughter, nor was there any rape in the two traditions antecedent to Demeter's mythology.

Archaeology has supported[7] what Diodorus wrote concerning the flow of Egyptian culture into Greece via Crete: "the whole mythology of Hades" was brought from Egypt into Greece and the mysteries of Isis are just like those of Demeter, "the names only being changed."[8] Isis was Queen of the Underworld, sister of Osiris, and passed freely to and from the netherworld. Demeter's other antecedent was Gaia,[9] the ancient Earth-Mother who had power over the underworld because

Charlene Spretnak is author of The Spiritual Dimension of Green Politics, Green Politics: The Global Promise, Lost Goddesses of Early Greece, *and editor of* The Politics of Women's Spirituality.

the earth is the abode of the dead.[10] At certain sites in Greece, Demeter was worshipped as "Demeter Chthonia,"[11] and in Athens the dead were called *Demetreioi*, "Demeter's People"; not only did she bring all things to life, but when they died, she received them back into her bosom.[12] That the maiden form (Kore) of the Goddess would share the functions of the mature form (Demeter), as giver of crops on the earth and ruler of the underworld, is a natural extension. The early Greeks often conceived of their Goddesses in maiden and mature form simultaneously; later the maiden was called "daughter."[13]

In addition to the connections with Isis and Gaia, another theory holds that Persephone (also called Phesephatta) was a very old Goddess of the underworld indigenous to Attica, who was assimilated by the first wave of invaders from the north; the myth of the abduction is believed to be an artificial link that merged Persephone with Demeter's daughter, Kore.[14] Whatever the impulse behind portraying Persephone as a rape victim, evidence indicates that this twist to the story was added after the societal shift from matrifocal to patriarchal, and that it was not part of the original mythology. In fact, it is likely that the story of the rape of the Goddess is a historical reference to the invasion of the northern Zeus-worshippers, just as is the story of the stormy marriage of Hera, the native queen who will not yield to the conqueror Zeus.

Although the exact delineation of the pre-Olympian version of the myth of Demeter and Persephone has been lost, the following version seeks to approximate the original by employing the surviving clues and evidence. This extremely ancient and widely revered sacred story of mother and daughter long pre-dates the Christian deification of father and son.

DEMETER AND PERSEPHONE

There once was no winter. Leaves and vines, flowers and grass grew into fullness and faded into decay, then began again in unceasing rhythms.

Men joined with other men of their mother's clan and foraged in the evergreen woods for game. Women with their children or grandchildren toddling behind explored the thick growth of plants encircling their homes. They learned eventually which bore fruits that sated hunger, which bore leaves and roots that chased illness and pain, and which worked magic on the eye, mouth, and head.

The Goddess Demeter watched fondly as the mortals learned more and more about Her plants. Seeing that their lives were difficult and their food supply sporadic, She was moved to give them the gift of wheat. She showed them how to plant the seed, cultivate, and finally harvest the wheat and grind it. Always the mortals entrusted the essential process of planting food to the women, in the hope that their fecundity of womb might be transferred to the fields they touched.

Demeter had a fair-born Daughter, Persephone, who watched over the crops with Her Mother. Persephone was drawn especially to the new sprouts of wheat that pushed their way through the soil in Her favorite shade of tender green. She loved to walk among the young plants, beckoning them upward and stroking the weaker shoots.

Later, when the plants approached maturity, Persephone would leave their care to Her Mother and wander over the hills, gathering narcissus, hyacinth, and garlands of myrtle for Demeter's hair. Persephone Herself favored the bold red poppies that sprang up among the wheat. It was not unusual to see Demeter and Persephone decked with flowers dancing together through open fields and gently sloping valleys. When Demeter felt especially fine, tiny shoots of barley or oats would spring up in the footprints She left.

One day They were sitting on the slope of a high hill looking out in many directions over Demeter's fields of grain. Persephone lay on Her back while Her Mother stroked Her long hair idly.

"Mother, sometimes in my wanderings I have met the spirits of the dead hovering around their earthly homes and sometimes the mortals, too, can see them in the dark of the moon by the light of their fires and torches.

"There are those spirits who drift about restlessly, but they mean no harm.

"I spoke to them, Mother. They seem confused and many do not even understand their own state. Is there no one in the netherworld who receives the newly dead?"

Demeter sighed and answered softly, "It is I who has domain over the underworld. From beneath the surface of the earth I draw forth the crops and the wild plants. And in pits beneath the surface of the earth I have instructed the mortals to store My seed from harvest until sowing, in order that contact with the spirits of My underworld will fertilize the seed. Yes, I know very well the realm of the dead, but My most important work is here. I must feed the living."

Persephone rolled over and thought about the ghostly spirits She had seen, about their faces drawn with pain and bewilderment.

"The dead need us, Mother. I will go to them."

Demeter abruptly sat upright as a chill passed through Her and rustled the grass around Them. She was speechless for a moment, but then hurriedly began recounting all the pleasures they enjoyed in Their world of sunshine, warmth, and fragrant flowers. She told Her Daughter of the dark gloom of the underworld and begged Her to reconsider.

Persephone sat up and hugged Her Mother and rocked Her with silent tears. For a long while They held each other, radiating rainbow auras of love and protection. Yet Persephone's response was unchanged.

They stood and walked in silence down the slope toward the fields. Finally They stopped, surrounded by Demeter's grain, and shared weary smiles.

"Very well. You are loving and giving and We cannot give only to Ourselves. I understand why You must go. Still, You are My Daughter and for every day that You remain in the underworld, I will mourn Your absence."

Persephone gathered three poppies and three sheaves of wheat. Then Demeter led Her to a long, deep chasm and produced a torch for Her to carry. She stood and watched Her Daughter go down farther and farther into the cleft in the earth.

In the crook of Her arm Persephone held Her Mother's grain close to Her breast, while Her other arm held the torch aloft. She was startled by the chill as She descended, but She was not afraid. Deeper and deeper into the darkness She continued, picking Her way slowly along the rocky path. For many hours She was surrounded only by silence. Gradually She became aware of a low moaning sound. It grew in intensity until She rounded a corner and entered an enormous cavern, where thousands of spirits of the dead milled about aimlessly, hugging themselves, shaking their heads, and moaning in despair.

Persephone moved through the forms to a large, flat rock and ascended. She produced a stand for Her torch, a vase for Demeter's grain, and a large shallow bowl piled with pomegranate seeds, the food of the dead. As She stood before them, Her aura increased in brightness and in warmth.

"I am Persephone and I have come to be your Queen. Each of you has left your earthly body and now resides in the realm of the dead. If you come to Me, I will initiate you into your new world."

She beckoned those nearest to step up onto the rock and enter Her aura. As each spirit crossed before Her, Persephone embraced the form and then stepped back and gazed into the eyes. She reached for a few of the pomegranate seeds, squeezing them between Her fingers. She painted the forehead with a broad swatch of the red juice and slowly pronounced:

> "You have waxed into the fullness of life
> And waned into darkness;
> May you be renewed in tranquility and wisdom."

For months Persephone received and renewed the dead without ever resting or even growing weary. All the while Her Mother remained disconsolate. Demeter roamed the earth hoping to find Her Daughter emerging from one of the secret clefts. In Her sorrow She withdrew

Her power from the crops, the trees, the plants. She forbade any new growth to blanket the earth. The mortals planted their seed, but the fields remained barren. Demeter was consumed with loneliness and finally settled on a bare hillside to gaze out at nothing from sunken eyes. For days and nights, weeks and months She sat waiting.

One morning a ring of purple crocus quietly pushed its way through the soil and surrounded Demeter. She looked with surprise at the new arrivals from below and thought what a shame it was that She was too weakened to feel rage at Her injunction being broken. Then she leaned forward and heard them whisper in the warm breeze: "Persephone returns! Persephone returns!"

Demeter leapt to Her feet and ran down the hill through the fields into the forests. She waved Her arms and cried: "Persephone returns!" Everywhere Her energy was stirring, pushing, bursting forth into tender greenery and pale young petals. Animals shed old fur and rolled in the fresh, clean grass while birds sang out: "Persephone returns! Persephone returns!"

When Persephone ascended from a dark chasm, there was Demeter with a cape of white crocus for Her Daughter. They ran to each other and hugged and cried and laughed and hugged and danced and danced and danced. The mortals saw everywhere the miracles of Demeter's bliss and rejoiced in the new life of spring. Each winter they join Demeter in waiting through the bleak season of Her Daughter's absence. Each spring they are renewed by the signs of Persephone's return.

NOTES

1. Lewis R. Farnell, *The Cults of the Greek States*, vol. 3 (Oxford: Oxford University Press, 1907), 28, 48–50.
2. Jane Ellen Harrison, *The Religion of Ancient Greece* (London: Archibald Constable & Co. Ltd., 1905), 51–52.
3. Jane Ellen Harrison, *Prolegomena to the Study of Greek Religion* (Cambridge: Cambridge University Press, 1922), 120–31; see also R. F. Willetts, *Cretan Cults and Festivals* (London: Routledge and Kegan Paul, 1962), 152.
4. Harrison, *Prolegomena*, 120.
5. Harrison, *The Religion of Ancient Greece*, 51.
6. E. O. James, *The Cult of the Mother Goddess: An Archeological and Documentary Study* (New York: Frederick A. Praeger, 1959), 153.
7. Sir Arthur Evans, *The Earlier Religion of Greece in the Light of Cretan Discoveries* (London: Macmillan and Co. Ltd., 1931), 8.
8. Harrison, *The Religion of Ancient Greece*, 52.
9. Farnell, *Cults of the Greek States*, 28, 48–50.
10. Ibid., 8.
11. Ibid., 48–50.
12. Jane Ellen Harrison, *Myths of Greece and Rome* (London: Ernest Benn Ltd., 1927), 73.
13. Harrison, *Prolegomena*, 263, 274.
14. Gunther Zuntz, *Persephone: Three Essays on Religion and Thought in Magna Graecia* (Oxford: Oxford University Press, 1971), 75–77.

Entering into the Serpent

GLORIA ANZALDÚA

Mi mamagrande Ramona toda su vida mantuvo un altar pequeño en la esquina del comedor. Siempre tenía las velas prendidas. Allí hacía promesas a la Virgen de Guadalupe. [My grandmother Ramona all her life maintained a small altar in the corner of the dining room. She always had candles lit. There she made vows to the Virgin of Guadalupe.] My family, like most Chicanos, did not practice Roman Catholicism but a folk Catholicism with many pagan elements. *La Virgen de Guadalupe*'s Indian name is *Coatlalopeuh*. She is the central deity connecting us to our Indian ancestry.

Coatlalopeuh is descended from, or is an aspect of, earlier Mesoamerican fertility and Earth goddesses. The earliest is *Coatlicue*, or "Serpent Skirt." She had a human skull or serpent for a head, a necklace of human hearts, a skirt of twisted serpents and taloned feet. As creator goddess, she was mother of the celestial deities, and of *Huitzilopochtli* and his sister, *Coyolxauhqui*, She With Golden Bells, Goddess of the Moon, who was decapitated by her brother. Another aspect of *Coatlicue* is *Tonantsi*.[1] The Totonacs, tired of the Aztec human sacrifices to the male god, *Huitzilopochtli*, renewed their reverence for *Tonantsi* who preferred the sacrifice of birds and small animals.[2]

The male-dominated Azteca-Mexica culture drove the powerful female deities underground by giving them monstrous attributes and by substituting male deities in their place, thus splitting the female Self and the female deities. They divided her who had been complete, who possessed both upper (light) and underworld (dark) aspects. *Coatlicue*, the Serpent goddess, and her more sinister aspects, *Tlazolteotl* and *Cihuacoatl*, were "darkened" and disempowered.

Tonantsi—split from her dark guises, *Coatlicue*, *Tlazolteotl*, and *Cihuacoatl*—became the good mother. The Nahuas, through ritual and prayer, sought to oblige *Tonantsi* to ensure their health and the growth of their crops. It was she who gave *México* the cactus plant to provide her people with milk and pulque. It was she who defended her children against the wrath of the Christian God by challenging God, her son,

---

Gloria Anzaldúa is a Chicana lesbian feminist poet and fiction writer. She has been active in the migrant farm workers movement and has taught at various universities. Coeditor of *This Bridge Called My Back: Writings by Radical Women of Color* and author of *Borderlands/La Frontera*, her work has appeared in numerous collections.

to produce mother's milk (as she had done) to prove that his benevolence equalled his disciplinary harshness.[3]

After the Conquest, the Spaniards and their Church continued to split *Tonantsi/Guadalupe*. They desexed *Guadalupe*, taking *Coatlalopeuh*, the serpent/sexuality, out of her. They completed the split begun by the Nahuas by making *la Virgen de Guadalupe/Virgen María* into chaste virgins and *Tlazolteotl/Coatlicue/la Chingada* into *putas* [whores]; into the Beauties and the Beasts. They went even further; they made all Indian deities and religious practices the work of the devil. Thus *Tonantsi* became *Guadalupe*, the chaste protective mother, the defender of the Mexican people.

Guadalupe appeared on December 9, 1531, on the spot where the Aztec goddess, *Tonantsi* ("Our Lady Mother"), had been worshipped by the Nahuas and where a temple to her had stood. Speaking Nahua, she told Juan Diego, a poor Indian crossing Tepeyac Hill, whose Indian name was *Cuautlaohuac* and who belonged to the *mazehual* class, the humblest within the Chichimeca tribe, that her name was *María Coatlalopeuh*. *Coatl* is the Nahuatl word for serpent. *Lopeuh* means "the one who has dominion over serpents." I interpret this as "the one who is at one with the beasts." Some spell her name *Coatlaxopeuh* (pronounced "*Cuatlashupe*" in Nahuatl) and say that "*xopeuh*" means "crushed or stepped on with disdain." Some say it means "she who crushed the serpent," with the serpent as the symbol of the indigenous religion, meaning that her religion was to take the place of the Aztec religion.[4] Because *Coatlalopeuh* was homophonous to the Spanish *Guadalupe*, the Spanish identified her with the dark Virgin, *Guadalupe*, patroness of West Central Spain.[5]

From that meeting, Juan Diego walked away with the image of *la Virgen* painted on his cloak. Soon after, Mexico ceased to belong to Spain, and *la Virgen de Guadalupe* began to eclipse all the other male and female religious figures in Mexico, Central America, and parts of the U.S. Southwest. "*Desde entonces para el mexicano ser Guadalupano es algo esencial*/Since then for the Mexican, to be a *Guadalupano* is something essential."[6]

Mi Virgen Morena	My brown virgin
Mi Virgen Ranchera	my country virgin
Eres nuestra Reina	you are our queen
México es tu tierra	Mexico is your land
Y tú su bandera.	and you its flag.

—"*La Virgen Ranchera*"[7]

In 1660 the Roman Catholic Church named her Mother of God, considering her synonymous with *la Virgen María*; she became *la Santa Patrona de los mexicanos* [the patron saint of Mexicans]. The role of defender (or patron) has traditionally been assigned to male gods. During the Mexican Revolution, Emiliano Zapata and Miguel Hidalgo used her image to move *el pueblo mexicano* [the Mexican people] toward freedom. During the 1965 grape strike in Delano, California, and in subsequent Chicano farmworkers' marches in Texas and other parts of the Southwest, her image on banners heralded and united the farmworkers. *Pachucos* (zoot suiters) tattoo her image on their bodies. Today, in Texas and Mexico she is more venerated than Jesus or God the Father. In the Lower Rio Grande Valley of south Texas it is *la Virgen de San Juan de los Lagos* (an aspect of *Guadalupe*) that is worshipped by thousands every day at her shrine in San Juan. In Texas she is considered the patron saint of Chicanos. *Cuando Carito, mi hermanito* [when Carito, my brother] was missing in action and, later, wounded in Viet Nam, *mi mamá* got on her knees *y le prometío a Ella que si su hijito volvía vivo* [and promised Her that if her son returned alive] she would crawl on her knees and light novenas in her honor.

Today, *la Virgen de Guadalupe* is the single most potent religious, political, and cultural image of the Chicano/*mexicano*. She, like my race, is a synthesis of the old world and the new, of the religion and culture of the two races in our psyche, the conquerors and the conquered. She is the symbol of the *mestizo* true to his or her Indian values. *La cultura chicana* identifies with the mother (Indian) rather than with the father (Spanish). Our faith is rooted in indigenous attributes, images, symbols, magic, and myth. Because *Guadalupe* took upon herself the psychological and physical devastation of the conquered and oppressed *india*, she is our spiritual, political, and psychological symbol. As a symbol of hope and faith, she sustains and insures our survival. The Indian, despite extreme despair, suffering, and near genocide, has survived. To Mexicans on both sides of the border, *Guadalupe* is the symbol of our rebellion against the rich, upper and middle class; against their subjugation of the poor and the *indio*.

Guadalupe unites people of different races, religions, languages: Chicano protestants, American Indians, and whites. "*Nuestra abogada siempre serás*/Our *mediatrix* you will always be." She mediates between the Spanish and the Indian cultures (or three cultures as in the case of *mexicanos* of African or other ancestry) and between Chicanos and the white world. She mediates between humans and the divine, between this reality and the reality of spirit entities. *La Virgen de Guadalupe* is the symbol of ethnic identity and of the tolerance for ambiguity that Chicanos-*mexicanos*, people of mixed race, people who have Indian blood, people who cross cultures, by necessity possess.

La gente Chicana tiene tres madres. [The Chicana people has three mothers.] All three are mediators: *Guadalupe*, the virgin mother who has not abandoned us, *la Chingada* (*Malinche*), the raped mother whom we have abandoned, and *la Llorona*, the mother who seeks her lost children and is a combination of the other two.

Ambiguity surrounds the symbols of these three "Our Mothers." *Guadalupe* has been used by the Church to mete out institutionalized oppression: to placate the Indians and *mexicanos* and *Chicanos*. In part, the true identity of all three has been subverted—*Guadalupe* to make us docile and enduring, *la Chingada* to make us ashamed of our Indian side, and *la Llorona* to make us long-suffering people. This obscuring has encouraged the *virgen/puta* (whore) dichotomy.

Yet we have not all embraced this dichotomy. In the U.S. Southwest, Mexico, Central and South America the *indio* and the *mestizo* continue to worship the old spirit entities (including *Guadalupe*) and their supernatural power, under the guise of Christian saints.[8]

> Las invoco diosas mías, ustedes las indias
> sumergidas en mi carne que son mis sombras.
> Ustedes que persisten mudas en sus cuevas.
> Ustedes Señoras que ahora, como yo,
>   están en desgracia.

FOR WAGING WAR IS MY COSMIC DUTY: THE LOSS OF THE BALANCED OPPOSITIONS AND THE CHANGE TO MALE DOMINANCE

Before the Aztecs became a militaristic, bureaucratic state where male predatory warfare and conquest were based on patrilineal nobility, the principle of balanced opposition between the sexes existed.[9] The people worshipped the Lord and Lady of Duality, *Ometecuhtli* and *Omecihuatl*. Before the change to male dominance, *Coatlicue*, Lady of the Serpent Skirt, contained and balanced the dualities of male and female, light and dark, life and death.

The changes that led to the loss of the balanced oppositions began when the Azteca, one of the twenty Toltec tribes, made the last pilgrimage from a place called Aztlán. The migration south began about the year C.E. 820. Three hundred years later the advance guard arrived near Tula, the capital of the declining Toltec empire. By the 11th century, they had joined with the Chichimec tribe of Mexitin (afterwards called Mexica) into one religious and administrative organization within Aztlán, the Aztec territory. The Mexitin, with their tribal god *Tetzauhteotl Huitzilopochtli* (Magnificent Humming Bird on the Left), gained control of the religious system.[10] (In some stories *Huitzilopochtli* killed his sister, the moon goddess *Malinalxoch*, who used her supernatural power over animals to control the tribe rather than wage war.)

Huitzilopochtli assigned the Azteca-Mexica the task of keeping the human race (the present cosmic age called the Fifth Sun, *El Quinto Sol*) alive. They were to guarantee the harmonious preservation of the human race by unifying all the people on earth into one social, religious, and administrative organ. The Aztec people considered themselves in charge of regulating all earthly matters.[11] Their instrument: controlled or regulated war to gain and exercise power.

After one hundred years in the central plateau, the Azteca-Mexica went to Chapultepec, where they settled in 1248 (the present site of the park on the outskirts of Mexico City). There, in 1345, the Azteca-Mexica chose the site of their capital, Tenochtitlan.[12] By 1428, they dominated the Central Mexican lake area.

The Aztec ruler, *Itzcoatl*, destroyed all the painted documents (books called codices) and rewrote a mythology that validated the wars of conquest and thus continued the shift from a tribe based on clans to one based on classes. From 1429–1440, the Aztecs emerged as a militaristic state that preyed on neighboring tribes for tribute and captives.[13] The "wars of flowers" were encounters between local armies with a fixed number of warriors, operating within the Aztec World, and, according to set rules, fighting ritual battles at fixed times and on predetermined battlefields. The religious purpose of these wars was to procure prisoners of war who could be sacrificed to the deities of the capturing party. For if one "fed" the gods, the human race would be saved from total extinction. The social purpose was to enable males of noble families and warriors of low descent to win honor, fame, and administrative offices, and to prevent social and cultural decadence of the elite. The Aztec people were free to have their own religious faith, provided it did not conflict too much with the three fundamental principles of state ideology: to fulfill the special duty set forth by *Huitzilopochtli* of unifying all peoples, to participate in the wars of flowers, and to bring ritual offerings and do penance for the purpose of preventing decadence.[14]

Matrilineal descent characterized the Toltecs and perhaps early Aztec society. Women possessed property, and were curers as well as priestesses. According to the codices, women in former times had the supreme power in Tula, and in the beginning of the Aztec dynasty, the royal blood ran through the female line. A council of elders of the Calpul headed by a supreme leader, or *tlactlo*, called the father and mother of the people, governed the tribe. The supreme leader's vice-emperor occupied the position of "Snake Woman" or *Cihuacoatl*, a goddess.[15] Although the high posts were occupied by men, the terms referred to females, evidence of the exalted role of women before the Aztec nation became centralized. The final break with the democratic Calpul came when the four Aztec lords of royal lineage picked the king's successor from his siblings or male descendants.[16]

La Llorona's wailing in the night for her lost children has an echoing note in the wailing or mourning rites performed by women as they bid their sons, brothers, and husbands good-bye before they left to go to the "flowery wars." Wailing is the Indian, Mexican, and Chicana woman's feeble protest when she has no other recourse. These collective wailing rites may have been a sign of resistance in a society that glorified the warrior and war and for whom the women of the conquered tribes were booty.[17]

In defiance of the Aztec rulers, the *macehuales* (the common people) continued to worship fertility, nourishment, and agricultural female deities, those of crops and rain. They venerated *Chalchiuhtlicue* (goddess of sweet or inland water), *Chicomecoatl* (goddess of food), and *Huixto-cihuatl* (goddess of salt).

Nevertheless, it took less than three centuries for Aztec society to change from the balanced duality of their earlier times and from the egalitarian traditions of a wandering tribe to those of a predatory state. The nobility kept the tribute, the commoner got nothing, resulting in a class split. The conquered tribes hated the Aztecs because of the rape of their women and the heavy taxes levied on them. The *Tlaxcalans* were the Aztec's bitter enemies and it was they who helped the Spanish defeat the Aztec rulers, who were by this time so unpopular with their own common people that they could not even mobilize the populace to defend the city. Thus the Aztec nation fell not because *Malinali* (*la Chingada*) interpreted for and slept with Cortés, but because the ruling elite had subverted the solidarity between men and women and between noble and commoner.[18]

SUEÑO CON SERPIENTES

Coatl. In pre-Columbian America the most notable symbol was the serpent. The Olmecs associated womanhood with the Serpent's mouth which was guarded by rows of dangerous teeth, a sort of *vagina dentate*. They considered it the most sacred place on earth, a place of refuge, the creative womb from which all things were born and to which all things returned. Snake people had holes, entrances to the body of the Earth Serpent; they followed the Serpent's way, identified with the Serpent deity, with the mouth, both the eater and the eaten. The destiny of humankind is to be devoured by the Serpent.[19]

> Dead,
> the doctor by the operating table said.
> I passed between the two fangs,
> the flickering tongue.
> Having come through the mouth of the serpent,
> swallowed,
> I found myself suddenly in the dark,
> sliding down a smooth wet surface
> down down into an even darker darkness.
> Having crossed the portal, the raised hinged mouth,
> having entered the serpent's belly,
> now there was no looking back, no going back.
>
> Why do I cast no shadow?
> Are there lights from all sides shining on me?

Ahead, ahead,
curled up inside the serpent's coils,
the damp breath of death on my face.
I knew at that instant: something must change
or I'd die.

Algo tenía que cambiar.

After each of my bouts with death I'd catch glimpses of an other-world Serpent. Once, in my bedroom, I saw a cobra the size of the room, her hood expanding over me. When I blinked she was gone. I realized she was, in my psyche, the mental picture and symbol of the instinctual in its collective impersonal, pre-human form. She, the symbol of the dark sexual drive, the chthonic (underworld), the feminine, the serpentine movement of sexuality, of creativity, the basis of all energy and life.

THE PRESENCES

She appeared in white, garbed in white,
standing white, pure white.

—Bernardino de Sahagún[20]

On the gulf where I was raised, *en el Valle del Río Grande* in South Texas—that triangular piece of land wedged between the river *y el golfo* [and the gulf] which serves as the Texas–U.S./Mexican border—is a Mexican *pueblito* [little village] called Hargill (at one time in the history of this one-grocery-store, two-service-stations town there were thirteen churches and thirteen *cantinas* [bars]). Down the road, a little ways from our house, was a deserted church. It was known among the *mexicanos* that if you walked down the road late at night you would see a woman dressed in white floating about, peering out the church window. She would follow those who had done something bad or who were afraid. *Los mexicanos* called her *la Jila.* Some thought she was *la Llorona.* She was, I think, *Cihuacoatl,* Serpent Woman, ancient Aztec goddess of the earth, of war and birth, patron of midwives, and antecedent of *la Llorona.* Covered with chalk, *Cihuacoatl* wears a white dress with a decoration half red and half black. Her hair forms two little horns (which the Aztecs depicted as knives) crossed on her forehead. The lower part of her face is a bare jawbone, signifying death. On her back she carries a cradle, the knife of sacrifice swaddled as if it were her papoose, her child.[21] Like *la Llorona, Cihuacoatl* howls and weeps in the night, screams as if demented. She brings mental depression and sorrow. Long before it takes place, she is the first to predict something is to happen. Back then, I, an unbeliever, scoffed at these Mexican superstitions as I was taught in Anglo school.

Four years ago a red snake crossed my path as I walked through the woods. The direction of its movement, its pace, its colors, the "mood" of the trees and the wind and the snake—they all "spoke" to me, told me things. I look for omens everywhere, everywhere catch glimpses of the patterns and cycles of my life. Stones "speak" to Luisah Teish, a Santera; trees whisper their secrets to Chrystos, a Native American. I remember listening to the voices of the wind as a child and understanding its messages. *Los espíritus* [the spirits] that ride the back of the south wind. I remember their exhalation blowing in through the slits in the door during those hot Texas afternoons. A gust of wind raising the linoleum under my feet, buffeting the house. Everything trembling.

We're not supposed to remember such otherworldly events. We're supposed to ignore, forget, kill those fleeting images of the soul's presence and of the spirit's presence. We've been taught that the spirit is outside our bodies or above our heads somewhere up in the sky with God. We're supposed to forget that every cell in our bodies, every bone and bird and worm has spirit in it.

Like many Indians and Mexicans, I did not deem my psychic experiences real. I denied their occurrences and let my inner senses atrophy. I allowed white rationality to tell me that the existence of the "other world" was mere pagan superstition. I accepted their reality, the "official" reality of the rational, reasoning mode which is connected with external reality, the upper world, and is considered the most developed consciousness—the consciousness of duality.

The other mode of consciousness facilitates images from the soul and the unconscious through dreams and the imagination. Its work is labeled "fiction," make-believe, wish-fulfillment. White anthropologists claim that Indians have "primitive" and therefore deficient minds, that we cannot think in the higher mode of consciousness—rationality. They are fascinated by what they call the "magical" mind, the "savage" mind, the *participation mystique* of the mind that says the world of the imagination—the world of the soul—and of the spirit is just as real as physical reality.[22] In trying to become "objective," Western culture made "objects" of things and people when it distanced itself from them, thereby losing "touch" with them. This dichotomy is the root of all violence.

Not only was the brain split into two functions but so was reality. Thus people who inhabit both realities are forced to live in the interface between the two, forced to become adept at switching modes. Such is the case with the *india* and the *mestiza*.

Institutionalized religion fears trafficking with the spirit world and stigmatizes it as witchcraft. It has strict taboos against this kind of inner knowledge. It fears what Jung calls the Shadow, the unsavory aspects of ourselves. But even more it fears the supra-human, the god in ourselves. Voodoo, Santeria, Shamanism and other native religions are called cults and their beliefs are called mythologies. In my own life, the Catholic Church fails to give meaning to my daily acts, to my continuing encounters with the "other world." It and other institutionalized religions impoverish all life, beauty, pleasure.

The Catholic and Protestant religions encourage fear and distrust of life and of the body; they encourage a split between the body and the spirit and totally ignore the soul; they encourage us to kill off parts of ourselves. We are taught that the body is an ignorant animal; intelligence dwells only in the head. But the body is smart. It does not discern between external stimuli and stimuli from the imagination. It reacts equally viscerally to events from the imagination as it does to "real" events.

So I grew up in the interface trying not to give countenance to *el mal aigre*,[23] evil non-human, non-corporeal entities riding the wind, that could come in through the window, through my nose with my breath. I was not supposed to believe in *susto*, a sudden shock or fall that frightens the soul out of the body. And growing up between such opposing spiritualities how could I reconcile the two, the pagan and the Christian?

No matter to what use my people put the supranatural world, it is evident to me now that the spirit world, whose existence the whites are so adamant in denying, does in fact exist. This very minute I sense the presence of the spirits of my ancestors in my room. And I think *la Jila* is *Cihuacoatl*, Snake Woman; she is *la Llorona*, Daughter of Night, traveling the dark terrains of the unknown searching for the lost parts of herself. I remember *la Jila* following me once, remember her eerie lament. I'd like to think that she was crying for her lost children, *los* Chicanos/*mexicanos*.

NOTES

1. In some Nahuatl dialects *Tonantsi* is called *Tonatzin*, literally "Our Holy Mother." "*Tonan* was a name given in Nahuatl to several mountains, these being the congelations of the Earth Mother at spots convenient for her worship." The Mexica considered the mountain mass southwest of Chapultepec to be their mother. Burr Cartwright Brundage, *The Fifth Sun: Aztec Gods, Aztec World* (Austin, TX: University of Texas Press, 1979), 154, 242.
2. Ena Campbell, "The Virgin of Guadalupe and the Female Self-Image: A Mexican Case History," in *Mother Worship: Themes and Variations*, ed. James J. Preston (Chapel Hill, NC: University of North Carolina Press, 1982), 22.
3. Alan R. Sandstrom, "The Tonantsi Cult of the Eastern Nahuas," in Preston, *Mother Worship*.
4. Andres Gonzales Guerrero, Jr., *The Significance of Nuestra Señora de Guadalupe and La Raza Cósmica in the Development of a Chicano Theology of Liberation* (Ann Arbor, MI: University Microfilms International, 1984), 122.
5. *Algunos dicen que Guadalupe es una palabra derivida del lenguaje arabe que significa "Río Oculto."* [Some say that Guadalupe is a word derived from Arabic that means "Hidden River."] Tomie de Paola, *The Lady of Guadalupe* (New York: Holiday House, 1980), 44.
6. "*Desde el cielo una hermosa mañana,*" from *Propios de la misa de Nuestra Señora de Guadalupe*, in Guerrero, 124.

7. From "*La Virgen Ranchera*," Guerrero, *The Significance of Nuestra Señora*, 127.

8. *La Virgen María* is often equated with the *Aztec Teleoinam*, the Maya *Ixchel*, the Inca *Mamacocha*, and the Yoruba *Yemayá*.

9. Levi-Strauss's paradigm which opposes nature to culture and female to male has no such validity in the early history of our Indian forebears. June Nash, "The Aztecs and the Ideology of Male Dominance," *Signs* (Winter 1978): 349.

10. Geoffrey Parrinder, ed., *World Religions: From Ancient History to the Present* (New York: Facts on File Publishers, 1971), 72.

11. Parrinder, 77.

12. Nash, "The Aztecs," 352.

13. Ibid., 350, 355.

14. Parrinder, 355.

15. Jacques Soustelle, *The Daily Life of the Aztecs on the Eve of the Spanish Conquest* (New York: Macmillan Publishing Co., 1962). Soustelle and most other historians got their information from the Franciscan father, Bernardino de Sahagún, chief chronicler of Indian religious life.

16. Nash, "The Aztecs," 252–53.

17. Ibid., 358.

18. Ibid., 361–62.

19. Karl W. Luckert, *Olmec Religion: A Key to Middle America and Beyond* (Norman, OK: University of Oklahoma Press, 1976), 68, 69, 87, 109.

20. Bernardino de Sahagún, *General History of the Things of New Spain* (Florentine Codex), vol. 1 revised, trans. Arthur Anderson and Charles Dibble (Santa Fe, NM: School of American Research, 1950), 11.

21. The Aztecs muted Snake Woman's patronage of childbirth and vegetation by placing a sacrificial knife in the empty cradle she carried on her back (signifying a child who died in childbirth), thereby making her a devourer of sacrificial victims. Snake Woman had the ability to change herself into a serpent or into a lovely young woman to entice young men who withered away and died after intercourse with her. She was known as a witch and a shape-shifter. See Brundage, *The Fifth Sun*, 168–71.

22. Anthropologist Lucien Levy-Bruhl coined the term *participation mystique*. According to Jung, "It denotes a peculiar kind of psychological connection . . . [in which] the subject cannot clearly distinguish himself from the object but is bound to it by a direct relationship which amounts to partial identity." Carl Jung, "Definitions," in *Psychological Types, The Collected Works of C. G. Jung*, vol. 6 (Princeton, NJ: Princeton University Press, 1953), par. 781.

23. Some *mexicanos* and Chicanos distinguish between *aire*, air, and *mal aigre*, the evil spirits that reside in the air.

Ancestor Reverence

LUISAH TEISH

Birth is the beginning of physical life and Death is the end of it. But the essential energy of existence continues beyond physical life. Both Life and Death simply exist and are two sides of the same coin of existence.

> Those who are dead are never gone:
> They are there in the thickening shadow.
> The dead are not under the earth:
> they are in the tree that rustles,
> they are in the wood that groans,
> they are in the water that sleeps,
> they are in the hut, they are in the crowd,
> the dead are not dead.
>
> Those who are dead are never gone,
> they are in the breast of the woman,
> they are in the child who is wailing
> and in the firebrand that flames.
> The dead are not under the earth:
> they are in the fire that is dying,
> they are in the grasses that weep,
> they are in the whimpering rocks,
> they are in the forest, they are in the house,
> the dead are not dead.
>
> —Birago Diop

From among the many African traditions remembered in the Americas comes the belief that those who go before us make us what we are. Accordingly, ancestor-reverence holds an important place in African belief systems. Through reverence for them we recognize our origins and ensure the spiritual and physical continuity of the human race.

Obviously, ancestors influence human life through hereditary physical and personality traits, but in African views they continue to exist and act in the world. Not only does their energy find a home in the "wood that groans" but at the proper time and under the right circumstances they can be reborn. . . .

Luisah Teish, author of *Jambalaya,* is an initiated priestess in the Yoruba-Lucumi spiritual tradition of West Africa (Nigeria). A writer, lecturer, and storyteller, she has appeared in a play about Zora Neale Hurston. She is an activist in the Black Women's health movement and the Womanspirit Community.

Ancestors function as guides, warriors, and healers. These roles are not mutually exclusive of each other. A given ancestor may act in any number or combination of these capacities. It depends on what the person was like during her lifetime and on what work she was doing in the spirit world.

Was your grandmother a seamstress? Yes? Then take her shopping with you. She'll lead you to the best bargain on attractive, durable, and low-cost clothing. You'll have to acquaint her with your style and color preferences but you should also pay attention to hers. Was Papa a handy man? Yes? Then take him with you when you go house hunting. He can sense the bad wiring, leaky pipes, and deteriorating foundation of the place. He'll steer you toward a better house and then suggest ways to make necessary repairs. Having trouble dieting? Perhaps your great-aunt realizes now that her heart attack was due to wrong diet. Perhaps she will help you keep to your diet as part of *her work* in the spirit world.

You don't know how much they are willing to help you until you contact them.

SHRINE BUILDING

The first step in communicating with your ancestors is building a shrine. Your ancestor shrine is an all-purpose altar. By adding different things in varying proportions, it can become a shrine for any element or attribute you desire—meditation space, abundance altar, oracular chamber.

One of my greatest pleasures is witnessing the variety of altars built by members of my extended family. Here everyone's artistic ability comes out. People mold, carve, arrange, and combine until they have an altar that is useful and pleasing.

Shop in the Mother's market for altar objects—driftwood, seashells, stones, and so on. Begin to see the beauty in things that you might have called *trash* before. Understand that "They—the ancestors—are in the whimpering rocks," and bring them home.

Altars move themselves (inspire you to move them) from room to room, change levels, take on different dimensions.

Following are *guidelines* for building altars to the ancestors or *eguns*. Use these guidelines initially, but know that once you contact your *eguns* they will give you new instructions.

I am assuming that your house is "cleaned."

THE SMALLEST ALTAR

If you live in a studio apartment, a room, or other small space, the smallest altar is your cup of tea. It consists of a piece of white cloth; a crystal chalice filled with water and a tablespoon of anisette, white rum, or white wine (this water is called *spirit water*) a white candle, and four stones. You will also need family pictures.

Place the stones in the four corners, the spirit water chalice at the center, the candle in front of it, and pictures of your family members behind it. Food offerings can be put either side of the chalice, or directly in front of the picture. The only place you *cannot* put them is on top of the chalice.

This is a humble altar but your ancestors understand your limitations. If they want a bigger altar, they will help you find a bigger space. It is better to construct a small altar and begin the attunement between you than to wait for more space.

THE NINE-DAY ALTAR

The nine-day altar is constructed at the time a family member surrenders the last breath. This altar can be built within the space of a larger altar, or in another room specifically for this member. If the departure of this member is your inspiration for taking up *egun* work, then build and use this altar first and expand on it later, for general use. Regardless of its future, this altar is designed to send comfort to the recently expired member.

Use a piece of white cloth, preferably a piece of a garment belonging to the *egun*. Tear the cloth so that its edges are stringy, fringed. Think of this fringed end as *Da* or life force in the form of nerve endings, connecting your intelligence with that of the new ancestor.

Place four stones in the four corners. If they are stones from the *egun*'s yard or house, they have more power; if not, simply wash some stones in natural water and breathe on them before placing them on the altar.

Now place the chalice with spirit water in the center of the altar and surround it with eight clear glasses of plain water. This is the "circle of waters."

If the ancestor was a Christian in this life, place a crucifix in the chalice; if not, a simple X or cross for the four directions will suffice. The Egyptian ankh, or any other symbol representing death and resurrection that the *egun* will recognize, can be used.

Place an image (picture, drawing) of the *egun* in front of the circle of waters. Place flowers behind the circle of waters. Offerings of food, and certain tools, favorite jewels, or other materials that the *egun* may need on the other side of the veil can be placed on either side of the circle of waters.

The important action you will take is this: every day for the next nine days, you will place a white candle on top of the image and bid the *egun* farewell.

Of course, the other option is to visit the cemetery each day for nine days after burial. In this case you bring candles and flowers and sit in front of the earth womb (grave) and have lunch with the *egun*.

If you are unusually uncomfortable in the cemetery, don't go in. If you are comfortable there, just be sure to enter and leave with respect.

THE OUTDOOR ALTAR

Some people have beautiful gardens in private yards. If you have been so blessed, perhaps you will want to construct an altar in the garden. In this case, simply mark off the space with rocks. Place the chalice of spirit water in the center and surround it with fruit, leaves, and pieces of wood; stick your candles in the earth in front of the chalice and bid the *egun* farewell.

THE ELABORATE INDOOR ALTAR

My favorite altar is the elaborate indoor altar. Choose a corner in a private room. Assuming the house has been cleaned, lay brown or dark green fabric on the floor (to represent the earth) and stabilize it with four stones in the corners. Now place the circle of waters in the center. Place flowers wherever it pleases you. Get nine white candles and one seven-day black candle. Place the black candle in front of the circle of waters and the nine white candles around the outside of the circle. Distribute images of the *eguns* at various places on the altar; and place images of living relatives on the wall above the altar. . . . Now arrange these objects on the altar in a way that makes you feel good about them. *Voilà!* You have a beautiful altar.

Some people say, "I'm not good at altar building!" That's only because they are thinking of it as a task. If you're having trouble, just set a glass of spirit water and a candle in the area and gaze until the altar tells you how to build it.

I am amazed at how much of what we call interior decorating is really just subconscious altar building. I've been in homes of people who swear they are "not the least bit spiritual," yet I find Grandma's picture standing next to a lovely bouquet, on a hand-crocheted doily and a lamp nearby. All that's needed is a glass of water.

Whatever your choice of altars, understand that as soon as it is built it becomes "sacred space"; a place between the physical and spiritual world where the *eguns* and the living can communicate in peace. . . .

RITUALS FOR THE EXTENDED FAMILY

Rituals and exercises create attunement with your ancestors. By *attunement*, I mean sacred acts that will help you to realize your kinship with them. . . .

POURING LIBATIONS

Libations should always be poured for the ancestors. Remember that the continuous creation of the *Da* is fluid. Water, juices, or alcohol can all be used. Simply pour the liquid on the ground or floor of the altar three times and say, "May my hands be fresh. May the road be clear. May the house be clean." After your ancestors have drunk, each person should take a sip of the liquid.

FIRST FEAST

Your first feast for the ancestors should be as elaborate as your means allow. There's only one rule on cooking for the *eguns*—no salt. Salt repels spirits, and you are asking them to focus some attention on you. Coffee, bread, sweets, fruit, soup, stews, meats, and so on—they eat it all. It is good to cook a special something characteristic of their and your motherland, such as cornbread, challah bread, scones, tortillas.

At this first feast, lay all the food on your altar and bless the food. Then take a small portion from each dish and place it on a saucer. Breathe on the food and touch it to the top of your head, your heart, and your pubis. Put a white candle in the center of the food, light it, and place it in a corner of the room. Then say,

O blood of my blood. This is your child _____ *(name yourself, all others name themselves)*. I bring you _____ *(name the foods)* for your nourishment. Know that you are loved and respected. Accept this offering for our good. Watch over your descendant: Let there be no death, let there be no illness, let there be no accident, let there be no upheaval, let there be no poverty, let there be no ill fate *(name all attributes you want to dispel)*. Stand fast for me, for my good fortune, for my wealth, for my happiness, for my home, for my health *(name all the attributes you want to attract)*.

Thank you, blood of my blood. Thank you, O mighty dead.

The traditional Yoruba invocation is much longer than this one. But we are talking to kind spirits who are appreciative of our attention, so you can begin with this humble invocation. Later you will write your own.

ATTENDANCE

You should have as many of your family members in attendance at your feast as possible. If they are far away or are hostile to your spiritual practice, have friends represent them. After the ritual, call your mother. You need not tell her what you are doing, just call to say Hi.

After this first feast, develop the habit of taking a small saucer of food out of the pot *before* dinner is served. If you make this a weekly habit, the *eguns* will be happy.

Do you find yourself habitually dropping food while cooking? Do yams seem to fly from your fingers and slide across the kitchen floor? Maybe it's time to feed your ancestors.

I have said that cooking for your ancestors is simple. It is, with one exception. Do not think that you can *impose* your diet on them. It won't work for long.

I knew a woman who tried to force her ancestors to keep a vegetarian diet. The oracle kept saying that they were not satisfied. I suggested she make some meatballs for them. She did and got "great good fortune" from the oracle. I could advise her this way because I'd tried to impose a pork-free diet on my ancestors, but much to my disgust they insisted on pork chops to accompany their greens, yams, and cornbread.

By now a few of you are saying, "This is absurd! Why should I give food to somebody who can't eat it?" Remember, everything including food is made of energy. You are simply returning energy to those who gave you the energy of existence. Feed them, and they'll feed you.

The day after your first feast, take the food on the saucer and place it at the foot of a tree, or throw it in the compost heap. Give it back to Eartha, and She'll give it back to you in the forms of fruit, flowers, and vegetables.

Part 2

NAMING THE SACRED

Naming the Sacred

A growing feminist consensus, expressed in the essays in this section, maintains that androcentric perspectives have affected not only the language and the images we use to name the sacred, but also the underlying conceptions we hold of God's *transcendence*. We not only call God "Lord," "King," and "Father" and think of "him" as "big and old and tall and grey-bearded and white," we also conceptualize God as radically separate from and more perfect than humanity and nature, and we think of ourselves as "godlier" than the rest of nature because we think of ourselves as created in the image of God.

Traditional notions of God's transcendence are expressed mythically through images of God as residing in heaven, creating the earth out of nothing, ruling over the earth like a king, and judging and destroying the earth. Philosophically, God's transcendence is frequently understood to mean that God is different from humanity and nature because God is pure spirit uncorrupted by a physical body. The human body with its connections to nature then is said to keep us from God. The mind must rule over the passions of the body, and humans must rule over "brute" nature. In such traditions, woman is often viewed as the source of sin who through her sexuality leads man away from God, binding him to his animal passions. Given that woman is viewed as closer to the animal and nature, it is logical that God would be imaged as male within such a system.

Though expressed in different languages and through images drawn from different traditions, most of the essays in this section criticize traditional notions of God's transcendence, suggesting that thealogy or theology take a more *immanental*, or earth and body-centered, direction. Though there are differences in the conceptions of God expressed in these varied feminist voices, each calls us to rethink the traditional dualisms through which we have understood the relation of the divine to humanity and nature. In different ways they suggest that we are connected to the divine through the body and nature.

Each of these feminist images of the sacred challenges traditional conceptions of divine transcendence that have been identified with *monotheism*, the doctrine or belief in one God. It is tempting to label these feminist views *animism*, the belief that everything has a soul or spirit, *pantheism*, the belief that all is God or God is all, or *polytheism*, the belief in many divinities. But these terms derive from the attempts of Western male theologians and scholars to understand and categorize religions they viewed as radically different from and inferior to biblical monotheism. Before rushing to label the new feminist namings of the sacred, it is important to *listen deeply* and to ask whether any of these categories is appropriate. Perhaps the new feminist namings of the sacred call us to develop new thealogical, theological, and philosophical categories and languages that are less dualistic and value-laden.

While such categories might help to reorient our thinking, the authors of the essays in this section would probably agree with Nelle Morton that philosophical concepts are secondary to images or metaphors, because "we act out of images rather than concepts." While the authors agree on the inadequacy of exclusive focus on the image of a white male God, they offer different images to replace or complement it: It, birds, trees, sexual feelings, feelings of oneness with all that is, the earth as my sister, the light in us, the Goddess, Spider Goddess, the goddess and the goddesses, Artemis, the source of life, God as Mother, God/ess as once and future Shalom of being, God our Mother and Father. Yet most would probably agree that respect for a plurality of images and metaphors for the sacred is another teaching of the turn toward the immanent in feminist namings of the sacred.

The image of God that emerges in Shug's conversation with Celie in Alice Walker's novel *The Color Purple* articulates the intuitions of many feminists and has been widely quoted. The image of God in *The Color Purple* is a product both of Shug's individual meditation and of her conversation with Celie which "hears her into speech." According to Shug, "God ain't a he or a she, but a It." Though many feminist theologians have named God "She" and "Goddess," most would agree that these names too are metaphorical. Besides challenging the image of God as an old man, Walker reminds us that God is commonly imaged not only as a man, but as *white*. When Shug says "God is inside you and inside everybody else . . . God is everything," her words point to the presence of God in the black female body as well as to the vivid experience of God in nature, as in "the color purple in a field." "It sort of like you know what, she say, grinning and rubbing high up on my thigh." Far from being a source of sin and temptation, sexuality for Shug—both homosexuality and heterosexuality—is a path to God. Shug's vision of God incorporates suffering and loss, "if I cut a tree, my arm would bleed." But Shug rejects the Christian notions of sin and salvation. Her relation with God is rooted in love and connection.

Susan Griffin, like Alice Walker, experiences the sacred through passionate connection. For Griffin the sacred is found within this earth who is called "she" and "my sister." In her meditations on the earth,

NAMING THE SACRED / 97

the forest, the wind, and matter, Griffin evokes a deep connection between woman and nature. Challenging the scientific worldview which says that through knowledge humans can control nature, Griffin hears the trees saying, "You know we have grown this way for years. And to no purpose you can understand." Nature provokes us to understand ourselves more deeply. "Are we afraid of this wind? Will we go where we are afraid to go?" When Griffin asserts, "we know ourselves to be made of this earth . . . everything moves, everything changes . . . we are nature," she rejects 2500 years of Western philosophy and theology which have stated that there is a reality beyond change, that our destiny is to rise above nature or to control it with our "superior" intelligence.

Griffin interweaves her love for women, including images of lesbian sexuality, with her love for nature. The "she" who is passionately loved is simultaneously earth, mother, daughter, lover. "As I go into her, she pierces my heart." Her "she" is both the earth and the female lover. "Her renewal washes over me endlessly" is an image of the sea, the seasons, and her lover's orgasm. Images of dominance and submission are absent. Rather Griffin calls us to imagine our love for each other, the earth, and the sacred without hierarchy.

Nelle Morton's "The Goddess as Metaphoric Image" reminds us that "Goddess" is not simply a female name for the God of the Bible. The words "Now, SHE is a new creation" spoken in the context of women's space, women's community, and women's liturgy shattered Morton's image of the patriarchal God and its glorification of hierarchical power. Morton's experience of the Goddess in the storm evokes the bond between woman and nature celebrated by Griffin. Whereas Morton had prayed to the patriarchal God to protect her *from* the storm, the Goddess enabled Morton to "become part of the rhythm" of the storm. Morton's dramatic revelation—of her mother floating on a river of blood—made her realize how deeply she had been wounded by her mother's internalizing the patriarchal fear of woman's blood. This vision enabled Morton to forgive her mother. The gray and orange spider that unexpectedly appeared, later recognized as Spider Woman, the Native American Creator Goddess, demonstrates that non-Indian North American women are being healed by the Grandmothers of our land.

Morton insists that Goddess is "metaphoric image" who "works herself out of the picture." For Morton, "She" is *necessary* to shatter the image of the male God. But the image of the Goddess for Morton is a transition to a still more immanental spirituality, linking us to "our full and whole inheritance that would make us one in our bodies, minds, and spirits."

For Christine Downing, the images of the Goddesses point to the depths of the self: living a myth connects us to archetypal, or universal and impersonal dimensions of experience. A dream sent Downing "in search of Her," "the goddess and the goddesses," leading her to confront herself through mirrors of the various Greek Goddesses—Gaia, Athene, Persephone, Ariadne, Aphrodite, Artemis. Downing weaves her personal experience and stories into her discussion of the myths and images of the Goddesses, in order to develop a female-centered archetypal psychology that reveals how women's lives are shaped by mythic themes.

For Downing, who writes, "I am no monotheist," the plurality of images of the Goddesses is celebrated as reflecting the many faces of the self. In the selection included here, Downing confronts Artemis as "She who comes from afar," and "She who slays." Artemis, Goddess of the wild and untamed places, is for Downing the most unfamiliar and difficult of the Greek Goddesses, calling her to explore unknown dimensions of herself. Artemis's devotion to female companions, the nymphs, requires Downing to "look honestly at the role in my life of deep and passionate friendships with women." Yet the Goddess's austere solitude calls Downing away from relationship, challenging her to "learn what is meant by the phrase 'monogamy of soul,'" a task Downing finds a fitting initiatory ordeal for her fiftieth birthday, her turning toward death. In her explorations of the meaning of Artemis, Downing acknowledges her hesitancy and fear, admitting that as she approaches Artemis, this Goddess retreats further into her wilderness, her wildness, revealing and concealing her numinousity, her otherness.

Marcia Falk's blessing of the "source of life," her invocation of "the holiness of the body," and her celebration of "the breath of all living things" resonate with the spiritual visions of Walker, Griffin, and Morton. But Falk's use of biblical Hebrew and her discipline of meditation and reflection on traditional Jewish prayers deliberately situates her work within the Jewish community. Falk's intention is not to deny monotheism, but to expand its meaning. *"In the name of monotheism, for the sake of an inclusive unity, I would like to see our God-talk articulate mutually supportive relationships between female and male, between immanence and transcendence, between our lives and the rest of life on the planet."* Falk's inclusive image "the source of life" is grammatically feminine in Hebrew, thus shattering the power of language that is grammatically masculine, but "the image itself cannot be said to have gender, being nonpersonal and inanimate." Although other Jewish feminists have advocated that God be invoked as "She" and even "Goddess," Falk does not choose to translate the male imagery of traditional prayers into female imagery. For Falk the image of God as "Queen of the Universe," is human-centered and hierarchical. Falk's imagery stresses the interconnectedness of all life on the planet and expresses an understanding of life as cyclical and changing. "Source of life" in

Hebrew evokes the waters of spring and womb, while images of ripening fruit, flow of life, and bringing forth bread celebrate change and transformation.

Sallie McFague's reflections on "God as Mother" are part of a longer study in which she experiments with a metaphorical Christian theology that can aid in healing the ecological and nuclear crises. Her reflections on "The World as God's Body," and on God as "Mother," "Lover," and "Friend," provide an incisive critique of the reclusive, transcendent God of Western, especially Protestant, theology. According to McFague, the image of God as Mother must not be used to perpetuate stereotypes about male and female characteristics or roles. Rather the image of God as Mother expands our conception of God, and exposes the sterility of the Christian image of God as Father. This Father God has been pictured more as redeemer from sins than as giver of life, and his love for creation, his *agape*, has been understood as "disinterested," as involving no need, no desire, no feeling, for the objects of his love. In contrast, the God who gives birth expresses joy in her creation, desires it to come to fulfillment. God as Mother is associated also with feeding and nurturing, adding a dimension of concreteness to the central Christian symbol of eucharist. Finally the image of God as Mother of the whole creation, human and nonhuman, is an image of inclusive love, shattering the fantasies that our family, our nation, our species is more deserving of life and nourishment than other members of God's family.

Rosemary Radford Ruether identifies the "male monotheism" of Christian culture in which spirit rules over matter as man rules over women, children, slaves, as a product of a revolt of the male ruling class against the ancient myth of "one physical-spiritual reality." This revolution was not completed in Hebrew culture: there the Goddess continued to be worshiped; the male God of the Hebrews appropriated some of the immanental qualities of the Goddesses; and female imagery resurfaced in the Wisdom traditions. In mainstream Christianity, however, the Goddess was eliminated, and the Wisdom tradition was absorbed by a male Christ as *Logos*, or Word. Yet Ruether finds "critical elements in Biblical theology" that contradict "male monotheism." The prophetic God who liberates the slaves and sides with the poor and the dispossessed "established at the heart of Biblical religion a motif of protest against the status quo of ruling class privilege." God as liberating sovereign calls people to break ties with familial and ethnic traditions (both understood as being oppressive), in order to "obey God rather than men." According to Ruether, the proscription of idolatry can be used to critique idolatrous adherence to male God-language, a theme also developed by Falk and McFague. Ruether argues that a "feminist reconstruction of God/ess" must draw on all these traditions, while guarding against dualism and stereotyping of the feminine principle: "God/ess as the *Shalom* of being" images liberation and new being as rooted in the matrix of being.

The Inclusive Language Lectionary is a new translation of passages from the Bible read each Sunday in the more liberal Protestant churches. The lectionary committee was asked to find nonsexist and nonracist alternatives to traditional translations of the Bible, but was not free to change the text. Though both the Hebrew and Greek texts of the Bible commonly refer to God using words that are masculine in gender ("he," "him," "father," "king," etc.), the lectionary committee decided that the *intention* of such language was to convey God's personal character and God's rulership, not to present God as a male figure. (This point is a matter of interpretation: some Christians and some feminists disagree.) Thus in the lectionary masculine pronouns are never used with reference to God. The Greek and Hebrew words that had been translated "Lord," are translated "Sovereign" or "the Sovereign One." The image of God as a ruler standing in hierarchical relation to his subjects remains intact. To change it would have required going beyond *retranslation* into *reconstruction* of biblical imagery. The most radical step taken by the lectionary committee was to use the words "Father [and Mother]" or "[Mother and] Father" with reference to God, with the word "Mother" enclosed in brackets in order to indicate that it is not found in the original text. In comparison to other selections in the section, *The Inclusive Language Lectionary* is relatively traditional and conservative. Yet it has generated a great deal of heated and even violent controversy in some churches and denominations, indicating that it too poses a radical challenge to traditional conceptions of God's nature and authority.

God Is Inside You and Inside Everybody Else

ALICE WALKER

Dear Nettie,

I don't write to God no more, I write to you.

What happen to God? ast Shug.

Who that? I say.

She look at me serious.

Big a devil as you is, I say, you not worried bout no God, surely.

She say, Wait a minute. Hold on just a minute here. Just because I don't harass it like some peoples us know don't mean I ain't got religion.

What God do for me? I ast.

She say, Celie! Like she shock. He gave you life, good health, and a good woman that love you to death.

Yeah, I say, and he give me a lynched daddy, a crazy mama, a low-down dog of a step pa and a sister I probably won't ever see again. Anyhow, I say, the God I been praying and writing to is a man. And act just like all the other mens I know. Trifling, forgitful and lowdown.

She say, Miss Celie, You better hush. God might hear you.

Let 'im hear me, I say. If he ever listened to poor colored women the world would be a different place, I can tell you.

She talk and she talk, trying to budge me way from blasphemy. But I blaspheme much as I want to.

All my life I never care what people thought bout nothing I did. I say. But deep in my heart I care about God. What he going to think. And come to find out, he don't think. Just sit up there glorying in being deef, I reckon. But it ain't easy, trying to do without God. Even if you know he ain't there, trying to do without him is a strain.

I is a sinner, say Shug. Cause I was born. I don't deny it. But once you find out what's out there waiting for us, what else can you be?

Sinners have more good times, I say.

Alice Walker, short story writer, poet, essayist, and novelist, received the American Book Award and Pulitzer Prize for her novel *The Color Purple* in 1983. In the same year, she published *In Search of Our Mothers' Gardens: Womanist Prose*, and in 1984, she published her fourth volume of poetry, *Horses Make a Landscape Look More Beautiful*.

You know why? she ast.

Cause you ain't all the time worrying bout God, I say.

Naw, that ain't it, she say. Us worry bout God a lot. But once us feel loved by God, us do the best us can to please him with what us like.

You telling me God love you, and you ain't never done nothing for him? I mean, not go to church, sing in the choir, feed the preacher and all like that?

But if God love me, Celie, I don't have to do all that. Unless I want to. There's a lot of other things I can do that I speck God likes.

Like what? I ast.

Oh, she say. I can lay back and just admire stuff. Be happy. Have a good time.

Well, this sound like blasphemy sure nuff.

She say, Celie, tell the truth, have you ever found God in church? I never did. I just found a bunch of folks hoping for him to show. Any God I ever felt in church I brought in with me. And I think all the other folks did too. They come to church to *share* God, not find God.

Some folks didn't have him to share, I said. They the ones didn't speak to me while I was there struggling with my big belly and Mr. _____ children.

Right, she say.

Then she say: Tell me what your God look like, Celie.

Aw naw, I say. I'm too shame. Nobody ever ast me this before, so I'm sort of took by surprise. Besides, when I think about it, it don't seem quite right. But it all I got. I decide to stick up for him, just to see what Shug say.

Okay, I say. He big and old and tall and graybearded and white. He wear white robes and go barefooted.

Blue eyes? she ast.

Sort of bluish-gray. Cool. Big though. White lashes, I say.

She laugh.

Why you laugh? I ast. I don't think it so funny. What you expect him to look like, Mr. _____?

That wouldn't be no improvement, she say. Then she tell me this old white man is the same God she used to see when she prayed. If you wait to find God in church, Celie, she say, that's who is bound to show up, cause that's where he live.

How come? I ast.

Cause that's the one that's in the white folks' white bible.

Shug! I say. God wrote the bible, white folks had nothing to do with it.

How come he look just like them, then? she say. Only bigger? And a heap more hair. How come the bible just like everything else they make, all about them doing one thing and another, and all the colored folks doing is gitting cursed?

I never thought bout that.

Nettie say somewhere in the bible it say Jesus' hair was like lamb's wool, I say.

Well, say Shug, if he came to any of these churches we talking bout he'd have to have it conked before anybody paid him any attention. The last thing niggers want to think about they God is that his hair kinky.

That's the truth, I say.

Ain't no way to read the bible and not think God white, she say. Then she sigh. When I found out I thought God was white, and a man, I lost interest. You mad cause he don't seem to listen to your prayers. Humph! Do the mayor listen to anything colored say? Ask Sofia, she say.

But I don't have to ast Sofia. I know white people never listen to colored, period. If they do, they only listen long enough to be able to tell you what to do.

Here's the thing, say Shug. The thing I believe. God is inside you and inside everybody else. You come into the world with God. But only them that search for it inside find it. And sometimes it just manifest itself even if you not looking, or don't know what you looking for. Trouble do it for most folks, I think. Sorrow, lord. Feeling like shit.

It? I ast.

Yeah, It. God ain't a he or a she, but a It.

But what do it look like? I ast.

Don't look like nothing, she say. It ain't a picture show. It ain't something you can look at apart from anything else, including yourself. I believe God is everything, say Shug. Everything that is or ever was or ever will be. And when you can feel that, and be happy to feel that, you've found It.

Shug a beautiful something, let me tell you. She frown a little, look out cross the yard, lean back in her chair, look like a big rose.

She say, My first step from the old white man was trees. Then air. Then birds. Then other people. But one day when I was sitting quiet and feeling like a motherless child, which I was, it come to me: that feeling of being part of everything, not separate at all. I knew that if I cut a tree, my arm would bleed. And I laughed and I cried and I run all around the house. I knew just what it was. In fact, when it happen, you can't miss it. It sort of like you know what, she say, grinning and rubbing high up on my thigh.

Shug! I say.

Oh, she say. God love all them feelings. That's some of the best stuff God did. And when you know God loves 'em you enjoys 'em a lot more. You can just relax, go with everything that's going, and praise God by liking what you like.

God don't think it dirty? I ast.

Naw, she say. God made it. Listen, God love everything you love—
and a mess of stuff you don't. But more than anything else, God love
admiration.

You saying God vain? I ast.

Naw, she say. Not vain, just wanting to share a good thing. I think
it pisses God off if you walk by the color purple in a field somewhere
and don't notice it.

What it do when it pissed off? I ast.

Oh, it make something else. People think pleasing God is all God
care about. But any fool living in the world can see it always trying to
please us back.

Yeah? I say.

Yeah, she say. It always making little surprises and springing them
on us when us least expect.

You mean it want to be loved, just like the bible say.

Yes, Celie, she say. Everything want to be loved. Us sing and dance,
make faces and give flower bouquets, trying to be loved. You ever notice that trees do everything to git attention we do, except walk?

Well, us talk and talk bout God, but I'm still adrift. Trying to chase
that old white man out of my head. I been so busy thinking bout him
I never truly notice nothing God make. Not a blade of corn (how it
do that?) not the color purple (where it come from?). Not the little
wildflowers. Nothing.

Now that my eyes opening, I feels like a fool. Next to any little scrub
of a bush in my yard, Mr. _____'s evil sort of shrink. But not altogether.
Still, it is like Shug say, You have to git man off your eyeball, before
you can see anything a'tall.

Man corrupt everything, say Shug. He on your box of grits, in your
head, and all over the radio. He try to make you think he everywhere.
Soon as you think he everywhere, you think he God. But he ain't.
Whenever you trying to pray, and man plop himself on the other end
of it, tell him to git lost, say Shug. Conjure up flowers, wind, water, a
big rock.

But this hard work, let me tell you. He been there so long, he don't
want to budge. He threaten lightening, floods and earthquakes. Us
fight. I hardly pray at all. Every time I conjure up a rock, I throw it.

Amen

This Earth Is My Sister

SUSAN GRIFFIN

THIS EARTH

WHAT SHE IS TO ME

> One should identify oneself with the universe itself. Everything that is
> less than the universe is subjected to suffering . . .
> —SIMONE WEIL, *Notebook*

As I go into her, she pierces my heart. As I penetrate further, she
unveils me. When I have reached her center, I am weeping openly. I
have known her all my life, yet she reveals stories to me, and these
stories are revelations and I am transformed. Each time I go to her I
am born like this. Her renewal washes over me endlessly, her wounds
caress me; I become aware of all that has come between us, of the noise
between us, the blindness, of something sleeping between us. Now my
body reaches out to her. They speak effortlessly, and I learn at no
instant does she fail me in her presence. She is as delicate as I am; I
know her sentience; I feel her pain and my own pain comes into me,
and my own pain grows large and I grasp this pain with my hands,
and I open my mouth to this pain, I taste, I know, and I know why
she goes on, under great weight, with this great thirst, in drought, in
starvation, with intelligence in every act does she survive disaster. This
earth is my sister; I love her daily grace, her silent daring and how
loved I am *how we admire this strength in each other, all that we have lost,
all that we have suffered, all that we know: we are stunned by this beauty*, and
I do not forget: what she is to me what I am to her.

FOREST

THE WAY WE STAND

> The poor little working-girl who had found strength to gather up the
> fragments of her life and build herself a shelter with them seemed to
> Lily to have reached the central truth of existence.
> —EDITH WHARTON, *The House of Mirth*

Susan Griffin, poet and social thinker, is the author of *Women and Nature, Pornography and Silence*, and a recent collection of poetry, *Unremembered Country*.
Her play *"Voices"* won an Emmy award for its televised version. She is currently
at work on a book about nuclear war, *The First and the Last: A Woman Thinks
About War*.

> The bank was dense with magnolia and loblolly bay, sweet gum and
> gray-barked ash. . . . He went down to the spring in the cool darkness
> of the shadows. A sharp pleasure came over him. This was a secret,
> lovely place. —MARJORIE KINNAN RAWLINGS, *The Yearling*

*The way we stand, you can see we have grown up this way together, out of
the same soil, with the same rains, leaning in the same way toward the sun. See
how we lean together in the same direction. How the dead limbs of one of us
rest in the branches of another. How those branches have grown around the
limbs. How the two are inseparable. And if you look you can see the different
ways we have taken this place into us. Magnolia, loblolly bay, sweet gum, Southern bayberry, Pacific bayberry; wherever we grow there are many of us; Monterey
pine, sugar pine, white-bark pine, four-leaf pine, single-leaf pine, bristle-cone
pine, foxtail pine, Torrey pine, Western red pine, Jeffrey pine, bishop pine. And
we are various, and amazing in our variety, and our differences multiply, so
that edge after edge of the endlessness of possibility is exposed. You know we
have grown this way for years. And to no purpose you can understand. Yet what
you fail to know we know, and the knowing is in us, how we have grown this
way, why these years were not one of them heedless, why we are shaped the way
we are, not all straight to your purpose, but to ours. And how we are each
purpose, how each cell, how light and soil are in us, how we are in the soil,
how we are in the air, how we are both infinitesimal and great and how we are
infinitely without any purpose you can see, in the way we stand, each alone, yet
none of us separable, none of us beautiful when separate but all exquisite as
we stand, each moment heeded in this cycle, no detail unlovely.*

THE WIND

> Ask who keeps the wind
> Ask what is sacred —MARGARET ATWOOD, "CIRCE POEMS"

*Yes, they say our fate is with the wind. The wind? Yes, they say when the
wind blows this way one thing will happen, and when it blows the other way,
something else will be. Something else will be? Yes, these are the questions. Does
the wind blow for us? This is what we must ask. Are we ready for this wind?
Do we know what this wind will bring us? Will we take what the wind gives,
or even know what is given when we see it? Will we see? Will we let the wind
blow all the way through us? Will the wind know us? These are the questions
to ask. Will we let the wind sing to us? Do our whole bodies listen? When the
wind calls, will we go? Will this wind come inside us? Take from us? Can we
give to the wind what is asked of us? Will we let go? Are we afraid of this
wind? Will we go where we are afraid to go? Will the wind ask us? This is
the question. Are we close to the wind? Will the wind ask much of us, and will
we be able to hear the wind singing and will we answer? Can we sing back,
this we ask, can we sing back, and not only sing, but in clear voices? Will this
be, we ask, and will we keep on answering, keep on with our whole bodies? And
do we know why we sing? Yes. Will we know why? Yes.*

MATTER

HOW WE KNOW

Because we know ourselves to be made from this earth. See this grass. The patches of silver and brown. Worn by the wind. The grass reflecting all that lives in the soil. The light. The grass needing the soil. With roots deep in the earth. And patches of silver. Like the patches of silver in our hair. Worn by time. This bird flying low over the grass. Over the tules. The cattails, sedges, rushes, reeds, over the marsh. Because we know ourselves to be made from this earth. Temporary as this grass. Wet as this mud. Our cells filled with water. Like the mud of this swamp. Heather growing here because of the damp. Sphagnum moss floating on the surface, on the water standing in these pools. Places where the river washes out. Where the earth was shaped by the flow of lava. Or by the slow movements of glaciers. Because we know ourselves to be made from this earth, and shaped like the earth, by what has gone before. The lives of our mothers. What she told me was her life. And what I saw in her hands. The calcium in the joints, the aching as she hemmed my dress. These clothes she made for me. *The pools overgrown by grass, reed, sedge, the marsh over time, becoming dry, over centuries, plankton disappearing, crustaceans gone, clams, worms, sponges, what we see now floating in these pools, fish, birds flying close to the waters. The bird with the scarlet shoulders. This bird with the yellow throat. And the beautiful song. The song like flutes. Like violoncellos in an orchestra. The orchestra in our mind. The symphony which we imagine. The music which was our idea. What we wanted to be. The lives of our grandmothers. What we imagined them to be.* She told me what she had wanted to be. What she had wanted to do. That she wanted to act on the stage. To write. She showed me the stories she wrote before she was married. Before I was born. *Why we were born when we were, as we were, we imagined. We imagined what she imagined then, what lay under the surface, this still water, the water not running over rocks, lacking air, the bacteria, fungi, dwelling at the bottom, without light, no green bodies, freeing no air, the scent of marsh gas, this bog we might lose ourselves in, sink in, the treachery here, our voices calling for help and no one listening, the silence, we made from this earth, returning to earth, the mud covering us, we giving ourselves up to this place, the fungi, bacteria, fish, everything struggling for air in this place, beetles capturing air bubbles on the surface of the pond, mosquitoes reaching with tubes to the surface of the water, fish with gills on the outsides of their bodies, fish gulping air at the surface, air captured in small hairs on the bodies of insects, stored in spaces in the stems of plants, in pockets in the tissue of leaves, everything in this place struggling for light, stems and leaves with thin skins, leaves divided into greater surfaces, numerous pores, tall plants in shallow water, open to the light; a jungle of growth in the shallow water at the edge, interwoven stems, matted leaves, places for wrens to hide, for rails, bitterns, for red-winged blackbirds to protect their nests. Fish hiding in plants underwater, insects' and snails' eggs, pupa cases, larvae and nymphs and crayfish. Sunlight pouring into plants, ingested into the bodies of fish, into the red-winged black-bird, into the bacteria, into the fungi, into the earth itself, because we know ourselves to be made of this earth, because we know sunlight moves through us, water moves through us, everything moves, everything changes, and the daughters are returned to their mothers. She always comes back. Back from the darkness. And the earth grows green again. So we were moved to feel these things. The body of the animal buried in the ground rotting feeds the seed. The sheaf of grain held up to us silently.* Her dreams, I know, she said, live on in my body as I write these words. *This proof. This testimony. This shape of possibility. What we dreamed to be. What we labored for. What we had burned desiring. What always returns. What she is to me. What she is to me, we said, and do not turn your head away, we told them, those who had tried to name us, those who had tried to keep us apart, do not turn your head away when we tell you this, we said,* how she was smaller than I then, *we try to tell you,* what tenderness I then felt for her, *we said,* as if she were my daughter, as if some part of myself I had thought lost forever were returned to me, *we said,* and then held her fiercely, *and we then made you listen, you turning your head away, you who tried to make us be still, you dividing yourself from this night we were turning through, but we made you listen, we said, do not pretend you do not hear what we say to each other, we say,* when she was returned to me and I to her that I became small to her, that my face became soft against her flesh, that through that night she held me, as if part of herself had returned, like mother to daughter *because we know we are made of this earth, and we know these meanings reach you, we said, the least comment of the stare, we said, the barely perceptible moment of despair,* I told her, *the eloquence of arms, those threaded daily causes, the fundaments of sound, cradling the infant's head, these cries,* the crying I heard in her body, *the years we had known together,* I know these meanings reach you, *we said, and the stars and their light we hold in our hands, this light telling the birds where they are, the same light which guides these birds to this place, and the light through which we imagine ourselves in the bodies of these birds, flying with them, low over the grass, weaving our nests like hammocks from blade to blade, from reed to reed. We standing at the edge of the marsh. Not daring to move closer. Keeping our distance. Watching these birds through the glass. Careful not to frighten them off. As they arrive. First the males, jet black, with a flash of red at their shoulders, a startling red which darts out of their blackness as they spread their wings. First the males and then the females flying together in the winter, now joining the males. The females with yellow throats, their wings brown and black, and light around their eyes. Now all of them calling. Calling or singing. Liquid and pleasant. Like the violoncello. We imagine like the violoncello, the cello we have made in our minds, the violin we have imagined, as we have imagined the prison, as we have made up boundaries, or decided what the fate of these birds should be, as we have invented poison, as we have invented the cage, now we stand at the edge of this marsh and do not go closer, allow them their distance, penetrate them only with our minds, only with our hearts, because though we can advance upon the blackbird, though we may cage her, though we may torture her with our will, with the boundaries we imagine, this bird will never be ours, he may die, this minute heart stop beating, the body go cold and hard, we may tear the wings apart and cut open the body and remove what we want to see, but still this blackbird will not be ours and we will have nothing. And even if we keep her alive. Train her to stay indoors. Clip her wings. Train her to sit on our fingers, though we feed her, and give her water, still this is not the blackbird we have captured, for the blackbird, which flies now over our heads, whose song reminds us of a flute, who migrates with the stars, who lives among reeds and rushes, threading a nest like a hammock, who lives in flocks, chattering in the grasses, this creature is free of our hands, we cannot control her, and for the creature we have tamed, the creature we keep in our house, we must make a new word. For we did not invent the blackbird, we say, we only invented her name. And we never invented ourselves, we admit.* And my grandmother's body is now part of the soil, she said. *Only now, we name ourselves. Only now, as we think of ourselves as passing, do we utter the syllables. Do we list all that we are. That we know in ourselves. We know ourselves to be made from this earth. We know this earth is made from our bodies. For we see ourselves. And we are nature. We are nature seeing nature. We are nature with a concept of nature. Nature weeping. Nature speaking of nature to nature. The red-winged blackbird flies in us, in our inner sight. We see the arc of her flight. We measure the ellipse. We predict its climax. We are amazed. We are moved. We fly. We watch her wings negotiate the wind, the substance of the air, its elements and the elements of those elements, and count those elements found in other beings, the sea urchin's sting, ink, this paper, our bones, the flesh of our tongues with which we make the sound "blackbird," the ears with which we hear, the eye which travels the arc of her flight. And yet the blackbird does not fly in us but in somewhere else free of our minds, and now even free of our sight, flying in the path of her own will,* she wrote, the ink from her pen flowing on this paper, her words, she thought, having nothing to do with this bird, except, she thought, as she breathes in the air this bird flies through, except, she thought, as the grass needs the body of the bird to pass its seeds, as the earth needs the grass, as we are made from this earth, she said, and the sunlight in the grass enters the body of the bird, *enters us,* she wrote on this paper, and the sunlight is pouring into my eyes from your eyes. Your eyes. Your eyes. The sun is in your eyes. I have made you smile. Your lips part. The sunlight in your mouth. Have I made the sun come into your mouth? I put my mouth on yours. To cover that light. To breathe it in. My tongue inside your mouth, your lips on my tongue, my body filled with light, filled with light, with light, shuddering, you make me shudder, you make the movement of the earth come into me, you fill me, you fill me with sound, is that my voice crying out? The sunlight in you is making my breath sing, sing your name, your name to you, beautiful one, I could kiss your bones, put my teeth in you, white gleam, whiteness, I chew, beautiful one, I am in you, I am filled with light inside you, I have no boundary, the light has extinguished my skin, I am perished in light, light filling you, shining through you, carrying you out, through the roofs of our mouths, the sky, the clouds, bursting, raining, raining free, falling piece by piece, dispersed over this earth, into the soil, deep, deeper into you, into the least hair on the deepest root in this earth, into the green heart flowing, into the green leaves and they grow, they grow into a profusion, moss, fern, and they bloom, cosmos, and they bloom, cyclamen, in your ears, in your ears, calling their names, this sound from my throat echoing, my breath in your ears, your eyes, your eyes continuing to see, continuing, your eyes telling, telling the light, the light. And she wrote, when I let this bird fly to her own purpose, when this bird flies in the path of his own will, the light from this bird enters my body, and when I see the beautiful arc of her flight, I love this bird, when I see, the arc of her flight, I fly with her, enter her with my mind, leave myself, die for an instant, live in the body of this bird whom I cannot live without, as part of the body of the bird will enter my daughter's body, because I know I am made from this earth, as my mother's hands were made from this earth, as her dreams came from this earth and all that I know, I know in this earth, the body of the bird, this pen, this paper, these hands, this tongue speaking, all that I know speaks to me through this earth and I long to tell you, you who are earth too, and listen *as we speak to each other of what we know: the light is in us.*

The Goddess as Metaphoric Image

NELLE MORTON

When I speak of the Goddess as metaphoric image I am in no way referring to an entity "out there" who appears miraculously as a fairy godmother and turns the pumpkin into a carriage. I am not even referring to a Goddess "back there" as if I participate in resurrecting an ancient religion. In the sense that I am woman I see the Goddess in myself, but I need something tangible, a concrete image or a concrete event, to capture my full attention to the present and draw me into the metaphoric process. . . .

The context in which I experienced the Goddess the first time grew out of a kind of unconscious awareness that, even though conceptually I no longer accepted a God "out there" nor defined a "God within" as male, on the level of imagery the maleness was still alive and functioning in me on most unexpected occasions.

In 1972 at Grailville[1] the second national conference on women exploring theology was held. One morning its sixty-five or so women delegates gathered for worship sitting informally in semicircular fashion on the floor of the oratory. The atmosphere of conditioned meditation—soft lighting, high altar up front, much space—was bypassed by the women perhaps intuitively, perhaps by overt intent of the leaders. A space indicated by cushions on the floor set aside was marked off as sacred. A screen hid the phallic symbol up front. A bouquet of wildflowers on the low table in front of the screen added to the informality. The women faced one another.

Most of us did not understand at the beginning what was taking place. I was aware early, however, that something new and different was happening to me—something far more than the caring I experienced in the presence of an all-woman community. The climax came near the end when the leader said: "Now, SHE is a new creation." It was not something I heard with my ears, or something I reasoned, or something I was being told. Everything seemed to coalesce and I felt

---

Nelle Morton, the first theologian to teach a university course on women and religion, was a long-time activist in the peace, human rights, and women's liberation movements. A mentor to many of the current generation of feminists in religion, her major feminist thealogical work is *The Journey is Home*.

hit in the pit of my stomach. It was as if the reader had said, "You are now coming into your full humanity. That which has been programmed out is authentically yours—essentially you." It was as if intimate, infinite, and transcending power had enfolded me, as if great wings[2] had spread themselves around the seated women and gathered us into a oneness. There were no ifs or buts. I was not hearing a masculine word from a male priest, a male rabbi, or a male minister. I was sensing something direct and powerful—not filtered by the necessity to transfer or translate from male experience and mentality into a female experience and then apply to myself. The words used in the service were exclusively female words.

Suddenly I came to, my hand on my stomach, my mouth open. I was almost sure I had said aloud, "Oh!" I wondered if I had made a fool of myself! When I looked about me, it seemed many other women were responding as I had. The leader paused. Then one of the women lifted her fist into the air and shouted "Yeah! Yeah!" All the women followed as the oratory rang with "Yeah! YEAH! YEAH!"

That is the first time I *experienced* a female deity. I had conceptualized one before, but I had not experienced one directly. It was also the first time I realized how deeply I had internalized the maleness of the patriarchal god and that in so doing I had evoked cosmic support of male rulership of the earth and had reneged on my own woman identity. Not until that moment did I realize that women had no cosmic advocate in any of the five major patriarchal religions of the world. I knew that I had much unfinished business, which I have been working on now for ten years.

My second experience of the Goddess occurred in 1976. I had already moved to a retirement community in California.[3] In August, en route to Dublin to address the World Federation of Methodist Women, I had stopped at Grailville as resource leader to the Seminary Quarter for Women.[4] Soon after my flight to New York had left the Cincinnati airport, the sky turned dark and we were caught in extremely turbulent weather. All my life I had been frightened of heights. I couldn't remember a time when I was at ease in the air—even in smooth skies. I must have had some traumatic experience with heights when a child, since each time I boarded a plane I reverted to a most irrational state, far from the mature faith I considered I now had. Usually I clasped my hands together and called on the powerful male deity in the sky for protection. I must have reverted to the faith I had when the phobia first latched itself in my unconscious; the phobia and the child faith images surfaced simultaneously. I usually asked the God Father to keep the plane safe. I even made promises and confessed my wrongdoing. I always asked safety for others in the plane and for all the planes flying as "He had the whole world in His hands." Once seized by such fear I had to keep up the pleas for safety throughout the journey. Then at the end of the journey, there was always much thanking to do.

In this particular storm en route to New York I decided it was past time to let my mature intelligent self take over. The thought came—what would happen if I invoked the Goddess! How does one call on the Goddess anyway? And which Goddess? I no sooner had such a thought than I leaned back in my seat and closed my eyes. Suddenly, it was as if someone had eased into the vacant seat next to me and placed her hand on my arm. "Relax," she said. "Let go of all your tightness. Feel your weight heavy against the seat and your feet heavy on the floor. The air has waves as does the ocean. You can't see them, but if you let yourself be carried by them you can feel their rhythm—even in turbulence. The pilot has been here before. He knows what he is doing. Even in the worst weather. Ever so faintly . . . now . . . can you feel the currents, the ordinary currents of the air? Now breathe, breathe deeply. Ride the waves. Let yourself become a part of the rhythm."

I did as she directed. Fear left my muscles. I did indeed feel the rhythm. Soon, I was enjoying the ride. Then came the question, How does one thank the Goddess? I opened my eyes. The seat was vacant. She had gone. I began to feel such power within, as if she had given me myself. She had called up my own energy. I was unafraid. Nor have I been afraid in a plane since that day. A new thing I recognized immediately: the Goddess works herself out of business. She doesn't hang around to receive thanks. It appears to be thanks enough for her that another woman has come into her own. I did not feel guilty. . . .

It was midafternoon some years later. I sat in my living room in a large armchair with my feet on a hassock, facing windows that opened onto the street. I could not throw off a blueness that had nagged me off and on all day. As I relaxed, I decided to give myself to it wholly, go to the root of it, release its energy and learn at least why it had not let go of me. As I began following it down, ready to face most anything to be rid of it, I thought of the Goddess and how she had come to my rescue on the plane, and nurtured me in other situations. As I let go and opened myself to her, in she swept suddenly through the left side of the windows in front of me. As she reached my chair she stepped aside, bowed my mother into the room, then disappeared. My mother floated in on a river of blood. It seemed all the blood in front of her was blood she had shed in her lifetime, and behind her, all the blood I had shed. She came directly to my chair, bent over me, and began speaking: "Nelle, I have made a great mistake with you children. I have allowed you to think—no, I have *taught* you—that menstruation is an illness. You were the oldest and I did learn something from you, but you suffered more than your two sisters. Never did I let you go swimming, play tennis, or hike during your periods. I didn't even let you do dishes, or take your turn with the chores about the house. It seemed the more I cared for you, the more pain your period brought. Huge clots of blood could not be absorbed by any napkin. Often the first day you had to miss school. Many times we had to have a doctor give you a shot, the pain was so intense. He kept promising that having a baby would be your only cure. Not only did you learn from me that menstruation was an illness but also that it was something to be ashamed of.

"I began sensing my mistake when you reached menopause and your doctor suggested that your dread of menopausal distress might be due to internalized negative attitudes toward blood and the body. He then proposed you purchase bath oils, bubble bath soap, bath powders, and luxuriate in your body, revel in its sensuousness. You did and have never to this day had a hot flash. Now I have learned that many of these conditions derived from patriarchal attitudes toward women and the mysterious power women possess. While I had these negative attitudes and passed them on to you girls, you, Nelle, internalized them—so deeply that they are now in your very bone marrow and too deep to be exorcised.

"Remember years ago your doctor prescribed sperm to start a baby. Now another doctor has fed you male hormones for six years. Both referred you to a male for a cure of patriarchal attitudes. Ha! Forget it! And forget all this visualizing of whole red blood cells that you will never have. Remember the hematologist who described your cells as shown under a microscope—'wild and bizarre.' Be thankful for your 'wild and bizarre' blood cells. They are keeping you alive. They are now normal for you."

My depression lifted immediately as I received this beautiful gift from my mother. I jumped from my chair and kissed her on the mouth, which she had never allowed us to do because of a lung disease she feared she might transmit to us. But in that kiss I had all the loving hugs she had ever given me. Then she disappeared.

Immediately on the right side of the window appeared an enormous spider with a gray body and large orange legs. She lifted one leg high above the other as she walked toward me on the darkness. I was not afraid, somehow. As the spider reached me she held out her two front legs on which hung some woven material. All she said was, "Your mother spun this for you." As I took the material the spider dissolved into me, as did the Goddess and then my mother. I opened my eyes. It was dark outside. My entire attitude toward my illness[5] had changed. But I remained puzzled by the spun cloth, which was neither practical nor by my standards particularly beautiful.

In not one of the above incidents was the Goddess actually summoned or invoked. Therefore, her coming, and the way she came in each case, was a surprise. . . . My greatest surprise and shock came perhaps in the last experience—the surprise of relating my internalized male attitudes toward women's blood to my present very serious blood difficulty—"too deep to exorcise." I am able now to receive the "bizarre and wild cells" as a special gift. In that sense the Goddess gave me back my life and called me to live fully with what I have, adjusting my activities to what energy I can summon and use creatively. Since then I have resumed my writing. I participate in social and political issues as I am able. It is as if the Goddess restored that part of myself that was wasted with fear from false images in my unconscious.

I began to see more clearly how we act out of images rather than concepts, especially in crisis situations; how the fear of heights automatically summoned up the God-image I had as a child when the phobia first planted itself as image deep in my unconscious. The Goddess caused the old image to surface and shatter so I could experience the flight from a more mature perspective which in many ways was mine already, but unused. I began to see more clearly how the God of patriarchal religions could have been a living metaphor at one time. But over the centuries the word has been filled with such male, power-over, and status quo images it has become a dead metaphor.

The Goddess ushered in a reality that respects the sacredness of my existence, that gives me self-esteem so I can perceive the universe and its people through my woman-self and not depend on the perception conditioned by patriarchal culture and patriarchal religion. I do not have to receive my identity or renew it through another gender, be the representative of that gender a minister, father, boss, professor, colleague, husband, or male lover. As I see the gift of myself aborted by social and political structures I renew my responsibility to the world—to help break the patriarchy that creates discriminations, oppressions, poverty, and wars. These for me have become woman issues and never again "causes." I perceive the world and its people from the perspective of where women have been put as women in the hierarchy.

The Goddess introduced me to a profound sense of community I had never before experienced. The bonding of women—from that small group at Grailville in 1972 to the small ritual, working, and action groups to which I now belong and the celebrating groups and the networks of women across the country and even around the world—continuously energizes and supports me. Beyond these groups, or because of them, rises the vision of what women can be and will become as we receive our full humanity and achieve political power. The vision enlarges to include those women still blinded by the patriarchal fog,[6] and imprisoned in a seemingly unbreakable vise. There is something of the past the vision resurrects (as Virginia Woolf urges us to resurrect Shakespeare's sister). Our research in history, literature, theology, and other fields is beginning to break open the tombs of our foresisters and enable them to walk the earth again, to claim the earth as sacred and for the good, health, and justice of all people.

The Goddess has cleared away much of the theological mystification to which I had subjected myself—which kept me from seeing and enjoying the sheer humanness of another as we came into physical proximity. Human beings did not come from another world nor are we headed for one. Nor did we descend from the sky but out of the womb of our mother, our mother's mother, and our mother's mother's mother. Recognizing our origin, we experience *presence*. . . . This kind of physical experience that is nourishing and loving and in touch with cosmic energy rises out of our common bonding and vision and our rootedness in the earth. Julia Kristeva[7] pointed out that such an experience is answerable to "a logic other than scientific," that it is experience dedicated to the search for "a little more truth" and for power shared and power from within rather than power-over.

Since the Goddess works herself out of the picture, we are better able to come into our full and whole inheritance that would make us one in our bodies, minds, and spirits. We can claim our sexuality as pervasive and as ourselves. We can claim our bodies as ours and as ourselves and our minds as our own and ourselves. This sense of oneness within and with one another has brought us into more erotic relationship with one another as women. For once a woman comes to see beauty in another woman's mind and in her own mind and to love with the mind, she discovers another dimension of power that is self-fulfilling.

The Goddess shattered the image of myself as a dependent person and cleared my brain so I could come into the power that was mine, that was me all along, but that could never have been appropriated until the old limiting image was exorcised or shattered.

The last experience with the Goddess ushering in my mother has proved most profound of all—the gift of my mother herself. Since blood is a powerful symbol of life, I see her blood as saying she has rebirthed me, and my blood as saying I have given birth to my mother. The kiss, still vivid, remains the seal of that blood covenant.

The spider! Surprise again! Who could have imagined a spider in this sequence! Especially one so large (about my size), orange and gray with elegant long legs stepping so lightly on the dark, and one that did not evoke fear!

I have not been able to identify the spider scientifically. The spider that comes closest to her color and shape is a tiny American House Spider—the *Sisyphoides*—a cobweb weaver. But since the Goddess does not allow herself to be limited to patriarchal time or space, the myth of the spider should be much more fruitful than the scientific identification or study of it.

Several tribes of the early American Indians, especially the Hopi, reverenced the Spider Woman as Creator of the earth and all underneath the earth. Making her home underneath the earth, she was known as the Earth Mother, "as old as time . . . as young as eternity." She was said to croon, "I receive Light and nourish Life. I am the Mother of all that shall ever come." Yet the Spider Woman resided in the Underground.[8]

The Mexicans saw the spider in a great hole in the west where the sun went down and perceived her as an archetypal womb sucking into death all who have ever been born. The Aztecs called her the "place of the Women" from which all humankind once crawled. The spider as this womb represented life and "time before time . . . before the birth of the sun."[9]

As Goddess of life and death the spider was also the Great Mother, a spinner of destiny. The new child is the fabric of her body or, to turn that about, the fabric of her body is the new child.[10] Finally, the Spider Goddess appears as a "journey or a way, always as walked or danced archetype," as labyrinth or spiral.

Relating myth to my experience, I see that the spider's prominent legs "walking on the darkness" affirm my journey; the spun cloth—fabric of my mother's body—affirms my own new birth. Yet the cloth being not usable in patriarchal time and space, and the Goddess not limited to time or space, the cloth could have a double meaning—death as well as birth. Since I possess no tangible evidence of the cloth, it must have disappeared in me along with the Goddess, my mother, and the spider. So *I am the new child.*

The afternoon's journey brought the relationship with my mother into sharp consciousness. "The true mystery," declared Erich Neumann, "through which the primordial situation is restored on a new plane is this: the daughter becomes identical with the mother [and she is] transformed in every respect. This unity . . . is the central content of the Eleusinian mysteries."[11]

The triple appearance of the Goddess—as herself, as my mother, as the spider—and ME! Blessed thrice! . . .

The appearance of the Goddess in the present wave of the woman movement looms as an important phenomenon and promises to become more so as the people of the world turn to our own inner power and integrity. . . . The Goddess has begun to expose the artificiality in the elaborate hierarchical system of a male-oriented deity. But perhaps the most important function of the Goddess is the transformation of women ourselves. . . . The reappearance of the Goddess at this time in history takes on profound metaphorical significance and global proportions. Women are no longer minus a cosmic advocate, rooted in creation itself, to provide legitimation for and to affirm our experiences.

NOTES

1. Grailville, located near Cincinnati, Ohio, is a Catholic Women's Community, the entire structure of which allows for full and mutual participation of all its members.
2. The image is of Isis with great, outstretched wings as if to enfold all who approach her. A silver replica of her was given to me by Carole Etzler.
3. Pilgrim Place in Claremont, California.
4. The Seminary Quarter for Women held at Grailville was a six-week course open to women enrolled in accredited seminaries. Academic credit was available. It dealt with feminist theory, theology, and practice.
5. Sideroblastic anemia is a disease of the bone marrow in which the excess iron forms a ring around young red blood cells and does not allow them to mature. No known cure. Certain medications and blood transfusions are required at frequent intervals.
6. See Susan Griffin, *Women and Nature* (New York: Harper & Row, 1978).
7. Julia Kristeva, *Desire in Language* (New York: Columbia University Press, 1980). See entire first essay, "The Ethics of Linguistics," 23ff.
8. See G. M. Mullet, *Spider Woman: Stories of the Hopi Indians* (Tucson, AZ: University of Arizona Press, 1979), 15.
9. Erich Neumann, *The Great Mother*, The Bollingen Series XL, VII (Princeton, NJ: Princeton University Press, 1972), 184–85.
10. Ibid., 177.
11. Ibid., 305–8.

Artemis

The Goddess Who Comes from Afar

CHRISTINE DOWNING

I have learned about myth from myth—from the discovery of what it means to live a myth. I have learned my way of attending to myth as I went along. . . . I have learned that recognition of the archetypal and universal dimensions of one's experiences can help free one from a purely personal relation to them. I also believe that one can celebrate the mythic patternings without losing an appreciation of the concrete and unique moments that constitute one's existence. This is what Freud meant by transference—knowing that one is Sigmund Freud *and* Oedipus, that I am Christine Downing *and* Persephone. Either description alone is insufficient. Recognition of the many goddesses that inform one's life also helps protect one against inflationary identifications and against the sense of being swallowed up by some fatally determining mythic pattern. The goddesses also seem to find ways of reminding us that they are indeed numinous forces, never reducible to our attempts at psychological interpretation. . . .

We need images and myths through which we can see who we are and what we might become. As our dreams make evident, the psyche's own language is that of image, and not idea. The psyche needs images to nurture its own growth; for images provide a knowledge that we can interiorize rather than "apply," can take to that place in ourselves where there is water and where reeds and grasses grow. Irene Claremont de Castillejo speaks of discovering the inadequacy of all *theories* about the female psyche, including the Jungian framework into which she had for so long tried to fit her own experience and that of her female patients. For now, she suggests, we need simply to attend lovingly and precisely to the images spontaneously brought forward in our dreams and fantasies.[1]

For me the quest for the goddess began with a dream:

Christine Downing is Chair of Religious Studies at San Diego State University and a Senior Core Faculty Member of The California School of Professional Psychology. The first woman president of the American Academy of Religion, she is author of *The Goddess, Journey Through Menopause,* and *Psyche's Sisters.*

In the dream I find myself in a state of confusion and despair. I decide to drive into the desert alone, hoping there to rediscover the still center I have lost. I drive far into the night on unfamiliar and seemingly rarely traveled byways. Then, in what feels like the middle of nowhere, a tire goes flat and I remember I have no spare. It seems unlikely that anyone would come by soon to offer help, but far in the distance I see a light which might mean someone available to assist me or at least a telephone. I set out toward it and walk and walk. It is some time before I realize the light is no closer and that I am no longer sure it is there at all. I turn around, thinking it might be better after all to wait by my car; but it has disappeared, as has the road.

At that point a figure appears from behind a sagebrush in the strangely moonlit desert night, the figure of a wizened but kindly appearing old man. "Can I help?" he asks. "No," I say. "You and I have been through this before. This time I need to go in search of Her."

So I set out across the desert, seeming now to know in what direction to proceed, though there are no marked ways and I know I had never been there before. Hours later I find myself at the foot of some steeply rising sandstone cliffs. I make my way up the cliffs, heading straight for a deep small cave just large enough for me to lie down. Still seeming to know exactly what I must do, I prepare myself to sleep there, as though to fall asleep were part of my way toward Her.

While I sleep there in the cave I dream that within the cave I find a narrow hole leading into an underground passage. I make my way through that channel deep, deep into another cave well beneath the earth's surface. I sit down on the rough uneven floor, knowing myself to be in her presence. Yet, though She is palpably there, I cannot discern her shape. Though I wait and wait, expecting to be able to see Her once my eyes grow accustomed to the darkness, that does not happen.

I returned to waking consciousness, aware that, though I did not know who *She* was, it was indeed time for me to go in search of Her.

I sensed that the pull to Her was a pull to an ancient source. "In the beginning, people prayed to the Creatress of Life, the Mistress of Heaven. At the very dawn of religion, God was a woman. Do you remember?"[2] To remember is to be remembered, to have our own lives made whole and our connections with others healed. . . .

I soon discovered that my search was not mine alone, that in recent years many women have rediscovered how much we need the goddess in a culture that tears us from woman, from women, and from ourselves.[3] To be fed only male images of the divine is to be badly malnourished. We are starved for images that recognize the sacredness of the feminine and the complexity, richness, and nurturing power of female energy. We hunger for images of human creativity and love inspired by the capacity of female bodies to give birth and nourish, for images of how humankind participates in the natural world suggested by reflection on the correspondences between menstrual rhythms and the moon's waxing and waning. We seek images that affirm that the love women receive from women, from mother, sister, daughter, lover, friend, reaches as deep and is as trustworthy, necessary, and sustaining as is the love symbolized by father, brother, son, or husband. We long for images that name as authentically feminine courage, creativity, loyalty, and self-confidence, resilience and steadfastness, capacity for clear insight, inclination for solitude, and the intensity of passion. We need images; we also need myths—for myths make concrete and particularize; they give us situations, plots, relationships. We need the goddess and we need the goddesses. . . .

Artemis is for me the most mysterious of the Greek goddesses.

> None of us ever sees Her in the dark
> or understands Her cruel mysteries.
> —Euripides[4]

So speaks Iphigenia after years of devotion to Artemis. Even Hippolytus, who prides himself as alone among mortals having the privilege of conversing with her, confesses, "True I may only hear. I may not see God face to face."[5] For one like myself who has fought to evade such devotion, it cannot help but be even more true. Artemis claims me now, calls me to her cruel mysteries with a power I can no longer withstand. The other goddesses who have presented themselves to me seemed to come forward out of the past, out of my childhood and youth and the early years of my marriage, or like Gaia as a reminder of some even more remote, prepersonal, transhuman past. They helped me to re-member who I have been and am; whereas Artemis seems to beckon from the future, to call me toward who I am now to become. . . .

I understand the turning toward Artemis as a ritual observance, this time of my forty-ninth birthday. Endings and beginnings have always been important to me, perhaps naturally so for someone born at just that moment in the astrological calendar (on the cusp between Pisces and Aries) when one year ends that another may begin. Every birthday invites celebration, but this one has for several years loomed as singularly significant. Seven times seven suggests a completion and a turning around, a birth into the rest of my life. I had looked to this birth as an easy one, like the ("only symbolic") rebirth of a snake shedding its skin or the emergence of a butterfly from its chrysalis. I had imagined it as a sloughing off of what was worn out and used up, so that what was viable and vital might emerge less fettered. Perhaps I had forgotten it would have to be a human birth, a birth into the human. Or perhaps I had expected the birth to be assisted by gentle Eileithyia rather than by Artemis. Though Artemis is a skillful and compassionate midwife, in her realm childbirth is painful and difficult and always accompanied by the threat of death. (The priestess of Artemis inherited the clothes of those who died in childbirth.) The first labor she attended (her mother's delivery of Artemis's own twin brother, Apollo) took nine desperately agonizing days (though her own birth had been without travail). I (whose literal birth-ings were all so easy) am now discovering what it is to be engaged in a giving birth that one resists, twists away from in pain, despairs of being done with. . . .

I had thought at first I could easily name what was being born. A few months before my birthday an annual checkup suggested I might have cancer of the uterus. "So, it is my death I am to give birth to," I thought. "Perhaps the reason I have for so long looked forward to this birthday is that somewhere deep inside me something knew it was to be the last." That very literal threat was proven illusory before it led me to call on Artemis whose arrows bring a swift and gentle death to women. Then a love affair which I had felt from its beginning was in some way a last time around seemed to be coming to an end. "So that's what it is," I mused; "I am going to be abandoned into an evaded solitude for which I have always known myself to be destined.". . .

I did not consciously think of Artemis, "the mercurial queen of solitude," during the interval before I realized that in my love affair it was a time for changes, not for endings. Again, I felt both relieved and cheated. What *was* going to happen? For a time it seemed that a job I knew I would not stay with much longer might come to an end earlier than I would have chosen; for a time my former husband and I considered remarriage. Both possibilities would have represented genuinely significant transitions, but I knew even before they dissolved that neither was what this birthday was really "about." It was not so much that these changes would have been too partial or too concrete as that they were too passive. The transition I anticipated would not happen until I turned around to confront "Her." This huntress insists on being hunted; she will never overtake. It is just that which makes it so difficult. *I* have to give birth—or struggle to be born; neither giving birth nor coming to birth are things that happen *to* one.

I understood that when I discovered that the most adequate name for this particular liminal space is simply: Artemis. The name does not eliminate the mystery; it honors it with an appellation that suggests its complexity and depth.

I must admit some puzzlement and even resentment at the youth of this goddess who stands so powerfully before me now. "What does *she* know?" I want to ask. Though I could have accepted the appearance of some divine child (for after all the child is symbol of all new beginnings), the archetypal image I really expected at this point in my life was that of the wise old woman. Finding myself under Artemis's tutelage at first made me feel somewhat embarrassed to be learning at fifty what others learn young. Like Slater and Pomeroy I saw the youth and virginity of the classic version of some of the goddesses only in negative terms; I believed it expressed male fear of mature femininity.[6] I now see that because Artemis has been the youthful virgin forever, she is, in her own paradoxical way, herself a wise old woman. I realize how truly timely it is to be pulled to doing therapy now (in the full ancient sense of *therapeia*) with this ancient huntress who surely and fearlessly follows any scent and who trusts us to learn to do the same. My familiar evasive games lose their efficacy in her wilderness; she will not be seduced into a relationship nor diverted by my storytelling skill. This ever-evanescent goddess appears only to say: "Here you are alone, as you have said you were ready to be."

As Walter Otto saw, manifold as Artemis's manifestations may be, we discover their unity and thus apprehend her essence, when we know her as the goddess who comes from afar, whose realm is the ever-distant wilderness. To this primary remoteness he appropriately connects her virginity, her solitariness, and her strangely cruel solicitude.[7]

Though others have found Artemis more accessible, I have learned by now that I need to start with what is darkest, with what I like least but which cannot be eluded. . . .

Born on unpeopled Delos, Artemis is really only at home in the wilderness, far from the haunts of men. A different logic, a different strength and wisdom, rules there. The romantic view of Arcadia as an idyllic pastoral realm inhabited by nymphs and shepherds does not do full justice to the Arcadia of ancient mythology: a wild and dangerous, rude and barbarous land. Arcadia is an imaginal realm, set apart from the everyday world, where things are as they are in themselves, not as shaped and manipulated by humankind. Artemis represents the form of imagination most foreign to me—the one connected to the psychological realm Jungians call sensation (as opposed to thinking, feeling, or intuition). There is nothing spiritual or sentimental or even sensual in Artemis's response to the wild things in whose company she lives. She does not respond to them as vehicles of symbolic meaning nor on the basis of their capacity to bring pleasure or displeasure. She knows each tree by its bark or leaf or fruit, each beast by its footprint or spoor, each bird by its plumage or call or nest. Only such carefully attendant seeing allows one to know why the black poplar that bears no fruit should be emblem of the underworld goddesses, the rose Aphrodite's flower, or the wild fig the fruit of Artemis; why the migratory quail should be Artemis's bird while the night-preying owl is Athene's. The woods and fields belong to Artemis and her nymphs: each tree, laurel or myrrh, oak or ash, is truly recognized only when we know with which nymph(s) to associate it; each wild flower, each brook and stream, also evokes a particular sacred presence. Artemis's imagination is concrete and specific, bespeaks a loving respect for the unique essence of everything as it lives in its natural state. It would be a wrong to mis-take her mode of perception for literalism: her response is animistic, anima-istic. Each creature—each plant, each wood, each river—is to her a Thou, not an it. Unlike Aphrodite she never confuses this I-Thou relation with merging. To know Artemis is to understand what Buber means by "*distance* and relation." . . . I have come to trust that the meaning of her remoteness will be transformed as I am willing to acknowledge it. So long as I deny that she is, indeed, "She Who Slays," I am still evading Artemis.

Artemis is the Lady of the Wild Things, a title that encompasses much more than is acknowledged in the post-Homeric image of her as the shaft-showering huntress.[8] As Aeschylus reminds us, she is not only the hunter but protector of all that is wild and vulnerable:

> Artemis the undefiled
> is angered with pity
> at the flying hounds of her father
> eating the unborn young in the hare and the
>   shivering mother.
> She is sick at the eagles' feasting.
> Sing sorrow, sorrow: but good wins out in the end.
> Lovely you are and kind
> to the tender young of ravening lions.
> For sucklings of all the savage
> beasts that lurk in the lonely places you
>   have sympathy.[9]

Artemis represents the mystic, primitive identity of hunter and hunted.[10] There are indications that the worship of Artemis in Arcadia and Attica included an initiation ceremony for pre-pubescent girls in which the goddess, her worshipers, and the bear whose skin the maidens wore were "considered to be as of one nature and called by the same name."[11] Artemis is intimately associated with the wild beasts of the field, the animals of the chase: the hare, the lion, the wolf, the wild boar, the bear, the deer. The earliest artistic representations show her holding one or another of these animals in her hands, often wearing the fruit of some wild tree on her head or with the branches of a wild fig tree above her. Artemis is herself the wilderness, the wild and untamed, and not simply its mistress.

She is uncivilized nature in quite a different sense from Gaia. Gaia is *there* before gods or mortals; she represents the ceaseless, irrepressible fecundity of nature. . . . In the world of Artemis, as Nilsson puts it, what "interests man is not Nature in herself, but the Life of Nature in the measure in which it intervenes in human life and forms a necessary and obvious basis for it."[12] Although Artemis may originally have been an oriental goddess, may have come from the fringes of the Greek world, in the classical period she is particularly identified with Arcadia, the wild, mountainous, forested center of the Peloponnesus. This reinforces my discovery that though we may first know her as the other without, she is more truly the other within. . . .

Besides being goddess of the wild, Artemis is also known as she who consorts with women. I had at one time understood Artemis's dramatic rejection of any male other than her brother (and perhaps a few brotherly companions like Herakles and Orion) as simply the obverse of her devotion to women. I had imagined that the most promising access to this most woman-identified of the Greek goddesses would be by way of an exploration of her relation to the nymphs in whose company we so consistently find her. Indeed, Nilsson suggests she is essentially nymph epitomized, *the* nymph who rises to prominence from amidst the company of nymphs.[12]

Here was Artemis prodding me to look honestly at the role in my life of deep and passionate friendships with women. Even this Artemis threatened me, portended a judgment from which I flinched. I saw her as having wholeheartedly chosen the love that women share with women, and as disdaining someone like myself who cannot say that friendships with women are the only ones really needed, the only ones that truly nurture. Even the patriarchally determined classical versions of the myths reveal Artemis as a woman who loves women. (Perhaps the most compelling evidence is to be found in the story of Zeus's rape of Callisto, the most beautiful of Artemis's nymphs, the one most dear to her. To win the nymph's love Zeus disguises himself as Artemis; in that guise Callisto welcomes his embrace.) But to see the relationship between Artemis and her nymphs primarily in sexual terms is simplification and distortion. It transposes their relationship into an Aphroditic key and thus ignores the testimony of the Homeric hymn to Aphrodite that alone among gods and mortals, Hestia, Athene, and Artemis are immune to Aphrodite's power. Artemis does not say, "Choose women," but "Choose yourself." The meaning of her primary association with women is that in loving women we are loving our womanly self. . . .

Fully to understand Artemis's connection to women demands relating it to that virginity so essential to her nature. Even in her association with women Artemis points to a communion not identical with sexual union and possibly subverted by it. The deep bonding of woman to women that Artemis encourages may, indeed, encompass passionate attraction, sensual delight, and sexual consummation. Yet she reminds us that the sexual may be surrogate for a more profound affirmation of one another and of our shared womanliness than we quite know how to express, an evasion of spiritual connection more fearful than the physical one. We mis-take Artemis's chastity if we interpret it only as patriarchal culture's attempt to suppress her lesbianism, her refusal of men and her love of women. Her chastity represents something more essential to her nature. It surely does not mean that she is not stirred by feminine beauty; it does not necessarily mean that she refuses sexual intimacy with women; it does mean that she never wholly gives herself to another, female or male. . . . Artemis's refusal to give herself bespeaks her respect, not her rejection, of the other; it is an expression not of frigidity but of passion. She gives herself to her own passion, her own wildness. Though invoked as the "frenzy-loving" goddess, Artemis is not driven mad by her passion as are the maenads when they leave their husbands' beds for their mountaintop orgies. Neither does she feel the need to find some appropriate sublimated expression for it, as might bright-eyed Athene, nor to transpose it immediately into the interpersonal erotic realm as would Aphrodite. Because Artemis is at home in the wilderness, she is comfortable with her own wildness. . . .

Artemis is who she is with an ease and simplicity that indeed seems divine. She does not suffer self-doubt or inner division and has little patience with those of us who do. Thus she often appears as a harsh judge of women. . . .

As I look at each aspect of Artemis in turn, again and again I discover She Who Slays, she who comes from afar, she who is other. Paradoxically, the reaffirmation of Artemis's otherness has made me more aware than ever of the power of Aphrodite in my life. How spontaneously, when confronting Artemis's claims on me, I respond by pleading, "Let's play Aphrodite instead." I have never been so aware of my tendency to devote my energies to love affairs rather than to soul, to discriminate on the basis of what I find pleasing or displeasing; how naturally I seek to transform all feelings into sexual passion, all potentially transformative experience into well-shaped story, and to make all my therapists, including Artemis herself, fall in love with me. That attending to Artemis should bring Aphrodite so prominently into view seems surprising, until I remember the story of Hippolytus and how it is his monolatrous devotion to Artemis that provokes Aphrodite's disastrous intervention. It is as though exclusive attention to Artemis—which she plainly demands—inevitably stirs Aphrodite. I understand better now how it can be that so many of the oriental and Cretan goddesses—Cybele, Bendis, Astarte, Ariadne, to name but a few—are as-sociated with both Artemis and Aphrodite, as though they are so essentially complementary as to be one.

I have seemingly always known I am no monotheist. Yet it is too simple to leave Artemis with that affirmation—and denial. I know that she is still *the* goddess to whom I now must attend. Her wilderness may indeed be a liminal space, but it is precisely the character of such "be-tweens" that while one is in them *that* is where one is, that is all there is. This is a time for me to turn away from that reliance on Aphrodite's ways which have for so long sustained me. I must begin to learn what is meant by the phrase "monogamy of soul." The cruel mystery inherent in that phrase led me to this attempt to expose myself to Artemis's mysteries. The birth into the rest of my life which she midwifes still feels incredibly painful. I still find it unspeakably difficult to join my voice with Iphigenia's as she, from her funeral pyre, cries:

Dance!
Let us dance in honor of Artemis . . .
O lift your voices
Lift them to Artemis
In honor of my fate
And of my dying.[14]

NOTES

1. Irene Claremont de Castillejo, *Knowing Woman* (New York: Harper & Row, 1974), 165ff.
2. Merlin Stone, *When God Was a Woman* (New York: Dial Press, 1976), 1.
3. See especially Carol P. Christ, "Why Women Need the Goddess," in *Womanspirit Rising*, ed. Carol P. Christ and Judith Plaskow (New York: Harper & Row, 1979).
4. Euripides, *Iphigenia in Tauris* 476–77, trans. Witter Bynner, in *The Complete Greek Tragedies: Euripides*, ed. David Grene and Richmond Lattimore (Chicago: University of Chicago Press, 1959), 3:361.
5. Euripides, *Hippolytus* 86–87, trans. David Grene, vol. 3, 166.
6. See Philip E. Slater, *The Glory of Hera* (Boston: Beacon Press, 1968), 12; Sarah B. Pomeroy, *Goddesses, Whores, Wives, and Slaves* (New York: Schocken Books, 1975), 10.
7. Walter F. Otto, *The Homeric Gods* (Boston: Beacon Press, 1954), 82.
8. Martin P. Nilsson, *Greek Folk Religion* (New York: Harper Torchbook, 1961), 16.
9. Aeschylus, *Agamemnon* 132–43, trans. Richmond Lattimore, in Grene and Lattimore, *The Complete Greek Tragedies: Aeschylus* (Chicago: University of Chicago Press, 1959), 1:39.
10. W. K. C. Guthrie, *The Greeks and Their Gods* (Boston: Beacon Press, 1955), 100.
11. Lewis Richard Farnell, *The Cults of the Greek States* (Chicago: Aegean Press, 1971), 2:435–6.
12. Martin P. Nilsson, *Greek Folk Religion* (New York: Harper Torchbook, 1961), 49.
13. Ibid., 112.
14. Euripides, *Iphigenia in Aulis* 1479–80, 1466, trans. Charles R. Walker, in Grene and Lattimore, *The Complete Greek Tragedies: Euripides* (Chicago: University of Chicago Press, 1958), 4:377.

Notes on Composing New Blessings

Toward a Feminist-Jewish Reconstruction of Prayer

MARCIA FALK

The recent past has seen amazing breakthroughs in Jewish ideas and practices, brought about in large part by the emerging feminist-Jewish community. Inevitably, theology has been the focus of some of the most profound changes. Feminist theologians have called for new God-language;[1] and in many circles, Jewish women have been emending the prayerbook and even structuring whole new services to replace the traditional ones.[2] Recognizing the enormous power of God-talk to educate and shape our lives, feminist Jews in our time are taking back the power of naming, addressing divinity in our own voices, using language that reflects our own experiences. We do this because we take theology seriously and we want to affirm ourselves back into the place from which, we deeply intuit, we have been erased.

We have begun with relatively small amendments, such as introducing the pronoun "she" to refer to divinity. With this change we have started to uproot the "he" that has been so deeply planted in us, the all-pervasive "he" that blocks our attempts to read ourselves, in any satisfying way, into the theological relationship. With this small change we are redeeming the forgotten half of the all-inclusive monotheistic divinity. Yet when we do so we are frequently accused of the deeply threatening "heresy" of "paganism." From a purely rational viewpoint, this reaction is ridiculous. For, as others have pointed out, if God is not really male, why should it matter if we call God "she"?[3] Clearly, it is not the inclusive "one God" that is being threatened. The ultimacy

Marcia Falk, Visiting Associate Professor of Religious Studies at Stanford University, is author of a new translation and critical study of the biblical *Song of Songs*. She has also written two books of poetry, a book of translations of the Yiddish poet Malka Heifetz Tussman, and a volume of translations of the Hebrew poet Zelda. She is currently writing *The Book of Blessings: A Feminist Jewish Reconstruction of Prayer*.

of an *exclusively male* God has come into question, and his defenders are ready to attack.

This is a crucial point, for nothing less than monotheism, Judaism's original raison d'être, is at stake. So let us think carefully: what is it we are affirming with a monotheistic creed? I believe monotheism means that, *with all our differences*, I am more like you than I am unlike you. It means that we share the same source, and that one principle of justice must govern us equally. Thus, monotheism would seem to imply that if we are all created in the image of divinity, the images with which we point toward divinity must reflect us all.

But what *single* image can do this? All images are necessarily partial. "Man" is no less partial than "woman" as clearly as "white" is no less partial than "black." It would seem, then, that the authentic expression of an authentic monotheism is not a singularity of image but an embracing *unity* of a *multiplicity of images*, as many as are needed to express and reflect the diversity of our individual lives. Indeed, much more than a feminine pronoun is needed; we must seek out a wide range of verbal imagery with which to convey our visions.

The search for theological imagery is a journey whose destinations are rarely apparent at the outset. As many feminists have discovered, it is not merely a matter of changing male images to seemingly equivalent female ones: the relatively simple (though still courageous) act of "feminizing" the male God has proved, to many of us, to be inadequate and often absurd. For a feminized patriarchal image is still patriarchal, though now in transvestite masquerade. The process has been instructive, however, in clarifying our theological concerns: in translating the king into a queen, for example, we realize that images of domination are not what we wish to embrace. We find instead that our search for what is authoritative leads us to explore more deeply what is just, and that the results of these explorations are not well represented by images of a monarch, either female or male.

And so we find we must create new images to convey our visions, and to do so we must be patient (though not passive), for images will not be called into being by sheer acts of will alone. Rather we learn what artists know well: that authentic images arise from our unconscious as gifts; that out of our living, from our whole, engaged selves, with the support of our communities, the images that serve us will emerge. We must trust the journey.

There are no shortcuts. The few female images already available in the tradition do not in themselves provide an adequate solution. The much-touted *Shekhinah*, used in recent times to placate uppity Jewish women (as in, "The tradition *has* a feminine image of God, what more do you want?"), will not suffice. The *Shekhinah* was not originally a female image; it did not become so until Kabbalistic times. And when it became explicitly associated with the female, it did not empower women, especially not in Kabbalistic thought, where male and female were hierarchically polarized. Nor has the *Shekhinah* fared much better in our century. I, for one, cannot think of the *Shekhinah* without recalling her burning tears as they fell on the young poet Ḥayyim Naḥman Bialik's *Gemara* page. In Bialik's poem *L'vadi*, "Alone," the *Shekhinah* was a pitiful mama bird with a broken wing, invoked to portray the frailty of Jewish tradition in the poet's time. "Alone, alone," was the *Shekhinah*'s cry, for all had abandoned her.

Not that tears are not valid. Not that I want my images of divinity to exclude solitude and suffering; these are important aspects of our experience that need expression in our theology. But should images of isolation and vulnerability alone be identified as the fundamental representation of God's "female side"? Do we wish to divide experience along these classically sexist lines? Sad as it is, I cannot help but feel that, far from redeeming women, the image of the *Shekhinah* has, until now, only supported the male-centered vision. In Jewish tradition, the *Shekhinah* has never been on equal footing with the mighty *Kadosh Barukh Hu*, the "Holy-One-Blessed-Be-He," her creator, her master, her groom, the ultimate reality of which she was only an emanation. And while I like the name itself—*Shekhinah*, from the Hebrew root meaning "to dwell"—I would like to see in-dwelling, or immanence, portrayed in ways that are not secondary to transcendence. So too, I would like to see autonomous female images, not ones that imply the essential otherness of women. *In the name of monotheism*, for the sake of an inclusive unity, I would like to see our God-talk articulate mutually supportive relationships between female and male, between immanence and transcendence, between our lives and the rest of life on the planet. In the end, it comes down to this: what I would like to see, I must help bring into being.

And so, I have been composing *b'rakhot*, new blessings in Hebrew and in English, as vehicles for new theological images, steps toward creating feminist-Jewish theology and practice. Why blessings? Because, in Jewish life, blessings are powerful tools for expressing spirituality and for forging community—tools that I have come to rely on in my daily life.

What is a blessing? A blessing is an event; a blessing is also that which turns a moment into an event. In Jewish tradition, blessings mark both extraordinary and ordinary occasions. Jews say blessings upon seeing a rainbow, or meeting a wise person, or hearing good news—occasions that take one of a sudden or by surprise. And Jews also bless before eating, and at the onset of every Sabbath—occasions that come with accustomed regularity. Jews are fond of "making blessings" (as the Yiddish expression goes); blessings enhance life, increase our awareness of the present moment. So Rabbi Meir tells us that we should utter daily a hundred blessings; and, indeed, the Hebrew liturgical tradition has produced a great number of benedictions with which to mark and sanctify the events of our lives. Yet, sadly and strikingly, few blessings exist for life-cycle events such as the onset of menstruation or menopause, or even the miracle of childbirth.

The traditional Hebrew blessings with which Jews today are most familiar all have essentially the same form. They consist of two parts: the opening address of divinity as that which is "blessed," and a phrase or phrases, varying in length and complexity, that relate to the specific occasion of the blessing. Thus, for example, the blessing over bread reads: *Barukh atah adonay eloheynu melekh ha-olam/ha-motzi lehem min ha-aretz*, "Blessed are you, Lord our God, king of the world, /who brings forth bread from the earth." It is in the latter halves of the blessings that the Hebrew poetic imagination has flourished; here, the liturgists have explored with verbal imagery a variety of life experiences. The first part of the traditional Hebrew blessing, on the other hand, is a strict formula: *barukh atah adonay eloheynu melekh ha-olam*, "blessed are you (masculine singular), Lord our God, king of the world." And this formula never varies, no matter what occasion is being marked, no matter what words comprise the rest of the speech.

To the traditional Jew, this formulaic opening is so absolute, so powerful, that, once it is said, it must not go to waste: it must never be said in vain. So, for example, when I utter the blessing over bread, I must immediately follow this speech-act with the act of eating bread. And without the formulaic address of divinity (an address referred to as *shem umalkhut*, "name and sovereignty"), the traditional Jew considers there to have been no blessing at all—nothing, that is, that bears the same kind of spiritual authority.

Yet criticism of this formulaic address of divinity may not sound surprising to feminist Jews. As I said above, it is obvious to many of us that no single set of names and images ought to monopolize religious authority, claiming the exclusive right to evoke monotheistic divinity, the exclusive power to make a moment sacred. Thus the formulaic opening of the traditional blessing, precisely because it is formulaic and unalterable, feels idolatrous to many feminist Jews. It seems to us that, through the repeated utterance of this phrase which is so indelibly fixed in the performance language of our liturgy, Jews come to worship the partial images themselves, rather than the inclusive monotheism for which these images are supposed to stand. And any worship of the partial in place of the whole, any equation of signifier with the ineffable that is signified, is nothing less than idolatry.

The way to avoid verbal idolatry is to keep reminding ourselves that *all* theological naming is really a naming-toward; all honest talk about divinity has an "as if" embedded in it. And when we recognize the naming of divinity for what it is—the act of *metaphor making*—we approach it with a new freedom, a new power that gives voice to our theological visions. For a metaphor is a transforming thing: it bridges and it leaps; it points out likeness even as it affirms difference; it connects without assimilating, without blurring distinction. But the empowering quality of metaphor exists only as long as we remember that it *is* metaphor we are speaking, not literal truth and not fiction. When a metaphor is treated as though it were literal truth, then it becomes a lie.[4]

Theological language that is so overused as to be absolutely predictable, so entrenched that it no longer reminds us that it is metaphorical, language that is so canonical and automatic that we forget the "as if" originally implied in it, is dead metaphor—in other words, a lie. Such is the case with the Hebrew words *adonay eloheynu melekh ha-olam,* "Lord our God, king of the world"—as it is the case with the Hebrew and English masculine pronouns when used to refer to the divine, or, as feminists in other traditions have noted, with the English word "God" itself. All these terms have ceased to remind us that divinity is not really male, not really human at all.

Dead metaphors make strong idols. Dumb as stone, they stand stubbornly in the way; like boulders jutting up in the desert, they block our view of any oasis that may lie ahead.

What shatters a verbal idol? Not hatchets, and not concepts—not the abstract idea that God is neither male nor female—but new, living metaphors, verbal images possessing powers of transformation. In its uneasiness with the arts, especially the visual arts, Judaism tacitly acknowledges the power of imagery. But there is no stopping the imagination from doing what it will do, and if as Jews we decline to make theological images out of clay or canvas, we must realize that we make them just as surely—perhaps even more effectively—out of words. This is an important part of why I compose new blessings: there is perhaps no more effective vehicle in Jewish life for conveying theological metaphors, verbal images of the divine.

When choosing new metaphors for my blessings, I try to confront the full extent of our liturgical idolatry. It is not just the exclusive maleness of our God-language that needs correction, but its anthropocentrism in *all* its ramifications. For as long as we image divinity exclusively as a person, whether female or male, we tend to forget that human beings are not the sole, not even the "primary," life-bearing creatures on the planet. We allow our intelligence and our unique linguistic capabilities to deceive us into believing that we are "godlier" than the rest of creation. And in so doing, we neglect the real responsibility attendant upon the gift of human consciousness: to care for the earth in ways that respect all human and nonhuman life upon it.

For this reason, when I compose my blessings, I draw my metaphors from all aspects of the creation—as did the biblical poets who created the metaphors *tzur yisrael,* "rock of Israel," and *etz hayyim,* "tree of life" (both of which phrases were adopted by later liturgists for prayers that eventually became part of synagogue services). I try to choose words whose meanings will expand in context, opening in more than a single direction. Recognizing that, no matter how resonant my language, any image I choose or create will necessarily be limited, I try to use theological metaphors that connect to the particular occasions being marked. When possible, I try also to draw upon the traditional versions of the blessings, focusing on the variable (nonformulaic) material as a source for my *kavvanah*, "spiritual direction."

Thus, for example, when I set out to compose a blessing to be said before eating, I considered the traditional blessing over bread quoted above: *Barukh atah adonay eloheynu melekh ha-olam/ha-motzi lehem min ha-aretz*, "Blessed are you, Lord our God, king of the world,/who brings forth bread from the earth." The phrase *ha-motzi lehem min ha-aretz*, "who brings forth bread from the earth," seemed especially powerful to me, because the picture it presented of bread being drawn from the earth was reminiscent of the biblical story of our own origins. Subtly but profoundly, a whole network of connections was being suggested here: between our food and the earth, ourselves and the earth, our food and ourselves. So rich was this phrase, I wanted not only to preserve it in my blessing but to let it inspire a new image.

In contrast to this phrase, the formulaic God-images opening the traditional blessing struck me as particularly inappropriate to the occasion. For it was certainly not as "lord" or "ruler" that I apprehended divinity at the moment before beginning a meal, but as nurturer, the source of all nourishment. And so I sought a metaphor that would embody this feeling in a vivid way, and I let the phrase *ha-motzi lehem min ha-aretz* guide me toward it. I searched until I came upon the following line in Deuteronomy 8:7: *eretz nahaley mayim ayanot ut'homot yotz'im ba-bikah uva-har*, "a land of watercourses, fountains, and depths springing from valleys and hills." In the fountains that rise from and flow back into the land, I found the image I was looking for: *ayin*, "fountain" or "well," with the figurative meaning of "source." In the springing up of the fountains, I had found an image to suggest the motion of bread being drawn from the earth: the image of a rising up from under, suggesting a deep ground-of-being. And out of this image, I made the metaphor *eyn ha-hayyim*, "fountain/well/source of life," to use for my blessing over bread: *N'varekh et eyn ha-hayyim/ha-motziah lehem min ha-aretz*, "Let us bless the source of life/that brings forth bread from the earth."

Readers of Hebrew may note that the phrase *eyn ha-hayyim* is grammatically feminine, although the image itself cannot be said to have gender, being nonpersonal and inanimate (in Hebrew, all nouns have grammatical gender, though not necessarily semantic gender). Therefore, the verb in the second phrase also takes the feminine form: *ha-*

motziah. Readers will also notice that I have changed the opening of the blessing from *barukh atah*, "blessed are you," with both "blessed" and "you" specified as masculine singular (in Hebrew grammar, the second person is always gender-specific), to the gender-inclusive first person plural verb *n'varekh*, "let us bless." This change allowed me to open up the speech of the blessing form and freely use images of both genders. It also had the powerful effect of emphasizing the "we" who are blessing, thus placing responsibility back on the community of living human speakers. *Lo ha-mettim yehalleluyah*, says the psalmist: it is not the dead but the living who will sing of God.

The very first time I uttered a blessing that began with *n'varekh*, I realized that I had long been uncomfortable with the passive "blessed are you" of the traditional blessing, not just because it is gender-re-strictive but because it is disempowering. With *n'varekh*, we reclaim our voices, take back the power of naming. When we say *n'varekh et eyn ha-hayyim*, we are reminded even as we speak that *eyn ha-hayyim is our met-aphor*, our naming toward the ultimately unnameable. And because our names and images can now take many forms, we begin to hear all the words of our sentences—verbs and adjectives as well as nouns—oc-curring in both genders, and in plural as well as singular constructions (for the many can represent the One in metaphor). And so in this new blessing we hear the grammatical shift from *ha-motzi* (masculine sin-gular), "who/that brings forth," to *ha-motziah* (feminine singular), "who/that brings forth"; and to many of us this small change in sound, the introduction of this tiny "ah," is refreshing, even liberating.

The blessing over bread was one of the first I grappled with when I began writing my own blessings. It was an obvious place to begin, since it was the prayer I used most frequently in my daily life; and the traditional version was fairly easy to adapt, once I had found what felt like an appropriate theological image for it. But when I tried to adapt the blessing over wine, another prayer used often in Jewish life, I quickly discovered that finding a new image for divinity was not always enough.

As with the blessing over bread, I considered the traditional version of the blessing over wine to see what in it was meaningful to me: *Barukh atah adonay eloheynu melekh ha-olam/bore p'ri ha-gafen*, "Blessed are you, Lord our God, king of the world, /who creates the fruit of the vine." And although once again I found the formulaic opening unsatisfying, I felt that the closing image, "the fruit of the vine," was full of reso-nance. I saw the vine as an image of interconnectedness, suggesting the intertwining paths of life; its fruit, then, might be seen as a met-aphor for community. This, I speculated, might be part of the reason why Jews use "the fruit of the vine" to make a *kiddush*, a blessing of sanctification, on occasions like the Sabbath and holidays, which unite the community.

I did not have to search long for a theological metaphor for this blessing: the image *eyn ha-ḥayyim*, which I had used in my blessing over bread, seemed fitting here too, for wine, like bread, has its origins in the earth. And I knew that I wanted to connect this theological image with the image of *p'ri ha-gafen*, "the fruit of the vine," understood literally, as part of the botanical world, and metaphorically, as representing human community. But when I looked at the verb connecting the two halves of the traditional blessing—*bore*, "create"—it seemed wrong. For *bore* means to "create" as the God of Genesis created, making, as the rabbis explain it, "something out of nothing"; and this image of creation did not feel true to the experience that my blessing was trying to evoke. Nothing in nature arises out of nothing; everything emerges from form to form, from seed to flower to fruit. So too, communities are not created full-blown out of nothing; they evolve gradually out of bonds sustained over time.

Thus the power I wished to invoke at the moment of my blessing—that flow connecting the divine with the realms of nature and humanity—was not a force that came down from above to command the fruit of the vine into being. Rather, it was a nurturance that enabled the vine's fruits to grow, sustaining them from within, allowing them to ripen. And so I substituted for *bore* the verb *l'hatzmiaḥ*, "to cause to grow," from the root *tzamaḥ*, meaning "grow from the ground." And I created this blessing: *N'varekh et eyn ha-ḥayyim/matzmiḥat p'ri ha-gafen*, "Let us bless the source of life/that ripens fruit on the vine."

As I continued in the creative process of composing new blessings, I found that the journey to create authentic prayers, useful and appropriate to their occasions, took many turns, few of which I was able to anticipate. With each new blessing I approached, I confronted and often wrestled with a different aspect of theology, and this grappling led to linguistic variations. For example, in my *havdalah* blessings, which close the Sabbath and begin the week, I experimented with the opening verb, substituting for *n'varekh* words such as *n'hallel*, "let us praise," and *n'vakkesh*, "let us seek." In other blessings, I varied the syntactic structures, so that images of divinity appeared in unexpected places, and sometimes appeared only in a veiled way. I tried to suggest, through syntax as well as vocabulary, that divinity is not necessarily to be found in predictable places; sometimes we must search for it where we do not expect it. I am looking for new ways to convey a theology of immanence, divinity encountered not from outside but from within.

In all my compositions, I try to preserve meaningful ties to the historical Hebrew tradition, interweaving images and phrases from a variety of biblical, midrashic, liturgical, and poetic sources. At the same time, as I have explained, I depart quite deliberately from the traditional prayers in as many ways as I need to. Perhaps equally important to my process is this: *I depart from my own departures, break my own forms,* as often as I have to, because I believe that no element of liturgical form or content ought to become completely automatic, even when the material is innovative. One of the deepest challenges for all feminist liturgy, I believe, is to keep our speech, like our thoughts, constantly evolving and responsive to change, even as we create forms to be used repetitively to build community and foster tradition.

How to do this successfully—how to create an exciting balance between spontaneity and repeated form—is a question that religious feminists, both "traditional" and "post-traditional," inevitably grapple with. This grappling, I believe, best takes place in the context of practical experimentation within communities. With Jewish feminism, as with other feminist religious contexts, experimentation is happening today in groups all across the country, in national and regional conferences, and in collectives that meet for retreats.[5] I have been deeply nourished by the feminist-Jewish network as a whole and by my own feminist-Jewish community, B'not Esh, in particular. I don't believe that I could have—or would have—written my blessings without the receptivity and support, not to mention inspiration, of this network; and I feel both grateful and gratified to know that my work finds a home not just on paper but in the voices of practicing feminist Jews.

And when, as inevitably will happen, critics question the authenticity of this work, denying feminist Jews the right to call our creativity and our creations Jewish, we—the members of the feminist-Jewish communities that help comprise *klal yisrael*, the community of Israel—need to remind them that Jewish prayer, like all of Jewish practice and belief, all of Jewish life, has never been finally "fixed." Rather, it has evolved, adapted, and changed throughout Jewish history. It is only recently, in fact, that the Hebrew liturgical tradition ossified; it is not too late, we must hope, to revive it. As we compose new prayers today to affirm diversity within unity, to express our visions of a true monotheism and our dedication to *tikkun olam*, repair of a fragmented world—as we compose and say such prayers, we place ourselves firmly *in the tradition*—a tradition that is still, always, in the process of becoming. We need to remind our critics, and ourselves, that tradition is not just what we inherit from the past; it is also what we create and pass on to the future. Tradition necessarily implies process, the continual forging of links on an unending chain. And the challenge to keep growing and changing even while forging an identity, to stay true to the present moment even while nurturing a sense of continuity with the past and with the future—is this not at the core of authentic living?

BLESSINGS[6]

Kabbalat Shabbat (Welcoming the Sabbath)

Hadlakat Nerot
Yitromeim libbeinu,
t'shovav nafsheinu
b'hadlakat neir shel shabbat.

Candlelighting
May this Sabbath
lift our spirits,
lighten our hearts.

Blessings for Leyl Shabbat Meal (Friday Evening Meal)

Kiddush L'leyl Shabbat
N'varekh et eyn ha-ḥayyim
matzmiḥat p'ri ha-gafen
un'kaddesh et yom ha-shabbat
zeikher l'maaseh v'reishit.

Sanctification over Wine
Let us bless the source of life
that ripens fruit on the vine
as we hallow the Sabbath day
in remembrance of creation.

N'tilat Yadayim
Tizkor nafsheinu et k'dushat ha-guf
bintilat yadayim.

Washing the Hands
Washing the hands, we call to
mind
the holiness of body.

Ha-Motziah
N'varekh et eyn ha-ḥayyim
ha-motziah leḥem min ha-aretz.

Blessing over Bread
Let us bless the source of life
that brings forth bread from the
earth.

Birkat Ha-Mazon
Nodeh l'eyn ha-ḥayyim
al ha-aretz v'al ha-mazon:
nishmor al ha-aretz
v'hi t'kayy' meinu,
un'vakkesh mazon la-sova
l'khol yoshvey teivel.

Blessing after the Meal
Let us acknowledge the source of
life
for the earth and for nourishment.
May we protect the earth
that it may sustain us,
and let us seek sustenance
for all who inhabit the world.

NOTES

This piece is part of a work in progress, *The Book of Blessings: A Feminist-Jewish Reconstruction of Prayer*, forthcoming from Harper & Row.

1. See, for example, Rita Gross, "Steps Toward a Feminine Imagery of Deity in Jewish Theology," in *On Being a Jewish Feminist*, ed. Susannah Heschel (New York: Schocken Books, 1983), 234–47; Judith Plaskow, "Language, God and Liturgy: A Feminist Perspective," *Response* 44 (Spring 1983): 3–14; Ellen Umansky, "Creating a Jewish Feminist Theology: Possibilities and Problems," *Anima* 10 (Spring 1984): 125–35.
2. For examples of liturgical experimentation in English, see Naomi Janowitz and Maggie Wenig, "Sabbath Prayers for Women," in *Womanspirit Rising*, ed. Carol P. Christ and Judith Plaskow (San Francisco: Harper & Row, 1979), 174–78; *Vetaher Libenu* (Sudbury, MA: Congregation Beth El, 1980). There has been some amount of experimentation in Hebrew as well, although far more has been done in English. Much of the available literature is circulating privately, and a great deal is undocumented.

3. Gross, "Female God Language," 170–71.
4. In this discussion, as indeed in all my thinking about liturgy, I am much indebted to Nelle Morton for her penetrating insights on metaphor, which may be found throughout her book *The Journey is Home* (Boston: Beacon Press, 1985), esp. pp. 147–75. I first heard Nelle Morton apply her ideas about theological metaphor to a Jewish context in a keynote address at a conference in November 1982, in Los Angeles, "God, Prayer, and the Jewish Woman," which I coorganized. Nelle's speech on that occasion empowered and impelled me to pursue the feminist reconstruction of Jewish liturgy that I was then just beginning, and which has since become an ongoing project.
5. For a description of one such collective, see Martha Ackelsberg, "Spirituality, Community, and Politics: B'not Esh and the Feminist Reconstruction of Judaism," *Journal of Feminist Studies in Religion* 2 (Fall 1986): 109–20. Much activity is also taking place in the Havurah and "Jewish-renewal" movements, which include feminist concerns in their creative agendas.
6. The new blessings and their English versions reprinted in this article are copyright © 1985 by Marcia Falk. If these blessings are used orally for religious or educational purposes, author attribution is requested. Any other use requires written permission of the author.

God as Mother

SALLIE McFAGUE

"Father-Mother God, loving me, guard me while I sleep, guide my little feet up to thee." This prayer, which theologian Herbert Richardson reports reciting as a child, impressed upon his young mind that if God is both father and mother, then God is not like anything else he knew.[1] The point is worth emphasizing, for as we begin our experiment with the model of God as mother, we recall that metaphors of God, far from reducing God to what we understand, underscore by their multiplicity and lack of fit the unknowability of God. This crucial characteristic of metaphorical language for God is lost, however, when only one important personal relationship, that of father and child, is allowed to serve as a grid for speaking of the God-human relationship. In fact, by excluding other relationships as metaphors, the model of father becomes idolatrous, for it comes to be viewed as a description of God.[2] Hence, one reason for including maternal language in a tradition where paternal language has prevailed is to underscore what the negative theological tradition has always insisted: God is unlike as well as like our metaphors.[3]

But there are additional reasons for using female as well as male metaphors of God. The most obvious is that since human beings are male and female, if we seek to imagine God "in the image of God"— that is, ourselves—both male and female metaphors should be employed. Because the point is self-evident, one wonders what all the fuss is about when the suggestion is made that God be imaged in female terms or addressed as "she." But fuss there is, and it is best to address it head on. For whatever reasons, Western thought—certainly Western theology—has been deeply infected by both a fear of and a fascination with female sexuality.[4] The most basic reason, it appears, for uneasiness with female metaphors for God is that unlike the male metaphors, whose sexual character is cloaked, the female metaphors seem blatantly sexual and involve the sexuality most feared: female sexuality.

There are at least three points being made here that need to be addressed briefly. First, to speak of God as father has obvious sexual

Sallie McFague teaches theology at Vanderbilt Divinity School in Nashville, Tennessee. Her interest in the nature and power of religious language is reflected in her books: *Speaking in Parables: A Study in Metaphor and Theology*, *Metaphorical Theology: Models of God in Religious Language*, and *Models of God: Theology for an Ecological, Nuclear Age*.

connotations (as is evident in the trinitarian language of the "genera-tion" of the Son from the Father), but given the Hebraic tradition's interest in distinguishing itself from Goddess religions and fertility cults, as well as the early and deep ascetic strain in Christianity, the sexual implications of paternal imagery were masked. This leads into the second point: the blatant sexuality of female metaphors. It is by introducing female metaphors for God that the sexuality of both male and female metaphors becomes evident, though it appears, because we are familiar with the male metaphors, that only the female ones are sexual. In other words, the shock of unconventional language for God—female imagery—jolts us into awareness that there is no gender-neutral language if we take ourselves as the model for talk about God, because we are sexual beings. Hence, traditional language for God is not nonsexual; on the contrary, it is male. The third point, the fear and fascination associated with female sexuality, is related to the first two points: female sexuality would not, I suspect, be so feared or found so fascinating if sexuality, both female and male, had been accepted in a more open and healthy manner both as a human good and as an important way to model the activity of God in relation to the world.[5] It is treated in this fashion in many religions, and Western thought, including Christianity, with its warped view of female sexuality as well as its reluctance to imagine God in female terms, has much to learn from these sources.

The first thing to insist upon, then, is that in spite of Western and Christian uneasiness over female imagery for God, since the *imago dei* is twofold, female as well as male, both kinds of metaphors ought to be used. The question then arises how God should be imaged as both female and male (as well as, of course, beyond both). I would make two points here: first, God should be imagined in female, not feminine, terms, and second, the female metaphors should be inclusive of but not limited to maternal ones. On the first point: the distinction between "female" and "feminine" is important, for the first refers to gender while the second refers to qualities conventionally associated with women.[6] The problem with introducing a feminine dimension of God is that it invariably ends with identifying as female those qualities that society has called feminine. Thus, the feminine side of God is taken to comprise the tender, nurturing, passive, healing aspects of divine ac-tivity, whereas those activities in which God creates, redeems, estab-lishes peace, administers justice, and so on, are called masculine. Such a division, in extending to the godhead the stereotypes we create in human society, further crystallizes and sanctifies them.

But to image God in female personal terms, as she as well as he, is a very different matter. It is not, at the outset, to identify God with any particular set of characteristics, unless one is slipping in feminine stereotypes under the cover of simple gender appellation. All that has been done is to use a personal pronoun for deity and this is not only our tradition, the tradition of addressing God as Thou, but desirable and necessary in our time. Since all agents are either male or female, either pronoun and both pronouns can and should be used. If we use only the male pronoun, we fall into idolatry, forgetting that God is beyond male and female—a fact that the use of both pronouns brings home to us as the opening prayer to "Father-Mother God" illustrated. If we refuse to use any pronouns for God, we court the possibility of concealing androcentric assumptions behind abstractions.[7] If we are, then, to be concrete, personal, and nonidolatrous in our talk about God, we have no alternative but to speak of God in female as well as male terms, to use "she" as well as "he," and to realize that in so doing we are not attributing passive and nurturing qualities to God any more than we are attributing active and powerful qualities. Or to say it differently, we are attributing human qualities: we are imaging God on analogy with human beings, and so far that is all that we are doing: God is she and he and neither.

We come now, however, to the second point: female metaphors for God should be inclusive of but not limited to maternal ones. One of the important insights emerging from current research into Goddess religions is that in these traditions all divine activities are imaged by both male and female deities: both Ishtar and Horus, for instance, engage in creating, governing, nurturing, and redeeming.[8] In other words, neither masculine nor feminine characteristics are attributed to deities; rather, divine activities are attributed equivalently to male and female agents. Both male and female deities operate in both the private and the public arena; both engage in activities of power as well as care.[9] The Christian tradition does not, of course, worship multiple deities, but this fact in no way lessens the point being made—that if we accept the reasoning behind addressing God as "she" as well as "he," we should do so in a fashion that does not stereotype divine activities. This is not a new or radical notion in Christianity, despite the fact that the only female "component" in the tradition has been the quasi-divine figure of Mary, whose characteristics have certainly been stereotypically feminine.[10] But an earlier hypostasis of God—Sophia, or Wisdom, in Hebrew religion—was identified not only with the earth and sexuality but also with order and justice.[11] Moreover, medieval piety freely attributed a wide range of activities to God, some in female form, some in male, some in both.[12]

What, then, about the model of God as mother? Is that not stereotyping by suggesting as a major model for God *one* activity of females and the one most closely identified as stereotypically feminine, namely, giving birth to and raising children? My answer is twofold. First, although this particular essay will focus on God as mother in order to balance and provide a new context for interpreting God as father, other divine activities will also be imaged in female form, especially those concerned with creation and justice. Second, although mothering is a female activity, it is not feminine; that is, to give birth to and to feed the young is simply what females do—some may do it in a so-called feminine fashion, and others may not. What is more important for our purposes is that the symbolic material from the birthing and feeding process is very rich and for the most part has been neglected in establishment Christianity. It is also, as I shall try to show, powerful imagery for expressing the interrelatedness of all life, which is a central component in both a holistic sensibility and an understanding of Christian faith as an inclusive vision of fulfillment.

In this essay the model I have employed has sometimes been "God as mother" and sometimes "God as parent"; the emphasis will be on the former, but the latter will have a role as well. Our tradition has thoroughly analyzed the paternal metaphor, albeit mainly in a patriarchal context. The goal of my work will be to investigate the potential of the maternal model but to do so in a fashion that will provide an alternative interpretive context for the paternal model—a parental one. . . .

THE LOVE OF GOD AS MOTHER: AGAPE

Hidden away in the third volume of Paul Tillich's *Systematic Theology* is the suggestion that the symbolic dimension of the "ground of being" "points to the mother-quality of giving birth, carrying, and embracing, and, at the same time, of calling back, resisting independence of the created, and swallowing it."[13] He goes on to say that the uneasy feeling that many Protestants have about the first statement about God—that God is the power of being in all being—arises from the fact that their consciousness is shaped by the demanding father image for whom righteousness and not the gift of life is primary. What the father-God gives is redemption from sin; what the mother-God gives is life itself. But there is another reason that one might feel uneasy about Tillich's suggestion, for it implies divine resistance to independence for created being, whereas Western thought has prized its image of independent individuals who are saved one by one, either by their own moral choices or by divine grace. But what if the power in us, that which gives us our very existence, is not primarily judging individuals but calling us back, wanting to be more fully united with us, or as Tillich graphically puts it, wanting to "swallow" us? Our first reaction is fear of the maternal maw and a cry that we are independent, owing nothing to anyone, ready to face the consequences of our own actions.

But Tillich's symbolic suggestion for imaging the ground of being, the depths of divinity, as mother-love, which both gives life to all and desires reunification with all life, is helpful as we attempt to answer the question of the kind of love implied in the model of God as mother. This love can be characterized as agape, but that designation needs considerable qualification since the usual understanding of agape sees it as totally unmotivated, disinterested love.[14] Obviously, if God as the power of being, God as mother, calls us back and wants to be reunited with us, her love is not totally disinterested. But one must ask, why should we *want* it to be? The discussions on the nature of divine love, principally in Protestant circles and principally motivated by the desire to expunge any trace of need or interest on the part of God toward creation, paint a picture of God as isolated from creation and in no way dependent on it. As C. S. Lewis says, God is " 'at home' in the land of the Trinity," presumably finding relations with the other "persons" sufficiently satisfying so that, needing nothing, God "loves into existence wholly superfluous creatures."[15] Discussions about agape as definitive of divine love have, unfortunately, usually focused on redemption, not creation, and as a result have stressed the disinterested character of God's love, which can overlook the sin in the sinners and love them anyway.[16] In other words, even though we are worthless, we are loved—but disinterestedly. Needless to say, this is a sterile and unattractive view of divine love and a view that most of us would not settle for even as a description of human love. If, among ourselves, we want to be loved not in spite of who we are but because in some sense we are valuable, desirable, and needed, then is this not the case also with divine love? If God's creative love is agapic love, then is it not a statement to created beings: "It is good that you exist!"?[17] Agape has been characterized as the love that gives (usually in contrast with eros as the love that takes), and as such it belongs with the gift of life, creation. If it is considered in that context instead of the context of redemption, it need not be disinterested; in fact, it should not be.

As "interested," divine agape cannot be isolated from the other forms of love, eros and philia. If, with Tillich, one understands love as the "moving power of life," as that "which drives everything that is towards everything else that is," then elements of need, desire, and mutuality are evident in all forms of love.[18] An understanding of love as unifying and reuniting is basic to an interpretation of Christian faith as destabilizing, inclusive, nonhierarchical fulfillment for all. It is the love that underscores the interdependence of life in all its forms, the desire to be with other beings in both their needs and their joy. Nonetheless, the *depth* of divine love can be characterized as agapic, for the distinctive feature of this love is its impartiality, its willing of existence and fulfillment for all being.

God as the giver of life, as the power of being in all being, can be imaged through the metaphor of mother—and of father. Parental love is the most powerful and intimate experience we have of giving love whose return is not calculated (though a return is appreciated): it is the gift of *life as such* to others. Parental love wills life and when it comes, exclaims, "It is good that you exist!" Moreover, in addition to being the gift of life, parental love nurtures what it has brought into existence, wanting growth and fulfillment for all. This agapic love is revolutionary, for it loves the weak and vulnerable as well as the strong and beautiful. No human love can, of course, be perfectly just and impartial, but parental love is the best metaphor we have for imaging the creative love of God.

An important caveat is necessary at this point: the parental model in its siding with life as such is not "pro-life" in the sense of being anti-abortion. This is the case because of two features of our model: it is concerned with all species, not just human beings (and not with individuals in any species), and it is concerned with the nurture and fulfillment of life, not just with birth. On the first point: whereas we as biological or adoptive parents are interested in only one species—our own—and with particular individuals within that species, God as the mother of the universe is interested in all forms of life. One indication of human pride is our colossal ego in imagining that of the millions of forms of life in the universe, we are the only ones that matter. Why should our birth, nurture, and fulfillment be the only concern of the power that gives life to all life? God as mother, on the side of life as such, does not therefore mean on the side of only one species or on the side of every individual human birth (or every individual birth in any other species). This first point on the goodness of creation, "It is good that you exist!" must be followed immediately by the second: the household or economy of the universe must be ordered and managed in a way so as to bring about the nurture and fulfillment of life—and again, this cannot mean every individual life that could be brought into existence. In a closed ecological system with limits on natural resources, difficult decisions must be made to insure the continuation, growth, and fulfillment of the many forms of life (not just one form and not all its individuals). Population control, both for our own species and other species, is one such decision. The balance between quantity and quality of life is one that a contemporary sensibility must keep to the forefront. To be on the side of life means participating in the decisions necessary to keep that balance. It cannot mean being "pro-life" in terms of one species or in terms of unlimited numbers, for such a perspective would in the long run mean being against life in its many and varied forms.

Let us now consider our model in more detail: the model of parental love for God's agapic, creative love. Why is this a powerful, attractive model for expressing the Christian faith in our time? If the heart of Christian faith for an ecological, nuclear age must be profound awareness of the preciousness and vulnerability of life as a gift we receive and pass on, with appreciation for its value and desire for its fulfillment, it is difficult to think of any metaphors more apt than the parental one. There are three features basic to the parental model that will give flesh to this statement: it brings us closest to the beginnings of life, to the nurture of life, and to the impartial fulfillment of life.

Much of the power in the parental model is its immediate connection with the mystery of new life. Becoming a biological parent is the closest experience most people have to an experience of creation, that is, of bringing into existence. No matter how knowledgeable one is biologically, no matter how aware that human beings by becoming parents are simply doing what all animals do in passing life along, becoming a biological parent is for most people an awesome experience, inspiring feelings of having glimpsed the heart of things. We are, after all, the only creatures who can think about the wonder of existence, the sheer fact that "things are," that the incredible richness and complexity of life in all its forms has existed for millions of years, and that as part of the vast, unfathomable network of life, we both receive it from others and pass it along. At the time of the birth of new life from our bodies, we feel a sense of being co-creators, participating at least passively in the great chain of being. No matter how trite and hackneyed the phrases have become—"the miracle of birth," "the wonder of existence," and so on—on becoming a parent one repeats them again and joins the millions of others who marvel at their role in passing life along.

There are other ways of being parental besides being a biological parent, and I want to stress this point at the outset, because much of the case for the models of mother (father), lover, and friend rests on their extensions beyond their physical and immediate base. One can, of course, be an adoptive parent as well as a biological one, but even more important for our purposes is that all human beings have parental inclinations. All human beings have the potential for passing life along, for helping to bring the next generation (of whatever kind of beings) into existence, nurturing and guiding it, and working toward its fulfillment. These tendencies are so basic, widespread, and various that it is difficult to catalogue all the ways they are expressed. Some of the ways that come most readily to mind, such as in teaching, medicine, gardening, and social work, are only the tip of the iceberg, for in almost any cultural, political, economic, or social activity, there are aspects of the work that could be called parental.

Having made this point, however, let us return to the base of the model, in the physical act of giving birth. It is from this base that the model derives its power, for here it joins the reservoir of the great symbols of life and of life's continuity: blood, water, breath, sex, and food. In the acts of conception, gestation, and birth all are involved, and it is therefore no surprise that these symbols became the center of most religions, including Christianity, for they have the power to express the renewal and transformation of life—the "second birth"—because they are the basis of our "first birth." And yet, at least in Christianity, our first birth has been strangely neglected; another way of saying this is that creation, the birth of the world and all its beings, has not been permitted the imagery that this tradition uses so freely for the transformation and fulfillment of creation. Why is this the case?

One reason is surely that Christianity, alienated as it always has been from female sexuality, has been willing to image the second, "spiritual," renewal of existence in the birth metaphor, but not the first, "physical," coming into existence.[19] In fact in the Jewish and Christian traditions, creation has been imaginatively pictured as an intellectual, aesthetic "act" of God, accomplished through God's word and wrought by God's "hands" much as a painting is created by an artist or a form by a sculptor. But the model of God as mother suggests a very different kind of creation, one in keeping with the world as God's body but not one that the central tradition has been willing to consider. And it is clearly the parent *as mother* that is the stronger candidate for an understanding of creation as bodied forth from the divine being, for it is the imagery of gestation, giving birth, and lactation that creates an imaginative picture of creation as profoundly dependent on and cared for by divine life.[20] There simply is no other imagery available to us that has this power for expressing the interdependence and interrelatedness of all life with its ground. All of us, female and male, have the womb as our first home, all of us are born from the bodies of our mothers, all of us are fed by our mothers. What better imagery could there be for expressing the most basic reality of existence: that we live and move and have our being in God?

If the symbol of birth were allowed openly and centrally into the tradition, would this involve a radical theological change? Would it mean a different understanding of God's relation to the world? The simple answer is yes, the view associated with birth symbolism would be different from the distant, anthropocentric view in the monarchical model: it would be an intimate view, inclusive of the cosmos, but not one that identifies God and the world. By analogy, mothers, at least good ones, encourage the independence of their offspring, and even though children are products of their parents' bodies, they are often radically different from them.

The power of the parental model for God's creative, agapic love only begins with the birth imagery. Of equal importance is the ability of the model to express the nurturing of life and, to a lesser extent, its impartial fulfillment. It is at these levels that the more complex theological and ethical issues arise, for the divine agapic love that nurtures all creatures is a model of justice at the most basic level of the fair distribution of the necessities of life, and divine agapic love impartially fulfilling all of creation is a model of *inclusive* justice. In our understanding of Christianity as a destabilizing, inclusive nonhierarchical vision of fulfillment for all, the parental model of God is especially pertinent as a way of talking about God's "just" love, the love that attends to the most basic needs of all creatures. It is important to look more closely at the way the model expresses the nurture and inclusion of all of life.

Parents feed the young. This is, across the entire range of life, the most basic responsibility of parents, often of fathers as well as of mothers. Among most animals it is instinctual and is often accomplished only at the cost of the health or life of the parent. It is not principally from altruistic motives that parents feed the young but from a base close to the one that brought new life into existence, the source that participates in passing life along. With human parents, the same love that says, "It is good that you exist!" desires that existence to continue, and for many parents in much of the world that is a daily and often horrendous struggle. There is, perhaps, no picture more powerful to express "giving" love than that of parents wanting, but not having the food, to feed their starving children.[21]

The Christian tradition has paid a lot of attention to food and eating imagery. In fact, one could say that such imagery is probably at the center of the tradition's symbolic power: not only does the New Testament portrait of Jesus of Nazareth paint him as constantly feeding people, and eating with outcasts, but the church has as its central ritual a eucharistic meal reminiscent of the passion and death of Jesus and suggestive of the eschatological banquet yet to come. Christianity may be reticent in regard to birth imagery, especially as associated with natural, female processes, but it has shown no comparable reluctance to use the experience of eating as a symbol of spiritual nourishment. In fact, as many have pointed out, the Christian eucharist has obvious overtones of cannibalism! But the power of the food imagery is precisely in not fearing the physical connection, for the use of food as a symbol of the renewal of life must be grounded in food's basic role as the maintainer of life. Unfortunately, however, although the power of food imagery has been preserved in Christianity, the practical truth that food is basic to all life has often been neglected. A tradition that uses food as a symbol of spiritual renewal has often forgotten what parents know so well: that the young must be fed.

A theology that sees God as the parent who feeds the young and, by extension, the weak and vulnerable, understands God as caring about the most basic needs of life in its struggle to continue. One can extend nurture to include much more than attention to physical needs, but one ought not move too quickly, for the concern about life and its continuation that is a basic ingredient in the sensibility needed in our time has too often been neglected by Christianity in its interest in "spiritual" well-being. An evolutionary, ecological sensibility makes no clear distinction between matter and spirit or between body and mind, for life is a continuum and cannot flourish at the so-called higher levels unless supported at all levels. God as parent loves agapically in giving, with no thought of return, the sustenance needed for life to continue. This is creative love, for it provides the conditions minimally necessary for life to go on.

Finally, God as parent wants *all* to flourish. Divine agapic love is inclusive and hence a model of impartial justice. This is a difficult point to make without falling back into the old view of agape as disinterested; moreover, parental love can model the impartiality of divine love only in a highly qualified way. Yet it is central to the essence of agapic love to stress that it is impartial, or as I would prefer to say, inclusive.[22] This is a better way to express what is at stake than to call the love disinterested, which suggests that God's love is detached, unconcerned, or perfunctory. In fact, the opposite is intended, for agapic love functions in spite of obstacles and in this way can be love of *all*, whatever the barriers may be. God as mother is parent to *all* species and wishes all to flourish. We can reflect this inclusiveness in the model of parent only in partial and distorted fashion, for as parents we tend by instinct to focus on our own species and on particular individuals within that species. To be sure, when we extend the model beyond its physical base to include our parental inclinations toward human children not our own, as well as toward life forms not our own, a measure of impartiality, of inclusiveness, emerges, but only as a faint intimation of divine agape. It is imperative to recognize when a model falters. This one falters here.

With most recent understandings of agape, however, our model would have faltered long ago, for if divine love is seen as totally different from all forms of love that we know, as entirely "giving" whereas human love is only "taking," no human love will serve as a metaphor for God's love. But we have maintained that dimensions of divine agapic love, especially those involved in the creating and sustaining of life, can be modeled with great power by parental love. What this model or any model cannot do is express the mystery that *all* are included, even the last and the least.

NOTES

1. Elizabeth Clark and Herbert Richardson, eds., *Women and Religion* (New York: Harper & Row, 1977), 164–65.
2. For a fuller treatment of this point, see my book *Metaphorical Theology: Models of God in Religious Language* (Philadelphia: Fortress Press, 1982; 2d printing with new preface, 1985), chap. 5.
3. Virginia Mollenkott makes this point eloquently in *The Divine Feminine: The Biblical Imagery of God as Female* (New York: Crossroad, 1983), 113–14.

4. For different but complementary views on this point, see Carolyn Merchant, *The Death of Nature: Women, Ecology, and the Scientific Revolution* (New York: Harper & Row, 1980); Brian Easlea, *Fathering the Unthinkable: Masculinity, Scientists, and the Nuclear Arms Race* (London: Pluto, 1983); Rosemary Radford Ruether, *Sexism and God-Talk: Toward a Feminist Theology* (Boston: Beacon Press, 1983), chap. 2; Mary Daly, *Gyn/Ecology: The Metaethics of Radical Feminism* (Boston: Beacon Press, 1978); and Rita M. Gross, "Hindu Female Deities as a Resource for the Contemporary Rediscovery of the Goddess," in *The Book of the Goddess Past and Present: An Introduction to Her Religion*, ed. Carl Olson (New York: Crossroad, 1983).

5. One example of the danger inherent in twisted thinking concerning sexuality surfaces in the birth metaphors used by scientists involved in creating the atomic bomb. Brian Easlea in his book *Fathering the Unthinkable* has collected these materials.

6. Many feminists are concerned to make this distinction. See, for example, Ruether, *Sexism and God-Talk*, 111.

7. Rosemary Radford Ruether makes this point tellingly with the comment that those unwilling to give up the male monopoly on God-language often reply to objectors, "God is not male. He is Spirit" (*Sexism and God-Talk*, 67).

8. For a sampling of this literature, see Judith Ochshorn, *The Female Experience and the Nature of the Divine* (Bloomington, IN: Indiana University Press, 1981); Carol P. Christ, "Symbols of Goddess and God in Feminist Theology" and Gross, "Hindu Female Deities," in Olson (ed.), *The Book of the Goddess*; and Ruether, *Sexism and God-Talk*, chap. 2.

9. This point is made by many feminist theologians and is succinctly summarized by Elizabeth A. Johnson: ". . . the goddess is not the expression of the feminine dimension of the divine, but the expression of the fullness of divine power and care shown in a female image." ("The Incomprehensibility of God and the Image of God Male and Female," *Theological Studies* 45 [1984]: 461.)

10. See, for example, Rosemary Radford Ruether, *Mary—The Feminine Face of the Church* (Philadelphia: Westminster Press, 1977), and E. Ann Matter, "The Virgin Mary: A Goddess?" in Olson (ed.), *The Book of the Goddess*.

11. In Elisabeth Schüssler Fiorenza's study of Sophia in Israelite religion, Sophia is in a symbiotic relationship to God with a variety of appellations (sister, wife, mother, beloved, teacher) and tasks (leading, preaching, teaching, creating, and so on). See *In Memory of Her: A Feminist Theological Reconstruction of Christian Origins* (New York: Crossroad, 1983), 130ff.

12. See Eleanor McLaughlin, " 'Christ My Mother': Feminine Naming and Metaphor in Medieval Spirituality," *St. Luke's Journal of Theology* 18 (1975): 356–86; and Caroline Walker Bynum, *Jesus as Mother: Studies in the Spirituality of the High Middle Ages* (Berkeley and Los Angeles: University of California Press, 1982).

13. Paul Tillich, *Systematic Theology* (Chicago: University of Chicago Press, 1963), 3:293–94.

14. Anders Nygren, with his much-discussed book *Agape and Eros* (trans. Philip S. Watson [Philadelphia: Westminster Press, 1953]), initiated the twentieth-century conversations on the issue, taking the extreme view that the two kinds of love are totally unrelated and incommensurable, with eros as the corruption of agape—the self-interest that creeps into disinterested love.

15. C. S. Lewis, *The Four Loves* (New York: Harcourt, Brace & Co., 1960), 176.

16. In Nygren's words, what is critical is to stress the "principle that *any thought of valuation whatsoever* is out of place in connection with fellowship with God. When God's love is directed to the sinner, then the position is clear; all thought of valuation is excluded in advance; for if God, the Holy One, loves the sinner, it cannot be because of his sin, but in spite of his sin" (*Agape and Eros*, 75–80).

17. This phrase comes from Josef Pieper's book *About Love*, trans. Richard and Clara Winston (Chicago: Franciscan Herald Press, 1974), 22.

18. Paul Tillich, *Love, Power, and Justice: Ontological Analyses and Ethical Applications* (New York: Oxford University Press, 1954), 25.

19. Another reason is the Christ-centeredness of the tradition, which overlooks the first birth because it wants to stress the second birth. In promoting Christ's mission of redemption, the tradition has failed to appreciate the gift of creation.

20. The Jewish and Christian traditions have carried imagery of gestation, giving birth, and lactation as a leitmotif that emerges only now and then over the centuries. For Hebraic use of the "breasts" and "womb" of God as metaphors of divine compassion and care, see Phyllis Trible, *God and the Rhetoric of Sexuality* (Philadelphia: Fortress Press, 1978), chap. 2.

21. The growing worldwide response to starving populations, response beyond anything expected and from all levels of society in all countries, is witness to the basic parental instinct to feed the young, the weak, the vulnerable. It need not (and should not) be named altruism, Christian love, or anything else grand; it is simply what all human beings want to be part of: passing along to others the gift of life.

22. Those who have written in the most balanced way about agape—including Josef Pieper, M. C. D'Arcy, Gene Outka, and Paul Tillich—all insist that although agape is not so completely different that there is nothing that unites the loves, it *is* different: agape qualifies the other loves, guarding against their distortions (as for Tillich), or it provides a base line (as in Outka's notion of agape as "equal regard," the "regard which is independent and unalterable; and which applies to each neighbor qua human existent," [in Nygren, *Agape and Eros*, 13]).

Sexism and God-Language

ROSEMARY RADFORD RUETHER

Male monotheism has been so taken for granted in Christian culture that the peculiarity of imaging God solely through one gender has not been recognized. But such an image indicates a sharp departure from all previous human consciousness. . . .

Male monotheism reinforces the social hierarchy of patriarchal rule through its religious system in a way that was not the case with the paired images of God and Goddess. God is modeled after the patriarchal ruling class and is seen as addressing this class of males directly, adopting them as his "sons." They are his representatives, the responsible partners of the covenant with him. Women as wives now become symbolically repressed as the dependent servant class. Wives, along with children and servants, represent those ruled over and owned by the patriarchal class. They relate to man as he relates to God. A symbolic hierarchy is set up: God-male-female. Women no longer stand in direct relation to God; they are connected to God secondarily, through the male. This hierarchical order is evident in the structure of patriarchal law in the Old Testament, in which only the male heads of families are addressed directly. Women, children, and servants are referred to indirectly through their duties and property relations to the patriarch.[i] In the New Testament this hierarchical "order" appears as a cosmic principle:

But I want to understand that the head of every man is Christ, the head of a woman is her husband, and the head of Christ is God. . . . For a man ought not to cover his head, since he is the image and glory of God, but the woman is the glory of man. (1 Cor. 11:3, 7)

Male monotheism becomes the vehicle of a psychocultural revolution of the male ruling class in its relationship to surrounding reality. Whereas ancient myth had seen the Gods and Goddesses as within the matrix of one physical-spiritual reality, male monotheism begins to split reality into a dualism of transcendent Spirit (mind, ego) and inferior and dependent physical nature. Bodiless ego or spirit is seen as pri-

---

Rosemary Radford Ruether is Georgia Harkness Professor of Theology at the Garrett Theological Seminary and member of the Graduate Faculty at Northwestern University in Evanston, Illinois. She is the author or editor of twenty-one books on Christian theology and social justice in such areas as feminism, Jewish-Christian relations, ecology, and militarism.

mary, existing before the cosmos. The physical world is "made" as an artifact by transcendent, disembodied mind or generated through some process of devolution from spirit to matter.

Both the Hebrew Genesis story and the Platonic creation story of *Timaeus* retain reminiscences of the idea of primal matter as something already existing that is ordered or shaped by the Creator God. But this now becomes the lower pole in the hierarchy of being. Thus the hierarchy of God-male-female does not merely make woman secondary in relation to God, it also gives her a negative identity in relation to the divine. Whereas the male is seen essentially as the image of the male transcendent ego or God, woman is seen as the image of the lower, material nature. Although both are seen as "mixed natures," the male identity points "above" and the female "below." Gender becomes a primary symbol for the dualism of transcendence and immanence, spirit and matter.

THE APPROPRIATION OF THE GODDESS IN JEWISH AND CHRISTIAN MONOTHEISM

In Hebrew religious development, male monotheism does not, by any means, succeed in simply supplanting the older world of Gods and Goddesses or the cult of salvation through renewal of nature-society. Rather it imposes itself on this older world, assimilating, transforming, and reversing its symbol systems. Thus, for example, the ancient myth of the Sacred Marriage lives on in Yahwism, but in a reversed form that uses this story to exert the possessive and judgmental relation of the patriarchal God over the people of agricultural society. The patriarchal God, not the Goddess, is the dominant partner in the Sacred Marriage. The female has been reduced to the human partner as servant to God. In the prophet Hosea, the marriage symbol is taken over judgmentally as a diatribe against the "harlotry" of Israelites, who prefer Baal, the vegetation and rain God of the Canaanites, to Yahweh, the nomadic patriarch. Yahweh is depicted as the angry and threatening husband who will punish his unfaithful bride with summary divorce. But he is also described as winning her back and making her faithful to him by drawing her out into the desert wildness. . . .

From archaeological evidence we know that Yahweh did not replace the Goddess in the affections of many people conquered or assimilated by the Israelites. Rather, for many people, Yahweh simply replaced Baal as the husband of the Goddess. Asherah, another form of the Canaanite Goddess, continued to be worshiped alongside Yahweh in the Solomonic temple for two-thirds of its existence.[2] Ordinary graves of Israelites show Yahwist and Goddess symbols together. The upper Egyptian Jewish colony at Elephantine worshiped Yahweh as husband of the Goddess in its temple.[3] Thus, behind the apparent conquest of

Yahweh over Anath-Baal lies a more complex reality. It is not insignificant that most of the polemics against Canaanite religion in the Old Testament are against Baal, not Anath or Asherah. Yahweh does not do warfare primarily against the Goddess. Rather it is Baal, her male consort, who must be replaced. The Goddess is not so much eliminated as she is absorbed and put into a new relationship with Yahweh as her Lord.

In addition to this transformation of the Sacred Marriage from a Goddess-king relation into a patriarchal God-servant wife, Yahwism appropriates female images for God at certain points. The male patriarchal image proves too limited to represent the variety of relationships to Israel that Hebrew thought wished to express. In certain texts Yahweh is described as like a mother or like a woman in travail with the birth of a child. These references occur particularly when the authors wish to describe God's unconditional love and faithfulness to the people despite their sins. They express God's compassion and forgiveness. God is seen as suffering on behalf of Israel, seeking to bring Israel to the new birth of repentance. As Phyllis Trible has pointed out, the root word for the ideas of compassion and mercy in Hebrew is *rechem*, or womb.[4] In ascribing these qualities to Yahweh, Hebrew thought suggests that God has maternal or "womblike" qualities. . . .

In addition to these appropriations of womb-qualities to Yahweh, there is a second important use of female imagery for God in the Scriptural and theological tradition. In the Wisdom tradition the female image appears as a secondary persona of God, mediating the work and will of God to creation. The Book of Proverbs describes Wisdom as an offspring of God, being brought forth from God before the beginning of the earth, cooperating with God in the creation of the world, rejoicing and delighting in the work of creation. In the Wisdom of Solomon, Wisdom is the manifestation of God through whom God mediates the work of creation, providential guidance, and revelation. She is the subtle power of the presence of God, permeating and enspiriting all things. . . . The wise man, represented by Solomon, takes Wisdom as his bride and brings her to live with him so she can give him good counsel (8:2, 9). Behind this powerful image of Wisdom lies the Goddess who was traditionally characterized as Wisdom. But in Hebrew thought she has become a dependent attribute or expression of the transcendent male God rather than an autonomous, female manifestation of the divine.

In Christianity the idea of a second persona of God expressing God's immanence, the presence of God in creation, revelation, and redemption, was taken over to explain the divine identity of Jesus. While the passages in Hebrews, chapters 1 and 2, and elsewhere in the New Testament echo the Wisdom tradition, the word *Logos* (word) used by the Jewish philosopher Philo is preferred to *Sophia* (wisdom). The roots of the *Logos* concept in the Wisdom tradition are evident at many points. Paul says, "We are preaching a crucified Christ . . . who is . . . the Wisdom of God" (1 Cor. 1:23–24). Several of the Christological hymns substitute the word *Logos* for the word *Sophia*. Theologically, *Logos* plays the same cosmological roles as *Sophia* as ground of creation, revealer of the mind of God, and reconciler of humanity to God. But the use of the male word *Logos*, when identified with the maleness of the historical Jesus, obscures the actual fluidity of the gender symbolism by appearing to reify as male a "Son of God" who is, in turn, the image of the Father. . . .

All speculation on a female side of God was not cut off despite the adoption of a male *Logos* symbol. The figure of the Holy Spirit picks up many of the Hebraic traditions of the female *Sophia* and *Hokmah* (spirit). Many early Christian texts refer to the Spirit as female. This is found particularly in the Apocryphal gospels. . . .

Female imagery for the Spirit continues to ferment under the surface of Christian theology, particularly in mystical writers. . . . A whole line of mystical thinkers, flowing from Jacob Boehme in the seventeenth century down into the nineteenth century, speculate on the androgynous nature of God. The eighteenth-century Shakers develop this concept in detail in new scriptures and a new vision of Christian messianism that includes a female Messiah who represents the Wisdom or Mother-aspect of God.[5]

Do these traditions of the androgyny of God and the female aspect of the Trinity resolve the problem of the exclusively male image of God? Some Christian feminists feel they do. God has both mothering or feminine as well as masculine characteristics. The feminine aspect of God is to be identified particularly with the Holy Spirit. It is doubtful, however, that we should settle for a concept of the Trinity that consists of two male and one female "persons." Such a concept of God falls easily into an androcentric or male-dominant perspective. The female side of God then becomes a subordinate principle underneath the dominant image of male divine sovereignty.

We should guard against concepts of divine androgyny that simply ratify on the divine level the patriarchal split of the masculine and the feminine. In such a concept, the feminine side of God, as a secondary or mediating principle, would act in the same subordinate and limited roles in which females are allowed to act in the patriarchal social order. The feminine can be mediator or recipient of divine power in relation to creaturely reality. She can be God's daughter, the bride of the (male) soul. But she can never represent divine transcendence in all fullness. For feminists to appropriate the "feminine" side of God within this patriarchal gender hierarchy is simply to reinforce the problem of gender stereotyping on the level of God-language. We need to go beyond the idea of a "feminine side" of God, whether to be identified with the

Spirit or even with the *Sophia*-Spirit together, and question the assumption that the highest symbol of divine sovereignty still remains exclusively male.

GOD-LANGUAGE BEYOND PATRIARCHY IN THE BIBLICAL TRADITION

THE PROPHETIC GOD

Although the predominantly male images and roles of God make Yahwism an agent in the sacralization of patriarchy, there are critical elements in Biblical theology that contradict this view of God. By patriarchy we mean not only the subordination of females to males, but the whole structure of Father-ruled society: aristocracy over serfs, masters over slaves, king over subjects, racial overlords over colonized people. Religions that reinforce hierarchical stratification use the Divine as the apex of this system of privilege and control. The religions of the ancient Near East link the Gods and Goddesses with the kings and queens, the priests and priestesses, the warrior and temple aristocracy of stratified society. The Gods and Goddesses mirror this ruling class and form its heavenly counterpart. The divinities also show mercy and favor to the distressed, but in the manner of noblesse oblige.

Yahweh, as tribal God of Israel, shows many characteristics similar to those of the Near Eastern deities, as mighty king, warrior, and one who shows mercy and vindicates justice. But these characteristics are put in a new and distinct context: Yahweh is unique as the God of a tribal confederation that identifies itself as liberated slaves. The basic identity of Yahweh as God of this confederation lies in "his" historical action as the divine power that liberated these slaves from bondage and led them to a new land. This confederation is not an ethnic people, but a bonding of groups of distinct backgrounds. A core group experienced the escape from bondage in Egypt that formed the primary identity of Israel. They were joined by nomadic groups from the desert and hill peoples in Canaan in revolt against the feudal power of the city-states of the plains. Norman Gottwald reconstructs the premonarchical formation of this tribal confederation (1250–1050 B.C.E.). The identification of Yahweh with liberation from bondage allowed this diverse group to unite in a new egalitarian society and to revolt against the stratified feudal society of the city-states that oppressed the peasant peoples of the hills with taxes and forced labor.[6]

The Davidic monarchy represents a capitulation of Judaic leadership to the city-state model of power, but the prophets of Israel continue the tradition of protests against the hierarchical, urban, landowning society that deprives and oppresses the rural peasantry. This established at the heart of Biblical religion a motif of protest against the status quo of ruling-class privilege and the deprivation of the poor. God is seen as a critic of this society, a champion of the social victims. Salvation is envisioned as deliverance from systems of social oppression and as restoration of an egalitarian peasant society of equals, "where each have their own vine and fig tree and none need be afraid" (Mic. 4:4). . . .

The New Testament contains a renewal and radicalization of prophetic consciousness, now applied to marginalized groups in a universal, nontribal context. Consequently, it is possible to recognize as liberated by God social groups overlooked in Old Testament prophecy. Class, ethnicity, and gender are now specifically singled out as the divisions overcome by redemption in Christ. In the New Testament stories, gender is recognized as an additional oppression within oppressed classes and ethnic groups.[7] Women, the doubly oppressed within marginalized groups, manifest God's iconoclastic, liberating action in making "the last first and the first last." All women are not doubly oppressed; there are also queens and wealthy women. But women's experience of oppression has begun to become visible and to be addressed by prophetic consciousness (very likely because of the participation of women in the early Christian movement).

THE LIBERATING SOVEREIGN

A second antipatriarchal use of God-language occurs in the Old and New Testaments when divine sovereignty and fatherhood are used to break the ties of bondage under human kings and fathers. Abraham is called into an adoptive or covenanted relation with God only by breaking his ties with his family, leaving behind the graves of his ancestors.[8] The God of Exodus establishes a relationship with the people that breaks their ties with the ruling overlords. As the people flee from the land of bondage, Pharaoh and his horsemen are drowned. God's kingship liberates Israel from human kings. The antimonarchical tradition inveighs against Israel's capitulation to the customs of the surrounding people by adopting kingship.

These Old Testament traditions are developed in Jesus' teaching. It has been often pointed out that Jesus uses a unique word for God. By adopting the word *Abba* for God, he affirms a primary relationship to God based on love and trust; *Abba* was the intimate word used by children in the family for their fathers. It is not fully conveyed by English terms such as *Daddy*, for it was also a term an adult could use of an older man to signify a combination of respect and affection.[9] But is it enough to conclude from this use of *Abba* that Jesus transforms the patriarchal concept of divine fatherhood into what might be called a maternal or nurturing concept of God as loving, trustworthy parent?

The early Jesus movement characteristically uses this concept of God as *Abba* to liberate the community from human dominance-dependence relationships based on kinship ties or master-servant relationships. In the Gospel tradition, joining the new community of Jesus creates a rupture with traditional family ties and loyalties. In order to follow Jesus one must "hate" (that is, put aside one's loyalty to) father and mother, sisters and brothers (Luke 14:26; Matt. 10:37–38). The patriarchal family is replaced by a new community of brothers and sisters (Matt. 12:46–50; Mark 3:31–35; Luke 8:19–21). This new community is a community of equals, not of master and servants, father and children. Matthew 23:1–10 states that the relationship to God as *Abba* abolishes all father-child, master-servant relations between people within the Jesus community: "You are to call no man father, master or Lord." The relationship between Christians is to be one of mutual service and not of mastery and servitude. At the end of the Gospel of John, Jesus tells the disciples that their relationship has now become one of equals. They now have the same *Abba* relation to God as he does and can act out of the same principles: "No longer do I call you servants, . . . but I have called you friends" (John 15:15). These traditions reverse the symbolic relation between divine fatherhood and sovereignty and the sacralization of patriarchy. Because God is our king, we need obey no human kings. Because God is our parent, we are liberated from dependence on patriarchal authority.

But the language used in this tradition creates an obvious ambivalence. It works to establish a new liberated relationship to a new community of equals for those in revolt against established authorities. This is true not only in the formation of Israel and in the rise of the Jesus movement; again and again throughout Christian history this antipatriarchal use of God-language has been rediscovered by dissenting groups. The call to "obey God rather than men" has perhaps been the most continuous theological basis for dissent in the Christian tradition. Throughout Christian history women discovered this concept of direct relation to God as a way to affirm their own authority and autonomy against patriarchal authority. God's call to them to preach, to teach, to form a new community where women's gifts were fully actualized overruled the patriarchal authority that told them to remain at home as dutiful daughters or wives.[10]

But once the new community becomes a part of the dominant society, God as father and king can be assimilated back into the traditional patriarchal relationships and used to sacralize the authority of human lordship and patriarchy. The radical meaning of *Abba* for God is lost in translation and interpretation. Instead, a host of new ecclesiastical and imperial "holy fathers" arises, claiming the fatherhood and kingship of God as the basis of their power over others. In order to preserve the prophetic social relationships, we need to find a new language that cannot be as easily co-opted by the systems of domination.

THE PROSCRIPTION OF IDOLATRY

A third Biblical tradition that is important to a feminist theology is the proscription of idolatry. Israel is to make no picture or graven image of God; no pictorial or verbal representation of God can be taken literally. By contrast, Christian sculpture and painting represents God as a powerful old man with a white beard, even crowned and robed in the insignia of human kings or the triple tiara of the Pope. The message created by such images is that God is both similar to and represented by the patriarchal leadership, the monarchs and the Pope. Such imaging of God should be judged for what it is—as idolatry, as the setting up of certain human figures as the privileged images and representations of God. To the extent that such political and ecclesiastical patriarchy incarnates unjust and oppressive relationships, such images of God become sanctions of evil.

The proscription of idolatry must also be extended to verbal pictures. When the word *Father* is taken literally to mean that God is male and not female, represented by males and not females, then this word becomes idolatrous. The Israelite tradition is circumspect about the verbal image, printing it without vowel signs. The revelation to Moses in the burning bush gives as the name of God only the enigmatic "I am what I shall be." God is person without being imaged by existing social roles. God's being is open-ended, pointing both to what is and to what can be.

Classical Christian theology teaches that all names for God are analogies. The tradition of negative or *apophatic* theology emphasizes the unlikeness between God and human words for God. That tradition corrects the tendency to take verbal images literally; God is like but also unlike any verbal analogy. Does this not mean that male words for God are not in any way superior to or more appropriate than female analogies? God is both male and female and neither male nor female. One needs inclusive language for God that draws on the images and experiences of both genders. This inclusiveness should not become more abstract. Abstractions often conceal androcentric assumptions and prevent the shattering of the male monopoly on God-language, as in "God is not male. He is Spirit." Inclusiveness can happen only by naming God/ess in female as well as male metaphors.

EQUIVALENT IMAGES FOR GOD AS MALE AND FEMALE

Are there any Biblical examples of such naming of God/ess in female as well as male metaphors that are truly equivalent images, that is, not "feminine" aspects of a male God? The synoptic Gospels offer some examples of this in the parallel parables, which seem to have been shaped in the early Christian catechetical community. They reflect the innovation of the early Christian movement of including women equally in those called to study the Torah of Jesus. Jesus justifies this practice in the Mary-Martha story, where he defends Mary's right to study in the circle of disciples around Rabbi Jesus in the words "Mary has chosen the better part which shall not be taken from her" (Luke 10:38–42).

In the parables of the mustard seed and the leaven the explosive power of the Kingdom, which God, through Jesus, is sowing in history through small signs and deeds, is compared to a farmer sowing the tiny mustard seed that produces a great tree or a woman folding the tiny bit of leaven in three measures of flour which then causes the whole to rise (Luke 13:18–21; Matt. 13:31–33). The parables of the lost sheep and the lost coin portray God seeking the sinners despised by the "righteous" of Israel. God is compared to a shepherd who leaves his ninety-nine sheep to seek the one that is lost or to a woman with ten coins who loses one and sweeps her house diligently until she finds it. Having found it, she rejoices and throws a party for her friends. This rejoicing is compared to God's rejoicing with the angels in heaven over the repentance of one sinner (Luke 15:1–10).

These metaphors for divine activity are so humble that their significance has been easily overlooked in exegesis, but we should note several important points. First, the images of male and female in these parables are equivalent. They both stand for the same things, as paired images. One is in no way inferior to the other. Second, the images are not drawn from the social roles of the mighty, but from the activities of Galilean peasants. It might be objected that the roles of the women are stereotypical and enforce the concept of woman as housekeeper. But it is interesting that the women are never described as related to or dependent on men. The small treasure of the old woman is her own. Presumably she is an independent householder. Finally, and most significantly, the parallel male and female images do not picture divine action in parental terms. The old woman seeking the lost coin and the woman leavening the flour image God not as mother or father (Creator), but as seeker of the lost and transformer of history (Redeemer).

TOWARD A FEMINIST UNDERSTANDING OF GOD/ESS

The preceding Biblical traditions may not be adequate for a feminist reconstruction of God/ess, but they are suggestive. If all language for God/ess is analogy, if taking a particular human image literally is idolatry, then male language for the divine must lose its privileged place. If God/ess is not the creator and validator of the existing hierarchical social order, but rather the one who liberates us from it, who opens up a new community of equals, then language about God/ess drawn from kingship and hierarchical power must lose its privileged place. Images of God/ess must include female roles and experience. Images of God/ess must be drawn from the activities of peasants and working people, people at the bottom of society. Most of all, images of God/ess must be transformative, pointing us back to our authentic potential and forward to new redeemed possibilities. God/ess-language cannot validate roles of men or women in stereotypic ways that justify male dominance and female subordination. Adding an image of God/ess as loving, nurturing mother, mediating the power of the strong, sovereign father, is insufficient.

Feminists must question the overreliance of Christianity, especially modern bourgeois Christianity, on the model of God/ess as parent. Obviously any symbol of God/ess as parent should include mother as well as father. Mary Baker Eddy's inclusive term, *Mother-Father God*, already did this one hundred years ago. Mother-Father God has the virtue of concreteness, evoking both parental images rather than moving to an abstraction (Parent), which loses effective resonance. Mother and father image God/ess as creator, as the source of our being. They point back from our own historical existence to those upon whom our existence depends. Parents are a symbol of roots, the sense of being grounded in the universe in those who have gone before, who underlie our own existence.

But the parent model for the divine has negative resonance as well. It suggests a kind of permanent parent-child relationship to God. God becomes a neurotic parent who does not want us to grow up. To become autonomous and responsible for our own lives is the gravest sin against God. Patriarchal theology uses the parent image for God to prolong spiritual infantilism as virtue and to make autonomy and assertion of free will a sin. Parenting in patriarchal society also becomes the way of enculturating us to the stereotypic male and female roles. The family becomes the nucleus and model of patriarchal relations in society. To that extent parenting language for God reinforces patriarchal power rather than liberating us from it. We need to start with language for the Divine as redeemer, as liberator, as one who fosters full personhood and, in that context, speak of God/ess as creator, as source of being.

Patriarchal theologies of "hope" or liberation affirm the God of Exodus, the God who uproots us from present historical systems and puts us on the road to new possibilities. But they typically do this in negation of God/ess as Matrix, as source and ground of our being. They make the fundamental mistake of identifying the ground of creation with the foundations of existing social systems. Being, matter, and nature become the ontocratic base for the evil system of what is. Liberation is liberation out of or against nature into spirit. The identification of matter, nature, and being with mother makes such patriarchal theology hostile to women as symbols of all that "drags us down" from freedom. The hostility of males to any symbol of God/ess as female is rooted in this identification of mother with the negation of liberated spirit. God/ess as Matrix is thought of as "static" immanence. A static, devouring, death-dealing matter is imaged, with horror, as extinguishing the free flight of transcendent consciousness. The dualism of nature and transcendence, matter and spirit as female against male is basic to male theology.

Feminist theology must fundamentally reject this dualism of nature and spirit. It must reject both sides of the dualism: both the image of mother-matter-matrix as "static immanence" and as the ontological foundation of existing, oppressive social systems and also the concept of spirit and transcendence as rootless, antinatural, originating in an "other world" beyond the cosmos, ever repudiating and fleeing from nature, body, and the visible world. Feminist theology needs to affirm the God of Exodus, of liberation and new being, but as rooted in the foundations of being rather than as its antithesis. The God/ess who is the foundation (at one and the same time) of our being and our new being embraces both the roots of the material substratum of our existence (matter) and also the endlessly new creative potential (spirit). The God/ess who is the foundation of our being-new being does not lead us back to a stifled, dependent self or uproot us in a spirit-trip outside the earth. Rather it leads us to the converted center, the harmonization of self and body, self and other, self and world. It is the *Shalom* of our being.

God/ess as once and future *Shalom* of being, however, is *not* the creator, founder, or sanctioner of patriarchal-hierarchical society. This world arises in revolt against God/ess and in alienation from nature. It erects a false system of alienated dualisms modeled on its distorted and oppressive social relationships. God/ess liberates us from this false and alienated world, not by an endless continuation of the same trajectory of alienation but as a constant breakthrough that points us to new possibilities that are, at the same time, the regrounding of ourselves in the primordial matrix, the original harmony. The liberating encounter with God/ess is always an encounter with our authentic selves resurrected from underneath the alienated self. It is not experienced against, but in and through relationships, healing our broken relations with our bodies, with other people, with nature. We have no adequate name for the true God/ess, the "I am who I shall become." Intimations of Her/His name will appear as we emerge from false naming of God/ess modeled on patriarchal alienation.

NOTES

1. Phyllis Bird, "Women in the Old Testament," in *Religion and Sexism: Images of Women in the Jewish and Christian Traditions,* ed. R. Ruether (New York: Simon and Schuster, 1974), 48–57.

2. Raphael Patai, *The Hebrew Goddess* (Philadelphia: Ktav, 1967), 36–45, 49–50 (236 out of 370 years).

3. Ibid., 99–100.

4. Phyllis Trible, *God and the Rhetoric of Sexuality* (Philadelphia: Fortress Press, 1978), 48.

5. Jacob Boehme, *Mysterium Magnum: An Exposition of the First Book of Moses Called Genesis*, trans. John R. Sparrow (London: John M. Watkins, 1924), 1:121–33. See R. Ruether and R. Keller, *Women and Religion in America: The Nineteenth Century: A Documentary History* (San Francisco: Harper & Row, 1981), 46–48, 60–65.

6. Norman K. Gottwald, *The Tribes of Yahweh: A Sociology of the Religion of Liberated Israel, 1250–1050 B.C.* (Maryknoll, NY: Orbis Books, 1979), 210–19, 489–587, 692–709.

7. See, for example, Matt. 15:21–28; Mark 5:25–33; Luke 7:11–17, 7:36–50, 10:38–42, 13:10–17.

8. Robert Hamerton-Kelly, *God the Father: Theology and Patriarchy in the Teachings of Jesus* (Philadelphia: Fortress Press, 1979), 21–28.

9. Ibid., 70–81.

10. The revolt of women against the patriarchal authority of fathers, husbands, or fiancés, as well as political authority, is found continuously in Christian popular literature of the second and third centuries, particularly in martyrologies and apocryphal Acts. See Stevan Davies, *The Revolt of the Widows: The Social World of the Apocryphal Acts* (Carbondale, IL: Southern Illinois University Press, 1980), 50–69. This theme is continued in medieval lives of female saints. See Eleanor McLaughlin, "Women, Power and the Pursuit of Holiness in Medieval Christianity," in *Women of Spirit: Female Leadership in the Jewish and Christian Traditions*, ed. R. Ruether and E. McLaughlin (New York: Simon and Schuster, 1979), 108–11. The theme is also typical in conversion stories of nineteenth-century Evangelical women. A dramatic example is found in the diary of the black Shaker Rebecca Jackson. See Jean McMahon Humez, *Gifts of Power: The Writings of Rebecca Jackson* (Amherst, MA: University of Massachusetts Press, 1981), 18–23 and passim.

Selections from *The Inclusive Language Lectionary*

INCLUSIVE LANGUAGE LECTIONARY COMMITTEE OF THE NATIONAL COUNCIL OF CHURCHES

A lectionary is a fixed selection of readings, taken from both the Old and the New Testament, to be read and heard in the churches' services of worship. Most lectionaries are simply tables or lists of readings to be used in weekly worship; some include daily readings. They cite the biblical book from which the reading is taken, as well as the chapter and verses: for example, Christmas Day: *Luke 2:1–20.* By contrast, this lectionary contains the full text of each reading.

WHY INCLUSIVE LANGUAGE?

The Inclusive Language Lectionary readings are based on the Revised Standard Version and original Greek and Hebrew texts, with the intent of reflecting the full humanity of women and men in the light of the gospel. A growing number of people feel they have been denied full humanity by a pattern of exclusion in English usage. Consider, for example, the traditional English use of the word "man." A man is a male human being, as opposed to a female human being. But in common usage "man" has also meant "human being," as opposed to "animal." On the other hand, "woman" means female, but never *human being.* No word that refers to a female person identifies her with humanity. So, in common English idiom, "man" has been defined by his humanity, but "woman" by her sex, by her relationship to man. "Woman" becomes a subgroup under "human." "Man" is the human race; "woman" is man's sexual partner, in traditional English usage.

This is but one example of how language *reflects* the way in which we think but also *informs* the way in which we think. The mandate to the Lectionary Committee is to seek "language which expresses inclusiveness with regard to human beings and which attempts to expand

---

The *Inclusive Language Lectionary Committee* was appointed by the Division of Education and Ministry of the National Council of Churches. The Committee's members come from a variety of denominations and liturgical traditions and represent expertise in Hebrew, Greek, linguistics, English, worship, Old and New Testaments, theology, and education.

the range of images beyond the masculine to assist the church in understanding the full nature of God."

The RSV (Revised Standard Version) is highly respected by biblical
scholars and is widely used in this country. However, in this lectionary
the wording of the RSV has been recast to minimize the gender-specific
language and other excluding imagery reflected in its language in reference to human beings, Christ, and God. Except for these changes
the text of the RSV, for the most part, has been retained.

Gender-specific language, however, is not unique to English translations of the Bible; it is characteristic of the languages in which the
Bible was written. Both the Old Testament and the New Testament
were written in languages and in cultures that were basically patriarchal; and as the English language is also patriarchal, the patriarchal
character of both Testaments has slipped easily into the great English
versions of the Bible.

LANGUAGE ABOUT HUMAN BEINGS

In a few instances the RSV Bible committee has already avoided
male-specific language in reference to human beings. For example, in
Rom. 7:1 the RSV has used "person" ("the law is binding on a *person*")
as a translation of the Greek word *anthropos* (meaning "man" or "person"). But most of the time *anthropos* is translated "man," or, in the
plural, "men." For example, Matt. 5:16 in the RSV reads, "Let your
light so shine before *men*" where the meaning of "men" is obviously
"people," but not male people exclusively. This verse can be rendered:
"Let your light so shine before *others*"—that is, men and women, which
represents the clear intention of the words.

Excluding language also appears when masculine pronoun subjects
are supplied with third person singular verbs when the context does
not require them. Compare, for example, the RSV of John 6:35–37:
"Jesus said to them, 'I am the bread of life; *he* who comes to me shall
not hunger, and *he* who believes in me shall never thirst . . . ; and *him*
who comes to me I will not cast out.'" What is the intention of this
passage? It surely is not that only *men* come to Jesus and believe in
Jesus. Why, then, does the RSV read "he" and "him"? It is because of
the assumption that "he" also means "she," though we know that it
does not.

In this lectionary all readings have been recast so that no masculine
word pretends to include a woman. For example, the word "brethren"
has been rendered in a variety of ways, including "sisters and brothers."
Formal equivalents have been adopted for other male-specific words
and phrases. For example, "kingdom" is usually rendered "realm" but
also by other terms such as "reign" or "dominion"; "king" in reference
to God or a messianic figure is rendered "ruler" and "monarch."

In a few instances, references to women have been added—for example, "Abraham [*and Sarah*]." Where the name of a person or details in the narrative make the gender clear, no change has been made. Thus, David is referred to as a "king," the wounded traveler in the parable of the Samaritan is a "man," and Jesus meets a "woman" by the well in Samaria. Where the gender of the person is not specified, the character is referred to as a "person" (e.g., John 9). Also, contemporary English usage suggests that we refer to a person as having a disabling condition, such as polio, rather than to a "cripple" or a "crippled person." So the biblical reference to "the blind and the lame" is rendered "those who are blind and those who are lame" (see Jer. 31:8). Where "darkness" is set in contrast with "light" and has a moral connotation, a substitute word for darkness is supplied—for example, "The light shines in the *deepest night*" (John 1:5).

LANGUAGE ABOUT JESUS CHRIST

Jesus was a male human being. But when the Gospel of John says, "The Word became flesh" (John 1:14), it does not say or imply that the Word became *male* flesh, but simply fl*esh*. Of course, to "become flesh," the one from God had to become male or female, but the language used in this lectionary tries to overcome the implication that in the incarnation Jesus' *maleness* is decisive—or even relevant—for the salvation of women and men who believe, or for matters in which the imitation or model of Christ is a concern.

In this lectionary the fact of Jesus' maleness is taken for granted. The historical Jesus is referred to as a man, and the pronouns "he," "his," and "him" are used when the reference is to that historical person. These male-specific pronouns, however, are not used to refer to the preexistent or postcrucifixion Jesus. They are replaced by proper names such as "Jesus," "Christ," and other words appropriate in the context, so that in hearing the gospel the church may recognize the inclusiveness of all humankind in the incarnation.

Formal equivalents adopted in this lectionary for "the Son of man," "Son," and "Son of God" are, respectively, "the Human One," "Child," and "Child of God."

LANGUAGE ABOUT GOD

The God worshiped by the biblical authors and worshiped in the church today cannot be regarded as having gender, race, or color. Such attributes are used metaphorically or analogically. Father is only one metaphor for God in the Bible; other personal metaphors include mother, midwife, and breadmaker. Less familiar, but equally appropriate, are such impersonal images for God as love, rock, and light.

Images for God in this lectionary are expressed in inclusive language so that when the church hears its scripture read, it is not overwhelmed by the male metaphors but is also enabled to hear female metaphors for God.

In the RSV Old Testament, the major names for God are "God" (*Elohim*), "Lord" (*Yahweh*), and "Lord" (*Adonai*), and several variations of these nouns—for example, "the Lord God" and "the Lord God." In this lectionary, "Lord" (*Yahweh*) is rendered "God" or "Sovereign," using an initial capital letter and small capitals, and "Lord" (*Adonai*) is rendered "God" or "Sovereign," using an initial capital letter and low-ercase letters.

In the New Testament lections, the formal equivalent adopted in this lectionary for "God the Father" or "the Father" is "God the Father [*and Mother*]" or "God the [*Mother and*] Father." The words that have been added to the text are italicized and in brackets. If the reader chooses to omit the bracketed words, the sentence will read exactly as rendered in the RSV. Where God is called "Father" several times in a single passage, as is often the case in the Gospel of John, the word "Father" is frequently rendered "God."

SELECTED LECTIONARY READINGS

EXODUS 20:1–17

God gives the Ten Commandments to Moses.

¹And God spoke all these words, saying,

²"I am the Sovereign [*or* Lord] your God, who brought you out of the land of Egypt, out of the house of bondage.

³"You shall have no other gods before me.

⁴"You shall not make for yourself a graven image, or any likeness of anything that is in heaven above, or that is in the earth beneath, or that is in the water under the earth; ⁵ you shall not bow down to them or serve them; for I the Sovereign [*or* Lord] your God am a jealous God, visiting the iniquity of the parents upon the children to the third and the fourth generation of those who hate me, ⁶ but showing stead-fast love to thousands of those who love me and keep my command-ments.

⁷"You shall not take the name of the Sovereign [*or* Lord] your God in vain; for God [*or* the Lord] will not hold anyone guiltless who takes God's name in vain.

⁸"Remember the sabbath day, to keep it holy. ⁹ Six days you shall labor, and do all your work; ¹⁰ but the seventh day is a sabbath to the Sovereign [*or* Lord] your God; in it you shall not do any work, you, or your son, or your daughter, or your manservant, or your woman-servant, or your cattle, or the resident alien who is within your gates;

[11] for in six days GOD [[or the LORD]] made heaven and earth, the sea, and all that is in them, and rested the seventh day; therefore GOD [[or the LORD]] blessed the sabbath day and hallowed it.

[12] "Honor your father and your mother, that your days may be long in the land which the SOVEREIGN [[or LORD]] your God gives you.

[13] "You shall not kill.

[14] "You shall not commit adultery.

[15] "You shall not steal.

[16] "You shall not bear false witness against your neighbor.

[17] "You shall not covet your neighbor's house; you shall not covet your neighbor's wife, [or husband,*] or manservant, or womanservant, or ox, or donkey, or anything that is your neighbor's."

PSALM 72:1–14

[1] Give the ruler† your justice, O God,
  and your righteousness to the royal heir!
[2] May the ruler judge your people with righteousness,
  and your poor with justice!
[3] Let the mountains bear prosperity for the people,
  and the hills, in righteousness!
[4] May the ruler defend the cause of the poor of the people,
  give deliverance to the needy,
  and crush the oppressor!
[5] May the ruler live while the sun endures,
  and as long as the moon, throughout all generations!
[6] May the ruler be like rain that falls on the mown grass,
  like showers that water the earth!

[7] In the ruler's days may righteousness flourish,
  and peace abound, till the moon be no more!
[8] May the ruler have dominion from sea to sea,
  and from the River to the ends of the earth!
[9] May the foes of the ruler bow down,
  and the enemies lick the dust!
[10] May the kings of Tarshish and of the isles
    render tribute,
  may the kings of Sheba and Seba
    bring gifts!
[11] May all kings bow down
    and all nations serve the ruler!
[12] For the ruler delivers the needy when they call,
    the poor and those who have no helper,

---

*Addition to the text.
†RSV Ps. 72:1 king.

¹³ and has pity on the weak and the needy,
  and saves the lives of the needy.
¹⁴ The ruler redeems their lives from oppression and violence,
  their blood is precious in the ruler's sight.

ISAIAH 63:16–19

Hear the prophet's intercessory prayer.

¹⁶ For you, O God, are our Father [*and Mother**],
  though Abraham [*and Sarah**] do not know us
  and Israel does not acknowledge us;
 you, O Sovereign [*or* Lord], are our Father [*and Mother**],
  our Redeemer from of old is your name.
¹⁷ O Sovereign [*or* Lord], why do you make us err from your ways
  and harden our heart, so that we do not fear you?
 Return for the sake of your servants,
  the tribes of your heritage.
¹⁸ Your holy people possessed your sanctuary a little while;
  our adversaries have trodden it down.
¹⁹ We have become like those over whom you have never ruled,
  like those who are not called by your name.

JOHN 12:20–33

John speaks of the glorification of the Human One.

²⁰ Now among those who went up to worship at the feast were some Greeks. ²¹ So these came to Philip, who was from Bethsaida in Galilee, and said, "Sir, we wish to see Jesus." ²² Philip went and told Andrew; Andrew went with Philip and they told Jesus. ²³ And Jesus answered them, "The hour has come for the Human One‡ to be glorified. ²⁴ Truly, truly, I say to you, unless a grain of wheat falls into the earth and dies, it remains alone; but if it dies, it bears much fruit. ²⁵ Whoever loves their life loses it, and whoever hates their life in this world will keep it for eternal life. ²⁶ Anyone who serves me must follow me; and where I am, there shall my servant be also; anyone who serves me will be honored by [*God*] the Father [*and Mother**]. ²⁷ "Now is my soul troubled. And what shall I say? 'God,** save me from this hour'? No, for this purpose I have come to this hour. ²⁸ God,** glorify your name." Then a voice came from heaven, "I have glorified it, and I will glorify it again." ²⁹ The crowd standing by heard it and said that it had thundered. Others said, "An angel has spoken to him." ³⁰ Jesus answered, "This voice has come for your sake, not for mine. ³¹ Now is the judgment of this world, now shall the ruler of this

---

*Addition to the text.
‡RSV *Son of man.*
**RSV *Father.*

world be cast out; [32] and I, when I am lifted up from the earth, will draw all people to myself." [33] Jesus said this to show by what death he was to die.

1 CORINTHIANS 1:3–9

Paul thanks the Corinthians because of the grace of God given them.

[3] Grace to you and peace from God our Father [*and Mother**] and from the Sovereign [*or* Lord] Jesus Christ. [4] I give thanks to God always for you because of the grace of God which was given you in Christ Jesus, [5] that in every way you were enriched in Christ with all speech and all knowledge—[6] even as the testimony to Christ was confirmed among you—[7] so that you are not lacking in any spiritual gift, as you wait for the revealing of our Sovereign [*or* Lord] Jesus Christ, [8] who will sustain you to the end, guiltless in the day of our Sovereign [*or* Lord] Jesus Christ. [9] God is faithful, by whom you were called into the community of God's Child,†† Jesus Christ our Sovereign [*or* Lord].

GALATIANS 4:4–7

Paul writes to the Galatians about the time of Christ's coming.

[4] But when the time had fully come, God sent forth God's Child,†† born of woman, born under the law, [5] to redeem those who were under the law, so that we might receive adoption as children of God. [6] And because you are children, God has sent the Spirit of the Child†† into our hearts, crying, "[*God! my Mother and*‡‡] Father!" [7] So through God you are no longer a slave but a child, and if a child then an heir.

---

*Addition to the text.
††RSV *his Son.*
‡‡Addition to the text. RSV "*Abba!*"

Part 3

SELF IN RELATION

Self in Relation

The authors of the essays in this section agree that the self is essentially relational, inseparable from the limiting and enriching contexts of body, feeling, relationship, community, history, and the web of life. The notion of the relational self can be correlated with the immanental turn in feminist views of the sacred: in both cases connection to that which is finite, changing, and limited is affirmed.

The notion of the self as relational is prominent in feminist thinking, and has an intuitive appeal to many people. Yet it is important to note that the relational self has not been affirmed within the dominant traditions of Western philosophy and theology. Descartes's famous statement, "I think, therefore, I am," is a concise expression of the dominant tradition's view that the self is essentially *rational, disembodied*, and *solitary*. Descartes's "I" constitutes itself through the dispassionate and solitary act of thinking. Descartes's self exists in an ideal world of rational thought that is not significantly affected by the body, feelings, relationships, community, or history.

Though the authors in this section take very different approaches to the theme of the relational self, they are united in their insistence that the self is essentially *embodied, passionate, relational*, and *communal*. Implicitly or explicitly, each challenges the view that selfhood is to be found in the rational self-reflection of the isolated ego. Instead, they affirm that knowledge arises from the body-mind continuum, which includes passions and feelings as well as thinking. They assert that the self cannot exist apart from relationships. And they insist that identity is found in community. While recognizing that most historical communities have not fully affirmed their female members, many of the authors in this section seek to find their integrity within ethnic, religious, and historical communities. Black womanist theologian Delores S. Williams coined the term "relational independence" to name black women's struggles for freedom from racist and sexist stereotypes within the context of relationships, family, and community. The other authors in this section agree with her in seeking to define women's independence as relational.

Community is central in Delores S. Williams's theology. Invoking

Alice Walker's term "womanist," which defines feminism out of black women's experience, she criticizes the false universalism of white feminist theology. If to be feminist means to "become white," to define the self exclusively or primarily through the work of white women authors and activists, black women do not need feminism, say Walker and Williams. Like Luisah Teish, Williams honors the ancestors: "Black mothers have passed on wisdom for survival . . . for as long as anyone can remember." She also remembers black heroines who provide models of selfhood for black womanists. Williams suggests that "the principal concerns of womanist theology should be survival and community building and maintenance." She names herself a "Christian womanist theologian," affirming the primacy for her of "black church women's faith, their love of Jesus, their commitment to life, love, family, and politics." Black women cannot afford the luxury of separation from the men of their communities. Reflecting on Walker's admonition that black women must love themselves "regardless," Williams warns black women to "avoid the self-destruction of bearing a disproportionately large burden in the work of community building and maintenance." Concluding her essay with the image of black girl children's game of the dandelion chain, Williams affirms both the particularity and the universal potential of womanist theology.

Ellen M. Umansky also affirms a particular communal starting point for feminist theology, when she insists that Jewish feminist theology must be situated within "the concept of *Klal Yisroel*"—"the Jewish people as members of a historical community that claims continuity with its own religious past, present, and future." While Marcia Falk's and Judith Plaskow's essays in this volume expand our conception of what a historical tradition can become, Umansky focuses on the limitations that she believes the Jewish tradition's understanding of monotheism imposes on Jewish feminist theologians. Umansky notes that many Jewish women are attracted to images of the Goddess, and considers the argument that a God who is not really male might also be addressed as "Goddess." But, she argues, the Jewish tradition's repeated, and she would maintain, fundamental, assertion that "to worship the Divine as Goddess is tantamount to idolatry" precludes that option for Jewish women. After exploring other resources that Jewish feminists have suggested as feminine or female names for God, Umansky returns to the difficult question of what loyalty to a tradition means. Once the Jewish feminist realizes that "the norms that have been established are *male* norms," she cannot be content with simply drawing out their implications. She "needs to hear her own voice and feel her own presence within the sources of Jewish tradition." Umansky's "received" retelling of the story of Sarah leads her to question traditional Jewish notions of not only men's, but also God's power. The conclusion of her essay is far more open than its beginning.

For Mary Daly, "Be-Friending" is the creation of feminist community through the naming of an intellectual climate in which women can be called forth from patriarchal bondage into authentic existence. Be-Friending "is the creation of a context/atmosphere in which acts/leaps of Metamorphosis can take place," sharing the "Realization of participation in Be-ing." Because Daly believes that language is one of the fundamental structures of patriarchy, she plays with it, teases it, and transforms it, in order to evoke a reality beyond its boundaries. Rage is an ongoing aspect of Be-Friending, she argues, because rage centers the self as it moves beyond patriarchy.

Daly is aware that women (for example, slave-holding women) have often expressed "unspeakable cruelty" to each other. But she understands this cruelty as rooted in patriarchal conditioning which has led women to identify with their oppressors. Claiming "phallocracy as the root of rapism, racism, gynocide, genocide, and ultimate biocide," Daly urges women to drop their ties to all patriarchally created groups and tribes, including ethnic, religious, and national identifications. Daly views black feminist Toni Morrison's novel *Sula* as an act of Be-Friending, because it names the power of female friendship. For Daly, the fact that *Sula* strikes chords of "Metamemory" in all women's psyches demonstrates the thesis that women's bonds are deeper than ethnic bonds. Daly's argument that women's primary loyalties should be to other women is controversial and disputed by other contributors to this volume who, while sharing Daly's commitment to women, also affirm other loyalties.

While Williams, Umansky, and Daly discuss the situation of the self within particular communities, Audre Lorde and Beverly Wildung Harrison reflect further upon its embodiment and the positive teaching of its passions. Black lesbian poet and theorist Audre Lorde writes, "As women, we have come to distrust that power which rises from our deepest and nonrational knowledge." According to Lorde, the suppression of the erotic, which she calls a deeply female and spiritual power, has been one of the tools in the oppression of women. She argues that learning to listen to and trust the power of the erotic is one of the keys to women's liberation. Lorde defines the erotic as "an internal sense of satisfaction," "a question of how acutely and fully we can feel in the doing," and an "assertion of the lifeforce of women." The erotic is a deeply spiritual power, because it puts us in touch with the creative energy of the life force. To reclaim the power of the erotic requires personal transformation, for we have been taught not to trust our feelings. This also requires rejection of those strands of both secular and religious culture that have defined the erotic as pornographic, the sexual power of women as source of sin, and all sexual feelings as lower, suspect. That we have difficulty even conceptualizing the erotic as spiritual power shows how deeply we have internalized centuries of patriarchal conditioning. For this reason, Lorde writes that to embrace the power of the erotic is to "do that which is most female and self-affirming in the face of a racist, patriarchal, and anti-erotic society."

Christian ethicist Beverly Wildung Harrison asserts that women's experiences must become the basepoints through which " 'the great commandment'—our love of God and our love of our neighbor" are reinterpreted. These basepoints are: activity as a mode of love; our bodies, ourselves as agents of love; and the centrality of relationship. Though women have often been defined as passive, Harrison argues that the actual historical experience of women is the social and cultural activity of love, not passive biological being. Like Williams, Harrison values our mothers' contributions to "the work of human communication, of caring and nurturance, of tending the personal bonds of community." Like Lorde, Harrison sees embodiment as the source of moral activity and power. She criticizes those Christians who have taught that feelings are not to be trusted. "We Christians have come very close to killing love precisely because we have understood anger to be a deadly sin." In contrast, Harrison argues with Daly that anger is a moral "signal that change is called for." Finally, Harrison argues that "relationality is at the heart of things." We are part of each other and of the larger web of life. Harrison believes that the life of Jesus calls us to "the radical activity of love, to a way of being that deepens relation, embodies and extends community, passes on the gift of life." Though many have defined Christian love as self-sacrifice, Harrison understands Jesus to be the embodiment of the activity of radical love, the power of relationality. Radical love may sometimes require sacrifice, but love, not sacrifice, is the goal.

According to Karen McCarthy Brown, "The moral wisdom of Vodou lies in its teaching that it is precisely in responsive and responsible relation to others that one has the clearest and most steady sense of self." The possession-performance dramatizes the relational notion of self, divinity, and community that is at the heart of Vodou. Brown argues that socialization for a life of relationship has made women leaders like Alourdes particularly adept at embodying this insight. In spirit possession, the self of the priestess or priest is said to leave the body and be replaced by the spirit, who then communicates with the community. To those who make a strong distinction between self and other and between self and divinity, the Vodou spirit possession ritual might seem ludicrous or blasphemous. Brown attempts to avoid these judgments, and instead to learn a different way of being a self in relation to spirit and community. The polyvalent nature of the self in Vodou is embodied in the ritual performance, especially drumming. In African and African-American drumming, there is not one rhythm. Only through active participation, through dancing or clapping, can the individual hear and participate in the harmonies and dissonances of the music which reflect the diverse rhythms of life. The goal is not to find one overarching theme, nor to play a solo, nor to lose oneself in the group, but rather to tap out one's own rhythm within the many patterns of the whole. Similarly Vodou does not seek to reduce the multiplicity of the world to a single law, nor to reduce the various manifestations of the sacred to a single "God." The essence of Vodou is to intensify and celebrate the diversity and difference, including conflict, pain, and suffering, which exist in the world as we know it.

Though reflecting a very different context from Brown, Rita Na-kashima Brock also speaks of the inevitability of suffering, the power of community, and the healing power of trance. Nakashima Brock writes as part of a community of theologically trained Asian American Christian women whose thealogical voices are just beginning to emerge. In her conversations with other Asian American women, Nakashima Brock discovered a shared quest for "an inclusive, pluralistic mono-theism, with room for a diversity of ways to speak about the sacred dimension of life [that] allows us to reclaim those aspects of Asian cul-ture that reconnect us to the presence of the sacred in Asian religions." In Asian American women's thealogy (Brock redefines the term to mean women's reflection on the divine), the subtle influence of Asian spiritual traditions transforms and reinvigorates Christian symbols. Though Asian American women have been counseled to avoid "pagan" or non-Christian influence, Nakashima Brock views the blending of traditions as a strength. Discussing the themes of suffering, community, and healing, Brock names Asian sources. Asian women's focus on suf-fering may have more in common with Buddhist notions of the inevi-tability of suffering in human life, than with traditional Christian con-ceptions of martyrdom and self-denial. A Buddhist-influenced notion of suffering stresses the creation of community with all beings through recognition of common pain. Nakashima Brock also argues that the shamanistic traditions of Asia (where female shamans are common) en-hance Asian American women's understanding of the incarnation. "The physical embodiment of the spirit" is not restricted to the life of Jesus; rather, "the earth is [understood as] the conduit through which we are touched by the spirit." Yet Nakashima Brock warns against ro-manticizing Asian traditions, for they too have deeply patriarchal ele-ments.

Though the last two essays in this section take a more abstract and conceptual form than the others, they reinforce its general direction, developing the notions of an embodied and relational self. Naomi R. Goldenberg asserts that Jungian theory, which has seemed to many—including herself—to offer a theoretical and spiritual alternative to the patriarchal traditions of Judaism and Christianity, is in reality deeply dualistic, antifemale, and antilife. Jung, like Plato and Socrates, was essentially suspicious of the world and the body, dissatisfied with the limitations of finitude. Therefore he located the archetypes in a time-less and unchanging realm not unlike that occupied by the Platonic forms and the Christian God. Goldenberg states that theories which despise the body have not only brought us to the brink of destroying the earth, but also inevitably devalue women as the symbolic and literal incarnation of bodily existence. Goldenberg then makes the controversial proposal that feminists should "be using psychoanalysis to think through the body." She offers a positive appraisal of Freud's focus on sexuality and childhood and notes that these have been prominent themes in feminist writing as well. The work of post-Freudian Melanie Klein and her followers that shifted the focus of psychoanalytic theory to the mother-child relationship of early infancy, symbolized by the "breast," can help us to better understand the deep ambivalence toward women and the body which is the legacy of the infant's dependence on the mother. According to Goldenberg, psychoanalytic theory can be of use to feminists because it is one of the few Western theories of the self that focuses on body, rather than denying it.

Catherine Keller asks if the "epiphany of interconnection" presented in Shug's vision of God can ground a feminist ethic. "How can a feeling of 'not being separate at all' do a woman any favors? Doesn't freedom demand a separation and independence?" she asks. Keller poses this question sharply through consideration of Simone de Beauvoir's argument that women must choose to be defined by "transcendence," or freely chosen projects, rather than "immanence," activities that sustain the world but do not change it. De Beauvoir views the activities of childbearing, childrearing, homemaking, cooking, gardening, and food producing (including the invention of agriculture!) as essentially limiting. When Keller subjects this theory to scrutiny, she discovers not only de Beauvoir's obvious contempt for ordinary women's lives, but also a very androcentric notion of the self, creativity, and freedom. For de Beauvoir, other people and the world are viewed as essentially hostile forces. The activities that she most values involve the "spear" as symbol of conflict, conquest, warfare, and killing. Turning to more recent feminist theory, Keller finds Shug's vision of connection confirmed in Carol Gilligan's *In a Different Voice*, which argues that for women "identity is defined in a context of relationship and judged by a standard of responsibility and care." Keller concludes that though freedom and transcendence are important, these values must be set within the context of connection and the "ethic of inseparability."

Womanist Theology

Black Women's Voices

DAUGHTER: Mama, why are we brown, pink, and yellow, and our cousins are white, beige, and black?
MOTHER: Well, you know the colored race is just like a flower garden, with every color flower represented.
DAUGHTER: Mama, I'm walking to Canada and I'm taking you and a bunch of slaves with me.
MOTHER: It wouldn't be the first time.

In these two conversational exchanges, Pulitzer Prize-winning novelist Alice Walker begins to show us what she means by the concept "womanist." The concept is presented in Walker's *In Search of our Mother's Gardens,* and many women in church and society have appropriated it as a way of affirming themselves as *black* while simultaneously owning their connection with feminism and with the Afro-American community, male and female. The concept of womanist allows women to claim their roots in black history, religion, and culture.

What then is a womanist? Her origins are in the black folk expression "You acting womanish," meaning, according to Walker, "wanting to know more and in greater depth than is good for one . . . outrageous, audacious, courageous and willful behavior." A womanist is also "responsible, in charge, serious." She can walk to Canada and take others with her. She loves, she is committed, she is a universalist by temperament.

Her universality includes loving men and women, sexually or nonsexually. She loves music, dance, the spirit, food and roundness, struggle, and she loves herself. "Regardless."

Walker insists that a womanist is also "committed to survival and wholeness of entire people, male and female." She is no separatist, "except for health." A womanist is a black feminist or feminist of color. Or as Walker says, "Womanist is to feminist as purple to lavender."

Delores S. Williams teaches in the Theological School at Drew University. Her articles have appeared in the *Journal of Feminist Studies in Religion, The Journal of Religious Thought, Christianity and Crisis,* and in several books. Along with other black women, she is contributing to the development of a newly emerging Womanist Theology.

Womanist theology, a vision in its infancy, is emerging among Afro-American Christian women. Ultimately many sources—biblical, theological, ecclesiastical, social, anthropological, economic, and material from other religious traditions—will inform the development of this theology. As a contribution to this process, I will demonstrate how Walker's concept of womanist provides some significant clues for the work of womanist theologians. I will then focus on method and God-content in womanist theology. This contribution belongs to the work of prolegomena—prefatory remarks, introductory observations intended to be suggestive and not conclusive.

THE MEANING OF WOMANIST

In her definition, Walker provides significant clues for the development of womanist theology. Her concept contains what black feminist scholar Bell Hooks in *From Margin to Center* identifies as cultural codes. These are words, beliefs, and behavioral patterns of a people that must be deciphered before meaningful communication can happen cross-culturally. Walker's codes are female-centered and they point beyond themselves to conditions, events, meanings, and values that have crystallized in the Afro-American community *around women's activity* and formed traditions.

A paramount example is mother-daughter advice. Black mothers have passed on wisdom for survival—in the white world, in the black community, and with men—for as long as anyone can remember. Female slave narratives, folk tales, and some contemporary black poetry and prose reflect this tradition. Some of it is collected in "Old Sister's Advice to her Daughters," in *The Book of Negro Folklore*.

Walker's allusion to skin color points to an historic tradition of tension between black women over the matter of some black men's preference for light-skinned women. Her reference to black women's love of food and roundness points to customs of female care in the black community (including the church) associated with hospitality and nurture.

These cultural codes and their corresponding traditions are valuable resources for indicating and validating the kind of data upon which womanist theologians can reflect as they bring black women's social, religious, and cultural experience into the discourse of theology, ethics, biblical and religious studies. Female slave narratives, imaginative literature by black women, autobiographies, the work by black women in academic disciplines, and the testimonies of black church women will be authoritative sources for womanist theologians.

Walker situates her understanding of a womanist in the context of nonbourgeois black folk culture. The literature of this culture has traditionally reflected more egalitarian relations between men and women, much less rigidity in male-female roles, and more respect for female intelligence and ingenuity than is found in bourgeois culture.

The black folk are poor. Less individualistic than those who are better off, they have, for generations, practiced various forms of economic sharing. For example, immediately after Emancipation mutual aid societies pooled the resources of black folk to help pay for funerals and other daily expenses. *The Book of Negro Folklore* describes the practice of rent parties which flourished during the Depression. The black folk stressed togetherness and a closer connection with nature. They respect knowledge gained through lived experience monitored by elders who differ profoundly in social class and world view from the teachers and education encountered in American academic institutions. Walker's choice of context suggests that womanist theology can establish its lines of continuity in the black community with nonbourgeois traditions less sexist than the black power and black nationalist traditions.

In this folk context, some of the black female-centered cultural codes in Walker's definition (e.g., "Mama, I'm walking to Canada and I'm taking you and a bunch of slaves with me") point to folk heroines like Harriet Tubman, whose liberation activity earned her the name "Moses" of her people. This allusion to Tubman directs womanist memory to a liberation tradition in black history in which women took the lead, acting as catalysts for the community's revolutionary action and for social change. Retrieving this often hidden or diminished female tradition of catalytic action is an important task for womanist theologians and ethicists. Their research may well reveal that female models of authority have been absolutely essential for every struggle in the black community and for building and maintaining the community's institutions.

The womanist theologian must search for the voices, actions, opinions, experience, and faith of women whose names sometimes slip into the male-centered rendering of black history, but whose actual stories remain remote. This search can lead to such little-known freedom fighters as Milla Granson and her courageous work on a Mississippi plantation. Her liberation method broadens our knowledge of the variety of strategies black people have used to obtain freedom. According to scholar Sylvia Dannett, in *Profiles in Negro Womanhood*:

Milla Granson, a slave, conducted a midnight school for several years. She had been taught to read and write by her former master in Kentucky . . . and in her little school hundreds of slaves benefited from her learning. . . . After laboring all day for their master, the slaves would creep stealthily to Milla's "schoolroom" (a little cabin in a back alley). . . . The doors and windows . . . had to be kept tightly sealed to avoid discovery. Each class was composed of twelve pupils and when Milla had brought them up to the extent of her ability, she "graduated" them and took in a dozen more. Through this means she graduated hundreds of slaves. Many of whom she taught to write a legible hand [forged] their own passes and set out for Canada.

Women like Tubman and Granson used subtle and silent strategies to liberate themselves and large numbers of black people. By uncovering as much as possible about such female liberation, the womanist begins to understand the relation of black history to the contemporary folk expression: "If Rosa Parks had not sat down, Martin King would not have stood up."

While she celebrates and *emphasizes* black women's culture and way of being in the world, Walker simultaneously affirms black women's historic connection with men through love and through a shared struggle for survival and for productive quality of life (e.g., "wholeness"). This suggests that two of the principal concerns of womanist theology should be survival and community building and maintenance. The goal of this community building is, of course, to establish a positive quality of life—economic, spiritual, educational—for black women, men, and children. Walker's understanding of a womanist as "not a separatist" ("except for health"), however, reminds the Christian womanist theologian that her concern for community building and maintenance must *ultimately* extend to the entire Christian community and beyond that to the larger human community.

Yet womanist consciousness is also informed by women's determination to love themselves. "Regardless." This translates into an admonition to black women to avoid the self-destruction of bearing a disproportionately large burden in the work of community building and maintenance. Walker suggests that women can avoid this trap by connecting with women's communities concerned about women's rights and well-being. Her identification of a womanist as also a feminist joins black women with their feminist heritage extending back into the nineteenth century in the work of black feminists like Sojourner Truth, Frances W. Harper, and Mary Church Terrell.

In making the feminist-womanist connection, however, Walker proceeds with great caution. With affirming an organic relationship between womanists and feminists, she also declares a deep shade of difference between them ("Womanist is to feminist as purple to lavender"). This gives womanist scholars the freedom to explore the particularities of black women's history and culture without being guided by what white feminists have already identified as women's issues.

But womanist consciousness directs black women away from the negative divisions prohibiting community building among women. The womanist loves other women sexually and nonsexually. Therefore, respect for sexual preferences is one of the marks of womanist community. According to Walker, homophobia has no place. Nor does

"Colorism" (i.e., "yella" and half-white black people valued more in the black world than black-skinned people), which often separates black women from each other. Rather, Walker's womanist claim is that color variety is the substance of universality. Color, like birth and death, is common to all people. Like the navel, it is a badge of humanity connecting people with people. Two other distinctions are prohibited in Walker's womanist thinking. Class hierarchy does not dwell among women who ". . . love struggle, love the Folks . . . are committed to the survival and wholeness of an entire people." Nor do women compete for male attention when they ". . . appreciate and prefer female culture . . . value . . . women's emotional flexibility . . . and women's strength."

The intimations about community provided by Walker's definition suggest no genuine community building is possible when men are excluded (except when women's health is at stake). Neither can it occur when black women's self-love, culture, and love for each other are not affirmed and are not considered vital for the community's self-understanding. And it is thwarted if black women are expected to bear "the lion's share" of the work and to sacrifice their well-being for the good of the group.

Yet, for the womanist, mothering and nurturing are vitally important. Walker's womanist reality begins with mothers relating to their children and is characterized by black women (not necessarily bearers of children) nurturing great numbers of black people in the liberation struggle (e.g., Harriet Tubman). Womanist emphasis upon the value of mothering and nurturing is consistent with the testimony of many black women. The poet Carolyn Rogers speaks of her mother as the great black bridge that brought her over. Walker dedicates her novel *The Third Life of Grange Copeland* to her mother ". . . who made a way out of no way." As a child in the black church, I heard women (and men) give thanks to God for their mothers ". . . who stayed behind and pulled the wagon over the long haul."

It seems, then, that the clues about community from Walker's definition of a womanist suggest that the mothering and nurturing dimension of Afro-American history can provide resources for shaping criteria to measure the quality of justice in the community. These criteria could be used to assure female-male equity in the presentation of the community's models of authority. They could also gauge the community's division of labor with regard to the survival tasks necessary for building and maintaining community.

WOMANIST THEOLOGY AND METHOD

Womanist theology is already beginning to define the categories and methods needed to develop along lines consistent with the sources of that theology. Christian womanist theological methodology needs to be informed by at least four elements: (1) a multidialogical intent, (2) a liturgical intent, (3) a didactic intent, and (4) a commitment both to reason *and* to the validity of female imagery and metaphorical language in the construction of theological statements.

A multidialogical intent will allow Christian womanist theologians to advocate and participate in dialogue and action with *many* diverse social, political, and religious communities concerned about human survival and productive quality of life for the oppressed. The genocide of culture and peoples (which has often been instigated and accomplished by Western white Christian groups or governments) and the nuclear threat of omnicide mandate womanist participation in such dialogue/ action. But in this dialogue/action the womanist also should keep her speech and action focused upon the slow genocide of poor black women, children, and men by exploitative systems denying them productive jobs, education, health care, and living space. Multidialogical activity may, like a jazz symphony, communicate some of its most important messages in what the harmony-driven conventional ear hears as discord, as disruption of the harmony in both the black American and white American social, political, and religious status quo.

If womanist theological method is informed by a liturgical intent, then womanist theology will be relevant to (and will reflect) the thought, worship, and action of the black church. But a liturgical intent will also allow womanist theology to challenge the thought/worship/action of the black church with the discordant and prophetic messages emerging from womanist participation in multidialogics. This means that womanist theology will consciously impact *critically* upon the foundations of liturgy, challenging the church to use justice principles to select the sources that will shape the content of liturgy. The question must be asked: "How does this source portray blackness/darkness, women, and economic justice for nonruling-class people?" A negative portrayal will demand omission of the source or its radical reformation by the black church. The Bible, a major source in black church liturgy, must also be subjected to the scrutiny of justice principles.

A didactic intent in womanist theological method assigns a teaching function to theology. Womanist theology should teach Christians new insights about moral life based on ethics supporting justice for women, survival, and a productive quality of life for poor women, children, and men. This means that the womanist theologian must give authoritative status to black folk wisdom (e.g., Brer Rabbit literature) and to black women's moral wisdom (expressed in their literature) when she responds to the question, "How ought the Christian to live in the world?" Certainly tensions may exist between the moral teachings derived from these sources and the moral teachings about obedience, love, and humility that have usually buttressed presuppositions about living the

Christian life. Nevertheless, womanist theology, in its didactic intent, must teach the church the different ways God reveals prophetic word and action for Christian living.

These intents, informing theological method, can yield a theological language whose foundation depends as much upon its imagistic content as upon reason. The language can be rich in female imagery, metaphor, and story. For the black church, this kind of theological language may be quite useful, since the language of the black religious experience abounds in images and metaphors. Clifton Johnson's collection of black conversion experiences, *God Struck Me Dead*, illustrates this point.

The appropriateness of womanist theological language will ultimately reside in its ability to bring black women's history, culture, and religious experience into the interpretive circle of Christian theology and into the liturgical life of the church. Womanist theological language must, in this sense, be an instrument for social and theological change in church and society.

Regardless of one's hopes about intentionality and womanist theological method, questions must be raised about the God-content of the theology. Walker's mention of the black womanist's love of the spirit is a true reflection of the great respect Afro-American women have always shown for the presence and work of the spirit. In the black church, women (and men) often judge the effectiveness of the worship service not on the scholarly content of the sermon nor on the ritual nor on orderly process. Rather, worship has been effective if "the spirit was high," i.e., if the spirit was actively and obviously present in a balanced blend of prayer, of cadenced word (the sermon), and of syncopated music ministering to the pain of the people.

The importance of this emphasis upon the spirit is that it allows Christian womanist theologians, in their use of the Bible, to identify and reflect upon those biblical stories in which poor oppressed women had a special encounter with divine emissaries of God, like the spirit. In the Hebrew Testament, Hagar's story is most illustrative and relevant to Afro-American women's experience of bondage, of African heritage, of encounter with God/emissary in the midst of fierce survival struggles. Kate Cannon among a number of black female preachers and ethicists urges black Christian women to regard themselves as Hagar's sisters.

In relation to the Christian or New Testament, the Christian womanist theologian can refocus the salvation story so that it emphasizes the beginning of revelation with the spirit mounting Mary, a woman of the poor: (". . . the Holy Spirit shall come upon thee, and the power of the Highest shall overshadow thee . . ." Luke 1:35). Such an interpretation of revelation has roots in nineteenth-century black abolitionist and feminist Sojourner Truth. Posing an important question and response, she refuted a white preacher's claim that women could not have rights equal to men because Christ was not a woman. Truth asked, "Whar did your Christ come from? . . . From God and a woman! Man had nothin' to do wid Him!" This suggests that womanist theology could eventually speak of God in a well-developed theology of the spirit. The sources for this theology are many. Harriet Tubman often "went into the spirit" before her liberation missions and claimed her strength for liberation activity came from this way of meeting God. Womanist theology has grounds for shaping a theology of the spirit informed by black women's political action.

Christian womanist responses to the question "who do you say God is?" will be influenced by these many sources. Walker's way of connecting womanists with the spirit is only one clue. The integrity of black church women's faith, their love of Jesus, their commitment to life, love, family, and politics will also yield vital clues. And other theological voices (black liberation, feminist, Islamic, Asian, Hispanic, African, Jewish, and Western white male traditional) will provide insights relevant for the construction of the God-content of womanist theology.

Each womanist theologian will add her own special accent to the understandings of God emerging from womanist theology. But if one needs a final image to describe women coming together to shape the enterprise, Bess B. Johnson in *God's Fierce Whimsy* offers an appropriate one. Describing the difference between the play of male and female children in the black community where she developed, Johnson says:

the boys in the neighborhood had this game with rope . . . tug-o'-war . . . till finally some side would jerk the rope away from the others, who'd fall down. . . . Girls . . . weren't allowed to play with them in this tug-o'-war; so we figured out how to make our own rope—out of . . . little dandelions. You just keep adding them, one to another, and you can go on and on. . . . Anybody, even the boys, could join us. . . . The whole purpose of our game was to create this dandelion chain—that was it. And we'd keep going, creating till our mamas called us home.

Like Johnson's dandelion chain, womanist theological vision will grow as black women come together and connect piece with piece. Between the process of creating and the sense of calling, womanist theology will one day present itself in full array, reflecting the divine spirit that connects us all.

Creating a Jewish Feminist Theology

Possibilities and Problems

ELLEN M. UMANSKY

American feminist theology has emerged primarily out of the experiences of women who have identified themselves as Christian, Christian-raised, post-Christian, or post-Jewish. Jewish women, thus far, with a few notable exceptions, have made no comparable attempt to create a theology out of their experiences as women and as Jews. In part, I think, the problem is one of numbers. It is undoubtedly true that there are significantly more non-Jewish women studying or "doing" theology than Jewish women, perhaps because their opportunities for study are greater, perhaps because "doing" theology is not viewed as a particularly Jewish enterprise. I suspect, however, that the problem lies deeper. Perhaps Jewish women have been reluctant or ill-equipped to create a Jewish feminist theology, not out of insensitivity to personal experience or ignorance of Jewish tradition but out of their awareness of the potentially irreconcilable conflict between the two.

This essay seeks to explore both the problems inherent in creating a Jewish feminist theology and the directions that such a theology, were it possible to create one, might pursue. It begins with an examination of previous attempts at creating a theology that is both feminist and Jewish. Evaluating the strengths and weaknesses of each, it then attempts to redefine the scope of a Jewish feminist theology through a reinterpretation of the word theology and a broadening of that experience that can be identified as legitimately Jewish.

DELINEATING THE PROBLEM: PERSONAL EXPERIENCE VERSUS TRADITION

Any feminist theology that identifies itself as Jewish acknowledges an *a priori* commitment to Jewish tradition. . . . What distinguishes a

Ellen M. Umansky is an Associate Professor of Religion at Emory University. The author of two books on Lily Montagu, founder and leader of the liberal Jewish movement in England, as well as several articles on women and Judaism, she is currently writing a book on Jewish Science, the twentieth century spiritual movement.

Jewish feminist theologian from a feminist theologian who sees herself as post-Jewish or Jewish raised, is that the latter can open herself to all forms of religious experience and self-expression, but the former, by choosing to identify herself and her visions as Jewish, attempts to place her experiences of the Divine within a specifically Jewish framework.

This recognition, I think, is implicit in Rita Gross's 1981 essay, "Steps Toward Feminine Imagery of Deity in Jewish Theology." Calling for a reimaging of the Hebrew God as male and female: God-He *and* God-She, God *and* Goddess, Gross explores a number of "feasible and traditional" steps through which this reimaging might begin. The first step, she writes, is that of rediscovering already existing, though scattered, Jewish feminine images of the Divine. She maintains that the rediscovery of these images would help call into question the false assumption "that 'God-He' is proper while 'God-She' is . . . [not]."

Gross further maintains that traditional images of God as female have been too firmly embedded in patriarchal contexts to be of sufficient use for Jewish feminists. "Almost entirely," she asserts,

traditional Jewish usage speaks of some variant of "God and *his Shekhinah*." Seeing feminine imagery of God as some sort of attachment to, or appendage of, the more familiar male images of God would only compound the current inadequacies.[1]

Thus, she suggests, a second, more useful step might be to incorporate non-Jewish feminine images of deity, culled from "religious symbol systems that have not been so wary of feminine imagery"[2] into a specifically *Jewish* understanding of the Divine. She suggests focusing on images of the Goddess as a coincidence of opposites ("She who gives and takes away"), as capable, strong, and beautiful, as mother, giver of wisdom, and sexual being. Gross makes a careful distinction between experiencing the Divine as Kali, Durga, Laksmi, or any other Hindu Goddess and using the symbolism of these and other Goddesses as a means of reimaging the Hebrew God. She is not, she maintains, "advocating mindless borrowing or wholesale syncretism."[3] Rather, she advocates translating non-Western images of the Divine into images that, in form and content, can be identified as Jewish.

The obvious strength of Gross's proposed theology lies in its incorporation of women's experience into a Jewish experience of deity. One might argue that to reimage the Divine as God and Goddess is to affirm both the feminist view and the Jewish conviction that men and women have been created in the Divine image. It also affirms that because the Jewish God is neither male nor female, female images are as "proper" (or improper) as are male images of the Divine. Yet the major weakness of Gross's proposal, as I understand it, is the unspoken assumption that the kind of reimaging she suggests is possible—that one *can* translate Hindu images of the Divine into "Jewish media" and that it is possible to exorcise what Sheila Collins refers to as the "patriarchal demon" from the Jewish concept of God.

Although it remains to be seen whether the kind of reimaging that she suggests can be accomplished, Gross at least needs to acknowledge the possibility of failure. More specifically, she needs to recognize that if her spiritual experiences as a woman/feminist and as a Jew are *not* compatible with one another, she would have to decide which voice to listen to: her own voice or the voice of Jewish tradition.

One major problem, I believe, in creating any Jewish feminist theology reflects the inherent tension between personal experience and tradition. I would argue that this tension, though it may also exist within Christian feminist theology, is not as great, or need not be as great as it is in a theology that is both feminist and Jewish. It may be possible to "reform" Christianity by reevaluating or reinterpreting its gospel as a gospel of liberation, but one cannot separate Jewish history from Jewish vision. Judaism is not based on a gospel but on the three-thousand-year-old history and experiences of the Jewish people. Consequently, one would be hard pressed to reduce Judaism to *any* given message.

Perhaps the first step that needs to be taken in establishing a Jewish feminist theology is the recognition that what is possible within a Christian context may not be possible within a Jewish one. In their introduction to *Womanspirit Rising*, Carol P. Christ and Judith Plaskow identify reformists as feminists who

are calling the church and synagogue back to an essential core of Christian or Jewish truth and are cleansing traditions of historical deviations from that core.[1]

The aim of the reformist, as they see it, is to discover, within tradition itself, "an authentic core of revelation pointing towards freedom from oppression." I would contend, however, that before Jewish reformists attempt to discover whether Judaism's core of revelation does, in fact, point towards freedom, they must decide whether Judaism even *has* a core of revelation. Indeed, I would argue that because Judaism is more than a religion, it is difficult if not impossible to reduce Judaism to *any* spiritual core.

FROM SPIRITUAL CORE TO HISTORICAL REALITY

The major strength of Judith Plaskow's more recent essay on "God and Feminism" lies in its honest and straightforward assessment of women's status throughout Jewish history. Without resorting to apologetics, she maintains that women's subordination is based on an understanding of women as " 'other than' the norm" and as "less than fully human." Women's otherness, she writes, "functions as a presupposition of Jewish law in its most central form." Consequently, attempts to improve women's status through legal mechanisms, i.e., through the amelioration or rejection of certain laws, are doomed to failure. As long as the Jewish woman, she insists, is seen as "other"—as "the stranger whose life is lived parallel to man's"—Judaism will continue to be shaped and will continue to reflect the experiences of Jewish *men*.[5]

Without searching for a liberating core of truth stripped of historical deviations, Plaskow lays bare the patriarchal foundations of Jewish history and thought. Rather than viewing *halacha* (Jewish law) as the cause of women's subordination, she maintains that *halacha* itself is a product of Judaism's deep-seated view of women as other, reinforced through a theology that continues to image God as exclusively male. "If God is male," she writes,

and we are in God's image, how can maleness *not* be the norm of Jewish humanity? If maleness is normative, how can women not be Other? And if women are Other, how can we not speak of God in language drawn from the male norm?[6]

Unlike Rita Gross, Plaskow does not suggest that we use contemporary Eastern religions as a resource for reimaging the Divine. Rather, she suggests looking within the history of Judaism itself. She reminds us that the ancient Israelites worshiped Gods and Goddesses, with the "exclusive worship of Jahweh . . . [the] product of a long, drawn-out struggle." Without arguing for a return to paganism, Plaskow boldly calls for a reimaging of the Goddess "through the lens of our monotheistic tradition." To acknowledge "the many names of the Goddess among the names of God," she writes,

becomes a measure of our ability to incorporate the feminine and women into a monotheistic religious framework. At the same time, naming women's experience as part of the nature of the deity brings the suppressed experience of women into the Jewish fold.[7]

Despite Plaskow's intriguing suggestions, the incorporation of Goddess imagery into a Jewish understanding of deity cannot be accomplished without an honest appraisal of the kinds of problems such a reimaging would entail. Plaskow and Gross are justified in arguing that a deity who is no more "He" than "She" can be imaged, and *should* be imaged, as both Father *and* Mother, King *and* Queen, Lord *and* Mistress of Heaven. Indeed, one might contend that talking of "God-She" and even "Goddess" in conjunction with "God-He" and "God" is more Jewish than adhering to a limited set of images that seem to suggest—despite protestations—that the Divine is really male. Yet before one can authenticate this claim, one needs to take into account the connection between Jewish history and Jewish vision. Although theologically, one may be justified in imaging the Divine as Goddess, the fact remains that Judaism clearly prohibits such worship. Even if it is possible to overcome this prohibition, to simply ignore it reflects an ignorance of the Hebrew language and of the notion of *Klal Yisroel*.

RENAMING THE GODDESS

There are two Hebrew words for Goddess: *Elah* (the feminine form of *El* or God) and *Elilah* (the feminine form of *Elil* or idol), both of which can be used interchangeably. Conversely, the God of Israel, although He is identified as *El* is never identified as *Elil*. It is He alone, in fact, who is *El*, with all other gods reduced to *Elilim* or idols. The message here seems clear: although Jews may worship the Divine as *El*, *Elohim*, and *Elyon* (God on High), to worship the Divine as Goddess is tantamount to idolatry. One sees this in the biblical condemnation of the Goddesses Asherah and Ashtoreth. In an effort perhaps to undermine their reality and/or legitimacy, biblical writers refrained from specific references to them as Goddesses. Despite their worship in ancient Israel, their names became synonymous with that which was abominable and therefore antithetical to the true—Hebrew—God.

Before Jewish feminist theologians can reappropriate the Goddess within the monotheistic framework of Judaism, they need to explore ways in which this appropriation can be accomplished. More specifically, they need to suggest a naming of the Goddess that would address her as the feminine aspect of the Divine and not as a separate and idolatrous Divine Being. To this end, there are a number of possible paths that can be pursued.

First, Jewish feminist theologians might seek to create an original Hebrew word that would mean "Goddess," a word that, because it would be new, would have no past or present association with idolatry. Perhaps a second, more feasible solution, would be to take an existing Hebrew word that refers to the Divine (but not necessarily to the Hebrew God) and reappropriate it as Goddess. Thus, for example, one could take the word *Elohut* (a feminine noun meaning Divinity or Deity) and claim that *Elohut* is feminine both grammatically and in gender. Although at present the grammatical form of *Elohut* is seen as inconsequential, the result of all Hebrew nouns being either masculine or feminine, one might transform *Elohut*, rename her, so to speak, from Divinity to female Divinity, from Deity to Goddess.

A third solution might be to retain *Elah*, a word that already means Goddess, yet deny the identification of *Elah* (Goddess) with *Elilah* (a female idol). To reclaim the right to say *Elah*—Goddess—is, in Mary Daly's words, to begin "wrenching back some wordpower."[8] Jewish feminist theologians might assert that *Elah* is not *Elilah*, that such "false naming" may reflect the experience of their ancestors, but it does not reflect their own. These theologians might suggest that the initial identification of *Elah* with *Elilah* was political rather than spiritual, reflecting priestly attempts to gain sole allegiance for the Hebrew God. Jewish feminist theologians might argue, then, that to reaffirm the Divine as *Elah* while denying any connection between *Elah* and *Elilah* articulates both their own experiences and the experiences of their ancestors, recalling early Jewish history and its earliest visions of the Divine.

My own hesitation, however, in reappropriating the name *Elah* stems from my understanding of the concept of *Klal Yisroel*. Literally meaning the totality of Israel, *Klal Yisroel* refers to the Jewish people as members of a historical community that claims continuity with its own religious past, present, and future. Bearing this in mind, I question whether a return to ancient Israelite religion, ignoring the last two thousand years of Jewish history, can claim to be authentically Jewish. Although it is possible to maintain that some Jews, especially Jewish mystics, continued and still continue to image the Divine as female, to name this Divinity *Elah* was, and still is, seen as idolatrous. My point, then, is that the feminist theologian who chooses the third path, that of reclaiming the word *Elah*, does so at the risk of breaking with the community of Israel. Even though one might argue that those who take this risk may help create a future notion of *Klal Yisroel* that includes the worship of *Elah* as Goddess, this argument may reflect too great a sense of optimism. In fact I suspect that for many, if not most Jews, *Elah* will continue to serve as an image of that which is other than the Hebrew God. Jewish feminist theologians must decide, then, whether reclaiming the right to name one's own experience is worth risking a separation (either by choice or necessity) from the Jewish community. If the answer is yes, this risk, I think, needs to be taken. If not, Jewish feminist theologians need to consider whether creating a new name for Goddess or transforming existing words like *Elohut* can adequately reflect the experience of female Divine power.

Lynn Gottlieb, a rabbi and storyteller, has chosen a fourth path. Retaining traditional Hebrew God language, she has begun to retranslate and reimage the words themselves, discovering new meaning in them. *Elohim* for her is not "God" but "all-spirits," a name reflecting *Elohim* as grammatically plural and as theologically beyond all gender. Her experience of *Elohim* as Creator is that of all-spirits who, in a "time before time . . . birthed creation." All-spirits does not hover over the face of the waters as does *Elohim* in traditional translations of Genesis, but rather "breaks the inner waters," an image that reflects women's own experience of birth. The world is created by *Elohim* and from her. She establishes neither hierarchies nor polarities and issues no commands. Without asserting "Let there be light," all-spirits simply says: "Light . . . behold light . . . it is good," and, separating light and darkness, creates distinction without polarization. Light is *distinguished* but not *divided* from darkness.

All-spirits then names the light and the darkness, "calling the light *yom* and the dark . . . *lilah*." Thus, the translation concludes, "Night passage, morning, one day." Lynn Gottlieb's retaining of the Hebrew words *yom* and *lilah* and her substitution of "night passage" for the more literal "and there was evening" are intentional. She envisions creation as process—night passing into light—and identifies this process as female, using the pronoun *she* to describe all-spirits as creator and the feminine noun *lilah* in place of the neuter English word, "night." Moreover, the retention of the Hebrew *lilah* suggests the linguistic and theological association of *lilah* with Lilith, the first created woman. According to rabbinic tradition, Lilith was a night demon who seduced men and killed children. Although Gottlieb chooses only to suggest the appearance of Lilith here, the image of *lilah* as female creative process emerges out of her own vision of Lilith as the "motherbed of creation" and the "progenitor of light."[9]

Combining a fluent knowledge of Hebrew, a mastery of Jewish texts, and her own spiritual experiences, Lynn Gottlieb continues to discover new meaning within traditional God language. *Adonai* is not "Lord" but the "I" as the ground of experience and the door to the mystery of life. This image is rooted in the letters Aleph, Nun, and Yod (*Ani* or I) and Daled, the mystical symbol for door, which become *Adonai* when joined together. Similarly, *Shaddai* is transformed from "the Almighty" to "my breasts," a literal translation of *Shad* (breast) and the possessive plural for "my," alternately imaged by Gottlieb as "the many breasted woman." She also finds meaning in *Shechinah*, not as the feminine element of God (the image that appears in the Kabbalah), but as She-Who-Dwells-Within (reflecting the feminine form of the Hebrew words for dwelling and neighbor). *Shechinah*, for her, is "immanent Presence," a crystal generating light. She is active, the source of vitality, through whom we discover our own energy and vision.[10]

JEWISH FEMINIST THEOLOGY AS RESPONSIVE THEOLOGY

Part of the difficulty in creating a Jewish feminist theology is that at times it may not be possible to harmonize personal experience and tradition. Thus, many Jewish feminist theologians may find themselves confronted with an insoluble dilemma. On the one hand, Judaism holds out a set of symbols for the Divine and demands that all Jews accept them; on the other hand, it expects us to see these symbols as personally meaningful even though they are not the products of our imagination. The theologies (or possible theologies) that I have discussed all seek to revive traditional images of the Divine by viewing them through the lens of personal experience. Yet when does a personally experienced image become Jewish? And what if this image cannot be reconciled with traditional Jewish visions of the Divine? Is the Jewish theologian (feminist or not) free to claim *all* personally experienced images as Jewish simply because she or he is a Jew? Or, might there be certain kinds of *a priori* restraints that need be imposed?

To answer these questions, one should define the theological enterprise more clearly. If one maintains, as Jacob Neusner does, that the major task of Jewish theology is

to draw out and make explicit the normative statements of the acknowledged sources of Judaism and to learn how to renew discourse in accordance with these norms,[11]

there can be no room for personally experienced images that are irreconcilable with the norms of Jewish tradition. Claiming Jewish self-identity is not enough. As Neusner writes, theological statements are more than "private opinion." They are, he insists, the products of visions "received . . . reformed . . . [and] transmitted."[12]

Yet, I think that, by definition, Jewish feminist theology must move in another direction. Rooted in the experiences of feminist theologians as women and as Jews, Jewish feminist theology begins with the recognition that we have received only male visions. As Judith Plaskow argues, the norms that have been established are *male* norms with women relegated to the role of other. Moreover, all of the sources of Jewish theology: the written and oral Torah, philosophical and mystical texts, and traditional liturgy were largely (if not exclusively) created by and for men. Thus, the first task of the Jewish feminist theologian is to recognize that the visions we have received are incomplete. Before the feminist theologian can reform or transmit Judaism's traditional visions, she needs to receive these visions herself. She needs to hear her own voice and feel her own presence within the sources of Jewish tradition. Before the feminist theologian can shape the content of religious expression she must discover what women's religious experience has been. To do so may require reading between the lines, filling in stories, writing new ones, making guesses. Consequently, Jewish feminist theology can best be described as "responsive theology."

As defined by Daniel Breslauer in his essay "Alternatives in Jewish Theology," responsive theology emerges out of an encounter with "images and narratives from the Jewish past" and from the experience of the theologian. Unlike normative theology, responsive theology does not begin with a set of norms delineating what is authentically Jewish. Rather, it begins with the "subjective response of the theologian to a set of experiences," encouraging, therefore, a "more fluid view of Judaism and the Judaic experience" itself.[13]

If Jewish feminist theology is responsive theology, its *a priori* commitment to Jewish tradition need not be a commitment to the norms of that tradition but to its sources and "fundamental categories" of God, Torah, and Israel.[14] Jewish feminist theology, then, is a theology that emerges *in response to* Jewish sources and Jewish beliefs. These responses are shaped by the experiences of the theologian as woman and as Jew. What may emerge is a transformation not only of Jewish theology but of the sources the feminist uses in transmitting her visions.

The most important source for Jewish feminist theology may well be *aggada*, Jewish legends and stories which themselves have often been subject to reinterpretation. Judith Plaskow's story of Lilith and Eve is an outstanding example of how traditional Jewish myths *as received by women* can be transmitted and transformed. In her myth, Plaskow places Lilith and Eve within the framework of their traditional setting. Eve is still in the garden with Adam, Lilith is Adam's ex-wife. Combining their myths, Plaskow retains much of the traditional content filtered through her own experience of self and of sisterhood with other women. Thus, she transforms, at first subtly, then radically, Eve and Lilith's relationship to Adam and to God and describes the ways in which each woman views herself and the world around her. She imagines what it might have been like had Eve and Lilith met one another and heard each other's story and at the end of the myth envisions a powerful Eve and Lilith returning to the garden to rebuild it together.[15]

Plaskow's myth emerges out of her own response to the traditional narrative. Thus, while she accepts the rabbinic image of Lilith as she who claimed equality with Adam (an image that speaks to her own experience of selfhood), she rejects the portrayal of Lilith as night demon, imaginatively suggesting that Adam created this falsehood to enlist Eve's aid in his battle against Lilith and to make sure that Eve and his former wife would not become friends. Similarly, she accepts the traditional image of Eve as created from Adam's rib to be his wife and helper but rejects the traditional assumption that Eve remained satisfied with her role. Moreover, by joining the Lilith and Eve myths together, Plaskow is able to move beyond the biblical and rabbinic materials completely. The new ending that Plaskow creates helps make the myth compelling, not just to herself but to those whose experience of sisterhood has been as powerful as her own.

A RE-VISIONING OF SARAH

One further direction that Jewish feminist theologians need to explore is related to but not identical with remythologizing. It involves paying attention to fantasies and dreams that seem to emerge out of our own experience of tradition. As an example, I offer the following story of Sarah, my own (unconscious) response to the traditional story of the binding of Isaac.

I first "received" this story several years ago, while celebrating Rosh Hodesh (the new moon) with a group of Jewish women. We were sitting in a circle, our eyes closed, and quite suddenly, I began to feel my voice become the voice of the biblical Sarah:

It was morning. Sarah had just awakened and reached over to touch her husband, Abraham, to caress him, but Abraham wasn't there. Neither, she discovered, was Isaac, her only son, Isaac, whom she loved more than anyone or anything in the world. She quickly dressed and went outside, hoping they'd be nearby. But they were gone, and so was Abraham's ass and his two young servants. It wasn't unusual for Abraham to take Isaac somewhere, but never this early and never without saying good-bye. And so she waited, and wept, and screamed.

And *I* screamed, I remember, feeling Sarah's pain, and bewilderment and sorrow.

Hours passed. It was hot and Sarah thought about going inside to escape the heat of the sun. But what if I miss them, she thought. I want to make sure that I catch the first glimpse of them, even if they're far away. And so she stood and waited . . . and waited . . . and waited. She felt anxious, nervous, upset. "Where could they be?" "Where has Abraham taken my son?" The sun began to set. She started to shiver, partly from the cold, mostly from fear. Again she cried, and wailed, and moaned. Isaac had been God's gift to her, a sign of His love and a continuing bond between them. She had laughed when God told her she was pregnant. She was old and no longer able to bear a child. But He had given her Isaac and filled her breasts with milk and for the first time in her life Sarah was happy.

She looked around her and saw the fields, now empty, and in the distance saw the mountains, sloping upwards into the sky. And then she saw them . . . Abraham walking with his ass and his servants and Isaac far behind, walking slowly, his head turning from side to side, his hands oddly moving as though he were trying to make sense of something, and Sarah knew in that instant where Abraham and Isaac had been and why they had gone. Though she could barely make out the features of Isaac's face, she could tell from his movements and his gestures that he was angry, that he wanted nothing to do with his father who had tried to kill him. Abraham was almost down the mountain by now and soon would be home. He'd try to explain, to make her understand *his* side of the story. But Sarah wanted no part of it. She was tired of hearing Abraham's excuses and even more tired of hearing what *he* thought God demanded. And so Sarah turned and went inside and prayed that, if only for one night, Abraham would leave her alone.

The theological image that emerges out of this vision, for me, is of a Divine Being who enters into a relationship not only with men but also with women. Though the biblical story speaks of Isaac only as Abraham's son, my vision reinforces the relationship between God, Isaac, and Sarah. Moreover, her giving birth can be seen as a sign, a sealing of the covenant that God has made with her. Just as He sealed His covenant with Abraham through circumcision, He chose to seal His covenant with Sarah through Isaac's birth. In some ways, this image is problematic. If God seals His covenant with women through childbirth, what of women who are unable to bear a child?

Were I to take this theological image as normative, I might be led to conclude that women who do not bear children are not included in God's covenant. Yet in doing responsive theology, I am only giving expression to what seems to me to be the significance of a particular biblical text. I do not see this text as setting norms for future behavior (fortunately, I think, for neither God's nor Abraham's behavior seems particularly commendable). Rather, I see this text, received and re-formed by me, as clarifying the relationship between God and Israel. God has chosen Abraham *and* Sarah and has sealed His covenant with them in different ways. Moreover, each has a separate understanding of what God demands. Though Abraham believes that God wants him to sacrifice Isaac, Sarah believes that their God—a God of love, not cruelty—would never have placed such a demand upon them.

Sarah's belief, which I experienced as my own, offers me another way of looking at the *Akedah* (the story of the binding of Isaac). As I retell my vision, I become more and more convinced that the *Akedah* as contained in the Bible is only half of the story. Perhaps Abraham did believe that it was his responsibility, as a man of faith, to do what-ever he felt God commanded. But the vision I received from Sarah is that God does not take back His gifts and that perhaps those who hear such commandments should at least question whether they have heard God correctly.

Although the God of my vision is clearly imaged as male, the rela-tionship between God and Sarah is a close one, far closer, in fact, than that between Sarah and her husband. Theologically, this seems to tell me that even though men, like Abraham, tried to impose their religious beliefs on their wives, women, like Sarah, listened to their own voices and to what *they* believe to be the voice of God. According to rabbinic legend, Sarah's death, referred to in the Bible immediately following the *Akedah*, was caused by her grief over (mistakenly) learning that Isaac had been sacrificed. My vision leads me to conclude that if the rabbis were right, Sarah died not only because she thought her son had been killed but also because she felt abandoned by her God.

These kinds of responses to the *Akedah*—from Sarah's point of view—provide a new means of understanding God's relationship to Israel and a new perspective from which to view God's demands. As Breslauer writes in describing responsive theology, its intent is to show that "reflecting on Jewish belief is not merely an elitist privilege but is open to every individual Jew."[16] Perhaps, then, it may encourage Jewish women to look again at myths that they have long ago abandoned, infusing them with new meaning and power.

As Jewish feminists work to create a theology of their own, they may find that not all Jewish sources can be resources for them, that some may have to be emended or rewritten. How much emendation one does will depend on adherence to *halacha* and loyalty to tradition. Yet before a feminist theology can be created, such emendations must be made. Despite protests from those who refuse to see past visions as anything less than complete, the feminist theologian who tries to respond to Jewish sources as a Jew and as a woman may find it difficult if not impossible to expound upon experiences that have not yet been given expression.

NOTES

1. Rita M. Gross, "Steps Toward Feminine Imagery of Deity in Jewish Theology," *Judaism* 30 (Spring 1981): 189.
2. Ibid.
3. Ibid.
4. Carol P. Christ and Judith Plaskow, "Introduction," in *Womanspirit Rising: A Feminist Reader in Religion,* ed. Carol P. Christ and Judith Plaskow (San Francisco: Harper & Row, 1979), 10.
5. Judith Plaskow, "God and Feminism," *Menorah* 3 (February 1982): 2.
6. Ibid., 6.
7. Ibid., 7.
8. Mary Daly, *Gyn/Ecology: The Metaethics of Radical Feminism* (Boston: Beacon Press, 1978), 9.
9. This interpretation and this translation of the Hebrew text were related to me orally by Lynn Gottlieb (16 December 1981, New York City). Her translation of Genesis 1:1–5 is as follows:

   > In a time before time, all-spirits birthed
   > creation. Creation was a dark howling wind
   > on the void.
   > All-spirits broke the inner waters
   > And said light . . . behold light . . .
   > It is good.
   > All-spirits separated among light and dark
   > Calling the light . . . yom
   > And the dark she called lilah.
   > Night passage
   > morning
   > One day.

10. This reimaging of *Adonai, Shaddai,* and *Shechinah* was passed on to me—again by oral tradition—by Lynn Gottlieb (17 December 1981, New York City).
11. Jacob Neusner, "The Tasks of Theology in Judaism: A Humanistic Program," *The Journal of Religion* (January 1979): 71.
12. Ibid.
13. S. Daniel Breslauer, "Alternatives in Jewish Theology," *Judaism* 30 (Spring 1981): 234.
14. Jacob Neusner, "Introduction," in Neusner, ed. *Understanding Jewish Theology: Classical Issues and Modern Perspectives* (New York: Ktav, 1973), 1.
15. Judith Plaskow, "The Coming of Lilith: Toward a Feminist Theology," in Christ and Plaskow, *Womanspirit Rising,* 206–7.
16. Breslauer, "Jewish Theology," 240.

Be-Friending

Weaving Contexts, Creating Atmospheres

MARY DALY

Spinsters, who have experienced something of the process/activity of Happiness, Lust to share such Realization of participation in Be-ing. The actualization of this desire requires *Be-Friending*. *Be-Friending* is the creation of a context/atmosphere in which acts/leaps of Metamorphosis can take place. Websters Weaving this context are inspired to do so by our knowledge of female potential. That is, it is not the supposition that women are "weak" that inspires the Weaving. Rather, it is certain knowledge of the potency of women—a potency that needs to be actualized—that emboldens us to continue the work.

While the knowledge of female potency is certain, it is far from certain that this will be Actualized/Realized by many women under the prevailing conditions of the State of Separation. Therefore, quantum leaps of Fate-identified faith, hope, and Lust are in order. These leaps are part of the process itself of Weaving. They are acts of Metamorphosis, for they strengthen and actualize spiritual capacities. As Lusty Leapers, women carry the threads of connectedness ever further, beyond already Realized limits. That is, we are actualizing psychic and physical ultimacy. This Leaping/Weaving is a continuing act of sharing Lust for Happiness.

In choosing/inventing the word *Be-Friending* to Name such Webster-identified activity, I do not mean to suggest that every woman, or even every feminist, can "be a friend to" or "be friends with" every other woman. It is clear, first of all, that there are limitations of time and energy. Second, there are serious differences of temperament and circumstances which make it impossible for some women to be friends with each other, no matter how well intentioned each may be. There are also, as Jan Raymond has pointed out, women who hate their Selves and other women, and there are histories of "unfulfilled expectations, betrayal, lack of real caring, and the wall of entrenched differences

Mary Daly, Associate Professor in the Department of Theology at Boston College, where she teaches feminist ethics, lectures widely across the United States and Canada, as well as internationally. She is author of numerous works of feminist philosophy, most recently *Webster's First Intergalactic Wickedary of the English Language*.

between friends that become insurmountable."[1] Moreover, a genuine friendship between any two women develops over a long period of time, and it requires basic creative harmony between the friends and a firmness of commitment to each other.

Although friendship is not possible among all feminists, the work of Be-Friending can be shared by all, and all can benefit from this Metamorphospheric activity. Be-Friending involves Weaving a context in which women can Realize our Self-transforming, metapatterning participation in Be-ing. Therefore it implies the creation of an atmosphere in which women are enabled to be friends. Every woman who contributes to the creation of this atmosphere functions as a catalyst for the evolution of other women and for the forming and unfolding of genuine friendships.

An example of Be-Friending will illustrate this process. In the late 1940s the publication of Simone de Beauvoir's great feminist work, *The Second Sex*, made possible dialogue among women about their own lives. For many years this work functioned as an almost solitary beacon for women seeking to understand the *connections* among the oppressive evils they experienced, for they came to understand the fact of otherness within patriarchal society. There were other feminist works in existence, of course, but these were not really accessible, even to "educated" women. *The Second Sex* helped to generate an atmosphere in which women could utter their own thoughts, at least to themselves. Some women began to make applications and to seek out less accessible sources, many of which had gone out of print. Most important was the fact that de Beauvoir, by breaking the silence, partially broke the Terrible Taboo. Women were Touched, psychically and e-motionally. Many such women, thus re-awakened, began to have conversations, take actions, write articles—even during the dreary fifties.

It could not accurately be said that de Beauvoir was a personal friend to the thousands of women awakened by her work. It can be said that she has been part of the movement of Be-Friending and that she has been a catalyst for the friendships of many women. The atmosphere to which her work contributed could not remain stagnant. The "air" was invigorating—a stimulant encouraging women to make those quantum leaps that bring us into Metamorphospheres.

Similarly today, any woman who makes leaps of metapatterning, whether these be in a personal relationship, in political activity, in a work of theory or of art, in spiritual understanding, or in all of the above, is a weaver of the network of Be-Friending. So also have been the Fore-Spinsters who have preceded us, Spinning and Weaving the context that makes our friendships possible.

BE-FRIENDING, BE-LONGING, AND RAGE

Be-Friending is radically connected with Be-Longing. The latter is that which metapatriarchal women wish for each other and en-courage in each other, for only the longing/Lusting for be-ing can bring about Happiness. Be-Friending arouses and awakens in a woman her Be-Longing, her telic focus. Be-Friending is both the flowering of Be-Longing and an important condition for the arousal and sustaining of this ontological Passion.

Be-Friending provides the context in which the low-grade multiple-personality disorder which I have suggested is the "contrary" of Rage can be confronted and overcome. The manner in which the context of Be-Friending functions to overcome this affliction of dissociation is analogous to the action of a magnet. That is, it attracts the telic focusing powers of be-ing in a woman. For, everything that is is connected with everything else that is. Only be-ing can call forth be-ing. Only confirmation of one's own Reality awakens that Reality in another.

As she is drawn into the Spiraling movement of Be-Friending, a woman becomes a friend to the be-ing in her Self, which is to say, her centering Self. The intensity of her desire focuses her energy, which becomes unsplintered, unblocked. This focusing, gathering of her dissociated energy, makes possible the release of Rage. The Metamorphosing Sage rides her Rage. It is her broom, her Fire-breathing, winged mare. It is her spiraling staircase, leading her where she can find her own Kind, unbind her mind.

Rage is not "a stage." It is not something to be gotten over. It is transformative, focusing Force. Like a horse who streaks across fields on a moonlit night, her mane flying, Rage gallops on pounding hooves of unleashed Passion. The sounds of its pounding awaken transcendent E-motion. As the ocean roars its rhythms into every creature, giving birth to sensations of our common Sources/Courses, Rage too, makes senses come alive again, thrive again.

Women require the context of Be-Friending both to sustain the positive force of moral Outrage and to continue the Fury-fueled task of inventing new ways of living. Without the encouragement of Be-Friending, anger can deteriorate into rancor and can mis-fire, injuring the wrong targets. One function of the work of Be-Friending, then, is to keep the sense of Outrage focused in a biophilic way.

THE CONTEXT OF OUTRAGE

The knowledge woven through acts of Be-Friending is characterized by the woman-identified recognition of connectedness that inspires and sustains the Weavers. Websters do not flinch from seeing the complicity of women as token torturers. At the same time, we struggle always to see who in fact holds the institutional power that man-ipulates and damages the consciousness/conscience of women who oppress other women. Examples of such complicity are legion. Crones know the horrifying history of mothers used as token torturers of their daughters. Crones born and brought up in America can hardly be unaware of the compounded complicity involved when phallocratic racial oppression further desensitizes and dissociates the woman who has "power" from her more oppressed sister.

The history of Black slavery in the United States illustrates this situation most tragically. A testimony of Sarah M. Grimké, abolitionist from South Carolina, published in 1839, concerns the torture of a young woman "whose independent spirit could not brook the degradation of slavery" and who repeatedly ran away. The young woman's back was lacerated to such an extent that "a finger could not be laid between the cuts." In addition:

A heavy iron collar, with three prongs projecting from it, was placed round her neck, and a strong and sound front tooth was extracted, to serve as a mark to describe her, in case of escape.[2]

Sarah Grimké, who personally saw this young woman, stated:

Her sufferings at this time were agonizing; she could lie in no position but on her back, which was sore from scourgings, as I can testify from personal inspection, and her only place of rest was the floor, on a blanket. These outrages were committed in a family where the mistress daily read the scriptures, and assembled her children for family worship. She was accounted, and was really, so far as alms-giving was concerned, a charitable woman, and tender-hearted to the poor; and yet this suffering slave, who was the seamstress of the family, was continually in her presence . . . with her lacerated and bleeding back, her mutilated mouth, and heavy iron collar without, so far as appeared, exciting any feelings of compassion.[3]

The passive complicity of the pious bible-reading mistress illustrates one way in which hatred could work itself out. Sometimes the cooperation has been more active. In 1853 Solomon Northup described the breaking of a high-spirited young woman whose back "bore the scars of a thousand stripes . . . because it had fallen her lot to be the slave of a licentious master and a jealous mistress." Northup testified concerning the agony of this woman:

Nothing delighted the mistress so much as to see her suffer. . . . Patsey walked under a cloud. If she uttered a word in opposition to her master's will, the lash was resorted to at once, to bring her to subjection; if she was not watchful while about her cabin, or when walking in the yard, a billet of wood, or a broken bottle perhaps, hurled from her mistress' hand, would smite her unexpectedly in the face. . . .

Finally, for a trifling offense, Patsey was given a savage whipping, while her mistress and the master's children watched with obvious satisfaction. She almost died.

From that time forward she was not what she had been.[4]

Black women, aware of this history and faced with the day-to-day experience of racial oppression, are faced with the dilemmas implied in bonding with white women. Together with other women of color, many are creating their own radical feminist analysis.[5] White women, especially in the United States, often feel discouraged by the knowledge of white patriarchal female indifference, racial hatred, and cruelty. In the face of such unspeakable cruelty, vividly illustrated in the accounts of the mistresses' behavior and repeated thousands of times over in the country of Reagan and Company, what can be said about Female-identified Outrage?

Considering the behavior of the slaveholders' wives described above may re-mind Hags of certain basic threads in the context of our Outrage. The bible-reading mistress of the tortured young seamstress was "supported" in her dissociation from the victimized Black woman by patriarchal religion, the patriarchal institutions of slavery and racism, and the patriarchal institution of marriage. The vicious mistress of the other young woman, whose jealousy was aroused by the fact that her lecherous lout of a husband raped his defenseless slave, was the product of these same soul-molding sado-institutions. None of these institutions were invented by women or have ever been under the control of women.

It would be not only absurd but ethically wrong to excuse the slaveholders' wives, or to excuse contemporary female racist oppressors, or to condone a Phyllis Schlafly for her gynocidal, genocidal, biocidal politics. As conscious carriers of phallocratic diseases and executors of phallocratic crimes, such women are indeed responsible. Furies, moreover, will recognize that the obvious corruption and cooptation of women under patriarchy can function to weaken Female-identified Outrage in women who are sincerely struggling to live a metapatriarchal morality. That is, token torturers function as instruments of the sadostate not only as the appointed executors of oppressive acts, but also as dis-couraging and confusing role models, driving other women into paralyzing guilt and misdirected anger. Patriarchal women, then, function as Rage-blockers/twisters.

It is predictable and already observable that as the biocidal nuclear arms race continues, as the destruction of Third World people by the United States and other powerful nations escalates, as racism and poverty "at home" worsens, many women's energy and motivation for Weaving tapestries of Female Be-Friending is undermined. This is partly traceable to disgust and horror at the increasing visibility and apparent moral bankruptcy of right-wing women and other female servants of the sadostate. It is also traceable to false guilt for putting the cause of feminism first.

Crones, then, can recognize the time-honored trick of the patriarchs efficiently operating in the eighties. This is the creation of a perpetual State of Emergency, in which some male-ordered activity is always made to appear prior in importance to the liberation of women. In the face of this onslaught, Metamorphic leaps of be-ing will be possible only if there is an intensification of intent and determination on the part of women who recognize phallocracy as the root of rapism, racism, gynocide, genocide, and ultimate biocide.

Only clearly focused Female Outrage can sustain the work of meta-patterning. Only continuous Weaving of tapestries of female-identified knowledge—that is, our work of Be-Friending—can further the de-velopment of metapatriarchal consciousness and behavior. These Crone-centered tapestries can serve as magic carpets for women who choose to fly beyond the sadostate's Eternal Lie. These vehicles can also serve as maps of passages to Metamemory.

BE-FRIENDING AND FEMALE FRIENDSHIP

There have been countless great and deep friendships among women. Without metapatriarchal consciousness, however, these are less than they might have been. A Metamorphic context is necessary for friendship to thrive. Since friendship implies a sharing of activity—in a special sense, intellectual activity—the necessary context will be one that awakens and encourages women to exercise their powers to full capacity. It will inspire women to share Happiness, to make Metamor-phic leaps and to encounter Metamemory. Such a context I have called Be-Friending.

Lacking such a context, women do sometimes reach immeasurable depths in their friendships, but there is almost always an atmosphere of tragedy about these relationships—a vague sense of something miss-ing, or something lost. Perhaps the most poignant words ever written concerning this subject are the closing lines of Toni Morrison's *Sula*, when Nel re-members her unfathomable connection with Sula, who had died twenty-five years before:

"All that time, all that time, I thought I was missing Jude." And the loss pressed down on her chest and came up into her throat. "We was girls together," she said as though explaining something. "O Lord, Sula," she cried, "girl, girl, girlgirlgirl." It was a fine cry—loud and long—but it had no bottom and it had no top, just circles and circles of sorrow.[6]

Musing women might well conclude that the words "We was girls together" *do* explain something, perhaps everything. It would seem that Nel's visit to the cemetery after the death of Eva (Sula's grandmother, who survived Sula by a quarter of a century) occasioned a volcanic eruption of Metamemory. For decades, Metamemory had been smoldering beneath the schemata, or categories, of "adult" memory. The "milestone" that had blocked Nel's deep Memory was having been deserted by her man, Jude, whom Sula had "taken."

This "milestone" of adult/male-identified memory is omnipresent among patriarchally possessed women. Even before it occurs, the "dreadful" event has already happened in the realm of anticipation. It therefore perpetually functions as a closure of deep Memory of female friendship, an alienating foreground "memory" of the future. Just before her death, Sula had intuited the way this Memory-block would continue to function in Nel.

When Nel closed the door, Sula reached for more medicine. . . . "So she will walk on down that road, her back so straight in that old green coat, the strap of her handbag pushed all the way to the elbow, thinking how much I have cost her and never remember the days when we were two throats and one eye and we had no price."[7]

The one word that was wrong in Sula's prophecy was "never." Although it required a quarter of a century, the volcanic eruption of Metamemory did take place. The landscape through which Nel's road had led became gynaesthetically perceptible. She Realized the truly significant events of the past, as distinct from those conventionally supposed to be significant.

The girlhood friendship of Nel and Sula was transcendent. They both were dreamers and both understood the odds against them:

Because each had discovered years before that they were neither white nor male, and that all freedom and triumph was forbidden to them, they had set about creating something else to be.[8]

The fact that so many women have responded deeply to this story suggests that such girlhood experiences are not isolated phenomena. *Sula* touches chords of remembrance of things past in women who seemingly are totally unlike Nel and Sula—unlike because of their racial and economic backgrounds, because of "training" and individual temperament. Yet there is a common Memory of setting about "creating something else to be."

When such chords are struck in women's psyches, the stirrings of Metamemory are felt. There are movements of re-membering beyond civilization. The tapestry of Be-Friending which such books as *Sula* help to Weave stirs the air, the atmosphere which women breathe. Breathing deeply, Muses recall those girlhood moments of be-ing in such a way that these become movements of be-ing. Each woman's ecstatic Metamemory is absolutely unique. Yet the threads of commonality are Luminously visible, harmoniously audible.

This ecstatic experience of Metamemory-bearing women suggests that it is primarily in the Realm of Metamorphospheres that Crones' genuine connections and true diversity can be discovered. When women bond solely on the basis of oppression, more and more forms of man-made "commonality" and "diversity" assume importance, masking the potential for deep woman-bonding. When women bond primarily on the grounds of male-identified "commonality" and "diversity," the hope of Metamorphosis becomes an elusive dream. The tragic spectacle of Arab and Jewish women misfiring rage at each other illustrates this patriarchally created scenario. One could think also of the women of Northern and Southern Ireland. One could think of one's local women's community, where divisions often have nothing to do with the common cause of feminism.

One need only think— if one can bear to do so—of one's local hospital. Although there are many skilled and sensitive nurses, it is not unknown for a nurse to identify more with "doctor's orders," even when she has certain knowledge that his orders are destroying the patient, than with the patient. If the patient is a woman, a nurse's dissociation from her Self and consequently from the woman patient can be astonishing and devastating. If the patient is a woman of color or is poor, the chances are that her mistreatment will be worse.

Women can easily fall (or be pushed) into forgetting that racial and ethnic oppression, like the sexual oppression that is the primary and universal model of such victimization, is a male invention. Seeking to uncover the causes of such amnesia and confusion, Furies find that the constructs of patriarchal civilization require the assimilation of women, and consequently our ghettoization from each other, from our Selves.

It is undeniable that women all over this planet have different exigencies and commitments that are overwhelming. Despite and because of this fact, Muses continue to Weave contexts of Be-Friending, which point beyond assimilation/ghettoization. Be-Friending beyond civilization, Sirens lure women to the places where female friendship comes alive, thrives. . . .

NOTES

1. Janice Raymond, "A Genealogy of Female Friendship," *Trivia: A Journal of Ideas* 1 (Fall 1982): 6.
2. Sarah M. Grimké, "A Seamstress Is Punished," in *Black Women in White America: A Documentary History*, ed. by Gerda Lerner (New York: Random House, Vintage Books, 1972), 18.
3. Ibid., 18–19.
4. Solomon Northup, "The Slaveholder's Mistress," in Lerner (ed.), *Black Women in White America*, 50–51.

5. See, for example, "Racism Is the Issue," *Heresies* 4, issue 15 (1982).
6. Toni Morrison, *Sula* (New York: Bantam Books, 1973), 149.
7. Ibid., 126.
8. Ibid., 44.

Uses of the Erotic

The Erotic as Power

AUDRE LORDE

There are many kinds of power, used and unused, acknowledged or otherwise. The erotic is a resource within each of us that lies in a deeply female and spiritual plane, firmly rooted in the power of our unexpressed or unrecognized feeling. In order to perpetuate itself, every oppression must corrupt or distort those various sources of power within the culture of the oppressed that can provide energy for change. For women, this has meant a suppression of the erotic as a considered source of power and information within our lives.

We have been taught to suspect this resource, vilified, abused, and devalued within western society. On the one hand, the superficially erotic has been encouraged as a sign of female inferiority; on the other hand, women have been made to suffer and to feel both contemptible and suspect by virtue of its existence.

It is a short step from there to the false belief that only by the suppression of the erotic within our lives and consciousness can women be truly strong. But that strength is illusory, for it is fashioned within the context of male models of power.

As women, we have come to distrust that power which rises from our deepest and nonrational knowledge. We have been warned against it all our lives by the male world, which values this depth of feeling enough to keep women around in order to exercise it in the service of men, but which fears this same depth too much to examine the possibilities of it within themselves. So women are maintained at a distant/inferior position to be psychically milked, much the same way ants maintain colonies of aphids to provide a life-giving substance for their masters.

But the erotic offers a well of replenishing and provocative force to the woman who does not fear its revelation, nor succumb to the belief that sensation is enough.

Audre Lorde, a black, lesbian, feminist, poet, mother of two children, activist, cancer survivor, is professor of English at Hunter College. Author of several books of poetry, her prose writings include *The Cancer Journals*, *Zami: A New Spelling of My Name*, *Sister Outsider*, and *A Burst of Light*.

The erotic has often been misnamed by men and used against women. It has been made into the confused, the trivial, the psychotic, the plasticized sensation. For this reason, we have often turned away from the exploration and consideration of the erotic as a source of power and information, confusing it with its opposite, the pornographic. But pornography is a direct denial of the power of the erotic, for it represents the suppression of true feeling. Pornography emphasizes sensation without feeling.

The erotic is a measure between the beginnings of our sense of self and the chaos of our strongest feelings. It is an internal sense of satisfaction to which, once we have experienced it, we know we can aspire. For having experienced the fullness of this depth of feeling and recognizing its power, in honor and self-respect we can require no less of ourselves.

It is never easy to demand the most from ourselves, from our lives, from our work. To go beyond the encouraged mediocrity of our society is to encourage excellence. But giving in to the fear of feeling and working to capacity is a luxury only the unintentional can afford, and the unintentional are those who do not wish to guide their own destinies.

This internal requirement toward excellence which we learn from the erotic must not be misconstrued as demanding the impossible from ourselves nor from others. Such a demand incapacitates everyone in the process. For the erotic is not a question only of what we do; it is a question of how acutely and fully we can feel in the doing. Once we know the extent to which we are capable of feeling that sense of satisfaction and completion, we can then observe which of our various life endeavors bring us closest to that fullness.

The aim of each thing which we do is to make our lives and the lives of our children richer and more possible. Within the celebration of the erotic in all our endeavors, my work becomes a conscious decision—a longed-for bed which I enter gratefully and from which I rise up empowered.

Of course, women so empowered are dangerous. So we are taught to separate the erotic demand from most vital areas of our lives other than sex. And the lack of concern for the erotic root and satisfactions of our work is felt in our disaffection from so much of what we do. For instance, how often do we truly love our work even at its most difficult?

The principal horror of any system which defines the good in terms of profit rather than in terms of human need, or which defines human need to the exclusion of the psychic and emotional components of that need—the principal horror of such a system is that it robs our work of its erotic value, its erotic power and life appeal and fulfillment. Such a system reduces work to a travesty of necessities, a duty by which we earn bread or oblivion for ourselves and those we love. But this is tantamount to blinding a painter and then telling her to improve her work, and to enjoy the act of painting. It is not only next to impossible, it is also profoundly cruel.

As women, we need to examine the ways in which our world can be truly different. I am speaking here of the necessity for reassessing the quality of all the aspects of our lives and of our work, and of how we move toward and through them.

The very word *erotic* comes from the Greek word *eros*, the personi-fication of love in all its aspects—born of Chaos, and personifying cre-ative power and harmony. When I speak of the erotic, then, I speak of it as an assertion of the lifeforce of women; of that creative energy empowered, the knowledge and use of which we are now reclaiming in our language, our history, our dancing, our loving, our work, our lives.

There are frequent attempts to equate pornography and eroticism, two diametrically opposed uses of the sexual. Because of these attempts, it has become fashionable to separate the spiritual (psychic and emo-tional) from the political, to see them as contradictory or antithetical. "What do you mean, a poetic revolutionary, a meditating gunrunner?" In the same way, we have attempted to separate the spiritual and the erotic, thereby reducing the spiritual to a world of flattened affect, a world of the ascetic who aspires to feel nothing. But nothing is farther from the truth. For the ascetic position is one of the highest fear, the gravest immobility. The severe abstinence of the ascetic becomes the ruling obsession. And it is one not of self-discipline but of self-abne-gation.

The dichotomy between the spiritual and the political is also false, resulting from an incomplete attention to our erotic knowledge. For the bridge that connects them is formed by the erotic—the sensual— those physical, emotional, and psychic expressions of what is deepest and strongest and richest within each of us, being shared: the passions of love, in its deepest meanings.

Beyond the superficial, the considered phrase, "It feels right to me," acknowledges the strength of the erotic into a true knowledge, for what that means is the first and most powerful guiding light toward any understanding. And understanding is a handmaiden which can only wait upon, or clarify, that knowledge, deeply born. The erotic is the nurturer or nursemaid of all our deepest knowledge.

The erotic functions for me in several ways, and the first is in pro-viding the power that comes from sharing deeply any pursuit with an-other person. The sharing of joy, whether physical, emotional, psychic, or intellectual, forms a bridge between the sharers that can be the basis for understanding much of what is not shared between them, and lessens the threat of their difference.

Another important way in which the erotic connection functions is the open and fearless underlining of my capacity for joy. In the way my body stretches to music and opens into response, hearkening to its deepest rhythms, so every level upon which I sense also opens to the erotically satisfying experience, whether it is dancing, building a bookcase, writing a poem, examining an idea.

That self-connection shared is a measure of the joy that I know myself to be capable of feeling, a reminder of my capacity for feeling. And that deep and irreplaceable knowledge of my capacity for joy comes to demand from all of my life that it be lived within the knowledge that such satisfaction is possible, and does not have to be called *marriage*, nor *god*, nor *an afterlife*.

This is one reason why the erotic is so feared, and so often relegated to the bedroom alone, when it is recognized at all. For once we begin to feel deeply all the aspects of our lives, we begin to demand from ourselves and from our life-pursuits that they feel in accordance with that joy which we know ourselves to be capable of. Our erotic knowledge empowers us, becomes a lens through which we scrutinize all aspects of our existence, forcing us to evaluate those aspects honestly in terms of their relative meaning within our lives. And this is a grave responsibility, projected from within each of us, not to settle for the convenient, the shoddy, the conventionally expected, nor the merely safe.

During World War II, we bought sealed plastic packets of white, uncolored margarine, with a tiny, intense pellet of yellow coloring perched like a topaz just inside the clear skin of the bag. We would leave the margarine out for a while to soften, and then we would pinch the little pellet to break it inside the bag, releasing the rich yellowness into the soft pale mass of margarine. Then taking it carefully between our fingers, we would knead it gently back and forth, over and over, until the color had spread throughout the whole pound bag of margarine, thoroughly coloring it.

I find the erotic such a kernel within myself. When released from its intense and constrained pellet, it flows through and colors my life with a kind of energy that heightens and sensitizes and strengthens all my experience.

We have been raised to fear the *yes* within ourselves, our deepest cravings. But, once recognized, those that do not enhance our future lose their power and can be altered. The fear of our desires keeps them suspect and indiscriminately powerful, for to suppress any truth is to give it strength beyond endurance. The fear that we cannot grow beyond whatever distortions we may find within ourselves keeps us docile and loyal and obedient, externally defined, and leads us to accept many facets of our oppression as women.

When we live outside ourselves, and by that I mean on external directives only rather than from our internal knowledge and needs, when we live away from those erotic guides from within ourselves, then our lives are limited by external and alien forms, and we conform to the needs of a structure that is not based on human need, let alone an individual's. But when we begin to live from within outward, in touch with the power of the erotic within ourselves, and allowing that power to inform and illuminate our actions upon the world around us, then we begin to be responsible to ourselves in the deepest sense. For as we begin to recognize our deepest feelings, we begin to give up, of necessity, being satisfied with suffering and self-negation, and with the numbness that so often seems like their only alternative in our society. Our acts against oppression become integral with self, motivated and empowered from within.

In touch with the erotic, I become less willing to accept powerlessness, or those other supplied states of being which are not native to me, such as resignation, despair, self-effacement, depression, self-denial.

And yes, there is a hierarchy. There is a difference between painting a back fence and writing a poem, but only one of quantity. And there is, for me, no difference between writing a good poem and moving into sunlight against the body of a woman I love.

This brings me to the last consideration of the erotic. To share the power of each other's feelings is different from using another's feelings as we would use a Kleenex. When we look the other way from our experience, erotic or otherwise, we use rather than share the feelings of those others who participate in the experience with us. And use without consent of the used is abuse.

In order to be utilized, our erotic feelings must be recognized. The need for sharing deep feeling is a human need. But within the european-american tradition, this need is satisfied by certain proscribed erotic comings-together. These occasions are almost always characterized by a simultaneous looking away, a pretense of calling them something else, whether a religion, a fit, mob violence, or even playing doctor. And this misnaming of the need and the deed give rise to that distortion which results in pornography and obscenity—the abuse of feeling.

When we look away from the importance of the erotic in the development and sustenance of our power, or when we look away from ourselves as we satisfy our erotic needs in concert with others, we use each other as objects of satisfaction rather than share our joy in the satisfying, rather than make connection with our similarities and our differences. To refuse to be conscious of what we are feeling at any time, however comfortable that might seem, is to deny a large part of the experience, and to allow ourselves to be reduced to the pornographic, the abused, and the absurd.

The erotic cannot be felt secondhand. As a Black lesbian feminist, I have a particular feeling, knowledge, and understanding for those sisters with whom I have danced hard, played, or even fought. This deep participation has often been the forerunner for joint concerted actions not possible before.

But this erotic charge is not easily shared by women who continue to operate under an exclusively european-american male tradition. I know it was not available to me when I was trying to adapt my consciousness to this mode of living and sensation.

Only now, I find more and more women-identified women brave enough to risk sharing the erotic's electrical charge without having to look away, and without distorting the enormously powerful and creative nature of that exchange. Recognizing the power of the erotic within our lives can give us the energy to pursue genuine change within our world, rather than merely settling for a shift of characters in the same weary drama.

For not only do we touch our most profoundly creative source, but we do that which is female and self-affirming in the face of a racist, patriarchal, and anti-erotic society.

The Power of Anger in the Work of Love

Christian Ethics for Women and Other Strangers

BEVERLY WILDUNG HARRISON

My basic thesis that a Christian moral theology must be answerable to what women have learned by struggling to lay hold of the gift of life, to receive it, to live deeply into it, to pass it on, cannot be fully defended here. My theological method is consonant with those other liberation theologies that contend that what is authentic in the history of faith arises only out of the crucible of human struggle. This I take to be *the* central, albeit controversial, methodological claim of all emergent liberation theologies. That the locus of divine revelation is in the concrete struggles of groups and communities to lay hold of the gift of life and to unloose what denies life has astonishing implications for ethics. It means, among other things, that we must learn what we are to know of love from immersion in the struggle for justice. I believe that women have always been immersed in the struggle to create a flesh and blood community of love and justice and that we know much more of the radical work of love than does the dominant, otherworldly spirituality of Christianity. A feminist ethic, I submit, is deeply and profoundly worldly, a spirituality of sensuality.

BASEPOINTS FOR A FEMINIST MORAL THEOLOGY

ACTIVITY AS THE MODE OF LOVE

The first point at which women's experience challenges the dominant moral theology is difficult to see historically because of the smoke screen created by a successful nineteenth-century male counterattack

Beverly Wildung Harrison is Carolyn Williams Beaird Professor of Christian Ethics at Union Theological Seminary in New York City. She teaches feminist theology and social ethics with particular concern for sexual and economic ethics. She is author of *Our Right to Choose: Toward a New Ethic of Abortion* and *Making the Connections: Essays in Feminist Social Ethics*.

on the first women's liberation movement. Because of this counterattack, most educated, middle-strata women have internalized an ideology about ourselves that contradicts our actual history. Historically, I believe, women have always exemplified the power of activity over passivity, of experimentation over routinization, of creativity and risk-taking over conventionality. Yet since the nineteenth century we have been taught to believe that women are, by nature, more passive and reactive than men. *If* women throughout human history had behaved as cautiously and as conventionally as the "good women" invented by late bourgeois spirituality, *if* women had acquiesced to "the cult of true womanhood," and *if* the social powerlessness of women that is the "ideal" among the European and American "leisure classes" had prevailed, the gift of human life would long since have faced extinction.

This very modern invitation to us women to perceive ourselves under the images of effete gentility, passivity, and weakness blocks our capacity to develop a realistic sense of women's historical past. The fact is that while there are few constants in women's experience cross-culturally, the biological reality of childbearing and nursing (never to be confused with the cultural power of nurturance) usually gave women priority in, and responsibility for, those day-to-day activities that make for human survival in most societies. For example, women—not men— are the breadwinners and traders in many precapitalist societies. If we modern women acquiesce in the seductive invitation to think of ourselves primarily as onlookers, as contemplators, as those who stand aside while men get on with the serious business of running the (public) world, we should at least recognize what a modern "number" we are doing on ourselves! The important point here, however, is that a theology that overvalues static and passive qualities as "holy," that equates spirituality with noninvolvement and contemplation, that views the activity of sustaining daily life as mundane and unimportant religiously, such a theology *could not have been formulated by women*. In contrast, Sojourner Truth spoke authentically, out of the real lived-world experience of women, when she defined her womanhood in this way:

Nobody ever helped me into carriages, or over mud puddles, or gave me the best place. And ain't I a woman? Look at me! Look at my arm! I have ploughed and planted and gathered into barns, and no man could head me! And ain't I a woman? I can work as much and eat as much as any man when I can get it and bear the lash as well. And ain't I a woman? I have borne thirteen children and seen most of them sold off to slavery, and when I cried out with my mother's grief, none but Jesus heard me. And ain't I woman?[1]

Women have been the doers of life-sustaining things, the "copers," those who have understood that the reception of the gift of life is no inert thing, that to receive this gift is to be engaged in its tending, constantly. I believe we have a very long way to go before the priority of activity over passivity is internalized in our theology and even farther to go before love, in our ethics, is understood to be a *mode of action*. In *Beyond God the Father*,[2] Mary Daly began the necessary theological shift by insisting that a feminist theism has no place for a God understood as stasis and fixity, that out of women's experience the sacred is better imaged in terms of process and movement. Her proposal that God be envisaged as Be-ing, as verb rather than as noun, struck a deep chord in her readers, and not merely in her women readers.

Even so, Daly's reformulation does not seem to me even to go far enough. Susanne Langer has rightly noted that philosophies of being—those philosophies that take the structures of nature as their starting point—have long since incorporated the notion that process is *the* basic structure of reality.[3] Process theologians rightly protest that Daly has not paid enough attention to, or given enough credit to, modern philosophy of religion for incorporating these new views of nature. However, not many process theologians—indeed, even Daly—recognize the further need to incorporate the full meaning of the human struggle for life into our understanding of God. It is necessary to open up the naturalistic metaphors for God to the power of human activity, to freedom not only as radical creativity but also as radical moral power. It is necessary to challenge the classic ontology of Be-ing even more deeply than Daly has done. Catholic natural law theologies, it has often been argued, fail to do justice to the fact that the power of nature passes through what Marx called "the species-being" of human nature. Our world and our faith are transformed, for good or ill, through human activity. A feminist moral theology needs to root its analysis in this realm of radical moral creativity. Such freedom is often abused, but the power to create a world of moral relations is a fundamental aspect of human nature itself. In my opinion, the metaphor of Be-ing does not permit us to incorporate the radicality of human agency adequately. *Do-ing* must be as fundamental as *be-ing* in our theologies. Both do-ing and be-ing are, of course, only metaphors for conceptualizing our world. Both are only "ways of seeing things." However, we can never make sense of what is deepest, "wholiest," most powerfully sacred in the lives of women if we identify women only with the more static metaphor of being, neglecting the centrality of praxis as basic to women's experience. We women have a special reason to appreciate the radical freedom of the power of real, concrete deeds.

To be sure, some male-articulated "theologies of praxis" have given feminist theologians pause on this point. Men often envisage the power of human activity under images that suggest that domination and control are the central modes of human activity, as though political or military conquest were the noblest expressions of the human power to act. Because of this, some women have urged that feminist theologies eschew historical categories and operate exclusively from naturalistic metaphors. I believe that such a theological move would have disastrous consequences. We dare not minimize the very real historical power of women to be architects of what is most authentically human. We must not lose hold of the fact that we have been the chief builders of what-ever human dignity and community has come to expression. *We* have the right to speak of *building* human dignity and community.

Just as do-ing must be central to a feminist theology, so too be-ing and do-ing must never be treated as polarities. Receiving community as gift and doing the work of community building are two ways to view the same activity. A feminist theology is not a theology of either/or.[4] Anyone who has lived in "women's place" in human history has had to come to terms with the responsibility of being a reciprocal agent. Women's lives literally have been shaped by the power not only to bear human life at the biological level but to nurture life, which is a social and cultural power. Though our culture has come to disvalue women's role, and with it to disvalue nurturance, genuine nurturance is a for-midable power.[5] Insofar as it has taken place in human history, it has been largely through women's action. For better or worse, women have had to face the reality that we have the power not only to create per-sonal bonds between people but, more basically, to build up and deepen *personhood itself*. And to build up "the person" is also to deepen rela-tionship, that is, to bring forth community.

We do not yet have a moral theology that teaches us the aweful, awe-some truth that we have the power through acts of love or lovelessness literally to create one another. I believe that an adequate feminist moral theology must call the tradition of Christian ethics to accountability for minimizing the deep power of human action in the work of or the denial of love. Because we do not understand love as the power to act-each-other-into-well-being we also do not understand the depth of our power to thwart life and to maim each other. The fateful choice is ours, either to set free the power of God's love in the world or to deprive each other of the very basis of personhood and community. This power of human activity, so crucial to the divine-human drama, is *not* the power of world conquest or empire building, nor is it control of one person by another. We are *not* most godlike in our human power when we take the view from the top, the view of rulers, or of empires, or the view of patriarchs.

I believe that our world is on the verge of self-destruction and death because the society as a whole has so deeply neglected that which is most human and most valuable and the most basic of all the works of love—the work of human communication, of caring and nurturance, of tending the personal bonds of community. This activity has been seen as women's work and discounted as too mundane and undramatic, too distracting from the serious business of world rule. Those who have been taught to imagine themselves as world builders have been too busy with master plans to see that love's work *is* the deepening and extension of human relations. This urgent work of love is subtle but powerful. Through acts of love—what Nelle Morton has called "hearing each other to speech"[6]—we literally build up the power of personhood in one another. It is within the power of human love to build up dignity and self-respect in each other or to tear each other down. We are better at the latter than the former. However, literally through acts of love directed to us, we become self-respecting and other-regarding persons, and we cannot be one without the other. If we lack self-respect we also become the sorts of people who can neither see nor hear each other.

We may wish, like children, that we did not have such awesome power for good or evil. But the fact is that we do. The power to receive and give love, or to withhold it—that is, to withhold the gift of life—is less dramatic, but every bit as awesome, as our technological power. It is a tender power. And, as women are never likely to forget, the exercise of that power begins, and is rooted in *our bodies, ourselves*.[7]

OUR BODIES, OURSELVES AS THE AGENTS OF LOVE

A second basepoint for feminist moral theology derives from celebrating "embodiment."[8] A moral theology must not only be rooted in a worldly spirituality but must aim at overcoming the body/mind split in our intellectual and social life at every level. Feminist historical theologian Rosemary Ruether and, more recently, a number of male theologians have begun to identify the many connections between this body/mind dualism and our negative attitudes toward women.[9] Ironically, no dimension of our Western intellectual heritage has been so distorted by body/mind dualism as has our moral theology and moral philosophy, which is why a feminist moral theology is so needed. A number of male theologians—notably my colleague Tom Driver[10]—have begun to reenvisage a Christian theology that repudiates the mind/body split. However, fewer men in the field of Christian ethics have grasped the connection between body/mind dualism and the assumption many moral theologians make that we are most moral when most detached and disengaged from life-struggle.[11] Far too many Christian ethicists continue to imply that "disinterestedness" and "detachment" are basic preconditions for responsible moral action. And in the dominant ethical tradition, moral rationality too often is *disembodied* rationality.

If we begin, as feminists must, with "our bodies, ourselves," we recognize that all our knowledge, including our moral knowledge, is body-mediated knowledge. All knowledge is rooted in our sensuality. We know and value the world, *if* we know and value it, through our ability to touch, to hear, to see. *Perception* is foundational to *conception*. Ideas are dependent on our sensuality. Feeling is the basic bodily ingredient that mediates our connectedness to the world. All power, including intellectual power, is rooted in feeling. If feeling is damaged or cut off, our power to image the world and act into it is destroyed and our rationality is impaired. But it is not merely the power to conceive the world that is lost. Our power to value the world gives way as well. If we are not perceptive in discerning our feelings, or if we do not know what we feel, we cannot be effective moral agents. This is why psychotherapy has to be understood as a very basic form of moral education. In the absence of feeling there is no rational ability to evaluate what is happening. Failure to live deeply in "our bodies, ourselves" destroys the possibility of moral relations between us.

These days there is much analysis of "loss of moral values" in our society. A feminist moral theology enables us to recognize that a major source of rising moral insensitivity derives from being out-of-touch with our bodies. Many people live so much in their heads that they no longer feel their connectedness to other living things. It is tragic that when religious people fear the loss of moral standards, they become *more* repressive about sex and sensuality. As a result they lose moral sensitivity and do the very thing they fear—they discredit moral relations through moralism. That is why the so-called "moral" majority is so dangerous.

By contrast, a feminist moral theology, rooted in embodiment, places great emphasis on "getting clear," on centering, on finding ways to enable us to stay connected to other people and to our natural environment.[12] Unless we value and respect feeling as the source of this mediation of the world, we lose this connection. To respect feeling is not, as some have suggested, to become subjectiv*istic*. To the contrary, subjectiv*ism* is not the result of placing too much emphasis on the body and/or feeling. Subjectiv*ism* and moral*ism* derive instead from evading feeling, from not integrating feeling deeply at the bodily level. This is not to suggest, however, that feelings are an end in themselves. We should never seek feelings, least of all loving feelings. Furthermore, the command to love is not now and never was an order to *feel a certain way*. Nor does the command to love create the power to *feel* love, and it was never intended to do so. Action does that. Feelings deserve our respect for what they are. There are no "right" and "wrong" feelings. Moral quality is a property of acts, not feelings, and our feelings arise in action. The moral question is not "what do I feel?" but rather "what do I do with what I feel?" Because this is not understood, contemporary Christianity is impaled between a subjectivist and sentimental piety that results from fear of strong feeling, especially strong negative feeling, and an objectivist, wooden piety that suppresses feeling under pretentious conceptual detachment. A feminist moral theology welcomes feeling for what it is—the basic ingredient in our relational transaction with the world.

The importance of all this becomes clear when we stop to consider the relation of our acts of love to our anger. It is my thesis that we

Christians have come very close to killing love precisely because we have understood anger to be a deadly sin. Anger is not the opposite of love. It is better understood as a feeling-signal that all is not well in our relation to other persons or groups or to the world around us. Anger is a mode of connectedness to others and it is always a vivid form of caring. To put the point another way: anger is—and it always is—a sign of some resistance in ourselves to the moral quality of the social relations in which we are immersed. Extreme and intense anger signals a deep reaction to the action upon us or toward others to whom we are related.

To grasp this point—that anger signals something amiss in relationship—is a critical first step in understanding the power of anger in the work of love. Where anger rises, there the energy to act is present. In anger, one's body-self is engaged, and the signal comes that something is amiss in relation. To be sure, anger—no more than any other set of feelings—does not lead automatically to wise or humane action. (It is part of the deeper work of ethics to help us move through all our feelings to adequate strategies of moral action.) We must never lose touch with the fact that all serious human moral activity, especially action for social change, takes its bearings from the rising power of human anger. Such anger is a signal that change is called for, that transformation in relation is required.

Can anyone doubt that the avoidance of anger in popular Christian piety, reinforced by a long tradition of fear of deep feeling in our body-denying Christian tradition, is a chief reason why the church is such a conservative, stodgy institution? I suggest, however, that while many of us actually hold out little hope for the moral renewal of the Christian church in our time, we are reluctant to face the cause of moral escapism in the church—namely, the fear of feeling and, more specifically, fear of the power of anger. We need to recognize that where the evasion of feeling is widespread, anger does not go away or disappear. Rather, in interpersonal life it masks itself as boredom, ennui, low energy, or it expresses itself in passive-aggressive activity or in moralistic self-righteousness and blaming. Anger denied subverts community. Anger expressed directly is a mode of taking the other seriously, of caring. The important point is that where feeling is evaded, where anger is hidden or goes unattended, masking itself, there the power of love, the power to act, to deepen relation, atrophies and dies.

Martin Buber is right that direct hatred (and hatred is anger turned rigid, fixated, deadened) is closer to love than to the absence of feeling.[13] The group or person who confronts us in anger is demanding acknowledgment from us, asking for the recognition of their presence, their value. We have two basic options in such a situation. We can ignore, avoid, condemn, or blame. Or we can act to alter relationship toward reciprocity, beginning a real process of hearing and speaking to each other. A feminist moral theology, then, celebrates anger's rightful place within the work of love and recognizes its central place in divine and human life.

THE CENTRALITY OF RELATIONSHIP

The final and most important basepoint for a feminist moral theology is the centrality of relationship.

As a feminist moral theology celebrates the power of our human praxis as an intrinsic aspect of the work of *God's* love, as it celebrates the reality that our moral-selves are body-selves which touch and see and hear each other into life, recognizing sensuality as fundamental to the work and power of love, so above all else a feminist moral theology insists that relationality is at the heart of all things.

I am perfectly aware that our current preoccupation with "human relations," with "skills of relationship" is such that some have declared that our modern concern for relationship is merely trendy and faddish. It is true that, like everything else in late capitalism, "relationship" becomes transformed into a commodity to be packaged and exchanged at a price. To speak of the primacy of relationship in feminist experience, and to speak of a theology of relation, however, is not to buy in on the latest capitalist fad. It is, above all, to insist on the deep, total sociality of all things. All things cohere in each other. Nothing living is self-contained; if there were such a thing as an unrelated individual, none of us would know it. The ecologists have recently reminded us of what nurturers always knew—that we are part of a web of life so intricate as to be beyond our comprehension.[14] Our life is part of a vast cosmic web, and no moral theology that fails to envisage reality in this way will be able to make sense of our lives or our actions today.

In a recent, powerful, and pioneering work that lays the groundwork for a feminist theology of relationship,[15] Carter Heyward has made clear how far traditional Christian theism has wandered from the central concern with relationality that characterized the faith of the Israelite community and that was so central to Jesus' ministry. She stresses that the basic images of God that emerged in patristic Christianity were devoid of relationship. By stressing that God is "being itself" or is "the wholly other," the Christian tradition implies that a lack of relatedness in God is the source of divine strength. And this image of divine non-relatedness surely feeds images of self that lead us to value isolation and monadic autonomy. In our dominant theologies and intellectual traditions, do we not think of ourselves as most effective, most powerful as moral agents when we are most autonomous and most self-reliant, when we least need anyone else's help or support? . . .

I submit that a theological tradition that envisaged deity as autonomous and unrelated was bound over time to produce a humanism of the sort we have generated, with its vision of "Promethean man," the individual who may, if he chooses, enter into relationship. Where our image of transcendence is represented to us as unrelatedness, as freedom from reciprocity and mutuality, the experience of God as living presence grows cold and unreal. But even after such a God is long dead, the vision of the human historical agent as one who may, or may not, choose relationship lingers with us.

Such notions of love as also linger in a world like this—whether they are images of divine or of Promethean human love—are images of heroic, grand gestures of self-possessed people. It is an image of patronizing love, the love of the strong for the weak, or, conversely, the sniveling gratitude of the weak toward those stronger who grant "favors."

Never mind that none of us wants, or has ever wanted or needed, transactions with this sort of love. Never mind that we all know—unless our sense of self has already been twisted almost beyond human recognition by sadism and brutality—that the love we need and want is deeply mutual love, love that has both the quality of a gift received and the quality of a gift given. The rhythm of a real, healing, and empowering love is take and give, give and take, free of the cloying inequality of one partner active and one partner passive.

I shudder to think how many times during my years of theological study I came upon a warning from a writer of Christian ethics not to confuse real, Christian love with "mere mutuality."[16] One senses that persons who can think this way have yet to experience the power of love as the real pleasure of mutual vulnerability, the experience of truly being cared for or of actively caring for another. Mutual love, I submit, is love in its deepest radicality. It is so radical that many of us have not yet learned to bear it. To experience it, we must be open, we must be capable of giving and receiving. The tragedy is that a masculinist reified Christianity cannot help us learn to be such lovers.

To dig beneath this reified masculinist idolatry is also, I believe, to move toward a recovery of a New Testament ethos of faith. Can Jesus' active embodiment of love be illumined by this image of mutuality? I believe it can. Orthodox Christological interpretations imply that somehow the entire meaning of Jesus' life and work is to be found in his headlong race toward Golgotha, toward crucifixion—as if he sought suffering as an end in itself to complete the resolution of the divine human drama once and for all.[17] I believe that this way of viewing Jesus' work robs it of its—and his—moral radicality. Jesus was radical not in his lust for sacrifice but in his power of mutuality. Jesus' death on a cross, his sacrifice, was no abstract exercise in moral virtue. His death was the price he paid for refusing to abandon the radical activity of love—of expressing solidarity and reciprocity with the excluded ones in his community. Sacrifice, I submit, is not a central moral goal or virtue in the Christian life. Radical acts of love—expressing human

solidarity and bringing mutual relationship to life—are the central virtues of the Christian moral life. That we have turned sacrifice into a
moral virtue has deeply confused the Christian moral tradition.

Like Jesus, we are called to a radical activity of love, to a way of being
in the world that deepens relation, embodies and extends community,
passes on the gift of life. Like Jesus, we must live out this calling in a
place and time where the distortions of loveless power stand in conflict
with the power of love. We are called to confront, as Jesus did, that
which thwarts the power of human personal and communal becoming,
that which twists relationship, which denies human well-being, community, and human solidarity to so many in our world. To confront
these things, and to stay on the path of confrontation, to break through
the "lies, secrets and silences"[18] that mask the prevailing distortions and
manipulations in relationship and the power of relations is the vocation
of those who are Jesus' followers.

It is one thing to live out a commitment to mutuality and reciprocity
as the way to bear up God in the world and to be clear-eyed and realistic
about what the consequences of that radical love may be. It is quite
another to do what many Christians have done—that is, to rip the
crucifixion of Jesus out of its lived-world context in his total life and
historical project and turn sacrifice into an abstract norm for the Christian life. To be sure, Jesus was faithful unto death. He stayed with his
cause and he died for it. He *accepted* sacrifice. But his sacrifice was *for*
the cause of radical love, to make relationship and to sustain it, and,
above all, to *righting* wrong relationship, which is what we call "doing
justice."

Needless to say, in the best of times and under the most propitious
of circumstances, it is risky to live as if the commonwealth of the living
God were present—that is, to live by radical mutuality and reciprocity.
Radical love creates dangerous precedents and lofty expectations
among human beings. Those in power believe such love to be "un-
realistic" because those touched by the power of such love tend to develop a reluctance to accept anything less than mutuality and self-respect, anything less than human dignity, anything less than authentic
relatedness. It is for that reason that such persons become powerful
threats to the status quo. As women have known, but also as men like
Martin Luther King, Jr., and Archbishop Oscar Romero understood,
as any must know who dare to act deeply and forcefully out of the
power of love, radical love is a dangerous and serious business. Without
blessed persistence, without the willingness to risk, even unto death,
the power of radical love would not live on in our world. There are
no ways around crucifixions, given the power of evil in the world. But
as that poetic theologian of the gay liberation movement Sandra Brow-
ders has reminded us, the aim of love is not to perpetuate crucifixions,
but to bring an end to them in a world where they go on and on and

on! We do this through actions of mutuality and solidarity, not by aiming at an ethic of sacrifice.

Mark the point well: *We are not called to practice the virtue of sacrifice.* We are called to express, embody, share, celebrate the gift of life, and to pass it on! We are called to reach out, to deepen relationship, or to right wrong relations—those that deny, distort, or prevent human dignity from arising—as we recall each other into the power of personhood. We are called to journey this way, to stay in and with this radical power of love. When you do that for me, I am often overwhelmed by your generosity, and I may speak of the sacrifice you make for me. But we both need to be perfectly clear that you are not, thereby, practicing the virtue of sacrifice on me. You are merely passing on the power of love, gifting me as others have gifted you, into that power to *do* radical love.

CONCLUSION

There is much more to be said about the envisionment of the work of radical love within a feminist moral theology that takes its signals from what is deepest and best in women's historical struggle. Certainly, more also needs to be said about the depth of sin and evil in the world. It is important to remember that a feminist moral theology is utopian, as all good theology is, in that it *envisages* a society, a world, a cosmos, in which, as Jules Girardi puts it, there are "no excluded ones."[19] But feminist theology is also mightily realistic, in that it takes with complete seriousness the radical freedom we human beings have for doing good *or evil.* Since we acknowledge that we have, literally, the power to person-each-other into love—that is, into relationship—we can also acknowledge our power to obliterate dignity, respect, care, and concern for humanity from our world. All of that *is* within our power.

Far more than we care to remember, though, the evil that we do lives on, after us. The radicality of our vision of love gains its urgency from that very knowledge. The prophets of Israel were right to insist, long ago, that the sins of the fathers (and the mothers) live on in us, corroding and destroying the power of relation. This is why our human moral task sometimes seems overwhelming. We live in a time when massive and accumulated injustice, acted out over time, encounters answer in the rising anger of those whose dignity and life are being threatened by collective patterns of privilege that have to be undone. In a world such as this, actively pursuing the works of love will often mean doing all we can to stop the crucifixions, resisting the evil as best we can, or mitigating the suffering of those who are the victims of our humanly disordered relations. In the midst of such a world, it is still within the power of love, which is the good news of God, to keep us in the knowledge that none of us were born only to die, that we were meant to have the gift of life, to know the power of relation and to pass it on.

A chief evidence of the grace of God—which always comes to us in, with, and through each other—is this power to struggle and to experience indignation. We should not make light of our power to rage against the dying of the light. It is the root of the power of love.

NOTES

1. See *The Feminist Papers*, ed. Alice Rossi (New York: Bantam Books, 1973), 426–29.
2. Mary Daly, *Beyond God the Father* (Boston: Beacon Press, 1973), 35, passim.
3. Susanne Langer, *Mind: An Essay on Human Feeling*, vol. 1 (Baltimore, MD: Johns Hopkins University Press, 1967).
4. See "Sexism and the Language of Christian Ethics" in my *Making the Connections: Essays in Feminist Social Ethics* (Boston: Beacon Press, 1985), 22–41.
5. See Eleanor Humes Haney, "What Is Feminist Ethics: A Proposal for Continuing Discussion," *Journal of Religious Ethics* 8 (Spring 1980): 115–24.
6. Nelle Morton, "The Rising Woman Consciousness in a Male Language Structure," *Andover Newton Quarterly* 12 (March 1972): 177–90.
7. The phraseology is from the Boston Women's Health Collective, *Our Bodies, Ourselves* (New York: Simon and Schuster, 1973).
8. See James B. Nelson, *Embodiment: An Approach to Sexuality and Christian Theology* (Minneapolis, MN: Augsburg Publishing House, 1979).
9. See especially Rosemary Ruether, *New Woman/New Earth* (New York: Seabury Press, 1975).
10. See especially Tom F. Driver, *Patterns of Grace: Human Experience As Word of God* (New York: Harper & Row, 1977).
11. See Nelson, *Embodiment*, and Daniel Maguire, *The Moral Choice* (New York: Doubleday, 1978).
12. See Haney, "What is Feminist Ethics," and Anne Kent Rush, *Getting Clear: Body Work for Women* (New York: Random House, 1972).
13. Martin Buber, *I and Thou*, trans. Walter Kaufmann (New York: Scribner's, 1970), 67–68.
14. See, for example, Barry Commoner, *The Closing Circle* (New York: Knopf, 1971).
15. Carter Heyward, *The Redemption of God: A Theology of Mutual Relation* (Washington, DC: University Press of America, 1982).
16. A major source for the deprecation of mutuality in Protestant Christian ethics was Anders Nygren's study *Agape and Eros* (Philadelphia: Westminster Press, 1953). Among those who followed Nygren was Reinhold Niebuhr. See Gene Outka, *Agape: An Ethical Analysis* (New Haven, CT: Yale University Press, 1972), 7–92. An early critique of Nygren never adequately appropriated was Daniel Day Williams, *The Spirit and Forms of Love* (New York: Harper & Row, 1968). Roman Catholic writers have usually included a more positive role for mutuality in ethics than have Protestants, but the critique of sacrifice proposed here is relevant to Roman Catholic writers.
17. For an excellent critique of orthodox christologies, see Heyward, *The Redemption of God*, and Dorothee Sölle, *Christ the Representative* (Philadelphia: Fortress Press, 1967) and *Political Theology* (Philadelphia: Fortress Press, 1974).
18. Adrienne Rich, *On Lies, Secrets, and Silence* (New York: Norton, 1979).
19. Jules Girardi, "Class Struggle and the Excluded Ones," trans. and distributed by New York Circus, from *Amor Cristiano y Lucha de Classes* (Sigueme, Spain, 1975).

Women's Leadership in Haitian Vodou

KAREN McCARTHY BROWN

Vodou was born on the slave plantations of eighteenth-century Haiti. A creative blend of several distinct West African traditions with the Catholicism of the French planter class, Vodou makes its many "spirits" (each is conflated with a Catholic saint) available to the people through trance-possession. It is the leaders within Vodou who are usually "ridden" by the spirits. Women and men, priestesses and priests, lend their bodies and voices to the Vodou spirits in order that the spirits can address the problems of the people in powerful, intimate, and direct ways.

The social control of the patriarchal extended family, which re-emerged after Haiti's successful slave revolution (1791–1804), recently has been broken in urban Haiti and in the growing Haitian expatriate communities. In contrast to those in most rural areas, religious leaders in the cities and among Haitians living abroad are women as often as men. A result of the breakup of the patriarchal family has been a dramatic growth in the number of multi-generational households where women are not only the main authority figures but also the major breadwinners. My impression is (there are no census data) that almost always women of this type—those who have both freedom and responsibility in large measures—are the successful Vodou priestesses.

Furthermore, it seems appropriate to suggest that women's leadership may well have influenced the shape of contemporary Vodou. Vodou, a deeply pluralistic religion, existentially and theologically, *accepts conflict as an inevitable, in fact essential, ingredient of life*. As a result, the moral vision of Vodou does not assume a dichotomy between good and evil. Moral discernment is focused on the health and liveliness of fluid relationships, not on the essence of persons or their acts. It is fair to say that all Vodou is about healing and that all healing work is aimed at the relations between people as well as those between the "living"

Karen McCarthy Brown is a Professor in the Graduate and Theological Schools of Drew University. She began research on Vodou in Haiti in 1973 and among Haitian immigrants in New York in 1978. She has written several articles on Vodou as a resource for North American feminists and is at work on *Mama Lola: A Vodou Priestess in Brooklyn*.

and the spirits. My contention is that women, who in Haiti as in the rest of the world devote a great deal of time and energy to the maintenance of relationships, enhance these key dimensions of the Vodou worldview when they are in positions of leadership. I will focus, in this essay, on certain aspects of Vodou that mesh with the social-relational skills that have been noted in women the world over. I hope this discussion will contribute to feminist analyses of women's relationality, a trait that has sometimes been mistaken for simple-minded selflessness.

For the past ten years I have worked closely with Alourdes (I use only her first name to protect her privacy), a Vodou priestess in her mid-fifties, who was born in Haiti but came to New York twenty-five years ago. The analysis that follows is based on observation of her performance as a successful and highly respected leader of a sizable immigrant community in Brooklyn.

The Vodou spirits become available to the members of Alourdes's community through her possession-performances. However, before any question can be raised as to whether Alourdes's successful possession-performances should be counted as evidence of her leadership capacities, some consideration must be given to the complex and contradictory indigenous understandings of the Vodou community. On one level those who serve the spirits make a clear distinction between what the spirits do and what Alourdes does. Her role as *chwal*, "horse," of the spirits is officially understood as a passive one.

The initial confusion that marks the onset of trance is said to arise from the struggle between the *gro bon ani*, "guardian angel," of the *chwal* and the Vodou spirit who seeks to displace it. Loss of the guardian angel leads to loss of conscious control, so the resistance is instinctive. Initiation into the priesthood begins a long process wherein Vodou technicians of the sacred learn how to manage this perilous ego-exchange. They learn how to summon the spirits; how to enter trance, and thus surrender control to the spirits more easily; and how to prevent trance when necessary. Alourdes, who is considered quite advanced as a *manbo*, "priestess," moves readily into trance states with a short, and more or less pro forma, period of struggle. She routinely claims to remember nothing of what transpired when the spirit had control of her body. These points are further ways of reiterating the Haitian belief that the spirit and the person possessed by that spirit are two separate entities.

With this, however, as with so many things in Vodou, conflicting perspectives coexist. There are several aspects of Vodou ritual and language that would reinforce a reading of the spirits as more closely tied to the person. For example, Haitians might remark: "Have you seen Alourdes's Ogou? He is strong!" This tying of person to spirit goes even further in the belief that spirits can be inherited in a family. So when Alourdes dies and her daughter takes over, as she likely will, people may talk of "Alourdes's Ogou in Maggie's head." A similar point is made in the initiation rituals that give persons access to, and to some extent control over, their protective spirits. In these rituals, equal attention is paid to "feeding" the spirits within the person and establishing repositories for the same spirits outside the person. In other words, the spirits are simultaneously addressed as "in there" and "out there."

In the possession-performances of the spirits that occur in Alourdes's rituals, these two perspectives on the divine/human relationship coexist. In part, it is this dual perspective that lies behind my use of the term possession-performance. The term invokes a theater context in which the individual actor's interpretation of a well-known character is one of the key ingredients in artistic success. Yet I do not wish to signal that Alourdes's possessions are in any sense playacting or pretense. The trance states are genuine. What is intended by the use of theater language is a point with which all Haitians would agree: some of the vehicles of the spirits are better than others, just as some actors are better at capturing a character than others. Alourdes has a sizable and faithful following in the New York Haitian community for many reasons, and one of the leading ones is she is a good *chwal*. People feel they have encountered the spirits and have been addressed by them when "the spirits come in Alourdes's head."

The interaction of a group of persons around someone possessed by a particular Vodou spirit is difficult to describe in language dependent on the assumptions we make about the nature of leaders and followers in Western, European-based culture. Our understanding of what it means to be a strong individual hinders our ability to comprehend a ritual scene such as the one that will be described below. In order to guard against importing such assumptions into the discussion, I have chosen to work with an interactional model indigenous to Haitian Vodou culture. This model is Vodou drumming and it will provide the means to analyze the complex exchanges described below. However, before quoting the relevant passage from my field notes and comparing it with a music model, it will be necessary to say a few things about drumming.

Vodou drumming is thoroughly African in character. In fact, some researchers claim that rhythms can still be heard in Haiti that have fallen into disuse in the areas of West Africa where they originated. Because of this close relationship between Haitian and African drumming, John Miller Chernoff's fine study of the structure of African drumming[1] can be put to full use in our analysis without fearing that it imports aesthetic values foreign to the Haitian Vodou context.

Chernoff argues that the context and the content of African music are identical. In other words, the content of the music is the community that performs it. In support of this point, he quotes a Takai drummer from Ghana. Chernoff asked, "What is music?" Ibrahim Abdulai replied, "Music is something which does not conceal things about us, and so it adds to us."[2] Such a claim may also be made for Vodou ritual, and, as we will see, Vodou carries on its socially revelatory work using many of the same interactional dynamics that Chernoff finds in African drumming.

African drumming is polyrhythmic. There are always at least two rhythms and often several more. The various rhythms, each carried by a separate drum, interweave in complex ways. Evidence of this complexity is illustrated by the fact that the music of African drumming ensembles cannot be reduced to Western-style notation without assigning different meters as well as different rhythms to each of the drums in an ensemble. Polymetric drumming creates the impression of different rhythms clashing and conflicting with one another.

Furthermore no one, not even the drummers, can listen to all the rhythms simultaneously. So what is, technically speaking, a simple repetition of the same patterning of sound is actually experienced as changing because the listener's focus shifts from one rhythmic line to another. The resulting dynamic and unresolved character of African drumming leaves ears trained to Western harmony thoroughly confused. Western listeners, at least those of us who are white, become confused because we try to listen the way we listen to our own music, passively. The only way to make sense of African music is to participate in it. When Africans are asked if they understand a certain type of music, Chernoff reports "they will say yes if they know the dance that goes with it."[3]

In this context, dancing is not simply an accompaniment to music but a crucial ingredient in the process of music making. Exactly where listeners accustomed to Western harmonic structure would expect to hear the most emphasis in this music, we hear the least. What we would call the main beat is missing.[4] The main beat in African music is supplied by clapping hands and pounding feet. It may also be supplied in the mind of the listener.

We can say that the musicians play "around" the beat, or that they play on the off-beat, but actually it is precisely the ability to identify the beat that enables someone to appreciate the music. We begin to "understand" African music by being able to maintain, in our minds or our bodies, an additional rhythm to the ones we hear. Hearing another rhythm to fit alongside the rhythms of an ensemble is . . . a way of being steady within a context of multiple rhythms.[5]

This capacity to identify and maintain the integrating beat is what Chernoff, following Waterman, calls "metronome sense."[6]

With this brief review of the structure of African drumming as background, I now turn to a selection from my field journals. In this passage Ogou, the somber warrior spirit, has possessed Alourdes and is just leaving. A chair is brought as her body collapses, signaling his departure.

July 21, 1979

Before Alourdes's body has time to occupy the seat offered to her, Gède arrives. He leaps from the chair with a mischievous laugh and a murmur of recognition and pleasure goes through the room. Gède's tricksterism always lightens the atmosphere and tonight, after more than two hours of Ogou, is a special relief. Gède [spirit of death and sexuality, protector of small children and social satirist] calls for his black bowler and the dark glasses with one lens missing. Then he frolics and gambols around the room pressing his body against the bodies of various women present in his hip-grinding imitation of lovemaking. He remains a long time, passing out drinks of his pepper-laced *tafya* [raw rum] and joking with everyone. Gède is merciless with one elegantly dressed young man. After directing him to sit on the floor in front of him, Gède asks him over and over if he has a big penis. He steals the hat of another man; and when I try to take a picture, demands money. I give him some change. Later he comes back and tells me that was not enough. I give a dollar and take pictures uninterrupted. . . .

Finally, Gède leaves and the singing picks up. In only a few minutes, Ezili Dantor arrives like an explosion and we are all suddenly awake. Alourdes's ample body crashes into that of a man standing nearby. The spirit seems to spread to him by contagion and he, in turn, goes crashing into the food-laden table. Dantor's eyes dart out of her head. She utters one sound over and over: "dè-dè-dè." The pitch and rhythm change but the sound remains the same. A gold-edged, blue veil is brought and draped over her head madonna-fashion so she looks like the chromolithograph of Mater Salvatoris [the Virgin with whom Dantor is conflated]. She goes up to one man standing at the edge of the crowd. "Dè-dè-dè-dè-dè-dè," she says softly. "Yes," he replies. "I will do it for you." She drags another to the elaborate table prepared for her and points to it emphatically: "Dè-dè-dè. Dè-dè-dè. Dè-dè-dè." A woman across the room yells out to the man: "She wants a table. She wants you to give her a party." "Dè-dè-dè-dè-dè-dè," she says to me, soothing, upbeat. Her hand brushes my cheek and she passes on. She strokes the belly of a pregnant woman next: "Dè-dè-dè-dè-dè-dè-dè," she almost whispers and then roughly grabs the hair of the same woman and jerks her head back and forth: "DÈ-DÈ-DÈ-DÈ-DÈ-DÈ-DÈ." "Your head washed," someone suggests. "She wants you to get initiated," another puts in. "That's right!" says a third, and heads nod all around.

To observe Gède and Ezili Dantor with the distanced eye of scholarly objectivity as they interact with others is one thing. It is quite another to be one—filled with questions concerning life issues and surrounded by people with whom one has interacted for years—who awaits the attention of the spirits. As we saw, African drumming requires that a person supply the integrating beat that clarifies what would otherwise be a chaotic clash of rhythms. Similarly, the participant in a Vodou ritual must pour her or his own life content into the polymorphic interplay of images found there, otherwise nothing will have meaning. Because people must bring their lives into conversation with this ritualizing to make sense of it, Vodou ritual, like the music Chernoff describes, becomes "an occasion for the demonstration of character."[7]

How I handle the intrusiveness of my camera; whether I try to buy my way into the community or pay appropriately and with humor; how I receive and how I am perceived as receiving the gentle acceptance of Ezili Dantor at a time (1979) when my presence in the community was a source of some contention: all these things become occasions not simply for me to demonstrate character but also for me to learn what it means to have character in that context.

The way in which one demonstrates character in African music making is through relationships.[8] No rhythm, not even the inner one, makes any musical sense in isolation. "Meaning" in African music arises from the mutual responsiveness of different rhythmic lines. For example, the dancers respond to the drummers *and* the drummers respond to the dancers. Drummers may shift their rhythmic patterning to match a particularly gifted dancer, and then intensify it even further to urge her on to yet more energetic self-expression. The necessary involvement of all persons present and their interdependency in the process of music making provides the key to Chernoff's insight that the content of African music is the social context in which it occurs. Furthermore, Vodou rituals, like African drumming, usually occur in thickly-meshed social situations, situations where people know one another well, and this is one of the key ingredients in their functioning.

In this situation Alourdes is like the lead drummer in an ensemble. Her role is not to emphasize her own beat but to use her beat to call the others into dialogue. Like the lead drummer she is also responsible for introducing the subtle changes that realign that "conversation." The criterion used to judge the success of an African drumming performance is not the virtuosity of the drummers or their creative innovations, but rather whether the entire social event goes well.[9] Similarly, Vodou ritualizing is considered successful if everything comes together in such a way that what is going on within and among the people gathered there is expressed and clarified. This cannot be accomplished by one person alone, not even one of Alourdes's stature. That is why in the early dawn when guests leave Alourdes's home after she has staged an elaborate Vodou feast, it is not only they who thank her. She also thanks them profusely for their help in the drama.

In the specifics of Ezili Dantor's possession-performance, we see even more precise parallels between Vodou ritualizing and African drumming. It is said that Ezili Dantor had her tongue cut out as punishment for participating in the Haitian slave revolution. That is why she cannot speak. Dantor's performance, like any single rhythm in an African ensemble, is meaningless in itself. Only as the spirit interacts with the group does her "dè-dè-dè" become articulate. As we saw in the passage quoted above, Ezili Dantor supplies the emotional tone and general context of her communications through body language and by varying the pitch and rhythm of the "dè-dè." Yet, the community, individually and collectively, actually supplies the specific content. It appears that the more conflict present in the message, the more the community is galvanized into offering interpretations. Such seemed to be the case when Dantor first soothingly patted the stomach of the pregnant woman and then roughly shook her by the hair. The interpretation of this message came from several sources and, in fact, drew the tacit approval of the whole group.

Ezili Dantor is the woman-who-bears-children. Through the complex ritualizing for Dantor, the many possibilities inherent in the mother-child relationship are played out—from the mutually nourishing to the mutually destructive. This spectrum of possibilities is quickly reviewed in the reaction of Dantor to the pregnant woman. She first gives soothing approval to the life growing in the woman's womb and then aggressively reminds the woman of her responsibilities to the larger kin group, the shoring up of which can be said to be the main function of the initiation Dantor urges.

Dantor's presence in the thick social weave of a Vodou ritual calls out meaning on many different levels and in many different directions. It would be impossible to describe all the ways in which persons present at that ceremony chose to bring their own life rhythms into dialogue with the "dè-dè-dè" rhythm of the spirit. But I did note one woman who used the occasion of Ezili's interaction with the prospective mother to communicate, without words, to her own daughter that she hoped the young woman would get to work on providing her with a grandchild. Dantor's cross-rhythms, in this case played out as soothing approval (rubbing the pregnant woman's belly) and forceful discipline (grabbing her by the hair), echoed through the room creating a variety of meanings as they combined with the cross-rhythms of different life contexts. Thus the ambiguous nature of the spirits' communications deepens and enriches their potential. This works in Haitian Vodou because the moral point in serving the spirits, like the aesthetic point in drumming, is not to strive toward an ideal form exterior to the context, but to ritualize, clarify, and balance the social forces already present within it.

Ritualizing is essentially about balancing. In the Vodou context, the Creole word *balanse* refers, among other things, to a kind of ritual movement or dance. By keeping the metronome beat with her or his own body, each dancer finds "a way of being steady within a context of multiple rhythms."[10] When this is happening—literally and figuratively—throughout a group, the situation "heats up," the singing and dancing become lively, many spirits arrive and stay long, and the rituals are declared successful.

One further parallel between musical structure and worldview should be noted. The polymetric clash and conflict of rhythms has cosmological, social, and personal counterparts in the Vodou system. Chernoff notes the parallel between "multiple rhythms in music and the religious conception of multiple forces in the world."[11] This point is extended to the social and personal realms by the Vodou system for describing the conflicting forces within and among persons according to the different spirits associated with them.

In Vodou, each person is said to have one spirit who is the *mèt tet*, "master of the head." To some extent the personality of this spirit mirrors that of the individual. For example, aggressive behavior can be explained by the observation that a person serves the warrior spirit, Ogou. Thus, because people have different *mèt tet*, there are somewhat different behavioral expectations around them. This is further complicated by the fact that, in addition to the *mèt tet*, there are two, three, or four other spirits who are also said to "love" each person. The character of individuals is consolidated by balancing in the midst of the polyrhythms of the different spirits "in" and "around the head." The neophyte who enters Vodou may be told: "You cannot pray to Ogou alone. He is too hot. Light a candle for Dambala too." A good and strong person is thus one who can *balanse*, "dance," in the midst of forces pulling in opposing directions without missing the beat. The moral person is one who has a strongly developed metronome sense, that is to say, a strongly developed sense of self. Chernoff calls the polyrhythmic structure of African drumming "music-to-find-the-beat-by."[12] We might call Vodou "ritual-to-find-the-self-by." Yet individual rhythms only make sense in relationship. So, the moral wisdom of Vodou lies in teaching that it is precisely in responsive and responsible relation to others that one has the clearest and most steady sense of self. In European-based cultures we tend to oppose individual and group concerns. The two coincide in Haitian Vodou, where developing a strong sense of self does not lead to self-sufficiency but to stronger and more sustaining social bonds.

The aesthetic sense that emerges from African drumming is one that delights in the skillful interweaving of rhythms that clash and conflict. The moral sense that emerges from Vodou is one that, if it does not always delight in life's conflicts, at least accepts them as somehow deeply and inevitably true. Vodou spirits are characters defined by conflict and contradiction. For example, Gède, patron of the dead and guardian of human sexuality, wears dark glasses with one lens missing because he is said to see simultaneously into the worlds of the living and the dead. This double vision is, no doubt, also the source of his humor. To laugh is to balance, and like all balancing within Vodou, is achieved not through resolving or denying conflict, but by finding a way of staying steady in the midst of it.

In or out of trance, Alourdes enjoys and is accomplished at the organization of power, of life energy. This is the key to her leadership. Her skill as a priestess derives from a consummate sense of relationships (among people as well as between "the living" and the spirits) and of how such relationships may be clarified and subtly changed to achieve a state that is at once dynamic and balanced. But Alourdes could not have developed this talent without coming to terms with herself. From one perspective, the priestly role—the initiation rituals that prepare one for it and the daily practices required to sustain it—can be seen as an elaborate system for solidifying the self. Leaders are not essentially different from followers in Vodou, but, amid the suffering, poverty, and chaos of life in urban Haiti, or life in Brooklyn for that matter, they must have a stronger and more constant "metronome sense." Many times I have heard Alourdes say, "I got plenty confidence in myself!" Alourdes has developed this confidence through careful attention to the spirits, who are, in one sense at least, the constituent parts of herself. Having claimed the spirits through ritual and prayer, she can call them into the midst of a community where, like crystals dropped into a supersaturated solution, they cause the group to realign and coalesce.

NOTES

1. John Miller Chernoff, *African Rhythm and African Sensibility: Aesthetics and Social Action in African Musical Idiom* (Chicago: University of Chicago Press, 1979).
2. Ibid., 35.
3. Ibid., 23.
4. Ibid., 47.
5. Ibid., 48–49.
6. Ibid. Richard Alan Waterman introduced the term "metronome sense" in "African Influence on the Music of the Americas," in *Acculturation in the Americas*, ed. Sol Tax. Proceedings and Selected Papers of the 29th International Congress of Americanists, vol. 2 (Chicago: University of Chicago Press, 1952).
7. Chernoff, *African Rhythm*, 151.
8. Cf. ibid., 126.
9. Ibid., 65.
10. Ibid., 49 and also p. 229 of this essay.
11. Chernoff, *African Rhythm*, 156.
12. Ibid., 50.

On Mirrors, Mists, and Murmurs

Toward an Asian American Thealogy

RITA NAKASHIMA BROCK

The *Kami no michi*, the way of the spirits, called Shinto in Japan, tells this story of Amaterasu, the Sun Goddess. Amaterasu's brother, Susanowo, the god of oceans and the underworld, is unhappy because, despite his attempts to overthrow his sister's life-giving, shining power, he is still a lesser god and he has been banned from the land of his dead mother. In a rage, he defiles Amaterasu's sacred Weaving Hall of Heaven by scattering his own feces in it and by destroying her sacred irrigation ditches. Amaterasu murmurs *kotodama*—spirit-empowered, generous words of good intention—that reinterpret the evil acts, giving Susanowo the benefit of the doubt. Her kindness does not halt his destructive acts. He skins a colt backwards and tosses it into the Weaving Hall, killing several sacred weavers. Amaterasu flees to her heavenly cave and bolts the door. The mists of night, winter, and sleep fall over the land as its Sun Goddess remains in silent, angry retreat.

Amaterasu's retreat is a disaster to the land, for it brings perpetual winter. Crowing cocks and entreaties from the heavenly deities fail to bring her out. The gods punish Susanowo by banning him from their community. They hang a mirror in the tree at the entrance to the cave. Nearby the goddess Amenouzume prepares for the shamanistic spirit trance that generates a raucous and bawdy celebration, a party oddly out of place in the sleepy winter. Amaterasu is puzzled by the noise. Curious, she emerges. As she stands fascinated by her own image in the mirror, the gods rope off the return route to her cave.

The mirror is one of the most sacred symbols in Shinto. Legendary beautiful mirrors, noted for their valuable decoration and the accuracy of their images, have been cherished legacies passed from mother to daughter for generations. A good mirror tells us the truth about our-

Rita Nakashima Brock is Director of Women's Studies at Stephen's College in Columbia, Missouri, and president of the Disciples Peace Fellowship. She is the author of *Journeys By Heart: A Christology of Erotic Power*, which was recently published by Crossroad.

selves and through its illuminating power gives us wisdom, the wisdom that comes with self-awareness and knowledge. Without a true mirror, we cannot know ourselves. And without mirrors we remain in caves of silence.[1]

The history of Asian American women in this country is a forced retreat into caves of silence. Asian American women, trained in seminaries, have fled the halls of theological academe where the activities of men have left only broken mirrors for Asian American women's identity. Naomi Southard and I have described the lack of a theological home for Asian American women.[2] Because we have largely lived our seminary experiences alone, we have struggled privately with our alienation, speaking generously of what we have learned and murmuring quietly, mostly to ourselves, about the absence of any theological mirrors that reflect ourselves back to us. We act on our theological concerns, but we continue to be alienated from writing about our thealogy. We are often lone women ministers in our churches and communities—sometimes the only Asian American. In the midst of marginalization, loneliness, and fragmentation, we have been struggling to live our thealogical concerns for justice, wholemaking relationships, suffering, healing, and peace and to integrate conflicting and often fragmented worlds of experience.* Our thealogical work is inaccessible to our sisters who need it and unavailable for educating others. The noise of various established theologies has been unable to lure us into visibility and speech.[3]

In our first meeting in 1978, forty Asian American women in ministry shared our previously unspoken and often lonely searches for thealogies that connect to our personal experiences, thealogies that would reflect our lives and enliven our ministries.[4] The first words we spoke startled and surprised us—we had been silenced so long. We search for clearer images as we seek to create a community of Asian American women that might become our truest mirror, even as we are scattered like solitary jewels across the miles that separate us. To emerge from our caves of silence will require that we find mirrors in a community that exists only sporadically. As a member of that group of women, I too have not found the theologies I was taught in seminary and graduate school satisfying, for each blurs me behind mists of race, sex, language, and culture. And so I continue to struggle with the task of hearing into speech the thealogy of Asian American women.[5]

As Naomi Southard and I have written, Asian American women seek "an inclusive, pluralistic monotheism, with room for a diversity of ways to speak about the sacred dimension of life . . . [and] a theological openness that allows us to reclaim those aspects of Asian culture that re-

*Theology describes the intellectual traditions of men who have reflected on their beliefs about divine reality. I use the word thealogy to describe the work of women reflecting on their experiences of and beliefs about divine reality.

connect us to the presence of the sacred in Asian religions."[6] In this essay, I shall be articulating what I think are important concerns of Asian American women's thealogy. I speak of a thealogical perspective that rises out of the mists of racism and sexism, embracing and affirming both the power of context and particularity—mirrors of identity—and our spiritual hunger for principles of connection and community—murmurs of speech.

My thoughts emerge from concerns I hold in common with many Asian American women and from my own life experiences and thealogical searching. I come from Japan, one of the cultures influenced by the Confucianism and Buddhism of China and India, but a culture also distinctly its own. I am also biracial, Japanese on my mother's side, in country of origin and mother tongue, and Puerto Rican on my genetic father's side. My mother married a white American soldier, like tens of thousands of Japanese women under the U.S. occupation, and we emigrated from Okinawa when I was six. I am what Japanese Americans call Issei and Happa, a Japanese-born U.S. citizen who is half non-Japanese. I do not seek to speak for all Asian American women, but only to begin to speak into the silence so that our many voices might begin to be heard.

A THEALOGY OF SUFFERING, COMMUNITY, AND HEALING

With my sisters, I seek mirrors for the creation of a thealogy that would empower our struggles with racism, sexism, economic exploitation, and narrow nationalism. In the search to create a thealogy that affirms our lives, we seek divine images and a spiritual depth that connect us to all our worlds—in their cultural and political complexity—in which we live and move and have our being. We seek a thealogy that binds our worlds in a life-giving wisdom. In that binding, we seek to integrate our concerns for *suffering, community, and healing*.[7]

Suffering in our thealogy is not the martyrdom of traditional Christian theology in which one more powerful or worthy than others takes on their suffering paternalistically, or in which we masochistically endure suffering for the improvement of our soul and character—the self-denying faith of orthodox dependence on god. These interpretations of suffering have been rightly rejected by feminists.

We must seek to embrace and acknowledge our own suffering and the suffering of all creation to bring healing to our broken world. This solidarity with a suffering world is not paternalistic rescue work. Our responsibility rests not in assuming others' suffering, but in acknowledging where we can change our own lives to cause less suffering and in offering what we can in solidarity with others for their own healing and liberation. We must learn to listen to, hold, and support others for their empowerment and ours.

This embrace of suffering comes through the concrete awareness of our own personal pain. The anger and grief revealed through that awareness lead us to heal our own woundedness in relationships of support with others. Without embracing suffering there is neither love and intimacy nor wisdom and compassion. With grief and healing come our ability to hear another's pain and to stand in solidarity with all who suffer. For at the deepest levels of our suffering, we encounter our profoundest connections to others as we come to know our relationships both hurt us and heal us. In this revelation we embrace fully the meaning of incarnation, the incarnation of both the divine spirit and the lives of others in our very being.

Asian American women often express this embrace of suffering in images of the cross, not as the symbol of a substitutionary death or self-sacrifice, but as the image of solidarity, of how God suffers with us and of what it means to suffer with another. While our language about the cross and liberation sounds Western, our words are spoken with a different undercurrent. To understand the Asian American approach to suffering, we need to shift our perspective from Western Christian to Mahayana Buddhist. This shift reveals the distinctive Asian American theological contribution to the meaning of suffering.

Buddhists assert that we must embrace suffering compassionately—to experience and acknowledge it—before it can be healed. To heal suffering, we must be willing to suffer. The Buddhist Joanna Macy, in *Despair and Personal Power in the Nuclear Age*, speaks of feeling our own despair and fear as the key to loving, to hoping, and to acting. But this ability runs against the dominant American preoccupation with success in which all pain is viewed as dysfunctional. "We lack the mirrors that tell us the truth about our lives.... A sanguine confidence in the future has been a hallmark of the American character and a source of national pride," and the admission that we know fear and pain "can appear to be a failure of maintaining stamina and even competence."[8]

To allow ourselves to suffer means risking feeling stupid, guilty, unpatriotic, doubtful, powerless, panicky, too emotional, or a failure. We can be accused of provoking disaster or causing others distress, but to deny our own suffering and the suffering of others leads us, according to Macy, to live an alienated double life haunted by self-doubt, to hedonistic or compulsive displacement activity, to passivity, to the psychological projection of our pain, to destructive behaviors, to burnout, to intellectual apathy, and to the inability to receive painful information. We choose these options instead of pain, "often immobilized by the fear of moving through that pain." But to be healed we must be willing to suffer.

No one is exempt from [pain for the world], any more than one could exist alone and self-existent in empty space.... It is inseparable from the currents of matter, energy and information that flow through us and sustain us as interconnected open systems.[9]

The Buddhist seeks to embrace the suffering of our whole aching and groaning cosmos. Denial of suffering severs life-giving connections to others and denies our experiences of the interdependence of all existence. And, as Macy asserts, our sense of radical interdependence is crucial to our survival as a species.

What is it [that] allows us to feel pain for our world? And what do we discover as we move through it? . . . It is interconnectedness with life and all other beings. It is the living web out of which our individual, separate existences have risen, and in which we are interwoven. Our lives extend beyond our skins, in radical interdependence with the rest of the world.[10]

Buddhists have tended to focus on intense inner self-awareness as the key to ethical behavior and to set compassion and wisdom in the larger aesthetic context of harmony and beauty, the beauty of the cosmos. I believe this Buddhist undercurrent in Asian American thought has much to offer Western Christianity, which has tended to split its concerns for the therapeutic, aesthetic, and ethical into competing spheres and disciplines.

In pointing to Buddhist undercurrents in the thealogical concerns of Asian American women, I am aware that Buddhism too is embedded in patriarchal cultures and carries its own misogyny. Buddhists are weak in their analyses of the political and social issues that lie between the intrapersonal and cosmic spheres. The Buddhist lack of social analysis renders talk of community vague or authoritarian. Buddhists often do not articulate differences between suffering that is caused and preventable, such as woman or child abuse or poverty, and suffering that is a part of the ebb and flow of life, such as death.[11] Lack of social analysis casts Buddhist language about suffering in a fatalistic mode, exemplified in Asian America by the Japanese concept of *shi kata ganai*—it can't be helped—a phrase murmured in the face of injustice and oppression.

Deficiencies in Buddhist and Christian analyses of the human condition intersect in their tendency to ignore or disparage feelings. Human passions—intimacy, anger, affection, and emotional pain—are not integrated into their analyses. Instead, they are usually rejected with the body as lower than mind and will. This lack is the point at which feminism, especially in its union of social, political, and psychological theories and its attention to passion and the body, is strong in its analysis.

Feminists address the question of the middle, interpersonal ground that Buddhism ignores. They have convincingly argued that patriarchy at its core is based on repression, oppression, and institutionalized violence.[12] Their work demonstrates how social, political, and economic factors in patriarchy affect intrapsychic processes and oppress us all. Alice Miller, for example, argues that the production of oppression and violence is grounded in social forces and relationships that hurt us and teach us to repress and project our feelings, especially pain, reproducing violence on a massive social scale. Repression becomes oppression.[13]

The embrace of our own pain cannot happen through vicarious identification with others' oppression or suffering—a strong emphasis in traditional Christology which allows us to project our suffering onto others and to take up everyone else's causes. Barbara Deming and Audre Lorde,[14] in exploring the roots of their own passions through love and anger, conclude that feeling anger for injustice directed against others—what Deming calls "anger by analogy," or identifying with the anger of another—is not enough. Such self-righteous anger can itself be a block to the empowering reality of our own pain. In our pain is the power of self-knowledge that brings us to a healing wisdom and compassion. We will not be made whole and healed until the truth of our lives can be seen and told. Asian American women have begun to understand this in our own journeys of speaking bitterness, of telling our own pain in a community of sisters who hear our gentle murmurs of loneliness and suffering and mirror ourselves back to us. We understand this mirroring as a way to embracing all suffering. The capacity to suffer with the world leads us to a sense of the community of all creation. However, in acknowledging suffering, I prefer to make the focus not so much a cross-centered suffering, but a community-centered one, the global community of all creation.

Asian American women hold the ties of community, no matter how frayed, as sacred. We have a greater global consciousness than many other Americans because we live with the reality that we are interconnected to many and often far-flung worlds. Sometimes this awareness is forced on us by a racist society, but it offers a strength, for we see the wider connections that affect our lives and we know we must overcome the narrow nationalisms that destroy our interconnections. Asian American women have spoken of this sense of community with profound insight.

Every cell in my body speaks to the ancients. I can understand in my body all the movements of faith that have been from the beginning.... We are all connected and feel the impact, literally and figuratively, of what happens on the other side of the globe.[15]

In creating a way toward an Asian American thealogy that affirms global community, I search all the places I feel rooted for my connections. I do not screen my sources for ideological purity, discriminating between Christian or pagan, Western or Eastern. I am not alone in this approach. In our interviews with Asian American women, Naomi Southard and I found that many spoke of their private searches for spiritual resources in Asian religions. They often spoke hesitantly, as if treading on forbidden ground, but they found there inner spiritual resources for strength and integrity. Some of us use the shamanistic resources of Asian religions, with their often women-centered activity and spiritual depth as resources for self and spiritual understanding.

Robert Ellwood argues that the shift from an earlier egalitarian, shamanistic religion with a horizontal cosmology to a male-dominant, priest-centered religion with a vertical cosmology characterizes the rise of patriarchy in Japan.[16] Ellwood argues what many Asian American women have intuitively felt: that the ancient shamanistic roots of our spirituality affirm our experience of incarnation. Shaman women felt internally the presence of spirits which guided their wisdom and spoke intimately through them. The move to male-dominance involves ascending and descending gods, mostly male, who visit priests in revelatory dreams and speak to, not through, them. The intimacies of spirit and flesh, wisdom and feeling, person and nature, are lost.

Shamanism provides a corrective to theologies that envision God as remote, apathetic, punitive, or alienated. Indigenous Asian spirituality is a thealogy of the incarnate spirit and not a theology of the transcendent father.

In my quest for a healing incarnate spirit, I find the ties that inspire and strengthen my connection to others not in universal abstractions and doctrines, but in attending to my love for the particular, ambivalent, and diverse worlds in which I live and move and have my being. The physical embodiment of spirit is crucial to understanding spirituality. The natural world is the root of our lives: the rivers, seas, trees, flowers, birds, animals, the very earth itself in its exuberant and sometimes terrifying power, the human body in all its sensuality, tactile pleasure, and joy. The earth is the conduit through which we are touched by the spirit.

Shamanistic healing trances reveal the spirit through the integration of feeling, thinking, and sensuality.[17] Trance allows us to touch the deepest parts of ourselves inaccessible to us when we focus on the cognitive aspects of doctrine and belief. In these deepest parts of ourselves we find the transformative, empowering, enlivening, and wholemaking spirit that connects us to all creation. Nelle Morton describes a similar healing trance state. She has a waking vision of the Goddess and her long dead mother who says healing and empowering words to her. Her visions dissolve into her and leave her feeling whole. To explore these deepest parts of ourselves involves surrendering control and giving ourselves to a process without a definable end or final goal. As in Morton's description of the journey of a metaphor, the ending cannot be determined in advance.[18]

Loss of control and an exploration of our deepest selves involve intense pain and facing our own capacity for destruction and hate as well as discovery of seeds of love and connection. If Asian American women are to explore the cultural resources of Asian spirituality, we must avoid creating a romanticized and nostalgic Asian spirituality. I would caution us, as we search for shaman rituals, to be aware that these ancient traditions have been transmitted and transmuted in patriarchal cultures. Crucial to our quest is a hermeneutics of suspicion about the patriarchal silencing of the authentic voices of our foresisters behind subtle and not so subtle misogyny and gynephobia.

This patriarchal mask is evident in the Amaterasu legends that contain an apologetic for imposing a feudal imperial line upon an indigenous shamaness and a spirit worshiping people.[19] What may have been an original celebration of the winter solstice has been turned into a political grab for power. The legend justifies the Goddess's absence from the male-dominated imperial palace. The sun's self-imposed rest is transmuted into silence in the face of male aggression, a response expected of docile Asian women. We must rethink our reactions of silence and retreat from the inhospitable world of theology. We must empower each other to speak our own spiritual words.

If we continue, as our mothers have done, to murmur *kotodama*, words of gentleness and generosity that speak from our hearts of the healing we seek, we must also speak bitterness. For only in the full self-knowledge of pain and the sharing of that pain with others will we be able to seek, with compassion, healing for the community of all creation.

The murmurs of our mothers have sustained us and brought us to the point where we can seek mirrors that do not distort or idealize the truth about our own pain and joy. In the layers of oppression and love we find in each of our worlds, there are no clear and easy enemies, no sides divinely ordained. In seeking to heal our own lives and the community of all creation, we bring only the resiliency of persistence, honesty, generosity, and hope.

NOTES

1. For different versions of the Amaterasu legend, see Donald L. Phillipi's *Kojiki* (Princeton, NJ: Princeton University Press, 1969) and Merlin Stone's *Ancient Mirrors of Womanhood: Our Goddess and Heroine Heritage*, vol. 2 (New York: Sybylline Books, 1979). The folk importance of mirrors is described in Juliet Piggott's *Japanese Mythology* (New York: Hamlyn Publishing Group, 1969), 46.
2. See Rita Nakashima Brock and Naomi Southard, "The Other Half of the Basket: Asian American Women and the Search for a Theological Home," *Journal of Feminist Studies in Religion* 3 (Fall 1987): 135–50.

   Asian American refers to women born both overseas and in the U.S. who see their lives based in the U.S. Because of this commitment, they have reflected on the U.S. experience, particularly as it relates to their Asian historical, social, and cultural heritage.
3. "The Other Half of the Basket" (see n. 2 above) contains interviews with Asian

American women about their dissatisfaction with the theologies we were taught in seminary.

4. This meeting was sponsored by the Pacific and Asian Center for Theology and Strategies (PACTS) in Berkeley, CA.
5. "Hearing into speech" is a phrase coined by Nelle Morton in her essay "The Rising Woman Consciousness in a Male Language Structure," in *The Journey Is Home* (Boston: Beacon Press, 1985), 11–30.
6. Brock and Southard, "The Other Half of the Basket," 149–50.
7. See Brock and Southard, "The Other Half of the Basket," for a discussion of these three main themes.
8. Joanna Macy, *Despair and Personal Power in the Nuclear Age* (New Haven, CT: New Society Publishers, 1983), 8. Macy is an American who has become a Buddhist. She therefore represents someone, like Asian American women, who has brought together in herself two cultures and value systems.
9. Ibid., 4.
10. Ibid., 24.
11. See Nelson Foster, "To Enter the Marketplace" and Gary Snyder, "Buddhism and the Possibilities of a Planetary Culture" in *The Path of Compassion: Contemporary Writings on Engaged Buddhism*, ed. Fred Eppsteiner and Denis Maloney (Buffalo, NY: White Pine Press, 1985).
12. See Nancy Chodorow, *The Reproduction of Mothering: Psychoanalysis and the Sociology of Gender* (Berkeley and Los Angeles: University of California Press, 1978); Susan Griffin, *Pornography and Silence: Culture's Revenge Against Nature* (New York: Harper & Row, 1981); Haunani-Kay Trask, *Eros and Power: The Promise of Feminist Theory* (Philadelphia: University of Pennsylvania Press, 1986); Catherine Keller, *From a Broken Web: Separation, Sexism, and Self* (Boston: Beacon Press, 1986); Gerda Lerner, *The Creation of Patriarchy*, vol. 1 (New York: Oxford University Press, 1986); Audre Lorde, *Sister Outsider* (Trumansberg, NY: The Crossing Press, 1984); Betty Reardon, *Sexism and the War System* (New York: Teachers College Press, 1985); Rosemary Radford Ruether, *Sexism and God-Talk: Toward a Feminist Theology* (Boston: Beacon Press, 1983); and Anne Wilson Schaef, *Women's Reality: An Emerging Female System in the White Male Society* (Minneapolis: Winston Press, 1981).
13. Alice Miller, *The Drama of the Gifted Child: How Narcissistic Parents Form and Deform the Emotional Lives of Their Talented Children* (New York: Basic Books, 1981), ix. See also Miller's *For Your Good: Hidden Cruelty in Childrearing and the Roots of Violence* (New York: Farrar Straus Giroux, 1984) and *Thou Shalt Not Be Aware: Society's Betrayal of the Child* (New York: Farrar Straus Giroux, 1984).
14. See Audre Lorde, *Sister Outsider*, and Barbara Deming, "On Anger," in *We Are All Part of One Another: A Barbara Deming Reader*, ed. Jane Meyerding (New Haven: New Society Publishers, 1984).
15. Brock and Southard, "The Other Half of the Basket," 140.
16. Robert Ellwood, "Patriarchal Revolution in Ancient Japan," *Journal of Feminist Studies in Religion* 2 (Fall 1986): 23–28.
17. Ibid. See also the discussion of healing trance in Marjorie Shostak's *Nisa: The Life and Words of a !Kung Woman* (New York: Vintage Books, 1983).
18. Morton, *The Journey Is Home*, 147–75 (her vision) and 210–21 (her discussion of metaphor).
19. See Ellwood, "Patriarchal Revolution."

Archetypal Theory and the Separation of Mind and Body

Reason Enough to Turn to Freud?

NAOMI R. GOLDENBERG

Belief in transcendent entities may well encourage the devaluation of physical life. In this paper, I look at the Jungian archetype as an example of an abstraction that is imagined as directing thought and behavior. I hope my critique of the archetype will be applicable to other theories that are based on similar disembodied constructs. The post-Freudian perspective I discuss here is important because it may offer a viable corrective to abstract theological systems. For me, then, this paper is an initial step toward a larger project and not just another critique of Jungian theory. . . .[1]

FORMS AND ARCHETYPES: IMMATERIAL FORCES OF THE WORLD BEYOND

The ancestors of the Jungian archetypes, the Platonic forms, were said to be transcendent entities that were reflected in the physical world, but were most definitely not *of* the physical world. . . . Whenever Plato discusses this "highest and most important class of existents," he stresses their vast superiority to anything that exists in this world. According to Plato, physical things partake of beauty and order only insofar as they imitate the unseen nature of forms. With good training, he thought, one could teach a soul to comprehend the forms. . . . In contrast to the perfect forms that can be known by the soul, in Platonic thought the body is a flawed, impermanent thing that does not warrant much attention. "I spend all my time," says Socrates, "going about trying to persuade you, young and old, to make your first and chief concern not for your bodies nor for your possessions, but for the highest welfare of your souls."[2] The two-fold task of the philosopher was

---

Naomi R. Goldenberg is Associate Professor of Religious Studies and Women's Studies at the University of Ottawa. Author of *Changing of the Gods* and *The End of God*, she is at work on a book titled *Returning Words to Flesh—Feminism, Psychoanalysis, and the Resurrection of the Body*.

seen as knowing the world of timeless perfection beyond body and all physical reality and then helping others to gain access to this glorious sphere.

Likewise, in Jungian theory, the task of the psychologist is defined as leading others to see the timeless archetypal reality behind their personal psychological experiences. Jung credits Plato with discovering the reality behind what we usually perceive.

In the products of fantasy the primordial images are made visible, and it is here that the concept of the archetype finds its specific application. I do not claim to have been the first to point out this fact. The honour belongs to Plato. . . . If I have any share in these discoveries, it consists in my having shown that archetypes are not disseminated only by tradition, language, and migration, but that they can rearise spontaneously, at any time, at any place, without any outside influence. . . .

The far-reaching implications of this statement must not be overlooked. For it means that there are present in every psyche forms which are unconscious but nonetheless active—living dispositions, *ideas in the Platonic sense*, that preform and continually influence our thoughts and feelings and actions.[3]

Jungian archetypes, like Platonic forms, influence the physical world but are not of the physical world. They are understood as transcending material reality. Jung stressed this transcendence in his last major statement on archetypes in *On the Nature of the Psyche*, written in 1954. In this essay, Jung speculates that perhaps "psyche and matter are two different aspects of the same thing." If this is so, he reasons, then archetypes "as such" must lie beyond psyche. He coins the term *psychoid* to name this locale beyond both body and soul.

The archetypal representations (images and ideas) mediated to us by the unconscious should not be confused with the archetype as such. They are very varied structures which all point back to one essentially "irrepresentable" basic form. . . . It seems to me probable that the real nature of the archetype is not capable of being made conscious, that it is transcendent, on which account I call it psychoid.

Those "irrepresentable" archetypes, Jung insists, "describe a field that exhibits none of the peculiarities of the physiological." "Their chiefest effect," he explains, lies in "spirit."[4]

Throughout *On the Nature of the Psyche*, which lays down the metaphysics of archetypal theory, Jung continually compares the archetype to more scientific-sounding concepts. He tells us that the archetype is "analogous to the position of physiological instinct" and states that when "psychology assumes the existence of certain irrepresentable psychoid factors, it is doing the same thing in principle as physics does when the physicist constructs an atomic model." The practice of using scientific analogies to explain archetypes is common in Jung's earlier writings as well. Sometimes he associated archetypes with instincts, presenting the "hypothesis that the archetypes are the unconscious images of the instincts themselves . . . that they are patterns of instinctual behavior." At other times he used metaphors from chemistry or physics, such as the comparison of an archetype "to an axial system of a crystal, which, as it were, preforms the crystalline structure in the mother liquid."[5] These scientific comparisons are often cited by Jungians concerned with popularizing archetypal theory.

It is important not to be misled by the frequent use of scientific analogies to explain the notion of archetypes. Science proceeds from the assumption that the composition of matter and energy can be known by means of careful observation and precise measurement. Jungian psychology starts from the premise that the physical universe is controlled by unseen, irrepresentable, and ultimately unknowable forces that are transcendent to the world itself. Although Jung sometimes refers to archetypes as within the stuff of matter, he quickly returns to the idea of the "content" of the archetype as something separate from people and physicality; archetypes are thus far removed from the sphere of science. . . .

THE CASE AGAINST SPLITTING MIND FROM BODY

Separating the "mind" or "soul" from the body is certainly a well-established practice in Western thought in general and in Western religious philosophy in particular. Whichever way the dichotomy is worded, body comes out as the thing valued less, while the mind or soul is seen as more permanent, more noble, and closer to the sphere of divinity.

It makes little difference whether the contrast is drawn between body and mind or body and soul. The important point is that one thing— mind or soul—is seen as qualitatively different from physical existence—as *separable* from the physical world and definitely superior to it. Although formulations of the soul/body or mind/body dichotomy can vary widely among philosophers, all will agree that one entity exists in some sense apart from the other, is better or higher than the other, and is meant to prescribe, to rule, or govern the other. Indeed, there are many ways of naming the higher parts: Plato generally employed the term *forms*. Jung used the word *archetypes*. Religions use the word *God* in singular or plural form. In each case the better thing is seen as more or less disembodied. Although minds, souls, forms, archetypes, and gods are all conceived of as interacting with the physical world in various ways and to various degrees, they are all said to be things apart, things that exist independently of this or that merely physical representation. The better thing is always thought to be closer to "mind," while the worse thing is seen as nearer to "body."

Debate about the mind/body split has proceeded for centuries among philosophers and religious theorists. It has only been in the last few decades, however, that the rather abstract discussion about mind and body has taken a practical, pragmatic turn. Thinkers other than professional philosophers and theologians have developed important critiques of mind/body dualism. These critiques insist that thinking in terms of the separateness of mind and body has serious effects—effects that constrict freedom in human life and that are perhaps destructive to all life on the planet. . . .

It is the recent work of ecologists and feminists that has questioned the separation of mind and body with an urgency that is new to the philosophical discussion. Ecologists have suggested that our environment is suffering from the notion that body (in this case, the body of the earth) is not of central importance. These people argue that the portion of the Western philosophical tradition that deprecates physical existence is in part responsible for the physical abuse that we have heaped on our planet and its plants and animals.[6] Thus, the age-old separation of mind and body may have abetted the inflicting of real damage on the earth.

Feminists have pointed to another kind of damage which is done by separation of mind and body—i.e., damage to women. Several feminist writers have argued that the oppression of women is linked to the identification of women with bodily nature.[7] It has even been suggested that the equation of women with "mother" nature herself reveals that the misuse of the environment and the oppression of women have much in common.[8] The existing body of feminist theory is so rich and varied and has raised so many issues around the consequences to women of the mind/body split that it argues powerfully for all future feminist theory to be firmly grounded in an understanding of the body's role in cognition.

Simone de Beauvoir was the first to draw the attention of feminists to the injustice of equating women with body and nature.

But to say that Woman is Flesh, to say that Flesh is Night and Death, or that it is the splendor of the Cosmos, is to abandon terrestrial truth and soar into an empty sky. For man also is flesh for woman; and woman is not merely a carnal object; and the flesh is clothed in special significance for each person and in each experience. And likewise it is quite true that woman—like man— is a being rooted in nature; her animality is more manifest; but in her as in him the given traits are taken on through the fact of existence, she belongs also to the human realm. To assimilate her to Nature is simply to act from prejudice.[9]

Woman, argues de Beauvoir, came to represent body both because her "animality is more manifest" and because her sociopolitical situation led her "to stress the importance of animal nature." But both sexes, she insists, must recognize and cope with the problematic reality of bodily existence. . . .

In order to begin to accept our physicality, we must search for theories that explain both why we associate corporeality with women and why we flee our bodies in the first place. We must look for the causes behind the equation of woman and body which de Beauvoir first described. Dorothy Dinnerstein attempts to find those causes in her book *The Mermaid and the Minotaur: Sexual Arrangements and Human Malaise.* Dinnerstein urges us to "look hard at what is very hard to look at." This is "the precise feature of childhood whose existence makes the adult situation de Beauvoir describes inevitable, and the consequent necessity for female abdication of unilateral rule over childhood, which she stopped short of facing."[10]

Dinnerstein argues that our sense of the transience of the human body is complicated by our memories of women as the first caretakers of our bodies. "The relation between our sexual arrangements and our unresolved carnal ambivalence," she explains, "begins with this fact: when the child first discovers the mystical joys and the humiliating constraints of carnality, it makes this discovery in contact with a woman. The mix of feelings toward the body that forms at this early stage, under female auspices, merges with our later acquired knowledge of the body's transience." It is because of the fact that women mother, Dinnerstein believes, that we come to equate women with body and mortality. Our hatred of the body is expressed in our hatred of women. In fact, it is the oppression of women that permits us to make women the scapegoats of our fear of aging and mortality. As long as we hate women we will fail to come to terms with our bodies and with mortality. We will continue "the self-contemptuous human impulse toward worship of dead automatic things and disrespect for what lives."[11]

Dinnerstein's answer to the problem of the human flight from carnality is to end the female monopoly on early childcare. If men too cared for infants, it would become impossible to see them as creatures beyond the concerns of human flesh. Women would no longer be scapegoats responsible for fleshly failings. Everyone would thus be forced to come to terms with her or his own mortality.

An end to female-dominated childcare is also a solution proposed by Nancy Chodorow in *The Reproduction of Mothering.*[12] Chodorow does not explicitly address the problem of identifying women with body, but rather seeks to explain why women become exclusively responsible for mothering. She concludes that women reproduce mothering to regain the physical and emotional intimacy that they enjoyed with their mothers and that they, unlike men, cannot get from heterosexual relationships. Chodorow's work implies that if men too cared for babies, intense physical intimacy would cease to be an experience that both sexes could only achieve with women. Her argument points to the same conclusion as Dinnerstein's—namely, that women will cease to be disproportionately associated with body only when childcare is in the hands of both sexes. Thus Dinnerstein and Chodorow present us with a solution from the viewpoint of psychology to the problem of equating women and body. Future work in psychology and the social sciences will reveal whether their ideas suggest societal directions that can lead to greater acceptance of both women and body.

Grounding our philosophical, psychological, and sociopolitical theory in a firm awareness of physicality will amount to a major change in the orientation of much of Western thought. Adrienne Rich has given us a vision of that change in *Of Woman Born*. Rich calls on feminists to build theories that "touch the unity and resonance of our physicality, our bond with the natural order, the corporeal ground of our intelligence." She urges us to transform "thinking itself" in order to transform contemporary culture, which, she says, "has . . . split itself off from life, becoming the death-culture of quantification."[13]

Adrienne Rich asks us to learn to "think through the body."[14] I endorse her plea. As feminist theory sets about constructing new systems of thought, let us make sure that those systems are life-enhancing. Let us not cling to disembodied ways of thinking that lead us to disparage women in particular and physical life in general. We need to show how the much-disparaged bodies of both women and men give rise to all so-called higher intellectual activity. We need to inspire thought that supports physical life by understanding in detail how physical life gives birth to thought.

I suggest that feminist theory radically depart from the Jungian archetype, from the Platonic form, from all systems of thought that posit transcendent, superhuman deities. We should study these outworn theories as history and not use them as models for present efforts at envisioning new ways of thought. I suggest that we seek our inspiration from theories and disciplines that see the body as the nexus of all human experience.

FREUDIAN AND POST-FREUDIAN PSYCHOANALYTIC THEORY: DIRECTIONS FROM THE BODY

Some useful directions for building feminist theories that "think through the body" might well come from a domain that is midway between art and science, i.e., from psychoanalysis, specifically Freudian and post-Freudian traditions. Psychoanalysis has produced an extensive body of theory based on the idea that human beings are essentially physical creatures whose mental and emotional experience is derived wholly from bodily life. Thus, analytic theory should be a natural ally in feminist efforts to explore the "corporeal ground of our intelligence." Unfortunately, this is not the case. The sexism in psychoanalytic theory has caused feminists to reject Freudian and post-Freudian thought almost completely. . . .

Although I support feminist criticism of psychoanalysis (and even plan to contribute to it myself), I maintain that there are other things we should be doing with Freudian and post-Freudian thought in addition to criticizing it. We should, I think, be using psychoanalytic theory to give us insight into the physical nature of human thought. We should, in short, be using psychoanalysis to think through the body. . . .

I was first struck by the degree to which Freud understood physical and mental processes as being continuous when I read the following statement: "The ultimate ground of all intellectual inhibitions and all inhibitions of work seems to be the inhibition of masturbation in childhood."[15] On the surface this is a rather astonishing statement (which might well stick in one's mind the next time a writer's block strikes). Actually the idea makes perfect sense if it is understood as part of the analytic view that the free flow of thought depends on the elimination of repressions. If there are significant areas of the imagination that are blocked from ever approaching consciousness, thought and action will be paralyzed. Since analysis considers early masturbation fantasies as being especially powerful in establishing the patterns of imagination, inhibitions arising in this area are seen as having long-range effects on all of mental life. The statement that masturbation and creative thought are intimately linked is an example of the way in which analysis recognizes that the contents of our minds are continuous with everything that has happened, is happening, and wants to happen in our bodies.

Freud is often reproached for seeing all psychical phenomena as derived from sex. It would be more accurate to say that Freud saw all psychical phenomena as derived from the body. In his final formulation of the principles of psychoanalysis, *An Outline of Psychoanalysis*, Freud defined "sexual life" as "the function of obtaining pleasure from zones of the body."[16] Freud arrived at defining sexuality as the pursuit of pleasure through all zones and organs of the body. He saw genital sexuality as only a part of the entire physical experience of the individual. Further, he understood that genital sexuality derived from earlier physical experiences involving nutrition, excretion, muscular excitation, and sensory activity. Reproaching Freud for his emphasis on sexuality is, in fact, reproaching him for his emphasis on physicality.

For Freud, genital experience is always metaphoric because it echoes the early intense experiences of infancy and early childhood. In fact, for Freud, all experience is metaphoric because all experience echoes feelings and perceptions that were experienced physically in the deep past. I suppose that in this sense Freudian theory is reductive—in the Latin usage of *reducere*—because it does lead us back, back to childhood, back to infancy, back to states of feeling that are structuring our being but that have slipped from conscious memory. I do not agree with those who find that this direction of Freudian theory diminishes human life. Instead, I feel that looking back in this way deepens experience and grounds it realistically in the physical being and personal history of an individual life.

Freudian theory links mind to body with the concept of the instincts. "We assume," Freud wrote, "that the forces which drive the mental apparatus into activity are produced in the bodily organs as an expression of the major somatic needs. . . . We give these bodily needs, in so far as they represent an instigation to mental activity, the name of 'Triebe'." The *Triebe*, or "drives," come to us in James Strachey's English translation of Freud as "instincts." The question of how to translate the term—whether as "drives" or as "instincts"—is rather unimportant. It is important to understand that by *triebe*, Freud meant to identify the essential determinants of human life as physical forces. Even though Freud saw the instincts as "mythical entities which were magnificent in their indefiniteness," he was always certain that they expressed physical needs and longings. He hoped that one day the theory of instincts would be based on a more precise "organic substructure."[17] As the instinct theory was improved upon, Freud envisioned it becoming even more precise about the physical mechanisms behind human thought.

It is worth stressing the degree to which thought is seen as arising from body in Freudian theory. Psychoanalysis views all of our thinking as motivated by instincts. "The whole flux of our mental life," said Freud, "and everything that finds expression in our thoughts are derivations and representatives of the multifarious instincts that are innate in our physical constitution." "An instinct," he insisted, "cannot otherwise be represented than by an idea."[18] Therefore, in Freudian thought, all of our notions, all of our images, all of our fantasies, and all of our ideals have their sources in our bodies. Our mental and physical lives are of one piece—just as a plant is continuous with both its foliage and its roots. . . .

As a specific example of how the psychoanalytic approach points theory in a physical direction, I turn to an essay by the British psychoanalyst D. W. Winnicott. The essay, "Mind and Its Relation to the Psyche-Soma," is particularly interesting to me because in it, Winnicott discusses how bodily experience may itself give rise to a feeling of estrangement between mind and body.

In his discussion of the mind-body split, Winnicott presents the clearest definition of psyche I have ever encountered. His concept of the psyche can clarify just what it is we are studying when we study imagery—whether in myth, art, dream, or reverie. Winnicott defines psyche as *"the imaginative elaboration of somatic parts, feelings, and functions."*[19] This definition captures what I have always felt as valuable about the concept of psyche and illuminates the vague insights about psyche in the works of Jung and some post-Jungians. Note that Winnicott's idea of the psyche includes no notions of transcendent, out-of-body forces influencing human imagination. Instead, in his definition he gives us an understanding of the sense of depth we convey when we use the word *soul* or *psyche*. When we say a person has soul, we are referring to someone who feels her or his physical and emotional being very deeply—who is connected to her or his particular physical and emotional fate profoundly and who somehow conveys that connection. . . .

After defining psyche as "the imaginative elaboration of somatic parts, feelings and functions," Winnicott uses this definition to discuss the origin of the idea of mind. He does not "think that the mind really exists as an entity,"[20] but that it develops differently in each person as a special function of the "psyche-soma." For optimum development of the psyche-soma, he thinks, a perfect environment is necessary. At the beginning of an infant's life, this need is absolute. However, in the normal development of an infant the environment will, of course, fail to be perfect. This is when the mind develops.

Winnicott believes that mental functioning begins as a compensation for environmental failure. Through cognitive understanding and mental control, the infant transforms the imperfect environment into the perfect one. Mind thus has its origins in the attempt to gain control of the environment.

In the healthy individual, the development of mind proceeds gradually. If the environment is not too unreliable, mind will be felt to be not too distinct from body. However, if the infant's environment is unpredictable, or if the care that the child receives is erratic, then mind will develop as a thing in itself which is felt as very much outside the problematic body and the physical environment. The most common way for this distancing to be imaged, Winnicott believes, is the false localization of the mind in the head.

When I read this theory, three ideas came to my mind. First, if Winnicott is right that the localization of the mind in the head is an attempt to dissociate oneself from a problematic psyche-soma, then theories of transcendent entities located outside and above the mind itself may be efforts to take this dissociation even further. Theories of forms and transcendent archetypes might be symptomatic of the tendency to escape from the psyche-soma and to imagine a degree of outside control.

Second, perhaps we should look more closely at the early lives of philosophers who have developed theories that are very much one-sided in their emphasis on the powers of mind and entities beyond. Carl Jung, for example, tells us that at night he feared his mother, who he felt became "strange and mysterious."[21] He thus hints that he experienced erratic mothering, which may partially be responsible for his lifelong effort to build a philosophical system in which destiny is governed by archetypes and not by people.

Third, perhaps Winnicott has indicated why it is that anti-body philosophies are so often also antiwoman. If he is right that an intense opposition between mind and body develops when the early environment of an infant fails, then it would be most likely that, in deep memory, a woman is held responsible, since women have been the most important factors in the environment of most babies. Thus, in cases in which the mind develops as an enemy to the early environment, it might be developing as an enemy to women. This phenomenon could be what is expressed in anti-body philosophy, which is invariably also misogynist.[22]

The hypothesis that the mind forms in opposition to the environment could be used to strengthen feminist arguments that women ought not to be the only people responsible for early childcare. If men shared the care of infants, women would no longer be seen as the only sex to represent body. Nor would women be the only sex that mind would tend to reject.

Winnicott does, I think, give us a useful theory about the context in which mental phenomena might develop and about how that development might be forming and deforming our philosophies. He points out that the separation of mind from body is an experiential matter. Although mind is essentially a bodily experience, we all feel "it" in some degree as something separate from our bodies. No philosophy can really change the experiential illusion that mind and body are separate. What can change, however, is our adherence to theories that are based on the illusion of mind/body dualism—theories that disparage bodily life and that keep us from understanding the bodily origin of thought.

Another psychoanalytic idea which is valuable in helping us to understand why we disparage the body is Melanie Klein's theory about the linking of guilt and sexuality.

Klein addresses a question that we should all be asking ourselves whenever we discuss guilt and sexuality: *Why* is it that sexual acts and thoughts are surrounded with so much guilt? Is it simply because conventional religions and conventional mores have taught that sex is a low and guilt-ridden thing? Or is the relationship between sex and guilt more complex? Do the religious restrictions around sex hide something more frightening than forbidden bodily pleasures?

Klein suggests that the guilt and shame around sexuality are cloaks for another emotion—anger—specifically, anger against parents. To arrive at this hypothesis, she applied to her work with children Freud's idea that guilt stems from a suppression of the aggressive instincts. She observed that a child's early sexual fantasies about masturbation are connected in varying degrees with sadistic wishes directed toward the parents. The wishes often involve angry attacks on the parents by means of the child's body and bodily functions. Klein concluded "that it is the sense of guilt arising from destructive impulses directed against its parents which makes masturbation and sexual behavior in general something wicked and forbidden to the child, and that this guilt is therefore due to the child's destructive instincts."[23]

In psychoanalytic theory, as goes the child, so goes the adult. If Klein is right about the relationship between sexual guilt and anger in the child, then the same relationship would apply to adults as well. We should thus seek the deep origin of feelings of shame, guilt, and contempt for bodies in feelings of anger. . . .

Perhaps the linking of sex and anger is also what lies in the imagination of the multitudes of philosophers and theologians who have written about sexuality with such distaste. It is, perhaps, not sex per se that is shunned, but rather the troublesome angry feelings connected with sex. Klein might very well have hit upon rage as the key motive behind the disparagement of sexuality in Western philosophical and religious thought.

These examples of psychoanalytic ideas about the body and sexuality illustrate the insight that analysis can give about the influence of physicality on cognition and imagination. I think we need such insight to build theories that give realistic support for human life. We have lived through at least 2,500 years of theory based on illusions of transcendent entities controlling our destinies. Whether they are called Platonic forms, Jungian archetypes, or religious deities, theories based on their existence have colluded with devaluation of physical life and of the physical environment. In order to stop disparaging the body, we might well have to give up all forms of theism and take our inspiration from ideas that see human beings as nothing more (or less) than human. We might well have to learn from theories that teach, as Rich has said, that "all our high-toned questions breed in a lively animal."[24]

NOTES

1. See Naomi R. Goldenberg, "Archetypal Theory After Jung," in *Spring 1975* (Zurich: Spring Publications, 1975), 199–220; "A Feminist Critique of Jung," *Signs* 2 (Winter 1976): 443–49; "Feminism and Jungian Theory," *Anima* 3 (Spring 1977): 14–17; *Changing of the Gods: Feminism and the End of Traditional Religions* (Boston: Beacon Press, 1979), 54–64.
2. Plato, *Apology* (trans. Hugh Tredennick), 30a–b, in Hamilton and Cairns, *Dialogues of Plato*, 16. Cited by Elizabeth V. Spelman, in "Woman as Body: Ancient and Contemporary Views," *Feminist Studies* 8 (Spring 1982): 111.
3. C. G. Jung, *The Collected Works of C. G. Jung*, ed. William G. McGuire et al., trans. R. F. C. Hull, Bollingen Series XX (Princeton, NJ: Princeton University Press, 1954–), 9, I: pars. 153–54.
4. Ibid., 8: pars. 418, 417, 420.
5. Ibid., pars. 420, 417, 91, 155.
6. See, for example, Lynne White, "The Religious Roots of Our Ecological Crisis," *Science* 155 (1967): 1203–7. Also, Elizabeth Dodson Gray, *Why the Green Nigger?* (Wellesley, MA: Roundtable Press, 1979).
7. Spelman, "Woman as Body," 109–131.
8. See Susan Griffin, *Women and Nature* (New York: Harper & Row, 1978).

9. Simone de Beauvoir, *The Second Sex*, trans. and ed. H. M. Parshley (New York: Knopf, 1952), 239.
10. Dorothy Dinnerstein, *The Mermaid and the Minotaur: Sexual Arrangements and Human Malaise* (New York: Harper & Row, 1976), 162.
11. Ibid., 130, 218.
12. Nancy Chodorow, *The Reproduction of Mothering* (Berkeley and Los Angeles: University of California Press, 1978).
13. Adrienne Rich, *Of Woman Born* (New York: Bantam Books, 1976) 21, 292.
14. Ibid., 290.
15. Sigmund Freud, *The Standard Edition of the Complete Psychological Works of Sigmund Freud*, ed. James Strachey (London: Hogarth Press, 1953–74), 23:300.
16. Ibid., 23:152.
17. Ibid., 20:200; 22:95; 14:78.
18. Ibid., 22:221; 14:177.
19. D. W. Winnicott, "Mind and its Relation to the Psyche-Soma," *Through Paediatrics to Psycho-Analysis* (London: Hogarth Press and the Institute of Psycho-Analysis, 1978), 254.
20. Ibid., 243.
21. C. G. Jung, *Memories, Dreams, Reflections* (New York: Random House, 1961), 18.
22. Spelman, "Woman as Body," 109–131.
23. Melanie Klein, *The Psycho-Analysis of Children* (New York: Dell Publishing Co., 1975), 171.
24. Adrienne Rich, from "Two Songs," as quoted in Spelman, "Woman as Body," 109.

Feminism and the Ethic of Inseparability

CATHERINE KELLER

She say, my first step from the old white man was trees. Then air. Then birds. Then other people. But one day when I was sitting quiet and feeling like a motherless child, which I was, it come to me: that feeling of being part of everything, not separate at all. I knew that if I cut a tree, my arm would bleed.

—ALICE WALKER

GITTING MAN OFF YOUR EYEBALL

When Shug experiences this epiphany of interconnection, she is female, black, and poor, living in a small town in the deep South between the wars. In other words, she dwells in the margins of the triply disestablished. No wonder her revelation comes as an ultimate answer to the "old white man," the establishment God—or, conversely, the establishment as God. She does not flee from her marginality into traditional spirituality, but rather discovers through a kind of *via negativa* by which she steps free of the ultimate image of oppression, a radical vision. "Being part of everything" evokes an anti-establishment metaphysic, divinely charged and ripe with ethical implications.

And yet this epiphany must give a feminist pause. No matter how well-credentialed by oppression, no matter how beautifully conjured by the black feminism moving Alice Walker's pen—a doubt arises. How can a feeling of being "not separate at all" do a woman any favors? Doesn't freedom demand separation and independence? Such inseparability blurs the boundaries between self and world, subject and object, spinning the universe into a web of relations. Does it not then threaten the self of woman so tenuously getting loose of the grip of defining and confining relations—above all to the traditional patrilineal family? Has not woman through great travail only begun to achieve a sense of distinct, focused, and intentional subjectivity? In other words, don't we as women need to move toward separateness

Catherine Keller, author of *From a Broken Web: Separation, Sexism, and Self*, teaches constructive theology in the Graduate and Theological Schools of Drew University. She is currently writing a book of feminist eschatology as part of a larger systematic project.

(which need not entail separatism) rather than toward this mystical state of pan-participation? Aren't women already all *too* empathetic—why should we now bleed with the *trees*?

Well, Shug might reply, it's not that we *should*: we already do; we are part of everything whether we realize it or not. So it might provide more power and indeed more self to feel *with* and *into* this reality of interconnection, rather than to flap about in the illusion of separateness, feeling "motherless." Separateness, her vision implies, characterizes the transcendent modality of the "old white man." Thus freedom requires iconoclasm, negation: "You have to git man off your eyeball, before you can see anything a'tall."[1] It is a matter of seeing things as they are: and the interdependence of all things summarizes the content, form, and force of the vision.

Let us then in response turn to the work of a pioneering feminist who pumped her lifeblood into the empowerment of an *independent* self for women. The Simone de Beauvoir of *The Second Sex*, which inaugurated the second wave of the woman's movement, would want nothing to do with such inseparability. We will examine certain fundamental presuppositions supporting her argument for woman's authenticity as a subject *over against* the object, the other, the world. This will focus our doubt (though this doubt may have intrinsically to do with the peculiarity of woman's oppression within a white bourgeois context). But if de Beauvoir's approach—taken as prototypical—itself arouses doubts, we will suggest in conclusion a strategy for considering Shug's epiphany in terms explicitly related to woman's experience. We will draw upon an example of contemporary theory that may corroborate the intuition of interconnection for precisely feminist purposes.

HOSTILE SUBJECTS, INESSENTIAL OBJECTS

Posing her famous question "What is woman?" de Beauvoir formulated what has remained perhaps the most incisive statement of the relationship between man and woman within patriarchal culture: "She is defined and differentiated with reference to man and not he with reference to her; she is the incidental, the inessential as opposed to the essential. He is the Subject, he is the Absolute—she is the Other."[2] Woman as the Other—de Beauvoir's brilliant deployment of Sartrian-Hegelian terms echoes throughout the work of women in religion.[3] It is the classic anti-Freudian declaration that anatomy is not only *not* destiny; gender difference is merely biological to whatever extent it is not culturally created. And the culture expresses the aims of the dominant male Absolute. She calls her perspective that of "existential ethics."

Because of the exclusive claim of the male upon normative subjectivity, he "represents both the positive and the neutral, as is indicated by the common use of man to designate human beings in general;

whereas woman represents only the negative, defined by limiting criteria, without reciprocity."[4]

Religion has been crucial in the maintenance of male absoluteness: "the males could not enjoy this privilege fully unless they believed it to be founded on the absolute and the eternal."[5] De Beauvoir traces the derivative status of woman as Other through its bountiful history in myth, psychoanalysis, economics, and literature, seeking to understand how it is that half the human race could seem to acquiesce in its own alterity—its identity as Other: "Why is it that women do not dispute male sovereignty? No subject will readily volunteer to become the Object, the inessential; it is not the Other, who in defining himself as the Other, establishes the One. The Other is posed as such by the One in defining himself as the One."[6] She will answer the question of woman's acceptance of her own otherness in terms both of man's coercion and woman's complicity. This arrangement suited not only men's economic aims but their "ontological and moral pretensions as well";[7] and at the same time a good many women could enjoy the derivative privileges of their class while being spared the existential burdens of "transcendence," of becoming an authentic, self-responsible subject. De Beauvoir's account of this elusive interplay of coercion and complicity relies upon two arguments: 1) women have always been subordinated to men and so lack, unlike other objectified groups, even the memory of a subjective existence, for they lack a historical religion or culture of their own; 2) every human consciousness is constantly tempted to retreat into its own subjectivity—i.e., into "immanence." De Beauvoir means by immanence the Sartrian sense of a fundamental stagnation, "the brutish life of subjection to given conditions," all that resists the "transcendence" of freely-chosen projects expanding "into an indefinitely open future."[8] But a problem with her fundamental approach disturbs both arguments, I believe.

She claims that "Otherness is a fundamental category of human thought."[9] Perhaps one cannot dispute this axiom without forfeiting any self, surrendering to a spiritual or a material monism in which there is no individuality at all. Rather than question that a relation of self to other "is as primordial as consciousness itself," I would draw attention to the particular sort of relation of Self and Other and hence the kind of consciousness her analysis presumes. For she draws the relation on the model of oppositions like right-left, good-evil, day-night. At least one culture-critic suggests that whenever "oppositionalism" appears we must be on the lookout for a particular kind of subject: the heroic ego, "who divides so he can conquer."[10] And the mythos of the hero as free-wandering warrior has provided the most pervasive or the most patriarchal of our culture-patterns. The heroic ego is not accidentally imaged as "he."

In fact we find the warrior-hero's metaphysically outfitted (and outmoded) descendant, the Hegelian absolute Ego, at work in de Beauvoir's own argument. The telling problem does not lie so much with de Beauvoir's own thinking as with what it presupposes. Recall that by catching such presuppositions at work we rehearse our ability to recognize their persistence in our own perspectives.

Duality is here the privileged form of plurality, for only the confrontation of the Hegelian subject with an object which it negates brings the subject into being at all; she explicitly follows Hegel (via Lévi-Strauss) in this analysis of all culture as a dialectic of symmetrical opposition: "We find in consciousness itself a fundamental hostility toward every other consciousness; as the subject can be posed only in being opposed—he sets himself up as the essential as opposed to the other, the inessential, the object."[11]

Ironically *The Second Sex*, which could be described as a single protest against the Freudian essentialism (that "anatomy is destiny"), lets echo in its very foundations another Freudian axiom: that of the "primary mutual hostility of human beings."[12]

Of course Freud did not invent the idea of an essential enmity, primal aggression, at the root of human relations. But even granted that such "a fundamental hostility" characterizes the psychological metaphysic of male sovereignty, does it disclose the essence of any human subject whatsoever? Or does de Beauvoir here succumb to an unnecessary generalization? In our dialogue with de Beauvoir, we must now ask: what price are we to pay as women if we "authentically assume" *this* subjective attitude? To what extent is culture's "inside man" authoring this authenticity? What are the consequences for the relation of self to other, for relatedness, including its most theological and cosmological limits?

COMPLICITY AND IMMANENCE

Above all, this subjective style would require us to forfeit any identity based on immanence, in favor of "transcendence," of the creative liberty whereby we become more than the natural, the given, the mechanical. As an act of the subject positing itself as One over against the Other, transcendence moves outward, forward, upward and can scarcely find itself in the circumscribed feminine spaces of house, garden, embrace.

The ideal relation between subjects is what de Beauvoir terms "reciprocity," in which selves are not vying to dominate one another but rather recognize one another as transcendences, face to face. However, in the field of consciousness generated by the supposedly inevitable hostility, can reciprocity finally mean more than an anxious peace treaty based on common projects? To be sure, such reciprocity would offer an immeasurable improvement over the continuing attempt to abort transcendence in self and other, to dominate or to submit. De Beauvoir demonstrates patriarchy's own refusal of freedom, and does not display its culture as facilitating even for males the expression of the transcendence she advocates; *au contraire*: "He would be liberated himself in their liberation. But this is precisely what he dreads. And so he obstinately persists in the mystifications intended to keep woman in her chains."[13]

As patriarchy learns at least in such statements to abort male transcendence as well, it is never for her a matter of simply achieving for women what men already have; of dressing women in masculine egos and three-piece suits (a contemporary Athena's armor). But at a deeper level do we discern after all a certain philosophical complicity—not to be reduced to a relationship to Sartre!—at work in her categories, a complicity between de Beauvoir and an ethic grounded in the culture of male dominance?

The presupposition of the unmitigated self-assertion of the transcendent subject shows its true colors in her historical account of the origins of culture. The critical balance of male coercion and female complicity has persisted in history so effectively, according to her analysis, because she believes male supremacy to have no beginning: "Slave or idol, it was never she who chose her lot."[14] It is true that little trustworthy work, anthropological or archaeological, had been accomplished suggesting any pre-patriarchal stages of culture: Lévi-Strauss's analysis of the universality of patriarchy was understandably more persuasive to her than Bachofen's speculations. I would here argue not so much with her choice of historical theory as with the assumptions that come to light in her evaluative descriptions of that history. The following account is telling. She discusses woman's role in the early agricultural communities to which patriarchal-patrilineal structures can only be attributed by inference:

In no domain whatever did she create: she maintained the life of the tribe by giving it children and bread, nothing more. She remained doomed to immanence, incarnating only the static aspect of society, closed in upon itself. Whereas man went on monopolizing the functions which threw open that society toward nature and toward the rest of humanity. The only employments worthy of him were war, hunting, and fishing; he made conquest of foreign booty and bestowed it on the tribe; war, hunting and fishing represented an expansion of existence, its projection toward the world. The male remained alone the incarnation of transcendence.[15]

According to this chain of thought, the labors that produce and nurture life, agriculture and child-rearing, count as "immanence"; whereas those privileged vocations of slaughter, either of humans or animals, count as "transcendence." Contrary to the previous passage, a patriarchal pastoral stimulates transcendence in men. Does "world-openness" mean warfare? The spear rises in this analysis as the symbol of tran-

scendence, and makes manifest the phallic-aggressive energy of the outward bound, projectile subject in its "fundamental hostility." Especially
disturbing is its ability to determine the thought of a most radical and
pioneering feminist!

We may acknowledge the strain of picturing any culture in which
"woman's work," especially mothering, does not circle aimlessly within
the confines of life-maintenance. But the question of the very relation
of self to other, to nature and to its world is at stake here. De Beauvoir
effectively exposes the use of the institution of motherhood as the privileged means for at once subjugating and valuing the privileged object
through which he subdues Nature. The dream of a rejuvenating, virgin, delightful nature joins the extremes of cultural artifice, out of
which "the feminine" is wrought. Thus the patriarch must dissociate
the "dreaded essence of the mother" from the woman he possesses.
For the mother holds for him the terror of an uncontrollable Mother
Nature along with its promises of security and refreshment: "Man is
on the defensive against woman in so far as she represents the vague
source of the world and obscure organic development."[16]

What is de Beauvoir's own attitude toward this "nature" men find
so threatening and yet so seductive, to be controlled through the subjugation of women? In her discussion of "Early Tillers of the Soil," she
speculates that history might have taken a different turn at the vital
juncture between the worship of the Great Mother (whom de Beauvoir
considers an idol, yet one that granted women at least the dignity of
idols) and the law-encoded patriarchy:

Perhaps, if productive work had remained within her strength, woman would
have accomplished with man the conquest of nature; the human species would
have made its stand against the gods through both males and females; but
woman was unable to avail herself of the promised benefits of the tool.[17]

By "tool" de Beauvoir means a technology based on "weapon," for she
attributes the invention of agricultural tools, which did not "conquer"
nature, to women. De Beauvoir simply does not question the absolute
right of the Absolute Ego to conquer and subdue the earth—she dis-
putes only the bad faith of its projection, its injustices, its denials of
finitude. "Nature" remains for her a means to human ends, "immanence" resisting "transcendence," cosmos devoid of the authenticity of
anthropos.

In this context her atheological commitment collaborates with the
existentialist alienation from the natural universe. She laments the failure of woman to divest herself of an identity invested in nature and
religion. The divine and the natural are both together to be van-
quished, drained of the projections of human subjectivity that keep
humans in bondage. The divine in her thought must stand over against
the human, as must the natural: both are inhuman objects *par excellence*,

awesomely Other than human, rendered alien in the course of human exploits of transcendence. As the embodiment of the zone between nature and spirit, subject and object, woman ever after "enables her group, separated from the cosmos and the gods, to remain in communication with them."

There can be no doubt that woman has been trapped, trivialized, and exploited in these margins of heaven and earth. Woman projected as Madonna mediates between the divine and the human; as Whore she seduces the human toward the animal. Woman has been rendered multilaterally marginal. In a certain sense, Shug's experience as socially marginal person confirms de Beauvoir's thesis. Shug blurs the boundaries between the natural, the divine, and the human in her normative epiphany. Yet where de Beauvoir might spy the effects of oppression, Shug locates the source of liberation.

Could it be, we must now ask, that the transcendent subject, in as much as it constitutes itself by a "fundamental hostility" toward the other, whether human, cosmic, or divine, is none other than the perennial "male ego," a cultural construct dependent on the nurture, flattery, and suspension of disbelief offered by its feminine counterpart? If so, the attempt to achieve the ethos of such a subject—requiring as it does the maintenance of the female Other—is doomed to failure from the outset. For its mode of consciousness might represent not human reciprocity but only the project of an essentially patriarchal self disguised as the normatively human. Yet de Beauvoir's analysis of the metaphysical conditions of subjectivity *within* the cultural status quo, which in its broadest self-definition means simply patriarchy, remains unsurpassed. Is there some way to receive back into a newly empowered sense of self certain of those values she discards as "immanent," without diluting the strength of freedom, individuality, and transcendence she has inspired within the feminist trajectory?

NOT SEPARATE AT ALL

Let us turn to the experience that inaugurated this discussion: to Shug's "feeling of being part of everything, not separate at all." As there is a profound problem with the sort of feminist position that stands against such inseparability, we may pursue Shug's sense of things with less anxiety. To support the intuition with a more systematic rationality, we could choose a method somewhat parallel to de Beauvoir's. That is, in the way that she uses existentialism as the basis for her ethic of transcendence, we could evoke that philosophical system that best elaborates the intuition of interconnection: the process, or process-relational metaphysic classically developed by Whitehead. In this organicist vision, the interrelatedness of every being to every other emerges— yet in conjunction with a doctrine of *mutual transcendence*. All beings take account of each other, take part in each other, literally internalizing one another, however unconsciously, as each others' very stuff. They then fashion their individuality out of this immanence of inflowing matter (the other, the world) in a momentary act of self-creation not unlike the existentialist transcendence. The ethic that emerges from this nondualistic account of subject-object relations approximates the sentiment that Shug summarizes as "if I cut a tree, my arm would bleed."[18]

Does any other method suggest itself, however, than such an immediate turn for legitimation to the male philosopher? Can we tread a path better coordinated with the feminist insistence upon woman's experience of herself as the basis for reflection and action? Indeed we need only look to the work of certain women in psychological theory to find both corroboration of Shug's intuition and an important explanation for the association of patriarchy with the separate self. Gilligan's *In a Different Voice*[19] proves especially valuable for the task of considering a specifically female structure of self as the basis for an alternative ethic.[20]

Gilligan found that women and men in fact understand and make moral decisions differently. The three studies that provided the data for her claim enable her to challenge normative theories of development and ethical maturation, especially Erikson's and Kohlberg's, and in the background, Freud's. In these maturity is identified with separation, independence, and autonomy; and women invariably seem to count as derivative or underdeveloped—if they are counted at all. While for women, she claims, "the moral problem arises from conflicting responsibilities" within an inclusive "network of relations," it is for men more a matter of "competing rights" requiring a hierarchical ordering of claims for its resolution.[21] Gilligan derives the difference between the two moralities from a radical difference in personality development between genders. Thus "the morality of rights differs from the morality of responsibility in its emphasis on *separation* rather than *connection*, in its consideration of the *individual* rather than the *relationship* as primary."[22]

The typically male sense of morality as Gilligan describes it presupposes a universe of aggressive others who must be kept in line, ordered, controlled. Through her critique of Freud, she illumines a crucial bond between the psychology of separateness and the primacy of aggression: the "primary separation" of infant-ego from object, "arising from disappointment and fueled by rage, creates a self whose relations with others or 'objects' must then be protected by rules, a morality that contains this explosive potential and adjusts 'the mutual relationships of human beings in the family, the state and the society.' "[23] De Beauvoir—naturally enough—presupposed precisely this sort of self, concocted of aggression and separation: the "fundamental hostility" of the subject as the very energy of transcendence. But Gilligan offers evidence that such a description at most fits the personality profile of typical males by demonstrating that women consistently describe *themselves* differently.

Thus in all of the women's descriptions, identity is defined in a context of relationship and judged by a standard of responsibility and care. Similarly, morality is seen by these women as arising from the experience of connection and conceived as a problem of inclusion rather than one of balancing claims.[24]

If de Beauvoir's acceptance of male preconceptions concerning the normative autonomy of a mature self has become more transparent, it is not surprising to find a sentiment echoing Shug's imagery voiced by one of the women interviewed in Gilligan's study:

You have to love someone else, because while you may not like them, you are inseparable from them. . . . *They are part of you*; that other person is part of that giant collection of people that you are connected to.[25]

This loving, derived from the intuition of interconnection, is vulnerable to criticisms of solipsism, narcissism, and stagnation if it collapses into sheer immanence. De Beauvoir's voice must not fade. Yet such loving need not eliminate transcendence and individuality. Taking part in each other presupposes and creates differentiated selves in which to take part! Then the ethic implied by the ecological—and almost animistic—sense that I harm myself by harming another, even nonhuman, creature embodies the ethic of loving-others-as-I-love-myself. But it corrects Christian anthropocentrism, while eliminating also the antinatural and antitheistic animus of de Beauvoir's ethic.

Gilligan's theory contributes to a growing commitment in feminism to tap the special strength of women's history trapped and hidden beneath the facades of femininity, rather than to flee to prevailing androcentric norms of subjectivity and ethics—norms that men themselves may begin to abandon. Of course any affirmation of gender "difference" raises the spectre of biologism, essentialism, and the stereotype. Yet the dangers of succumbing to apparently "human" and actually patriarchal values and ontologies is every bit as dire. As Gilligan says elsewhere, criticizing whatever tendency we may have today to consider gender a difference that makes no difference in any but the most limited biological sense, "femininity may contain values and ways of seeing whose release would benefit all." "Connection," as a value arising from a recent and rich variety of feminist perspectives offers a critical, perhaps the most important, key to such a release.[26] It may just happen to be a spacious, wildly diverse, and differentiated world of interwoven entities that comes into focus—when you "git man off your eyeball."

NOTES

1. Alice Walker, *The Color Purple* (New York: Harcourt Brace Jovanovich, 1982), 168.
2. Simone de Beauvoir, *The Second Sex*, trans. H. M. Parshley (New York: Vintage Books, Random House, 1974; original, 1949), xix.
3. For example, Mary Daly's first book, *The Church and the Second Sex* (New York: Harper & Row, 1975), is a straightforward application of de Beauvoir's notion of woman as "Other" to Roman Catholic treatment of women; Rosemary Ruether's influential work, *New Woman/New Earth* (New York: Seabury Press, 1975), also uses de Beauvoir's thesis as its starting point.
4. De Beauvoir, *The Second Sex*, xviii.
5. Ibid., xxv.
6. Ibid., xxi.
7. Ibid., 157.
8. Ibid., xxxiii.
9. Ibid., xix.
10. James Hillman, *The Drain and the Underworld* (New York: Harper Colophon, 1979), 82.
11. De Beauvoir, *The Second Sex*, xx.
12. Sigmund Freud, *Civilization and Its Discontents*, trans. James Strachey (New York: Norton, 1961), 59.
13. De Beauvoir, *The Second Sex*, 80.
14. Ibid., 89.
15. Ibid., 83.
16. Ibid., 170.
17. Ibid., 87.
18. Walker, *The Color Purple*, 167.
19. Carol Gilligan, *In a Different Voice: Psychological Theory and Women's Development* (Cambridge, MA: Harvard University Press, 1982).
20. Nancy Chodorow, who especially in *The Reproduction of Mothering* (Berkeley and Los Angeles: University of California Press, 1978) reaches similar conclusions by way of a more rigorous sociological and psychoanalytic argument, provides Gilligan her starting point. Dorothy Dinnerstein, Jean Baker Miller, and Ann Wilson Schaef are psychologists who propound related theses.
21. Gilligan, *In a Different Voice*, 19, 33.
22. Ibid., 19. My emphasis.
23. Ibid., 46.
24. Ibid., 160.
25. Ibid. Her emphasis.
26. For instance, Nancy Chodorow analyzes the gender-difference in a way that frees it of any biological or archetypal determinism, while Stephanie Demetrakopoulos, in *Listening to Our Bodies: The Rebirth of Feminine Wisdom* (Boston: Beacon Press, 1983), partially in response to Chodorow, would want to affirm some sort of innate, body-linked tendency. And the proliferating metaphor of web, of weaving, arising in the poetics of woman's vision (notably in Mary Daly and Adrienne Rich) depicts the dynamism of a collective female insight into a universe of interknit subjectivities.

Part 4

TRANSFORMING THE WORLD

Transforming the World

While the feminist activities of claiming history, naming the sacred, and defining the self are implicitly directed toward social change, the essays in this section focus more explicitly on transforming the world. The first three parts of this book make it clear that feminists envision a world of connection and relationship (not dualism, division, hierarchy), a world in which pluralism and diversity (not monolithic unity) are celebrated as contributing to the richness of the whole. There has been a consistent focus on the connection of humanity and nature and on the presence of the divine in nature, and on a positive valuing of the body. In this final section, these themes are developed with regard to the questions of racism, sexual orientation, violence against women, the ecological and nuclear crises, and the creation of community. The issues discussed here are suggestive, certainly not exhaustive, of the changes feminists seek.

Drawing on the practices of her Cherokee ancestors and non-Western meditation techniques, Dhyani Ywahoo discusses inner attitudes that can help foster deep commitment to working for nonviolent social change. She urges us to awaken the "caretaker mind," to practice "great generosity," and to remember that we all are connected in the "Sacred Hoop." The threat of destruction has come about, Ywahoo writes, because people have forgotten that everything is connected. "The big company that takes things out of the Earth, and poisons the ground . . . does so without even considering the effect on themselves." The practice of great generosity requires "strenuous discipline . . . courageously to speak what is correct and also to accept the softness of one's self." It also requires the Native American teaching that "our present actions will affect the world unto seven generations." This spirit can only be cultivated if we give up the notion that we are isolated individuals. Yet Ywahoo does not counsel self-sacrifice or self-abnegation. Understanding the self to be part of the Sacred Hoop means that "Whatever we're doing, we're doing it for one another, for ourselves, rather than, 'I do this for them.'" In order to cultivate the spirit of generosity it is necessary to affirm the life we have been given, "speaking of the best, seeing ourselves in process, and acknowledging the wisdom, the beauty, and the blessing of life in this time." For Native Americans the give-away is a concrete manifestation of this inner understanding. Because the habits of mind Ywahoo advocates are unfamiliar to many Westerners, including activists, Ywahoo emphasizes spiritually changing inner attitudes through meditative practices. But the goal is action, not contemplation. As she says, "Community building, relationship, is very active." Only through combining visualization, affirmation, and community building, will the Sacred Hoop be renewed.

Katie Geneva Cannon, a black American Christian ethicist, asserts that Christian ethics as practiced by white people has sanctioned racism when its ethical concerns have proved destructive *or* irrelevant to black people. Black American women's literary tradition is a repository of "moral wisdom" chronicling the ethical principles of the black community. Listening to the voices of black women could transform Christian ethics. Though black women's literature depicts black women's triple oppression by racism, sexism, and classism, black women are not portrayed solely as the objects of oppression, as stereotypical victims. Rather this literature speaks of "black women's survival," their ability not only to "get along," but also to "build churches, schools, homes, temples, and college educations out of soapsuds and muscles." Cannon insists that Christian ethics must focus on the struggles of the "most vulnerable and most exploited members of American society." In this context, "survival"—preserving the life and integrity of self, family, and community—is the highest ethical value. Like Delores S. Williams, Cannon turns to black women's literature as a theological and moral resource, and like Luisah Teish and Williams, she honors the ancestors whose survival has made the lives of black women, as Audre Lorde puts it, "richer and more possible." Though Cannon's essay is explicitly addressed to the male-created discipline of Christian ethics, she also challenges middle- and upper-class white feminists to understand that exclusive focus on their own struggles will replicate the structures of racism and classism that oppress other women.

Carter Heyward focuses on heterosexism as an aspect of the structures of oppression in women's lives. Heterosexism, "built and maintained upon patriarchy," presumes that everyone is or ought to be heterosexual, and maintains a system of power relations in which economic, social, political, legal, religious, and other privileges are conferred on those who conform to its norms. Heyward understands God to be the power of "right relationship," or just love. She argues that there is no love without justice: "Love does not come first, justice later." She states that in her experience the power of God's just love is more fully expressed in homosexual relationships where the structures of male domination are absent, than in heterosexual relationships.

The power of right relation that Heyward has experienced in lesbian relationships has been condemned as immoral by Christian and other

ethical systems. This is in part because Christianity has never fully affirmed sexuality as an aspect of the divine love ("It [God] sort of like
you know what, Shug say"), and in part because Christianity has sanc-
tified the structures of domination within sexual relationships. By
"coming out," publicly identifying herself as a lesbian priest, Carter
Heyward challenges the church and the world to affirm the sacredness
of sexuality, to affirm the divine power of just love in all its manifestations, *and* to reject the forms of so-called love that enshrine the domination of one person (the male) over the other (the female).

Susan Brooks Thistlethwaite concretely undergirds Heyward's argument that many women have understood love to require their submission to injustice. As Thistlethwaite notes, battering is a pervasive
reality in women's lives, not a deviation from the so-called norm. The
New Testament, traditionally interpreted as requiring wives to submit
to their husbands, and Christian piety's paean to love as long-suffering,
have taught women that God wishes them to remain in battering relationships. Many religious women reject the services of battered
women's shelters because they believe that to leave the "sacred *bonds*"
of marriage is contrary to the will of God.

Liberation hermeneutics, a method of biblical interpretation that focuses on God as the Liberator of the oppressed (a theme also discussed
by Rosemary Radford Ruether), enables women to understand that the
will and love of God are inseparable from justice. But as Thistlethwaite
shows, this process of reinterpreting the Bible is not a simple matter
of intellectual substitution of one set of interpretations for another.
"Feminist biblical interpretation for women who live with male violence
is a healing process that develops over time. It involves claiming self-
esteem, taking control, and owning one's anger." The implications of
Thistlethwaite's essay are far-reaching, creating a space for others to
write about their experiences of spiritual dimensions of the process of
healing from all forms of violence against women, including incest and
rape. For Alice Walker's Celie, healing from incest and rape came
through experiencing God in everything, while for other women the
path may lead to reinterpreting Jewish tradition or to the Goddess.

Developing the theological and thealogical dimensions of the theme
of connection to nature discussed by many contributors to this volume,
Carol P. Christ traces the roots of the ecological and nuclear crises to
the separation of humanity and divinity from nature. She argues that
"the preservation of the earth requires a profound shift in consciousness: a recovery of more ancient and traditional views that revere the
connection of all beings in the web of life, and a rethinking of the
relation of humanity and divinity to nature." She claims that the notion
of human and divine superiority to nature is deeply rooted in biblical
and theological traditions and the habits of mind derived from them.
Drawing on the work of Susan Griffin, Alice Walker, Paula Gunn Al-

len, and others, she contends that a thealogy and ethic for a nuclear age must repudiate the pretension to human and divine superiority over nature. Christ writes, "The supreme relativizing is to know that we are no more valuable to the life of the universe than a field flowering in the color purple . . . and no less." For Christ, ethics stem from our love for life in this universe, not from obligation to a God who stands beyond it. Arguing that we ought to reconsider the Native American Indian notion that "all beings, including rocks and rain, corn and coyote, as well as the Great Spirit, have intelligence," she concludes, "What I do know is that whether the universe has a center of consciousness or not, . . . the rainbow must be enough to stop us from destroying all that is and wants to be."

Starhawk puts this theory into practice as she contributes the insights of feminist Goddess spirituality to the direct action movement against nuclear power. She argues that ritual is part of every culture, that it creates "a heart, a center, for a people," and evokes the "Deep Self of a group." Rituals create community and build power by attuning the group to the values they share and to the circle of life from which all energy is drawn. Starhawk finds this theory tested as she, a feminist priestess, is called to help create rituals for the Diablo Canyon blockade, an attempt to prevent the opening of a nuclear power plant in California.

All of the participants in the blockade shared her commitment to saving the earth, but not all of them understood that commitment through Goddess spirituality. Starhawk found that speaking of the "*things* and people that embody the Goddess, that are manifestations of power-from-within—the earth, air, fire, and water, natural objects, each other," is a way of touching and unifying members of a group who hold different philosophies and ideologies. The Tree of Generations meditation that she shares is an example of this strategy. Starhawk also learned that rituals must be modified in sensitivity to the energy of the group. The rituals at the beginning and ending of the blockade and the equinox ritual celebrated by a group who breached the plant's security and were jailed were experienced by Starhawk and others as the magic that "spins the bond that can sustain us to continue the work over years, over lifetimes."

Sharon Welch joins the discussion of how to create communities of resistance by turning her attention to the ideological splits that often cripple social change movements. Reflecting on the nineteenth- and early twentieth-century feminist movements, Welch concludes that its failures were not failures of ideology as has been alleged by historians, but failures to marshall sufficient power to defeat the establishment. She argues that while theory is important in social change movements, its importance is often overestimated, especially by its creators. The purpose of theory is to embolden a movement, not to "get it right once and for all." Welch urges feminists to theorize boldly while making coalitions broadly, for in the end political power is required to create social change.

Though committed to plurality and diversity, members of the feminist movements in religion and spirituality have suffered from ideological divisions, as discussed in the introduction to this volume. Splits between Goddess and Christian feminists, arguments about anti-Judaism, divisions between white feminists and feminists of color, lesbians and heterosexuals, while often productive of growth, have sometimes weakened and debilitated our movements. But the truth is that we need each other. Welch warns us not to take our intellectual differences so seriously that we lessen our power to work together to transform the patriarchy.

Drawing on the tribal wisdom of her Native American ancestors, and evoking the spirit of connection discussed throughout this volume, Carol Lee Sanchez argues that American culture has become alienated, fragmented, and destructive of life on the planet because we have lost an understanding of the sacredness of everyday life. For Native Americans the sense of place, of being rooted in a land base is essential to the ability to "walk in balance and harmony" with everything that is. Many non-Native Americans, in contrast, view the earth as a resource to be exploited and fail to see that the "holy land" is here, where we live. Sanchez asserts that it is imperative that Americans develop a sense of spiritual connection to the American land base. This can be accomplished through attending to the spiritual teachings of Native Americans and through the creation of New World Tribal Communities in which Indian values are transformed in an urban, pluralistic context. The goal is not for others to become Indian. Through telling stories of immigration in a concrete way, non-Indians can create new tribal mythologies or origin stories that honor their ancestors (a theme also discussed by Luisah Teish) and celebrate the connection of all who live on it to the American land. In addition, Sanchez offers a set of journal meditations that enable us to reflect upon our connection to plants and animals, to become aware of our thoughts, our dreams, and the way we spend our time. She urges us to celebrate the spiritual significance of the technologies that have made our lives easier, while focusing on awareness of their consequences. In this way we can begin to create New World Tribal Communities that will heal and nurture us as we seek to heal the planet and enhance the lives of all beings in the circle of life.

Renewing the Sacred Hoop

DHYANI YWAHOO

The quality of our laughter and joy, the knowledge of our voices, thoughts, and actions are weaving beauty around the land. There is a harmony; there is a song. All things move in a circle. It is from the womb of emptiness that all is made manifest. Our thoughts make sound waves upon the planet, wind currents upon the stream. As our thoughts become clarified in the wind of our personal experience so, too, they become clarified around the planet through bioresonance.

We can sense at many levels an awakening, a song arising clearly in the hearts of many people, the community of human beings sharing an environment. The song is of planetary peace; individually it means each of us recognizing the beauty of ourselves and one another. What we see around us is people calling out for peace, for remembrance, and really wishing to recall the "how." How to set aside thought forms that battle in the angry mind? How to recognize the beauty of human beings in process? In this moment the caretaker mind of woman needs to hold forth the idea of abundance, to be joyous, to recognize the qualities of life—and to know that we can shape the world around us with our thoughts and feelings. Accepting the healing power of affirmation and action, speaking of the best, seeing ourselves in process and acknowledging the wisdom, the beauty, and the blessing of life in this time. Then to sense the interplay, the resonance of our being with all the world around us. That is the dream of this land, the dream of the child's heart; that is to renew the Sacred Hoop.

In finding peace and recognizing the light in yourself, we say there's a hearth in your heart where the Creator has given you something very sacred, a special gift, a special duty, an understanding. And now is the time for us to clean out those hearths, to let that inner light glow. Listen to the breath and know it is also the mountain's breath. Mother Mountain has many meridians of energy just as the human body does. You can feel the mountains in your cheeks, just by breathing. Your consciousness is not just in your body. It is in everything. Everything is

Dhyani Ywahoo is a member of the Etowah Band of the Eastern Tsalagi (Cherokee) Nation. Trained by her grandparents, she is the twenty-seventh generation to carry the ancestral wisdom of the Ywahoo Lineage. She is Spiritual Director of the Sunray Meditation Society, an international spiritual society dedicated to planetary peace.

related. The mountain, too, is your body, so all the better to treat it with respect.

As long as you are walking upon the Earth you are like a child in the womb, being fed by this Earth. And respect for the Earth and for one another is being called for right now. We each have a duty to the Earth and to each other. Each race, each nation, has its different purpose in maintaining the whole. The wisdom of all our ancestors, wherever they came from, basically points to one truth: everything is in relation to you. Native Americans say, "all my relations," acknowledging that connection to everything that is alive. All being is an aspect of yourself. So to listen to the elements of nature is to listen to the voice of yourself: to look at the fire and see what it has to show you; to listen to the wind and understand that it, too, is your mind. These are your relatives: the fire, the water, the wind, the Earth, all of the creatures that you meet upon this planet and within it. We see some places that are not as sparkling as they can be and that is because people are being untrue to themselves, to one another, to the planet. People are not keeping tradition in their hearts; they are digging too far and using without consideration of returning. In this time it is either yes or no. You are either in harmony with the planet, with that part of truth in yourself, or you are not.

The first step is to understand your own consciousness. Can we maintain spiritual dignity in an environment that denies more and more the grace of our inner beauty? We must. It is coming to that. Earth is asking. Our very inner nature is saying that to us now.

Let us all speak the best of one another and perceive the best in everything. It is a strenuous discipline in these times to practice this, courageously to speak what is correct and also to accept the softness of one's self; to realize that everything is Mother and Father. There is no form without the gift of the Mother and the Father. From Father Sky comes your consciousness and Mother Earth is your very bones. To sense the balance of the Mother/Father, Father/Mother within one's own being, one's own nature, is a way to renew the Earth, to renew our hearts, to renew the vision.

To see one's purpose is a very important moment in the vision. We can choose, we can weave. We hold the form, we dance it, and the moment comes when it is recalled in each of us. We are human beings; we can live in harmony and dignity. We can make peace. We can empower ourselves to be peaceful, to know that what manifests through our hands, our hearts, and our actions is a reflection of our thinking and our relationship. In this time of illusion many people feel they're not good enough or that somebody else is in control, so they hold back. People disavow their place in the circle of life when they think in that mind. So generosity is something that we first begin to look at in our own thought. When we give we must give with consideration, so that always there is that cycle of reciprocity. To come again to realize the circle of life and the wheel of cause and effect, to plant good seeds, it is important to affirm, "I have something to give, I am receiving, even this gift of the human body and I am thankful." In this way one's highest ideals and clarity of mind can manifest. This accomplishes the goal of realizing the great truth: having good relationship with everything around one, for the benefit of all.

In this industrial age, which has been described as paternalistic, we see how by moving away from the circle and working more in components, there is a loss of continuity and a forgetfulness of how what one does affects the Earth. So the big company that takes things out of the Earth and poisons the ground and the water and the atmosphere does so without even considering the effect on themselves. How do we turn the mind to realize that our actions have an effect, that things we do in this moment have an impact upon all of humanity now and unto seven generations down the road? It is in the reawakening of caretaker mind that we recognize our responsibility to right relationship and to nurture that which is good. It is the natural capacity of woman in her wombness to bring forth the good, to generate clear ideas; yet we are all caretakers and can come to see everyone we meet as a relative and ourselves as part of the great family called humanity. Seeing all in relationship, in the circle, is a part of the planetary healing. So it is very important that among ourselves we practice great generosity. This generosity carries over into respect for one another.

Native people have what is called the give-away. Very often people are so happy they have a party and give away everything. Then they find themselves renewed, emptied of attachment. This concept of the give-away comes from courageously affirming one's ability to act for what is good for other people and oneself, knowing that each day will be abundant because one is not grasping. The give-away is an outward expression of an understanding that all things are related in the circle of life.

How to hold the form that we are planetary beings, universal beings, and able to live in harmony? How to hold the form that we are abundant beings, capable of creating all that is needed for the people? Within our hearts and within our minds, within the imagination's light, we begin to see the way of resolution. This is known as visualization, where you see the accomplished goal of a world of enlightened action and good relationship. We must consider how our present actions will affect the world unto seven generations. This comes through stilling one's own mind and putting aside personal expectations and considering the balance of the Earth. This generates the mind of generosity.

Seeing the factions in one's own mind and community come to clarity is a first step to planetary enlightenment. It is to make peace with ourselves and all those we know; to feel confident that we are on the path of exploration, energetically seeking that full enlightenment. To know that anger, pain, shame, blame are only thought forms. We can end the formation of those thought forms by letting go of attachment to the idea of conflict. Can I make peace with my relatives? It is a great gift. How far will I go? Is there anything to lose? Nothing to lose. It is an awareness of the power of mind, an understanding of the process of unfolding and ultimately a freedom from the suffering of doubt. Doubt gives rise to fear and the idea that there is something to aggressively protect. Forgiveness is the balm, the soothing gel, so that one recognizes wisdom and the capacity to love, the compassion that turns aside fear and anger, the compassion that recognizes beauty and holds the form of planetary enlightenment.

The vision is the clear intention. It is a generosity of heart, the mothering heart, the caretaker heart, that holds the vision. In terms of practical envisioning and manifesting the ideals, one considers three principles. The first principle is the clear intention that something may manifest; the understanding of its relationship to your life's purpose and to those around you and its repercussions. The second principle is generosity of heart; the compassion of the heart to affirm it to be so. The third principle is the ability, the mind to make it manifest. So we visualize the goal being accomplished in clear light, in right relationship. We affirm daily in our mind and in our spiritual practice that it will happen. And we work to manifest it.

Say you want to see a piece of land in your area put in trust because it is sacred ground. How do you bring it about? The process works on many levels, and there are three basic steps: visualization, affirmation, and manifestation. First envision the land, the ideal situation and see your relationship to it. Is this action good for all the people? Understand its relationship to all things, to future generations, and know that it may return to you in the stream. Look and see if there are any thought forms or obscurations in your own nature or in the situation that may impede actualization of the ideal. If there are, then correct them through visualization and affirmation. Second, affirm and call forth the people through the certainty of your heart. Through visualization, affirmation, and chanting set up a magnet so that others of like energy will come and offer their resources. The third component is the manifestation, actively to manifest the goal. Carefully choose the team; attune with one another before you meet and during your meetings so you have unity of mind. Success comes from holding the ideal very clearly in your minds and making certain that the ideal is beneficial for the people unto seven generations. The idea is in the minds of the people rather than something imposed upon the people. To sit back and think it will happen because you visualize is not enough. You consciously look for the right connections, consciously weed the garden of the mind, consciously gather the funds to acquire the place. Community building, relationship, is very active.

The world of enlightened action and good relationship begins through the thoughts, words, and actions of today. People's methods, goals, or ideals may be different, but basically there is one truth in the community of human beings: we are all human beings, we are all relatives. There are many ways in which we can keep clear the stream of mind to bring forth enlightened community. First step, speak words in a building way, a constructive way; rather than pointing to the defects, point to the strengths. When recognizing defects in one's own nature or perception, make them correct through affirmation. As one is looking through the compassionate generosity of the heart, begin to notice the "empty bowl," the mind getting still. Set aside attachment to what "I said," "she said," and "they said" and understand what we are all doing together. Work by making agreement and evaluating what is possible. Set priorities. It is most important not to let actions become "charged" and held onto. Blaming doesn't accomplish; establishing a strong pattern does.

Many people abdicate self-empowerment by withdrawing their energies, rather than by making a change either in themselves or in the situation. Also consider that people are like musical notes and need to have a harmonious complement. Knowing how to establish the team is important. Understand the basic character of those you're working with and have no expectations beyond. Clarify your own heart and know that when working together you're doing the best for all the people. Affirm that you can do it and acknowledge the positive qualities in yourself and in the work team. Do certain prayer rituals and meditations together to keep your hearts and minds clear. At Sunray when we prepare to meet we attune through the heart center, the center of compassion.

There is a simple way to bring about enlightened action: knowing that whatever we're doing, we're doing it for one another, for ourselves, rather than "I do this for 'them'." Attuning to one another, working as a team, knowing that in the circle each person has a unique and necessary function, letting go of wanting one's ego stroked, this is generosity of mind.

Refinement, change, is a process of life. It's how we respond to the change that is significant. See change as a process, without grasping the pain of "right or wrong," and see "it seems to be unfolding in this way." How not to grasp the feeling of pain? Look at the feeling. Where did it come from? Where did it begin? It is a matter of knowing that people do go through suffering but we can also transform the suffering into a real understanding about life. What does one do in a moment of despair? Practice, do meditation, make a ritual of clarifying the mind. "Here, I offer my attachment, my suffering, to the elements. Take them away. I inhale peace and harmony and radiate it out."

The only way I know to see life as a process unfolding without becoming attached is to have clear practice, and when I say practice I mean regular meditation, reflection time. Too often people think that meditation and contemplation are separate from action. Meditation has several phases. It has an active moment of sitting down, visualizing, chanting, whatever means the person has; then stillness of mind; then action, going out and doing something. It may be doing what you saw in the stillness. It may be what you saw upon the screen of your mind before the stillness. The action is as much a meditation as are the sitting and the contemplation. Action is what manifests that which you perceive in the meditation.

In this time there needs to be a change in action to protect the Earth. The human mind affects the very elements themselves. The thought and action of the people has become imbalanced; elements out of balance are chaotic and chaos affects planetary mind. Through good relationship and through developing generosity of heart and action individuals clarify their minds, and this resonates throughout the planet.

Native peoples see that Earth is a living being, very much affected by people's thinking and actions. The ancient Native prophecies foretell for this time much change and breaking of earth forms, the thundering of ignorance and the lightning force of inspiration moving forth. They also speak of the possible negative effects of people's attachment to thought forms of conflict and dominion. Prophecies are the possibilities that may manifest based on the actions of a given moment. And in the moment each one has a choice. So the prophecies speak of these times as trying times, of many streams meeting—and the possibility of the Hoop being rebuilt. And ultimately the Hoop will be rebuilt.

I see a great turn in the spiral. The mind is very powerful and the voice is very strong. I see a world of beauty and right relationship unfolding. I see that nations will come to recognize the foolishness of nuclear armament and make changes in their actions, and that the means will come to defuse the poisonous weapons that have been made. And most important, the means will come to defuse the angry thinking that leads people to build weapons. The means are positive visualization, affirmation, and community building.

Visualize yourself as a great mother feeling all the beings upon this planet, sending forth loving thoughts of peace and harmony and certainty that the crops will be good and all will be fed. Imagine yourself a great lake sending forth endless ripples of compassion and care.

Let us all recall the sacred wisdom of all our relations and let that light move brightly in our hearts. Let our words be words of wisdom and creative energy, building stairways to our remembrance of the clan of humanity. In this way Mother Earth and Father Sky meet in our hearts and we know our wholeness. In this way the Sacred Hoop is renewed.

Moral Wisdom in the Black Women's Literary Tradition

KATIE GENEVA CANNON

I first began pondering the relationship between faith and ethics as a schoolgirl while listening to my grandmother teach the central affirmations of Christianity within the context of a racially segregated society. My community of faith taught me the principles of God's universal parenthood that engendered a social, intellectual, and cultural ethos embracing the equal humanity of all people. Yet my city, state, and nation declared it a punishable offense against the laws and mores for Blacks and whites "to travel, eat, defecate, wait, be buried, make love, play, relax and even speak together, except in the stereotyped context of master and servant interaction."[1]

My religious quest tried to relate the Christian doctrines preached in the Black Church to the suffering, oppression, and exploitation of Black people in the society. How could Christians who were white flatly and openly refuse to treat as fellow human beings Christians who had African ancestry? Was not the essence of the Gospel mandate a call to eradicate affliction, despair, and systems of injustice? Inasmuch as the Black Church expressed the inner ethical life of the people, was there any way to reconcile the inherent contradictions in Christianity as practiced by whites with the radical indictments of and challenges for social amelioration and economic development in the Black religious heritage? How long would the white church continue to be the ominous symbol of white dominance, sanctioning and assimilating the propagation of racism in the mundane interests of the ruling group?

In the 1960s my quest for the integration of faith and ethics was influenced by scholars in various fields who surfaced the historical contributions of Afro-Americans that had been distorted and denied. Avidly I read the analysis exposing the assumptions and dogmas that made Blacks a negligible factor in the thought of the world. For more than three and a half centuries, a "conspiracy of silence" rendered invisible the outstanding contributions of Blacks to the culture of hu-

---

Katie Geneva Cannon, a womanist ethicist, is Associate Professor of Christian Ethics at the Episcopal Divinity School in Cambridge, Massachusetts. She is the author of *Black Womanist Ethics* and is working on a book on moral wisdom in the black women's literary tradition.

mankind. From cradle to grave the people in the United States were taught the alleged inferiority of Blacks.

When I turned specifically to theological ethics, I discovered the dominant ethical systems implied that the doing of Christian ethics in the Black community was either immoral or amoral. The cherished ethical ideas predicated upon the existence of freedom and a wide range of choices proved null and void in situations of oppression. The real-lived texture of Black life requires moral agency that may run contrary to the ethical boundaries of mainline Protestantism. Blacks may use action guides that have never been considered within the scope of traditional codes of faithful living. Racism, gender discrimination, and economic exploitation, as inherited, age-long complexes, require the Black community to create and cultivate values and virtues in their own terms so that they prevail against the odds with moral integrity.

For example, dominant ethics makes a virtue of qualities that lead to economic success—self-reliance, frugality, and industry. These qualities are based on an assumption that success is possible for anyone who tries. Developing confidence in one's own abilities, resources, and judgments amidst a careful use of money and goods—in order to exhibit assiduity in the pursuit of upward mobility—have proven to be positive values for many whites. But the oligarchic economic powers, and the consequent political power they generate, own and control capital and distribute credit in a manner detrimental to Blacks. As part of a legitimating system to justify the supposed inherent inferiority of Blacks, the values so central to white economic mobility prove to be ineffectual. Racism does not allow all Black women and Black men to work and save in order to develop a standard of living that is congruent with the American ideal.

Theory and analysis demonstrate that to embrace work as a "moral essential" means that Black women are still the last hired to do the work that white men, white women, and men of color refuse to do, and at a wage that men and white women refuse to accept. Black women, placed in jobs proven to be detrimental to their health, are doing the most menial, tedious, and by far the most underpaid work, if they manage to get a job at all.

Dominant ethics also assumes that a moral agent is to a considerable degree free and self-directing. Each person possesses self-determining power. For instance, one is free to choose whether or not she or he wants to suffer and make sacrifices as a principle of action or as a voluntary vocational pledge of crossbearing. In dominant ethics a person is free to make suffering a desirable moral norm. This is not so for Blacks. For the masses of Black people, suffering is the normal state of affairs. Mental anguish, physical abuse, and emotional agony are all part of Black people's daily lives. Due to the white supremacy and male superiority that pervade this society, Blacks and whites, women and men are forced to live with very different ranges of freedom. As long as the white-male experience continues to be established as the ethical norm, Black women, Black men, and others will suffer unequivocal oppression. The range of freedom has been restricted by those who cannot hear and will not hear voices expressing pleasure and pain, joy and rage as others experience them.

In the Black community, qualities that determine desirable ethical values of upright character and sound moral conduct must always take into account the circumstances, paradoxes, and dilemmas that constrict Blacks to the lowest rungs of the social, political, and economic hierarchy. Black existence is deliberately and openly controlled.

> ... How we travel and where, what work we do, what income we receive, where we eat, where we sleep, with whom we talk, where we recreate, where we study, what we write, what we publish.[2]

The vast majority of Blacks suffer every conceivable form of denigration. Their lives are named, defined, and circumscribed by whites.

The moral wisdom of the Black community is extremely useful in defying oppressive rules or standards of "law and order" that degrade Blacks. It helps Blacks purge themselves of self-hate, thus asserting their own validity. But the ethical values of the Black community are not identical with the obligations and duties that Anglo-Protestant American society requires of its members. Nor can the ethical assumptions be the same, as long as powerful whites who control the wealth, the systems, and the institutions in this society continue to perpetuate brutality and criminality against Blacks.

BLACK WOMEN'S LITERATURE AS AN ETHICAL RESOURCE

The method used in this study departs from most work in Christian and secular ethics. Data is drawn from less conventional sources and probes more intimate and private aspects of Black life. The Black women's literary tradition has not previously been used to interpret and explain the community's socio-cultural patterns from which ethical values can be gleaned. I have found that this literary tradition is the nexus between the real-lived texture of Black life and the oral-aural cultural values implicitly passed on from one generation to the next.

Black women are the most vulnerable and exploited members of the American society. The structure of the capitalist political economy in which Black people are commodities, combined with patriarchal contempt for women, has caused the Black woman to experience oppression that knows no ethical or physical bounds.

> As a black, she has had to endure all the horrors of slavery and living in a racist society; as a worker, she has been the object of continual exploitation, occupying the lowest place on the wage scale and restricted to the most de-

meaning and uncreative jobs; as a woman she has seen her physical image defamed and been the object of the white master's uncontrollable lust and subjected to all the ideals of white womanhood as a model to which she should aspire; as a mother, she has seen her children torn from her breast and sold into slavery, she has seen them left at home without attention while she attended to the needs of the offspring of the ruling class.[3]

This essay shows how Black women live out a moral wisdom in their real-lived context that does not appeal to the fixed rules or absolute principles of the white-oriented, male-structured society. Black women's analysis and appraisal of right and wrong, good and bad develop out of the various coping mechanisms required by their own circumstances. Black women have justly regarded survival against tyrannical systems of triple oppression as a true sphere of moral life.

Black women are taught what is to be endured and how to endure the harsh, cruel, inhumane exigencies of life. The moral wisdom does not rescue Black women from the bewildering pressures and perplexities of institutionalized social evils; rather, it exposes those ethical assumptions that are inimical to the ongoing survival of Black womanhood. The moral counsel of Black women captures the ethical qualities of what is real and what is of value to women in the Black world.

Black women writers function as symbolic conveyors and transformers of the values acknowledged by the female members of the Black community. In the quest for appreciating Black women's experience, nothing surpasses the Black women's literary tradition. It cryptically records the specificity of the Afro-American life.

For instance, Zora Neale Hurston in *Jonah's Gourd Vine* recorded a series of proverbial sayings between a dying mother and her nine-year-old daughter. The mother is providing the child with the moral wisdom of coping when life goes awry.

Stop cryin', Isie, you can't hear whut Ahm sayin', 'member tuh git all de education you kin. Dat's de onliest way you kin keep out from under people's feet. You always strain tuh be de bell cow, never be de tail uh nothin'. Do de best you kin, honey, 'cause neither yo' paw or dese older chillun is goin' tuh be bothered too much wid you. But you goin' tuh git 'long. Mark mah words. You got spunk, but mah po' lil'l sandyhaired child goin' suffer uh lot 'fo' she git tuh de place she can 'fend fuh herself. And Isie, honey, stop cryin' and lissen tuh me. Don't you love nobody bettern'n you do yo'self. Do, you'll be killed 'thout being struck uh blow. Some us dese things Ahm tellin' yuh, you won't understand 'em fuh years tuh come, but de time will come when you'll know.[4]

The mother's instruction was concerned not so much with the ascertainment of fact or elaboration of theories as with the means and ends of practical life. The mother spelled out those things that the daughter needed to do in order to protect the quality and continuity of her life. The Black female need not be a muzzled, mutilated individual but must continue to grow as a woman-child with a vibrant, creative spirit. This moral wisdom, handed down from mother to daughter as the crystallized result of experience, aimed to teach the next generation not only how to survive but also how to consider more deeply the worth and meaning of their lives.

My goal is not to arrive at my prescriptive or normative ethic. Rather what I am pursuing is an investigation that will help Black women, and others who care, to understand and to appreciate the richness of their own moral struggle through the life of the common people and the oral tradition. I seek to further understandings of some of the differences between ethics of life under oppression and established moral approaches that assume freedom and a wide range of choices. I am being suggestive of one possible ethical approach, not exhaustive.

I make no apologies for the fact that this study is a partisan one. For too long the Black community's theological and ethical understandings have been written from a decidedly male bias. This study is not merely a glorification of the Black female community, but rather an attempt to add to the far too few positive records concerning the Black woman as moral agent. This method should enable us to use the lives and literature of Black women to recognize the contribution to the field of ethics that Black women have made. One test will be whether those who know this literary tradition find that I have done justice to its depth and richness. The second test is whether Black women recognize the moral wisdom they utilize. The third test is whether Black feminists who have given up on the community of faith will gain new insights concerning the reasonableness of theological ethics in deepening the Black woman's character, consciousness, and capacity in the ongoing struggle for survival. If these criteria are met, I will have reached my objective.

It is my thesis that the Black women's literary tradition is the best available literary repository for understanding the ethical values Black women have created and cultivated in their participation in this society. To prevail against the odds with integrity, Black women must assess their moral agency within the social conditions of the community. Locked out of the real dynamics of human freedom in America, they implicitly pass on moral formulas for survival that allow them to stand over against the perversions of ethics and morality imposed on them by whites and males who support racial imperialism in a patriarchal social order.

THE EVIDENCE OF BLACK WOMEN'S STORIES

The story of the Afro-American has been told quite coherently, but has repeatedly left out the Black woman. Seldom in history has a group of women been so directly responsible for insuring the well-being of both the Black family and the white. At the same time, this story has not been told. The work of Black women writers can be trusted as seriously mirroring Black reality. Their writings are important chronicles of the Black woman's survival.

Despite their tragic omission by the literary establishment, Black women have been expressing ideas, feelings, and interpretations about the Black experience since the early days of the eighteenth century. Throughout their history in the United States, Black women have used their creativity to carve out "living space." From the beginning, they contended with the ethical ambiguity of racism, sexism, and other sources of fragmentation in this acclaimed land of freedom, justice, and equality. The Black women's literary tradition delineates the many ways that ordinary Black women have fashioned value patterns and ethical procedures in their own terms, as well as transcending, radicalizing, and sometimes destroying pervasive, negative orientations imposed by the mores of the larger society.

Toni Morrison describes the moral agency of old Black women reared in the South in this way:

Edging into life from the back door. Becoming. Everybody in the world was in a position to give them orders. White women said, "Do this." White children said, "Give me that." White men said, "Come here." Black men said, "Lay down." The only people they need not take orders from were black children and each other. But they took all of that and recreated it in their own image. They ran the houses of white people, and knew it. When white men beat their men, they cleaned up the blood and went home to receive abuse from the victim. They beat their children with one hand and stole for them with the other. The hands that felled trees also cut umbilical cords; the hands that wrung the necks of chickens and butchered hogs also nudged African violets into bloom; the arms that loaded sheaves, bales and sacks rocked babies to sleep. They patted biscuits into flaky ovals of innocence—and shrouded the dead. They plowed all day and came home to nestle like plums under the limbs of their men. The legs that straddled a mule's back were the same ones that straddled their men's hips. And the difference was all the difference there was.[5]

The bittersweet irony of Afro-American experience forces Black women to examine critically the conventional, often pretentious, morality of middle-class American ideals.

The Black women's literary tradition provides a rich resource and a cohesive commentary that brings into sharp focus the Black community's central values, which in turn frees Black folks from the often deadly grasp of parochial stereotypes. The observations, descriptions, and interpretations in Black literature are largely reflective of cultural experiences. They identify the frame of social contradiction in which Black people live, move, and have their being. The derogatory caricatures and stereotypes ascribed to Black people are explicitly rejected. Instead, writings by Blacks capture the magnitude of the Black personality. Spanning the antebellum period to today's complex techno-logical society, Black women writers authenticate, in an economy of expressions, how Black people creatively strain against the external lim-its in their lives, how they affirm their humanity by inverting assump-tions, and how they balance the continual struggle and interplay of paradoxes.

PARALLELS WITH BLACK HISTORY

The Black women's literary tradition is a source in the study of ethics because it is tied historically to the origin of Black people in America. Most writing by Black women captures the values of the Black com-munity within a specific location, time, and historical context. The lit-erary tradition is not centered automatically upon the will and whims of what an individual writer thinks is right or obligatory, nor even upon whatever she personally believes to be true for her own localized con-sciousness. The majority of Black women who engage in literary com-positions hold themselves accountable to the collective values that un-derlie Black history and culture. Dexter Fisher makes the point this way:

... To be totally centered on the self would be to forget one's history, the kinship of a shared community of experience, the crucial continuity between past and present that must be maintained in order to insure the future.[6]

The patterns and themes in Black women's writings reflect historical facts, sociological realities, and religious convictions that lie behind the ethos and ethics of the Black community. As recorders of the Black experience, Black women writers convey the community's consciousness of values that enables them to find meaning in spite of social degra-dation, economic exploitation, and political oppression. They record what is valued or regarded as good in the Black community. Seldom, if ever, is their work art-for-art's-sake. "Whatever else may be said of it, Black American writing in the United States has been first and last, as Saunders Redding once observed, a 'literature of necessity.' "[7]

The appeal of a basically utilitarian literature written to meet the exigencies of a specific historical occasion usually declines after the occasion has passed. That this is much less true of Black literature is due to constant factors in Afro-American history—the Black presence and white racism.[8]

ORAL NARRATIVE DEVICES

The irresistible power in the Black women's literary tradition is its ability to convey the assumed values of the Black community's oral tradition in its grasp for meaning. The suppression of book learning and the mental anguish of intellectual deprivation obliged Black lit-erature to be expressed mainly in oral form. What is critical for my purpose is that these women reveal in their novels, short stories, love lyrics, folktales, fables, drama, and nonfiction, a psychic connection with the cultural tradition transmitted by the oral mode from one generation to the next. As serious writers who have mastered in varying degrees the technique of their craft, Black women find themselves causally dependent on the ethics of the Black masses. Black women writers draw heavily upon the Black oral culture.

The folk tales, song (especially the blues), sermons, the dozens, and the rap all provide Black writers with the figurative language and connotations of dim hallways and dank smells, caged birds and flowers that won't sprout, curdled milk and rusty razors, general stores and beauty parlors, nappy edges and sheened legs. The social and cultural forces within the Black oral tradition form the milieu out of which Black writers create.

Black women writers document the attitudes and morality of women, men, girls, and boys who chafe at and defy the restrictions imposed by the dominant white capitalist value system. They delineate in varying artistic terms the folk treasury of the Black community: how Black people deal with poverty and the ramifications of power, sex as an act of love and terror, the depersonalization that accompanies violence, the acquisition of property, the drudgery of a workday, the inconsistencies of chameleonlike racism, teenage mothers, charlatan sorcerers, swinging churches, stoic endurance, and stifled creativity. Out of this storehouse of Black experience comes a vitally rich, ancient continuum of Black wisdom.

This capacity to catch the oral tradition also means an ability to portray the sense of community. Barbara Christian in *Black Women Novelists: The Development of a Tradition, 1892–1976* recognizes this unique characteristic common to Black women's literature as the "literary counterpart of their communities' oral tradition."

The history of these communities, seldom related in textbooks, are incorporated into the tales that emphasize the marvelous, sometimes the outrageous, as a means of teaching a lesson. In concert with their African ancestors, these storytellers, both oral and literary, transform gossip, happenings, into composites of factual events, images, fantasies and fables.[9]

This important characteristic of Black women's writing is increasingly recognized by literary interpreters. Jeanne Noble says, "We would be scripted in history with little true human understanding without the black writer telling it like it is."[10] Mary Helen Washington says that this deeper-than-surface knowledge of and fondness for the verbal tradition is a truth that is shared by the majority of Black women writers. "This remembrance of things past is not simply self-indulgent nostalgia. It is essential to her vision to establish connections with the values that nourish and strengthen her."[11]

Verta Mae Grosvenor captures the essence of the oral tradition at the very outset of her book, *Vibration Cooking:* "Dedicated to my mama and my grandmothers and my sisters in appreciation of the years that they have worked in miss ann's kitchen and then came home to TCB in spite of slavery and the moynihan report."[12] Marcia Gillespie, in the 1975 May editorial of *Essence* magazine, concludes that recording the oral tradition is a way of releasing the memories of mamas and grand-mamas—"the race memory of our women who, though burdened, neither broke nor faltered in their faith in a better world for us all."[13]

Black women's combination of the Western literary form with oral narrative devices expresses with authority, power, and eloquence the insidious effects of racism, sexism, and class elitism on members of their communities. By not abandoning the deeply ingrained traditions of the Black community, these writers utilize common sources to illustrate common values that exist within the collective vision of Blacks in America.

THE INSULARITY OF THE BLACK COMMUNITY

Black women writers, as participant-observers, capsulize on a myriad of levels the insularity of their home communities. Due to systemic, institutionalized manifestations of racism in America, the Black community tends to be situated as marginated islands within the larger society. The perpetual powers of white supremacy continue to drop down on the inhabitants of the Black community like a bell jar—surrounding the whole, yet separating the Black community's customs, mores, opinions, and system of values from those in other communities. Black women authors emphasize life within the community, not the conflict with outside forces. In order to give faithful pictures of important and comprehensive segments of Black life, these writers tie their character's stories to the aesthetic, emotional, and intellectual values of the Black community.

For instance, Ann Petry's *The Street* (1946) depicts the inevitability of crime that Black mothers, who provide for their families against all odds in hostile urban environments, must face.

A lifetime of pent-up resentments went into the blows. Even after he lay motionless, she kept striking him, not thinking about him, not even seeing him. First she was venting her rage against the dirty, crowded street. She saw the rows of dilapidated old houses; the small dark rooms; the long steep flight of stairs; the narrow dingy hallways; the little lost girls in Mrs. Hedges' apartment, the smashed homes where the women did drudgery because their men had deserted them. She saw all of these things and struck them.

Then the limp figure on the sofa became in turn Jim and the slender girl she'd found him with; became the insult in the moist-eyed glances of white men on the subway; became the greasy, lecherous man at the Crosse School for Singers; became the gaunt Super pulling her down into the basement.

Finally, and the blows were heavier, faster, now, she was striking at the white world which thrust black people into a walled enclosure from which there was no escape; and at the turn of events which had forced her to leave Bub alone while she was working so that he now faced reform school, now had a police record.

She saw the face and the head of the man on the sofa through waves of anger in which he represented all these things and she was destroying them.[14]

Gwendolyn Brooks's novel *Maud Martha* (1953) focuses on the coming of age for the Black woman-child who has dark complexion and untameable hair and who must learn how to ward off assaults to her human dignity.

I am what he would call sweet. But I am certainly not what he would call pretty. Even with all this hair (which I have just assured him, in response to his question, is not "natural," is not good grade or anything like good grade) even with whatever I have that puts a dimple in his heart, even with these nice ears, I am still definitely not what he can call pretty if he remains true to what his idea of pretty has always been. Pretty would be a little cream-colored thing with curly hair. Or at the very lowest pretty would be a little curly-haired thing the color of cocoa with a lot of milk in it. Whereas, I am the color of cocoa straight, if you can be even that "kind" to me.[15]

Margaret Walker's *Jubilee* (1966) captures the richness of Black folk culture: the songs, sayings, customs, foods, medicinal remedies, and the language. This historical novel is the character Vyry's mosaic movement from slavery to freedom.

I wants you to bear witness and God knows I tells the truth, I couldn't tell you the name of the man what whipped me, and if I could it wouldn't make no difference. I honestly believes that if airy one of them peoples what treated me like dirt when I was a slave would come to my door in the morning hungry, I would feed 'em. God knows I ain't got no hate in my heart for nobody. If I is and doesn't know it, I prays to God to take it out. I ain't got no time to be hating. I believes in God and I believes in trying to love and help everybody, and I knows that humble is the way. I doesn't care what you calls me, that's my doctrine and I'm gwine preach it to my childrens, every living one I got or ever hopes to have.[16]

Black women writers find value consciousness in their home communities that serve as the framework for their circular literary structure. They transform the passions and sympathies, the desires and hurts, the joys and defeats, the praises and pressures, the richness and diversity of real-lived community into art through the medium of literature. As insiders, Black women writers venture into all strata of Black life.

Using the subject matter close to the heart of Black America, the Black women's literary tradition shows how slavery and its consequences forced the Black woman into a position of cultural custodian.

Black female protagonists are women with hard-boiled honesty, a malaise of dual allegiance, down-to-earth thinking, the ones who are forced to see through the shallowness, hypocrisy, and phoniness as they struggle for survival. Alice Childress paints the picture in this manner:

The emancipated Negro woman of America did the only thing she could do. She earned a pittance by washing, ironing, cooking, cleaning, and picking cotton. She helped her man, and if she often stood in the front line, it was to shield him from the mob of men organized and dedicated to bring about his destruction.

The Negro mother has had the bitter job of teaching her children the difference between the White and the Colored signs before they are old enough to attend school. She had to train her sons and daughters to say "Sir" and "Ma'am" to those who were their sworn enemies.

She couldn't tell her husband "a white man whistled at me," not unless she wanted him to lay down his life before organized killers who strike only in anonymous numbers. Or worse, perhaps to see him helpless and ashamed before her.

Because he could offer no protection or security, the Negro woman has worked with and for her family. She built churches, schools, homes, temples and college educations out of soapsuds and muscles.[17]

CONCLUSION

The work of Black women writers can be trusted as seriously mirroring Black reality. Their writings are chronicles of Black survival. In their plots, actions, and depictions of characters, Black women writers flesh out the positive attributes of Black folks who are "hidden beneath the ordinariness of everyday life." They also plumb their own imaginations in order to crack the invidiousness of worn-out stereotypes. Their ideas, themes, and situations provide truthful interpretations of every possible shade and nuance of Black life.

Black women writers partially, and often deliberately, embrace the moral actions, religious values, and rules of conduct handed down orally in the folk culture. They then proceed in accord with their tradition to transform the cultural limitations and unnatural restrictions in the community's move toward self-authenticity.

The distinctiveness of most Black women writers is their knack for keeping their work intriguing and refreshing amidst its instructiveness. They know how to lift the imagination as they inform, how to touch emotions as they record, how to delineate specifics so that they are applicable to oppressed humanity everywhere. In essence, there is no better source for comprehending the "real-lived" texture of Black experience and the meaning of the moral life in the Black context than the Black women's literary tradition. Black women's literature offers the sharpest available view of the Black community's soul.

NOTES

1. Pierre L. Van Der Berghe, *Race and Racism: A Comparative Perspective* (New York: Wiley, 1967), 77.
2. W. E. B. Du Bois, *Dusk at Dawn* (New York: Harcourt, Brace and Co., 1940).
3. Frances M. Beal, "Slave of a Slave No More: Black Women in Struggle," *The Black Scholar* 12 (November/December 1981): 16–17; reprinted from vol. 6 (March 1975).
4. Zora Neale Hurston, *Jonah's Gourd Vine* (Philadelphia: J. B. Lippincott Co., 1934; reprint, 1971), 206–7.
5. Toni Morrison, *The Bluest Eye* (New York: Holt, Rinehart and Winston, 1970), 109–10.
6. Dexter Fisher, ed., *The Third Woman: Minority Women Writers of the United States* (Boston: Houghton Mifflin Co., 1980), 148.
7. Quoted by Arna Bontemps in "The Black Contribution to American Letters: Part I," in *The Black American Reference Book*, ed. Mable M. Smythe (Englewood Cliffs, NJ: Prentice-Hall, Inc., 1976), 752.
8. Richard K. Barksdale and Kenneth Kinnamon, eds., *Black Writers in America: A Comprehensive Anthology* (New York: Macmillan Publishing Co., 1972), 59.
9. Barbara Christian, *Black Women Novelists: The Development of a Tradition, 1892–1976* (Westport, CT: Greenwood Press, 1980), 239.
10. Jeanne Noble, *Beautiful, Also, Are the Souls of My Sisters: A History of the Black Women in America* (Englewood Cliffs, NJ: Prentice-Hall Inc., 1978), 63.
11. Mary Helen Washington, *Midnight Birds: Stories of Contemporary Black Women Writers* (Garden City, NY: Doubleday, 1979), 95–96.
12. Verta Mae Grosvenor, *Vibration Cooking* (New York: Doubleday, 1970).
13. Marcia Gillespie. Editorial, *Essence*, May 1975, 39.
14. Ann Petry, *The Street* (1946; reprint, New York: Pyramid Books, 1961), 266.
15. Gwendolyn Brooks, "Maud Martha," in *The World of Gwendolyn Brooks* (New York: Harper & Row, 1971), 178–79.
16. Margaret Walker, *Jubilee* (1966; reprint, New York: Bantam Books, 1981), 406.
17. Alice Childress, "The Negro Woman in American Literature," in *Keeping the Faith: Writings by Contemporary Black Women*, ed. Pat Crutuchfield Exum (Greenwich, CT: Fawcett Publications, 1974), 32.

Sexuality, Love, and Justice

CARTER HEYWARD

> The role of the artist is exactly the same as the role of the lover. If I love you, I have to make you conscious of the things you don't see.
> —JAMES BALDWIN

If I love you, I have to make you conscious of the things you don't see. I read and understand this to be our common vocation.

My understanding of myself continues to evolve—often very roughly, sometimes abrasively even to myself, peppered with surprises about myself and others. I do not understand myself primarily in categories that suggest that anything about me is static, unchanging, finished. Even those categories that most of us assume to be basic—such as female or male gender, such as racial identity, such as the *Homo sapiens* species itself—seem to me more elusive, less static, than we often assume. I am tempted to say, and will for now, that nothing is fixed; nothing in the world is so essentially what it is today that tomorrow may not surprise us with something new—whether in the nations, governments, religions, economic and political structures of our own country, or in the ways in which we live our lives among friends, lovers, colleagues.

And yet, there is something basic among us, something evolutionary—and revolutionary; something more basic than femaleness or maleness, whiteness or blackness, gayness or straightness; something more basic than Christianity or any religion. Something that is unchanging, stable, constant, precisely in its dynamic, revolutionary movement in the world. I am speaking of the human experience, and perhaps also the experience of other creatures, of love—or, of our human experience of God in the world. And so, if there is one fundamental category that can be appropriately descriptive, even definitive, of who we are—of what we are here to do in the world—it is that of *lover*.

Because the word love has become a catchall for sweet and happy feelings; because we have learned to believe that love stories are warm and fuzzy tales about dewy eyes and titillating embraces; because we have been taught that love and marriage go together like a horse and carriage and that love means never having to say you're sorry; because,

---

Carter Heyward is Professor of Theology at Episcopal Divinity School, Cambridge, Massachusetts. Among her many books and articles are *The Redemption of God: A Theology of Mutual Relation* and *Our Passion for Justice: Images of Power, Sexuality, and Liberation.*

in short, love has been romanticized so poorly, trivialized so thoroughly, and perverted—turned completely around—from what it is, we find ourselves having to begin again to re-experience, re-consider, re-conceptualize what it means to say "I love you." What does it mean to believe that God is in the world, among us, moving with us, even by us, here and now? What does it mean to be a lover?

It occurs to me that it may be the special privilege of lesbians and gay men to take very seriously, and very actively, what it means to love. As lesbians and gay men, we have had to fall back on the category of lover in order to speak of our most intimate, and often most meaningful, relationships. Deprived of the categories that are steeped in the tradition of romantic love—categories like husband and wife, fiancée, marriage, masculinity and femininity, bride and bridegroom—deprived of the symbols of romantic love, such as rings and weddings and public displays of affection, both verbal and physical; deprived of the religious legitimation of romantic love—the blessing of our relationships; deprived of celebration, acceptance, even acknowledgment, of our relationships, we have had no other common word for ourselves, and for those whom we love, except the word lover. Deprived of civil and religious trappings of romantic love, we may well be those who are most compelled to plumb the depths of what it really means to love. Our deprivation becomes an opportunity and a vocation: to become conscious of the things we have not seen, and to make others conscious of these same things.

What might it mean—to love? I want to tell you what I am discovering, in the hope that you—each of you, all of you—will be moved to consider carefully your own experiences. There is a time, occasionally, for us to come to a consensus, for the purpose of corporate action. But my intention is not to gather a consensus on what it means to love, or even to suggest that a consensus would be helpful to us, or to anyone.

At this point, the last thing we need is a new set of commandments writ large in stone. I believe it is time to tell our stories, to listen carefully, to begin to experience our experience, to risk realizing and sharing our own senses of confusion, fear, frustration, anger, even rage, about what is done to us, and about what we do to ourselves and others, all in the name of a "love" that is too often not love at all, but only a sham. A perversion. A corruption of ourselves and the God that is with us.

And so I speak personally, as a *lesbian feminist Christian priest* and *teacher*. I use each of these words to describe myself, because each of them has grown in an evolving sense of how I might best be a lover of sisters and brothers in the world today. Lesbian. Feminist. Christian. Priest. Teacher. Either these dimensions of my identity enable me, as a lover of human beings and of creation itself, or they are destructive, dysfunctional dimensions of who I am that would best be somehow outgrown or discarded. For now, these overlapping, at times interchangeable, senses of myself ignite me, excite me, infuse me with a sense not only of what love means, but also that who I am—and who you are, and who we are together—matters. If we love the world, we matter. Lovers make all the difference in the world. Lovers re-create the world.

We must begin to see that *love is justice.* Love does not come first, justice later. Love is not a "feeling" that precedes right-relation among the persons in a family or the people of the world. We do not feel our ways into right-relation with other races, other people. We do not feel our way into doing what is just. We act our way into feeling. This was, by the way, the raison d'être of the Philadelphia ordination [of eleven women, myself included, as Episcopal priests before the church's hierarchy accepted us]: a conviction shared by many that we act our way into new feelings, new emotions, new ideas. And the act is love. The act is justice. Good feelings about love and justice may come later.

The same thing is true in friendship. The more just a personal relationship, the more loving this relationship, the more mutual, honest, beneficial, and creative for each friend, the more intense are the feelings of love between us. Speaking personally, the better the friendship, the more sustained and deeper and more precious to me is the erotic flow of energy that bonds us together. I find this terribly confusing, as you might imagine, in the context of a social order in which there is historically a great divide between friendship and sexual love—between philia and eros. Most of us have been out of touch, from the beginning, with the eroticism that draws us into friendship with persons of both sexes. Our sexuality is our desire to participate in making love, making justice, in the world; our drive toward one another; our movement in love; our expression of our sense of being bonded together in life and death. Sexuality is expressed not only between lovers in personal relationship, but also in the work of an artist who loves her painting or her poetry, a father who loves his children, a revolutionary who loves her people.

Sexuality is the undercurrent of the love that flows as justice in close friendship; in the victory salutation of a Sandinista rebel in Nicaragua; in the poetry of e. e. cummings, Emily Dickinson, Adrienne Rich; in the celebration of the Maundy Thursday Eucharist on behalf of Maria Cueto and Raisa Nemikin; in the genital embrace and ecstasy of two women, or two men, or a woman and a man, who are doing their best to make justice in their relationship. Where there is no justice—between two people or among thousands—there is no love. And where there is no justice/no love, sexuality is perverted into violence and violation, the effects of which most surely include rape, emotional and physical battering, relationships manipulated by control, competition, and contempt, and even war itself.

Love is passionate. If I love you, I am invested in our bonding. You are important to me, deeply so. Passion is a deep realization of our relation, of the significance of who we are together, of the fact that you matter/I matter/we matter. I may not always be able to show you or tell you. I may even be afraid of you. I may hurt you or be hurt by you. But I *care* about us, whether or not I "feel good" about us right now, and I do not want to leave you comfortless and without strength. If I love you, I am your advocate. If I love you, I will struggle for you/myself/us. My passion is my willingness to suffer for us, not masochistically, but rather bearing up who we are, enduring both the pain and the pleasure of what it means to love, to do what is just, to make right our relation. A person of passion, a lover of humanity, is she or he who enters seriously and intentionally into the depths of human experience, insists upon its value, and finds God in "the exchange of glances heavy with existence" (Elie Wiesel); or in refusing to live any longer with "someone's feet upon our necks" (Sarah Grimké); or in the vision of a promised land in which we are "free at last" (Martin Luther King, Jr.), a land in which love as justice is humanity's common experience.

Our passion as lovers is what fuels both our rage at injustice—including that which is done to us—and our compassion, or our passion, which is on behalf of/in empathy with those who violate us and hurt us and would even destroy us. Rage and compassion, far from being mutually exclusive, belong together. Each is an aspect of our honesty—and our integrity—for just as our rage is entirely appropriate to our experience of lovelessness in our own lives and elsewhere in the world, so too is our compassion the ongoing acknowledgment and confession of our own refusals to make love, to make justice, in the world—beginning in our own homes, in our own beds, at our own altars. How, in the name of either God or humanity, can we hear the frustrated and fear-laced protests against us raised by bishops, priests, and laypersons of our own church without experiencing both rage at what is being done to us in the name of love, and compassion for those who—like us, and with us—act, in some way, every day, on the basis of fear, projection, denial, scapegoating, and contempt for those who threaten us?

I am not suggesting that we be marshmallows. To the contrary. I would like us to continue to toughen up in our work for love and justice at every level of human life. And the way to move on through these trials by fire, being shaped by courage and passion, is actively to realize our own participation in fear and denial, in injustice and lovelessness;

and to do what we can each day "to go and sin no more." Regardless
of our good intentions, our feet will always be placed squarely on someone's neck—perhaps when we least realize it. And it is the loving, just
vocation of those whom we put down to ask us to remove our feet from
their necks; if need be, to tell us; and, finally—if we refuse—to knock
us off.

We, lesbians and gay men in the church, are in a social situation in
which we are asking ecclesiastical authorities to remove the feet of a
predominant theological tradition—both sexist and heterosexist—from
our necks. Some of us are telling these institutional authorities. And,
if it is not done, our loving and just vocation is to knock them off.

We need to remember something. Both as *oppressor* (white, male, up-
per-middle-strata people, capitalist dupes in a world yearning for common sources, unjust lovers in one-to-one relationships) and as *oppressed*
(females, homosexuals, poor, blacks, other colors and racial/ethnic mi-
norities, victims of domination in personal relationships)—we need to
remember that the oppressed set both the timetable and the agenda
for liberation. If we say now is the time, *now is the time!* Our compassion
is chastened and sustained by our rage.

Love is full of such yearning, such adamant insistence for right-
relation, such compassion, such rage. And it is absolutely irrepressible.

In a society, essentially a contemporary world order, built upon sex
roles; an economy—namely capitalism (although Marxism has a similar
set of sex-role problems)—maintained upon sex roles; a religion—
Christianity—thoroughly patriarchal and rooted in sex roles, the deepest currents of women's liberation and gay/lesbian liberation merge in
radical feminism and threaten to bring down the entire social/eco-
nomic/religious structure of reality.

Many fear that lesbian feminism poses a threat to the nuclear family,
the economic order, the religious assumptions about marriage as the
blessed state, the fatherhood of God and the motherhood of women,
the procreative norm of sexuality, and the high value of dominant-
submissive relationships beginning with male property rights and extending to God the Father. Those who fear that this is what we are
about fear rightly. As lesbian, feminist, Christian, I believe that our
vocation is to bring down the sacred canopy that has heretofore pre-
vented our active realization of love and justice in human life as the
only sacred—godly, right, and normative—dimension of our life together on earth. If economic structures do not support love, justice,
mutuality, and cooperation in human life, they should be undone.

Heterosexism is built and maintained upon patriarchy: patriarchal
definitions of what it means to be female and male and of what it
means to have sex—fantasies that rigidly delineate the male from the
female, the masculine from the feminine, the animus from the anima,

the top from the bottom, the initiator from the receiver, and the power of the phallus from the gratitude of the womb. Heterosexism is a social structure pervasive in our culture and worthy only of being undone.

And yet, to participate in its undoing is to feel a little crazy. For I, like you, like us all, have been raised and instructed in heterosexist values. I have come to realize that these heterosexist assumptions all but complete our sense of who we are in the world. To reject them privately is difficult and tedious, and leads us toward strange senses of schizophrenia. To reject them publicly is to take a step none of us is ever prepared to take. It is to begin to act our way into what we hope, believe, or trust will be new ways of feeling and thinking about ourselves and others in the world.

To state publicly that we are lesbians or gay men is to enter, for a time at least, into a sense of ourselves as crazy. Such has been my experience. By craziness, I mean that my own sense of what is important, of who I am in relation to others in the world, of what my vocation as priest and teacher is, even my sense of what is happening in my closest relations—with friends and lovers—is called into question, often as much by me as by others. To feel crazy is to wonder if I am concocting a reality meaningful only to me and a few folks who are crazy enough to agree with me; it is to feel as if I have stepped outside the arena of what is not only acceptable, but also intelligible—even, at times, to myself. My decision (years in the making) to state publicly that I am a lesbian was a decision central to my vocation as a teacher (of students, for whom sexuality is usually a primary concern); a priest (in a church in which sexuality is a bedrock of the entire corpus of theological tradition and praxis); a feminist (in a society founded upon unjust assumptions about female and male roles); a Christian (who believes that the command to love neighbor as self has as much to do with eros and philia as with agape, and that such love knows no gender confines); and a lover (a person in pursuit of friendship, justice, cocreativity in the world, including our most immediate and intimate relations).

To say I am a lesbian is to make a statement at once personal and political. It is to acknowledge the fact that, in our present social order, mutual sexual relationships are available largely in same-sex relationships. I have come to believe that it is unwise to expect true personal equality—mutuality of common benefit—between women and men in a sexist society. And, while I can appreciate the efforts of women and men toward this end, this is not where I choose to invest my self, my energy, my passion.

The lesbian relation, as I experience it, may be mutual, and as such may offer a glimpse into a way of being in the world that is as instructive for women and men in relation as for women and women and men and men. To be a lesbian is, for me, a way—the best way for me—of being lover.

To be a lesbian is to begin to untangle myself from the "lies, secrets, and silences" (Adrienne Rich) that have been draped as a shroud over our life together on earth. It is to invite projections onto myself, to trigger anxiety, to learn to bear—with others—a common pain, a common yearning, a common responsibility to make each other conscious of the things we do not see. It is to suggest that eros, philia, and agape are different words for the one experience of what it means to love. It is to affirm that lesbianism is a political act, a spiritual affirmation of God—the power of relation—in the world.

We are just learning to name ourselves, to experience our experience, to speak of these things without trembling or even apology. For me, lesbian sexuality is *loving* sexuality. It is *just* sexuality, rooted in and expressed between peers who have work to do together in the world—specifically, the liberation of women. It is to linger on the particularity of being women in patriarchal society. Lesbianism is cultivated in a vital intensity between/among women, an intensity vital at least for some of us—if all of us are ever to take ourselves and our sisters as seriously as we were born to believe we should take men: whether Church Fathers or natural fathers, employers, husbands, or sons, the Sonship of a Redeemer, or the Fatherhood of a Creator. Lesbian feminism is shaped in the struggle against the structures of male dominance—including such structures of one-to-one relationships as mating, dating, marriage.

And we who are lesbians—and perhaps gay men as well—need to be on guard against being washed away by the torrents of craziness (which is what has happened to many of our foremothers and forefathers), or—worse yet—finally engulfed by the powers that be, and convinced that the only way we can survive in the world is to accommodate ourselves—passively and invisibly—in conformity with the norms of the present order.

This is not a call to "come out." It is a call to be aware of what you are doing and why. It is a call to realize the depth of the dilemma in which feminists, lesbians, and gay men find ourselves—whether we are 100 percent in the closet, 95 percent out, 50 percent both ways, completely unclear on whether we are in or out, or even on whether or not we are gay/lesbian! It is a call to realize that what homosexuals are perceived to be about (and what some of us are about intentionally) is not simply the right to lead our own private lives, but rather an overhauling of the social structures of our time.

Those who resist us have good reason. The stakes are high. True sexual liberation—for homosexuals and for women—will happen only when our economic, religious, educational, business, and other structures and customs do not operate on the assumption that men will lead and women follow; that men work away from home and women in the home; that only a man and a woman constitute a creative couple; that only procreation is truly creative; and that in order to have a social order, someone must be on top and someone else on the bottom—economically, religiously, sexually, otherwise. To challenge these assumptions is, in some very real sense, to go mad. The "Fathers" are not with us. Our families do not know how to be with us. Our church believes it must be against us. The Bible admonishes us. Jesus was silent about us. The authorities that be despise the threat that we pose—and despise it all the more if we happen, or appear to be, wise and happy people. It is much easier to tolerate a sad and pitiful homosexual than a proud and creative gay man or lesbian. If we affirm ourselves, we are seen as sick; if we renounce ourselves, we are called healthy. And we think *we* are crazy!

All of which is to say that, for me, lesbianism has been, and is, a tedious but important way of my learning to love—myself, my friends, my God. Lesbianism is a sign of justice for women. Lesbianism signals the opportunity for creative cooperation among women on behalf of a humanity of women and men in which cooperation often gives way to competition, and love to coyness, manipulation, and contempt.

If our common vocation is to be lovers, perhaps we can be more conscious of what justice is in our own lives and in the world; conscious of our own passion with and for each other, as each of us seeks to make love; conscious of our own feelings of craziness—learning to see that we are not "out of our minds." We are beginning to live with integrity, to reclaim our minds as our own; integrity, in which personal life-style and political conviction converge; in which friendship, sexuality, love, and justice are a common stream flowing into righteousness at home and elsewhere in the world; in which we begin to understand that loving is always a revolutionary act. Among lovers and friends, as well as in our passion for justice for women, blacks, Native Americans, the poor in the United States, Latin America, the Middle East—true love is the *most* revolutionary act. It is exactly the opposite of romantic love. To really love is to topple unjust structures, bringing down the principalities and powers of domination and control at all levels of human social relations. Such loving needs no church blessing—although it is good when it is forthcoming, whether for a gay or lesbian couple, civil rights, or the revolution of the people in El Salvador.

To say I love you is to say that you are not mine, but rather your own.

To love you is to advocate your rights, your space, your self, and to struggle with you, rather than against you, in our learning to claim our power in the world.

To love you is to make love to you, and with you, whether in an exchange of glances heavy with existence, in the passing of a peace we mean, in our common work or play, in our struggle for social justice, or in the ecstasy and tenderness of intimate embrace that we believe is just and right for us—and for others in the world.

To love you is to be pushed by a power/God both terrifying and comforting, to touch and be touched by you. To love you is to sing with you, cry with you, pray with you, and act with you to re-create the world.

To say "I love you" means—*let the revolution begin!* God bless the Revolution! Amen.

Every Two Minutes

Battered Women and Feminist Interpretation

SUSAN BROOKS THISTLETHWAITE

All day long, every day, women are verbally intimidated, battered, injured, and killed by the men they live with. If, as Susan Brownmiller has said, "rapists are the shock troops of patriarchy," then batterers are the army of occupation. This essay is concerned with the way in which this climate of violence that touches women's lives affects biblical interpretations.

All women live with male violence. A survey conducted by the National Division of the United Methodist Church's Program of Ministries with Women in Crisis in 1980 and 1981 indicates that one in every twenty-seven United Methodist women had been raped, one in every thirteen had been physically abused by her husband, one in every four had been verbally or emotionally abused. Of the respondents, both male and female, one in nine knew of a close friend or relative who had been raped, one in six knew of physical abuse, one in five knew of emotional abuse.[1]

While the authors are aware of the limitations of their survey, as a random sampling of Protestants the survey seems to indicate that even scratching the surface of women's lives reveals the daily presence of violence.

The authors also observed, "Denial runs deep." Their report has met with "disbelief and an amazing capacity to rationalize the findings."[2] Denial is the way to the continuation of the abuse of women. Consciousness of the violence against women with which we all live every day is the beginning of its end.

A feminist biblical interpretation must have this consciousness at its center. The Christian scriptures are inextricably interwoven with this history of the belief systems that support the view of women as scape-

---

Susan Brooks Thistlethwaite is Associate Professor of Theology and Culture at Chicago Theological Seminary. She is an ordained minister of the United Church of Christ and a member of the National Council of Churches Inclusive Language Lectionary Committee. She is author of *Metaphors for the Contemporary Church* and editor of *A Just Peace Church*.

goats. In *Violence Against Women,* Emerson and Russell Dobash have a chapter on the relationship of biblical material to the problem of spouse abuse, in which they call women "the appropriate victim." They believe this problem requires intensive examination of history for the structures that support the legitimization of wife as victim.

The seeds of wife beating lie in the subordination of females and in their subjection to male authority and control. This relationship between women and men has been institutionalized in the structure of the patriarchal family and is supported by the economic and political institutions and by a belief system, *including a religious one,* that makes such relationships seem natural, morally just, sacred.[3]

There is apparent division over the question of whether the location of the authority (warrant, cause, justification) of a feminist interpretation of the Bible is in the text or in women's experience. I believe it is impossible to make this distinction with any clarity because women's experience in Western culture has been shaped by the biblical materials, and the biblical materials were shaped by a patriarchal culture.

Following a presentation I gave on the Bible and battered women in New York in October 1982, one member of the audience raised the question, "Why deal with the Bible at all?" But as anyone who works with abused women knows, this is not an option. Battered women frequently bring their religious beliefs to the process of working through a battering relationship. Phone calls to shelters often begin with the phrase, "I'm a Bible-believing Christian, but . . ." We begin to develop a feminist interpretation because the Bible is a part of the fabric of the oppression of battered women.

In the early 1970s I became involved as a pastor counseling abused women. I received calls from some women who were experiencing abuse but were reluctant to try to change their situation because they had been told the teaching of the Bible prohibited their protest. I organized Bible studies with some of these women, and I have continued this work in several locations. Many of the examples that follow are from such groups.

FEMINIST METHOD

A feminist method does not always come first chronologically. In Elisabeth Schüssler Fiorenza's landmark work *In Memory of Her: A Feminist Theological Reconstruction of Christian Origins,* method appears first in the volume, but it does not come first in the development of her thought. It was living with the texts themselves in the midst of the contemporary women's movement that shaped her method of investigation. Precisely because it is a method of investigation, it is a process for discovery of what has been hidden.

Moreover, a history of the *use* of biblical materials must become a part of the interpretation. John Cobb has noted that critical study recognizes, and indeed emphasizes, the socio-historical context in which the text functioned in the early church.[4] Feminist biblical interpretation has added a recognition of the patriarchal context in which the text functioned. But the text is still functioning, so to speak, and the patriarchal view that formed part of the formulation of the text is in turn supporting and supported by the text. All that history must become part of a feminist interpretation of the Bible.

Likewise, the origin of women's suspicions of the biblical interpretation of their situation is *both* the text *and* their life experience. Method emerges in this process of interrogation between text and experience. The key is that this process of interrogation proceeds over time.

Work with abused women is a process of support in which women who are physically safe, perhaps for the first time in many years, find self-esteem through affirmations of the gifts of women, through taking control of their lives, and through claiming their anger and finding in that anger a source of strength to act and to change. This process takes time. It cannot happen overnight.

Likewise, the development of a feminist method of biblical interpretation takes time. In Western philosophy, thought has been deemed a timeless, eternal absolute. But if that were the case, nothing new would ever emerge from human consciousness, because it would have to emerge full-blown. Plato wrestled with this problem in the *Meno* and decided that the way we come to know anything new is by remembering it from a formerly perfect state of knowledge before birth. Today we follow an investigative, scientific model of deduction that holds that thoughts proceed from first principles toward a logical conclusion. This is the grip of positivism that has held us in obeisance to science for more than two centuries.

In fact, it appears more likely that we think by analogy. When we want to ask about the unknown, we ask, "What is it like?" We learn something new both from the similarity and from the dissimilarity. The tension of the dissimilarity probes us to ask again. Thought moves by analogy and it moves through time. We have to live with something for a while before we can move on.

Over time, women come to varying levels of interpretation of biblical materials. Each of these levels is possible with the whole corpus, and all are necessary in order to deal with the varying attitudes toward women within the Bible.

THE LIBERATION IN THE TEXT: FINDING SELF-ESTEEM

The support given by programs and shelters is essential so that an abused woman can begin to see her life in a new way. Through her research, Lenore Walker has described the battered woman as follows:

1. Has low self-esteem.
2. Believes all the myths about battering relationships.
3. Is a traditionalist about the home, with strong beliefs in family unity and the prescribed feminine sex-role stereotype.
4. Accepts responsibility for the batterer's action.
5. Suffers from guilt, yet denies the terror and anger she feels.
6. Presents a passive face to the world but has the strength to manipulate her environment enough to prevent further violence.
7. Has severe stress reactions, with psychophysiological complaints.
8. Uses sex as a way to establish intimacy.
9. Believes no one will be able to help her resolve her predicament except herself.[5]

Abused women who receive support begin to learn that they have self-worth and to experience their anger as legitimate. Yet these women believe what they have been taught the Bible says about their situations: that women are inferior in status before husband and God and deserving of a life of pain. One woman said, "God punished women more" (see Gen. 3:16).

Frequently, women with strong religious backgrounds have the most difficulty in accepting that the violence against them is wrong. They believe what they have been taught, that resistance to this injustice is unbiblical and unchristian. Christian women are supposed to be meek, and claiming rights for oneself is committing the sin of pride. But as soon as battered women who hold rigidly traditional religious beliefs begin to develop an ideological suspicion that this violence against them is wrong, they react against it.

In workshops for persons who work with abused women, I have found that most social workers, therapists, and shelter personnel view religious beliefs as uniformly reinforcing passivity and tend to view religion, both traditional Christianity and Judaism, as an obstacle to a woman's successful handling of abuse. Unfortunately, they also say that many strongly religious women cease attending shelters and groups for abused women when these beliefs are attacked.

For women whose religious beliefs include extremely literal interpretations of the Bible as the norm, no authority except that of the Bible itself can challenge the image contained in these texts of woman as silent, subordinate, bearing her children in pain, and subject to the absolute authority of her husband. Yet in Bible study groups, these women can learn that the scriptures are much more on their side than they dared hope. They can become suspicious of a biblical exegesis that is a power play used against them. The process of critical interpretation is often painful and wrenching, because new ways of looking at the Bible have to be learned. But it is also affirming, because one is telling abused women, "You have a right both to your religious beliefs and to your self-esteem."

The core insight with which to begin such a process of interpretative suspicion is that the Bible is written from the perspective of the powerless.[6] The people of Israel, God's chosen, are a ragged band of runaway slaves. God, by identifying *this* people as chosen, is revealed as a God who sides with those who are out of power. It may be that to be out of power is a continuing metaphor in scripture for those who are especially valued by God.

Several types of texts have proved especially helpful to abused women. The theme of God's care for widows and orphans can be helpful in demonstrating that those who are oppressed by societal structures are especially dear to God. A widow in Israel was effectually without economic support and a nonperson in the eyes of that society. The children of a widow, because they lacked this economic support, were considered orphans. God's judgment on those who would afflict any woman or child was especially severe (Ex. 22:2–24).

Yet this does not mean that the impoverished condition of widows and orphans is legitimated because of God's care. God's identification with the oppressed helps them to value themselves as God values them and to recognize that their oppression is unjust. God does not want meek acceptance of oppression.

In *Liberation Preaching*, Justo and Catherine Gonzalez note, "God seems to choose those who have been made to feel like outcasts and then gives them a new sense of self-worth. God vindicates them in the eyes of their former oppressors."[7] This theme of the vindication of the powerless is a constant one in the Hebrew scriptures (see 1 Sam. 2:1–10). It is to be contrasted with the sinful arrogance of the powerful, who believe themselves secure in their own strength (see Psalm 73).

It is essential to see that the ministry of Jesus of Nazareth continued this identification of the chosen of God with the poor. Jesus announced his ministry as one who proclaimed "release to the captives, and recovering of sight to the blind, to set at liberty those who are oppressed, to proclaim the acceptable year of the Lord" (Luke 4:18–20).

Jesus included women in his ministry and ministered to their distress, both spiritual and socioeconomic. The striking amount of biblical material that recounts Jesus' special regard for women, despite androcentric reaction, was the beginning point for the development of a feminist interpretation of the Bible.

Examples of Jesus' care for women are seen in the story of the widow's mite (Luke 21:1–4; 15:8–10), the forgiveness of the prostitute who has faith (Mark 14:3–9), the healing of the woman with the bloody flux (Luke 8:43–48), and the defense of Mary's right to discipleship (John 4:16–30).

Raymond E. Brown has entertained the idea that the crucial role women play in discipleship and apostolic witness is evidence of female leadership in the Johannine community. Jesus' public ministry begins and ends with a story about women: Mary, the mother of Jesus, and Mary Magdalene. Several times, stories of the discipleship of women and that of men are paired: the faithfulness of Nicodemus is paired with the insight of the Samaritan woman; the christological confession of Peter is paralleled by that of Martha. Women's roles in the Fourth Gospel placed them as intimate disciples, those whom Jesus loved (Martha and Mary).

In researching the evidence of the Fourth Gospel, one is still surprised to see to what extent in the Johannine community women and men were already on an equal level in the Good Shepherd. This seems to have been a community where in the things that really mattered in the following of Christ there was no difference between male and female—a Pauline dream (Gal. 3:28) that was not completely realized in the Pauline communities.[8]

Yet the text with which many abused women find the most identification is John 7:53–8:11. Jesus' defense of the woman who would have been stoned (abused) for adultery, omitted in many manuscripts, including the earliest ones, appears to be an authentic incident in the life of Jesus. Some interpreters have argued that this pericope was not originally part of the Gospel of John. Yet the extraordinary position of women in this Gospel may be a reason for its later inclusion.

Whether or not the woman has already been tried, she is on the verge of execution, having been caught in the act of adultery. Adultery for Jewish women could consist merely in speaking to a male alone. Her crime is not specified beyond that text. But somehow she has transgressed patriarchal grounds.

Textual interpretation usually overlooks the woman's situation and stresses that the scribes and Pharisees wanted to put Jesus to the test and were looking for grounds on which to accuse him.[9] But women who have suffered physical violence hear that whatever human law or custom may legitimate violence against women, it cannot stand face to face with the revelation of God's affirmation of all humanity. Many abused women would echo the joy of the woman who exclaimed, "That's right! He [Jesus] broke the law for her!"

THE LIBERATION OF THE TEXT: TAKING CONTROL

Some biblical material that appears not to address women, or even appears hostile to them, can be reworked to bring out liberating themes for abused women. The opinion of women that prevailing androcentric interpretation of the Bible is wrong, coupled with the emphasis in a major portion of the biblical materials themselves on God's identification with the oppressed, creates critical interpretation. Consciousness-raising for these women has provided the essential catalyst: the insight that women are included in the category of the poor, the oppressed, and the outcast. Moving from that critical standpoint, women can begin to examine and reinterpret these texts, imagining new relationships between the texts and their experience.

An especially useful text is Luke 9:1–5, which ends, "And wherever they do not receive you, when you leave [there] shake off the dust from your feet as a testimony against them." One of the crucial issues for abused women is the psychological and physical intimidation they experience that prevents them from leaving. Shelters and safe houses can begin to help with the fear of destitution and further violence faced by a woman who contemplates leaving. But there are psychological factors as well that include religious sanctions against a woman's "breaking up the home."

What kind of people are my children going to become, seeing us or hearing us live this way? Will my son abuse his wife or girlfriend as he's seen his father do? Will my daughter live in fear and dread of every man she meets? For *them*, if not for me, I've got to do something. But instead, I stay, and stay, and stay for what seems like an eternal hell. I can't see my way out. I'm fearful of losing family respect for my failed marriage, *afraid of censure about my religious convictions*, fearful of a terrible reputation with my own friends (the few who are left). Finally I become obsessed with a fear of losing my respect for myself, and for my sanity—what's left of it.[10]

Because abused women experience themselves as out of control of their lives, part of working with them involves attempts to take control. One of the major obstacles to women's hearing the permission to leave where they are not valued is that they do not identify themselves with the disciples.

Disciples are followers of Jesus who hear the Word and do it (Mark 8:34–35). By this definition, the Synoptic Gospels agree that women were among the most faithful of Jesus' disciples, remaining at the foot of the cross even when others had fled. Jesus appeared first to women and commissioned them to tell of his resurrection, the central fact of the "good news," to the other disciples (Matt. 28:10; Mark 16:7; Luke 24:8–9).

The Roman Catholic Church has emphasized the absence of women among the twelve as indicative of Jesus' preference for male leadership.[11] While the New Testament authors are not uniformly in agreement on the role of the twelve, the theological function of the twelve is to represent the twelve tribes of Israel. In this way they provide a bridge between the Israelite past and the hoped-for future in which all Jews and Gentiles would be united as the People of God. The twelve thus have a largely symbolic role, not an administrative one, as evidenced by the fact that they were not replaced by the church after their deaths.[12]

Much of the New Testament material leads one to believe that the circle around Jesus was in fact quite fluid and did include women.

Another title for Jesus' followers throughout his ministry is apostles. Generally, the term "apostle" is thought to refer to the twelve, a point of view held by the framers of the Vatican Declaration. On the contrary: it is a much wider circle, according to some New Testament writers. Junia, considered a woman by John Chrysostom, is named by Paul as "outstanding among the apostles" (Rom. 16:7, NIV). The "apostle" Paul, of course, was not a member of the twelve at all (see Gal. 1:1–24).

It is therefore quite reasonable to decide that women were included in the most intimate circle around Jesus and that their inclusion was deliberate on his part. We begin to see how this text can be heard as addressing women. Power and authority are given to those who hear the Word of God and do it, the disciples. Women can claim this power and authority to heal their situation. One woman, reading the text in this way, remarked, "I thought that you always had to turn the other cheek."

For too long we have neglected the healing and casting out of demons that occurs so frequently in biblical materials in favor of discussions focused solely around the miraculous. But for abused women, women who study the Bible with bloodied noses, bruised ribs, and broken limbs, healing has a concrete and immediate reference. Likewise, the demonic has a concrete reference for those who have experienced the cycle of violence that builds in the home of an abuser.[13]

Women are not named in scripture as among the twelve. But women can learn to imagine themselves in the text on the basis of other textual material that does affirm women (such as women's discipleship) and on the basis of their own experience, which shows that they have been the ones to hear the Word of God and do it. This type of imagining challenges traditional interpretation, which has ignored women who are actually in the text or whose presence is implied by the text, and moves interpretation to a new level of engagement with the contemporary life of the church.

THE LIBERATION FROM THE TEXT: CLAIMING ANGER

Recently I have been conducting Bible study groups composed primarily of Catholic women over forty. Biblical material has not formed the religious framework for their acceptance of battering. Rather, it has been the church and its teaching about the role of women, divorce, and contraception that has provided religious legitimation for battering. Biblical study with these women has proceeded in a different manner because they did not regard the text as the primary religious authority in their lives. Rather, they were willing to enter into a suspicion of the many texts we examined that seemed to legitimize violence against women. These women found that they could not always trust the text or its traditional interpretations and that some of the texts are "harmful to their health."

Ephesians 5:21–23 is a very difficult passage for abused women struggling to find self-respect and some control over their lives. A preliminary study of this passage modifies extreme misinterpretation by demonstrating that to be "subject" (v. 21) does not mean specifically subject to physical violence: "For no man ever hates his own flesh, but nourishes and cherishes it, as Christ does the church" (v. 29). Husbands are admonished to love their wives "as their own bodies" (v. 28).

But physical violence is not the only form of abuse. Verbal intimidation, economic deprivation, and deliberate humiliation also characterize the violent relationship. One woman reported that her husband would deliberately keep her from arriving at family parties on time and then make her apologize to her relatives for being so late. This type of subjection appears compatible with the Ephesians passage, since only wives are admonished to "respect" their spouses.

Liberation from this text requires a recognition of its location within the biblical materials and of the function this particular emphasis in Ephesians played in the history of the church. In the pseudo-Pauline epistles, a shift away from the egalitarian ethos of the Jesus movement can be observed. Ephesians was written about the same time as Colossians, another epistle where the subjection of wives to husbands is emphasized. This is the first of the household duty codes, a series of exhortations to obedience in the households of the early Christian communities.

In Colossians 3:11, women are left out of the otherwise complete repetition of the baptismal formula of Galatians 3:28: "Here there cannot be Greek and Jew, circumcised and uncircumcised, barbarian, Scythian, slave, free man, but Christ is all, and all in all." "Neither male nor female" seems to belong to an earlier vision of human equality in Christ.

In Ephesians the household duty codes are limited to the relation of husbands and wives, combined with a theology of Christ and the church. This tends to reinforce the cultural notion of submission contained in the household duty codes with a theological legitimation of dominance and submission in the household of God. While the negative exhortation of Colossians ("Do not be harsh" to your wives) is softened ("Love" your wives), the inferior position of both wives and the church is cemented.

This is not the only pattern for divine-human relationships in the scripture. It is a pattern developed in response to social criticism of the newfound freedom of Christians, especially as this was reflected in the behavior of Christian wives and slaves. Other patterns exist, such as Galatians 3:28, and these can be drawn upon to critique patriarchal patterns such as Ephesians 5:21–23. The religious sanction in the household codes for the submission of women is a primary legitimation of wife abuse and must be challenged by women in order for them to gain some control over their own lives. A woman relates the traditional response of clergy:

Well, he spoke to both of us and he sat down for about an hour and he spoke about our financial situation and how having a child affected a marriage and things like that. Then he would bring in the vows of marriage—"to love, honor, and obey until death do us part." And I argued on the point of obeying because I feel, I felt at that time, to obey, it's all right in certain principles but you cannot obey all your life. I mean, if I asked him to stop gambling he would not obey me, but I have to obey all his rules. The minister would not talk about that fact.[14]

On the contrary, we must begin to talk about obedience and the role it has played in the cultural accommodation of religion to social mores, particularly to patriarchy. We must find strength to reject this notion of obedience to male authority in claiming our anger at the suffering that women have experienced in obedience.

A final text to consider within this rubric of liberation from the text involves a more subtle perception of the patriarchal violence against women that is in the biblical material. Genesis 2:21–24 is such a text.

Although Phyllis Trible has dealt with this text creatively in suggesting ways it can be understood as a basis of equality between woman and man, feminist interpretation must also recognize that the history of control of women's bodies is at stake in this text and must become part of its interpretation.[15] In the development of patriarchy, a very important issue has been control of women's abilities to procreate. The ability of women's bodies to create life has resulted in awe, fear, and the desire to control this power. While Freud may have discovered penis envy, womb envy has also played a role in human history.

This story is apparent in Genesis 2. A woman is born from a man in contrast to every other human birth. Perhaps, too, this interpretation of the first birth is also meant to symbolize control over woman's abilities to make decisions about whether to bear a child. From an early period the church has attempted to curtail knowledge of contraception and abortion. Puritanical Protestants led a late-nineteenth-century campaign to pass laws making contraceptive knowledge a crime. The current "Right to Life" movement is ecumenical in that its adherents are both Catholics and Evangelical/Fundamental Protestants. These movements are attacks on female autonomy that threatens patriarchal power at its core.

A Maryland woman who was severely abused over many years told me that when she complained after some attacks that she had sustained injuries, her husband would retort that "your bones are my bones— just like it says in the Bible." Less explicit reinforcement of patterns of domination and submission that legitimate violence against women can be found in interpretations of this text. Walter Brueggemann argues in the *Catholic Biblical Quarterly* that this text "suggests nothing of the superiority of the male as is often suggested." But Brueggemann correctly connects this text to marriage metaphors for divine-human relationship, such as "the Image of God and his [*sic*] bride Israel."[16] He then rightly draws the important analogy between Genesis 2:18–23 and Ephesians 5:21–33:

The same imagery in Paul [Ephesians 5:21–23] is illuminated. The relation of Christ and his bride-church is grounded in a commonality of concern, loyalty, and responsibility which is pledged to endure through weakness and strength.[17]

But the metaphor of patriarchal marriage for divine-human relationship is not one of mutuality; it is an image of dominance and subordination in that cultural context. Likewise, tying marriage to the divine-human relationship clearly divinizes male superiority in that relationship.

Brueggemann's interpretation of Genesis 2:18–23 illustrates the limits of a biblical interpretation that does not take a nuanced approach to the materials. There is much affirmation of women within the biblical materials, but grounds for violence against women exist as well, along with much material in between. This material has shaped cultural attitudes toward women. But contemporary experience also shapes our interpretation of the text.

Feminist biblical interpretation for women who live with male violence is a healing process that develops over time. It involves claiming self-esteem, taking control, and owning one's anger. Women's relationships to biblical materials need to undergo the same type of healing process. As Adrienne Rich has observed, "We have lived with violence far too long."[18]

NOTES

1. *Crisis: Women's Experience and the Church's Response. Final Report of a Crisis Survey of United Methodists*, The United Methodist Church (March 1982), 4–9.
2. Ibid.
3. R. Emerson Dobash and Russell Dobash, *Violence Against Wives* (New York: Free Press, 1979), 33–34. My emphasis.
4. John B. Cobb, Jr., *Process Theology as Political Theology* (Philadelphia: Westminster Press, 1982), 23.
5. Lenore E. Walker, *The Battered Woman* (New York: Harper & Row, 1979), 31.
6. Juan Luis Segundo, *The Liberation of Theology* (Maryknoll, NY: Orbis Books, 1976), 9.
7. Justo L. Gonzalez and Catherine G. Gonzalez, *Liberation Preaching* (Nashville: Abingdon Press, 1980).
8. Raymond E. Brown, "Roles of Women in the Fourth Gospel," *Theological Studies* 36 (1975): 688–89, reprinted in Brown's *Community of the Beloved Disciple* (Ramsey, NJ: Paulist Press, 1979), 183–98.

9. Rudolf Schnackenburg, *The Gospel According to St. John* (New York: Seabury Press, 1980), 165.
10. Quoted from *Introduction to Battered Women: One Testimony* (Southwest Community Mental Health Center, Columbus, Ohio). My emphasis.
11. "Declaration on the Question of Admission of Women to the Priesthood," in *Women Priests: Catholic Commentary on the Vatican Declaration*, ed. Leonard and Arlene Swidler (Ramsey, NJ: Paulist Press, 1977).
12. Elisabeth Schüssler Fiorenza, "The Twelve," in Swidler and Swidler, *Women Priests*, 138.
13. Lenore Walker has identified a three-stage cycle to the violence in homes of batterers: the "tension-building stage," the "acute battering incident," the "kindness and contrite, loving behavior" stage. Walker notes that women who kill their abusers do so in stage three (*The Battered Woman*, 55–70).
14. Dobash and Dobash, *Violence Against Wives*, 205.
15. Trible, *God and the Rhetoric of Sexuality* (Philadelphia: Fortress Press, 1978), 95–102.
16. Walter Brueggemann, "Of the Same Flesh and Bone, Genesis 2:23a," *Catholic Biblical Quarterly* 32 (1969): 532.
17. Ibid., 541.
18. Adrienne Rich, "Natural Resources," in her *Dream of a Common Language: Poems 1974–1977* (New York: W. W. Norton, 1978), 64.

Rethinking Theology and Nature

CAROL P. CHRIST

With many spiritual feminists, ecofeminists, ecologists, antinuclear activists, and others, I share the conviction that the crisis that threatens the destruction of the earth is not only social, political, economic, and technological, but is at root spiritual. We have lost the sense that this earth is our true home, and we fail to recognize our profound connection with all beings in the web of life. Instead many people uncritically accept the view that "man" is superior to "nature" and has the right to "use" the natural world in any way "he" sees fit. Though often clothed in the garb of modern science, such views have their root in theological conceptions that separate both God and humanity from nature and from finitude, change, and death.[1] The preservation of the earth requires a profound shift in consciousness: a recovery of more ancient and traditional views that revere the connection of all beings in the web of life and a rethinking of the relation of humanity and divinity to nature. I will explore some of the dimensions of this shift in consciousness by contrasting the work of Protestant theologian Gordon Kaufman with a variety of feminist voices that challenge the Western theological notion that human creation in the image of God sets us apart from the rest of nature.

Gordon Kaufman, whose views are typical of much recent Protestant theology and biblical criticism, articulates a widely held version of the Western theological separation of humanity and nature when he states:

The great religious struggle between Israel and Canaan was over the relative metaphysical importance of natural power and process on the one hand and personal moral will on the other. When Yahweh won that struggle it meant that the object of ultimate loyalty and devotion for humans in the West would be conceived increasingly in terms of models rooted in our moral and personal experience, not in our sense of dependence upon and unity with the orders and processes of nature.

Carol P. Christ, a feminist writer and thealogian who has taught at Pomona College and Harvard Divinity School, is author of *Laughter of Aphrodite: Reflections on a Journey to the Goddess* and *Diving Deep and Surfacing*, and coeditor of *Womanspirit Rising*. Currently living in Greece, she is completing a book about her life in a Greek village titled *A Year of Seasons*.

According to Kaufman, Western theological tradition considers nature to be without purpose or value: "Nature appears to be a nonteleological, nonaxiological order within which emerges purposive valuing activity." He states further that

the conceptions of God and humanity, as they have developed in Western religious traditions, work hand in hand toward distinguishing humankind from (the rest of) nature. Nature is *not* [my italics] conceived primarily as our proper home and the very source and sustenance of our being.[2]

He argues that in Western theology the concept of a personal moral will separates both humanity and God from nature. He also maintains that human agency and morality cannot be explained without positing a God who stands outside the natural world as their source.

Feminist philosopher, poet, and mystic Susan Griffin challenges the Western tradition's assertion that humanity is separate from nature and that our value lies in this alleged separation. She concludes her book *Woman and Nature* with a passage that reverses the imagery of Plato's vision in the cave. Plato equates the physical world and the body with darkness that can only be lit by the transcendent light of reason, while Griffin writes:

I know I am made from this earth, as my mother's hands were made from this earth, as her dreams were made from this earth and this paper, these hands, this tongue speaking, all that I know speaks to me through this earth and I long to tell you, you who are earth too, and listen *as we speak to each other of what we know: the light is in us.*[3]

Here she challenges the Western view that we are to understand ourselves as set apart from nature by our reason and moral will. But her work is imbued with what some might call a stunning moral consciousness and will. She writes of the intrinsic value of other beings:

... for the blackbird, which flies now over our heads, whose song reminds us of a flute, who migrates with the stars, who lives among reeds and rushes, threading a nest like a hammock, who lives in flocks, chattering in the grasses, this creature is free of our hands, we cannot control her.[4]

Griffin and Kaufman express two very different understandings of the human relation to nature: one asserts our ontological separation by virtue of personal moral will; the other names a felt connection. The voices, too, are different. One separates itself from whatever passions and emotions may have led to its assertions, affirming that only thus can we think clearly; the other tells us with its every word that "*we have cause to feel deeply.*"[5] Those of us who have been trained in the language and thought forms of patriarchy but who have not entirely forgotten our connections to the powers of other beings, understand both voices. Should we follow the voice of male philosophy and theology and assert that the woman whose words have named something we know deeply within ourselves is after all not a philosopher, but, at best, a poet? Should we accept his assertion that she cannot adequately account for our differences from nature, for the moral projects we propose as persons? Or can we respond to her call to enter into dialogue and "listen *as we speak to each other of what we know*."[6]

Susan Griffin has named the passionate conviction that "we are nature"—something I have always known deeply within myself, but which I have found lacking from both the form and content of much of theology and philosophy. As a mystic, she also calls us to rethink the separation of the divine from nature. But before adopting her vision as a foundation for feminist thealogy, it is important to consider several typical misinterpretations of her work. One misreading of Griffin asserts that she has simply reversed the dualisms we have inherited, naming men and rationality as essentially evil, and women, nature, and irrationality as essentially good. But Griffin explicitly counters this view when she begins her book with a prologue that states:

He says that woman speaks with nature. That she hears voices from under the earth. That wind blows in her ears and trees whisper to her. But for him this dialogue is over. He says he is not part of this world, that he was set on this world as a stranger. He sets himself apart from woman and nature.

Close reading of this text indicates that it is man's choice that sets him apart from woman and nature, not his essence. Griffin underscores this point when she writes:

(And when we hear in the Navajo chant of the mountain that a grown man sits and smokes with bears and follows directions given to him by squirrels, we are surprised. We had thought only little girls spoke with animals.)[7]

Because philosophy has been defined as a discipline in which reason is separated from passion and emotion, some have asserted that when Griffin affirms deep feeling as a source of knowledge, she accepts Western culture's designation of women as intuitive and irrational. But Griffin's poetic reflections on the human relation to nature have deeply philosophical implications and demonstrate mastery of the language and thought forms of Western so-called rational thought. If Griffin had intended to state that women and nature are irrational and inarticulate, then she would not have compared her consciousness of herself as a writer to the flight of a redwing blackbird:

yet the blackbird does not fly in us but somewhere else free of our mind, and now even free of our sight, flying in the path of her own will, she wrote, the ink from her pen flowing on this paper, her words, she thought, having nothing to do with this bird, except, she thought, as she breathes in the air this bird flies through.

and:

all that I know, I know in this earth, the body of the bird, this pen, this paper, these hands, this tongue speaking, all that I know speaks to me through this earth.[8]

Griffin is playing here with the expectations embedded in our language and way of thinking. We are used to thinking of the mystical experience with the bird—a bodily, preverbal experience—in relation to the earth that we think of as inarticulate. But we are not used to thinking of the book we read in relation to the paper it is written on, the hand that wrote it in a particular place on a particular day, and both the hand and the pen and the paper as earth. We are used to hearing that women and girls speak with nature, but we are not used to hearing that those same girls and women put pen to paper, consciously shaping their experience into naming, into words.

Griffin is not proposing that women remain within a mystical, perhaps even mantic, but ultimately inarticulable and inarticulate relation with nature. She calls us rather to rethink the notions of rationality and articulation we have inherited as we rename the relation with nature that we experience. Griffin is clearly aware that this will require a deconstruction and reconstruction of language when she writes: "And we are nature. We are nature seeing nature. We are nature with a concept of nature. Nature weeping. Nature speaking of nature to nature."[9] Here Griffin is consciously using words that are not adequate to her conceptions, deforming and stretching language.

Because the disjunction of divinity, humanity, and nature is deeply embedded in the words "God," "humanity," and "nature," articulating new conceptions is difficult. The three terms in the triad—"God, man, and nature"—must be rethought together. Simply to say that the divine is nature, for example, will not do, because concepts of nature have already been defined as excluding teleology and the kind of power commonly associated with divinity. Nor, on the other hand, will simply saying that nature is teleological do, since teleology has been defined as residing in the divine and human moral will that stands over against nature. Similarly, it cannot be asserted that humanity is nature, since to most people that would imply that humans are irrational, immoral, and inarticulate. What is required is a revolution in thought, a deconstruction and reconstruction of theology and language.

In his recent work *Theology for a Nuclear Age*, Gordon Kaufman takes some steps towards this reconstruction, departing from the notion of the radical separation between divinity, humanity, and nature that he had earlier characterized as constitutive of Western theology. In recognition of the very real possibility that human beings may destroy ourselves and much of the life on the planet, Kaufman writes:

We humans must understand ourselves in the first place, therefore, as one strand in the very ancient and complex web of life, a strand, moreover, which would not exist apart from this *context* [my italics] which has brought it forth and continues to sustain it at every point.

But note that for Kaufman the "web of life" is "context." This leads me to ask whether the web of life is granted intrinsic value, or whether it is valued because it supports and sustains human life. Kaufman confirms these suspicions when he asserts that understanding our connection to the biosphere is not sufficient for understanding human nature and its potentialities.

Once an animal had evolved with a sufficiently complex nervous system to sustain linguistic and other symbolic activity, thus making possible primitive consciousness, memory, and imagination, a long and complicated *historical* development was required before anything that we would recognize as a truly human mode of existence could appear on earth. . . . Human creativity was born together with *intention* and *action* [my italics], as humans found they could themselves actualize some of these possibilities and hopes. Thus human existence gradually developed capacities not found in any other form of life.

Though acknowledging that humans are rooted in and sustained by the web of life, Kaufman asserts that intention and action, self-reflection and choice, or finite freedom and self-consciousness, remain the marks of the distinctively human. This is expressed within an evolutionary perspective in which the two processes of nature and history have been guided by a "hidden creativity," symbolized by the name "God," that has produced human beings who are essentially different from nature. Kaufman writes that

in the course of time the cosmic and divine order has brought forth a mode of being, a dimension of itself, that transcends in a significant way even the luxuriant fecundity of life, namely history—the symbolic order, the realm of spirit—within which consciousness and meaning, self-conscious subjectivity and purposiveness and freedom have reality. We humans are the only creatures we know who are the living incarnations of that distinctive mode of being.[10]

In view of this statement, I wonder whether it would be misreading Kaufman to say that if self-consciousness and finite freedom could be sustained apart from continuing dependence on the web of life out of which they arose, then the death of the biosphere would not itself be a significant tragedy. If this conclusion is not intended, and I suspect it may not be, then a stronger affirmation needs to be made of the intrinsic value of the web of life and those parts of human nature that are similar to the rest of the web of life. As it is, there remains in *Theology for a Nuclear Age* a profound humanocentrism in regard to the web of life and the nature of God, as well as a focus on thought and choice as that which definitively characterizes humanity and divinity. Though God for Kaufman is the hidden creativity behind both historical and biological evolution, one is left to conclude, perhaps despite Kaufman's intentions, that for the God he describes, the primary goal in the creation of the universe is the creation of humanity. But this is precisely the notion that we must question and deconstruct.

Kaufman argues that theological positions ought to be judged by the following criterion:

The supreme test, one might say, of the ultimate viability, and thus finally of the truth . . . [of any] symbolic frame of orientation is [its] capacity to provide insight and guidance in our situation today, a situation in which humankind has come up against its own limits in a most decisive and paradoxical way: through gaining the power to obliterate itself.[11]

I agree, and add three other criteria: (1) a symbol system must aid us in overcoming historic injustices between women and men, between races, and between peoples; (2) it must strike a deep chord in our experience; and (3) it must help us better to understand, love, and enjoy the life that has been given to us.

Kaufman argues that the symbol of God that comes to us through Christian tradition meets his test by playing a *relativizing* and a *humanizing* function. The relativizing function is provided by the symbol of God: "God is understood as that ecological reality behind and in and working through all of life and history, and the service of God can consist thus only in universally oriented vision and work."[12] I agree with Kaufman that the relativizing function of God reminds us of the importance of universally oriented vision and work. But I am not happy with the asceticism and self-denial implicit in Kaufman's notion that "*service* of God can consist *only* [my italics] in universally oriented vision and work." I also agree with Shug, who in Alice Walker's novel *The Color Purple*, said, "God love all them feelings. That's some of the best stuff God did."[13] And with Z Budapest who said, "All pleasures are rituals to the Goddess."[14]

Kaufman proposes that the symbol of Christ serves a humanizing function, providing orientation by showing us that "radical self-giving in the struggle with the worst evils of contemporary human life, culminating perhaps in complete self-sacrifice—crucifixion—is what is to be expected." I wonder whether this image of Christ crucified can be separated from the other more dangerous image of Christ exalted to the right hand of the Father. Kaufman courageously criticizes and rejects that image because it has "laid foundations for later Christian imperialism, . . . crusades against infidels and inquisitorial tortures and executions of heretics, and . . . ultimately give[s] its blessing to Western imperialism."[15] I am not convinced that one can change the way images of Christ have functioned in Christian imagination through theological, that is, intellectual, assertion. Images of Christ exalted as well as crucified remain embedded in the Christian Bible and liturgy and continue to mold and shape the Christian imagination. In addition, Kaufman's image of Christ crucified is tinged with a masochism that goes

beyond recognizing that life has a tragic dimension. Kaufman, following the Japanese writer, Shusako Endo, states that Christ "understood
himself as coming into the world to be trampled on by his fellow humans."[16] While it is true that the just do not always prosper, to me, to
say that we come into the world to be trampled upon is an overly
pessimistic reading of life. I am not persuaded that such an image of
Christ provides a genuinely humanizing function.

In the remainder of this essay I will articulate and discuss the outlines
of an alternative thealogical vision that I believe meets Kaufman's criterion of providing orientation for the lives we are living under the
threat of nuclear war and ecological destruction. This vision resonates
with many feminist voices. In Alice Walker's *The Color Purple*, Shug
describes her vision of God to Celie in these words:

My first step from the old white man was trees. Then air. Then birds. Then
other people. But one day when I was sitting quiet and feeling like a motherless
child, which I was, it come to me: that feeling of being part of everything, not
separate at all. I knew that if I cut a tree, my arm would bleed. And I laughed
and I cried and I run all round the house. I knew just what it was. In fact,
when it happen, you can't miss it. It sort of like you know what, she say, grinning and rubbing high up on my thigh. . . . I think it pisses God off if you
walk by the color purple in a field and don't notice it. . . . Everything want to
be loved. Us sing and dance, make faces and give flower bouquets, trying to
be loved. You ever notice that trees do everything to git attention we do, except
walk?[17]

Anthropologist Paula Gunn Allen, who comes from a Keres Pueblo
background, expresses a strikingly similar understanding in her book
The Sacred Hoop:

We are the land. To the best of my understanding, that is the fundamental
idea that permeates American Indian life; the land (Mother) and the people
(mothers) are the same. As Luther Standing Bear has said of his Lakota people,
"We are of the soil and the soil is of us." The earth is the source and being
of the people and we are equally the being of the earth. The land is not really
a place separate from ourselves, where we act out the drama of our isolate
destinies; the witchery [disconnected power] makes us believe that false idea.
The earth is not mere source of survival, distant from the creatures it nurtures
and from the spirit that breathes in us, nor is it to be considered an inert
resource on which we draw in order to keep our ideological self functioning. . . . Rather for the American Indians . . . the earth *is* being, as all creatures
are also being: aware, palpable, intelligent, alive. . . . Many non-Indians believe
that human beings possess the only form of intelligence in phenomenal existence (often in any form of existence). The more abstractionist and less intellectually vain Indian sees human intelligence as rising out of the very nature
of being, which is of necessity intelligent in and of itself.[18]

For me the divine/Goddess/God/Earth/Life/It symbolizes the whole
of which we are a part. This whole is the earth and sky, the ground

on which we stand, and all the animals, plants, and other beings to which we are related. We come from our mothers and fathers and are rooted in community. We come from earth and to earth we shall return. Life feeds on life. We live because others die, and we will die so that others may live. The divinity that shapes our ends is life, death, and change, understood both literally and as metaphor for our daily lives. We will never understand it all. We do not choose the conditions of our lives. Death may come at any time. Death is never early or late. With regard to life and death there is no ultimate justice, nor ultimate injustice, for there is no promise that life will be other than it is. There are no hierarchies among beings on earth. We are different from swallows who fly in spring, from the many-faceted stones on the beach, from the redwood tree in the forest. We may have more capacity to shape our lives than other beings, but you and I will never fly with the grace of a swallow, live as long as a redwood tree, nor endure the endless tossing of the sea like a stone. Each being has its own intrinsic beauty and value. There will be no end to change, to death, to suffering. But life is as comic as it is tragic. Watching the sun set, the stars come out, eating, drinking, dancing, loving, and understanding are no less real than suffering, loss, and death. Knowledge that we are but a small part of life and death and transformation is the essential religious insight. The essential religious response is to rejoice and to weep, to sing and to dance, to tell stories and create rituals in praise of an existence far more complicated, more intricate, more enduring than we are.

How does this vision meet the test of the theological task as proposed by Kaufman? God/Goddess/Earth/Life/It, the whole of which we are a part, the unnameable beneath naming serves a profoundly relativizing function. The supreme relativizing is to know that we are no more valuable to the life of the universe than a field flowering in the color purple, than rivers flowing, than a crab picking its way across the sand—and no less. This vision of God/Goddess/Life/Earth/It has much to say to the ecological, social, and nuclear crises that we face. The ethic that would follow from this vision is that our task is to love and understand, to live for a time, to contribute as much as we can to the continuation of life, to the enhancement of beauty, joy, and diversity, while recognizing inevitable death, loss, and suffering. To understand and value the life we enjoy is to understand and value the lives of all other beings, human and nonhuman—and to understand that we are limited by the values inherent in other beings. We cannot live without taking the lives of other beings, but when we understand our profound connection to other beings, we begin to understand that it is a violation of the web of life to take more than we need. To poison rivers and seas and the ground on which we stand so that we can have televisions and air-conditioning, to engage in wars of conquest in order to exploit other people's labor and take the resources of their land, is to forget that we are all connected in the web of life. Death and killing are part of life. But to imagine something that we call "our way of life" justifies the creation of nuclear bombs with the capacity to destroy most of the life on this planet is ultimate arrogance. This ethic calls into question much of modern life that is based on the acceptance of the inevitability of war, and on the exploitation of other people, of plants, animals, and the rest of nature. But the difficulty of comprehending how to implement an ethic based upon reverence and respect for all life forms within the web of life should not lead us to dismiss it as romantic or impractical.

In addition to inspiring respect for all beings in the web of life, the vision of connection encourages greater appreciation for the diversity of human experience. If the essentially human is defined as consciousness and self-reflection, it is hard to avoid the conclusion that some humans, especially those educated within the Western intellectual tradition, are more human than others. This view has often been expressed through the naming of others—women, ethnic, cultural, and racial groups—as closer to nature, as barbarians, savages, peasants, slaves. However, *if the essentially human is to understand our connection to other people and to all other beings and to rejoice in the life that has been given to us*, then Western intellectuals are by no means self-evidently superior.

Further, this view offers a reason, rooted in vital feelings and instinct, to live. The great philosopher Simone de Beauvoir has written: "If we do not love life on our own account and through others, it is futile to seek to justify it in any way."[19] To seek to perpetuate and preserve life because we enjoy it, because we love it, seems to me to be more life-affirming than the somewhat ascetic notion of "service to God" and the somewhat masochistic notion of "radical self-giving" proposed by Kaufman.[20] To choose life because we love it, does not mean life is without risk, inevitable suffering, loss, and death. It is life that can end in death at any moment that we must love. Such love must inspire an ethic rooted in a desire to enhance the life possibilities of all beings, both human and nonhuman.

Objections could be raised against the view I have articulated. Kaufman states in *Theology for a Nuclear Age*:

We might then, attempt to think of God in terms defined largely by the natural processes of cosmic and biological evolution. This would result in a God largely mute: one who, though active and moving with creativity and vitality, was essentially devoid of the kind of intentionality and care which was characterized by the heavenly father of tradition. Such a God could certainly evoke a piety of a profound awe and respect, and even, in its own way, of love and trust. But it is not a God who could provide much guidance with respect to the great crises we today face, crises which are largely historical in character, not biological, crises of human motivation, policy, action, and institutions. . . . If we are to think of God as that reality which actually *humanizes* us, as well as *relativizes* us [my italics], these matters [history, language, human purpose] will have to be taken into account.[21]

Though there is a certain symmetry in this argument, I do not find it compelling. Let us approach the problem from the other side. Let us entertain the possibility that the divinity that shapes our ends is an impersonal process of life, death, and transformation. Let us imagine that the human spirit—history, language, human purpose—is not the goal of creation. Let us imagine that the life force does not care more about human creativity and choice than it cares about the ability of bermuda grass to spread or moss to form on the side of a tree. The human species, like other species, might in time become extinct, dying so that other lives might flourish. But then is there nothing that should stop the human species from poisoning the earth or blowing it up? Suppose there is no personal Goddess or God who would punish us for our act, or even weep over what we had done? Does it therefore follow that there is no reason for humans not to destroy a universe that has been created through aeons of life, death, and transformation? I suggest that what can stop us is not knowledge that our self-reflection and freedom are in the image of God, nor that self-sacrifice is in the image of Christ. What can stop us, I propose, is a deeply felt connection to all beings in the web of life. What can stop us is that we love this life, this earth, the joy we know in ourselves and other beings enough to find the thought of the end of the earth intolerable. We do not need to know that our moral will is in the image of a personal God in order to know that we have the capacity to create death or to love and preserve life.

But let us probe further. Is an image of Goddess/God that is based in our connection to all beings within the web of life necessarily impersonal and uncaring? Or is it our own Western consciousness that imports the notion that nature is "devoid" of "intention and care." Let us return to the words of Paula Gunn Allen:

Many non-Indians believe that human beings possess the only form of intelligence in phenomenal existence (often in any form of existence). The more abstractionist and less intellectually vain Indian sees human intelligence as arising out of the very nature of being, which is of necessity intelligent in and of itself.[22]

Allen's view is that all beings have a similar nature. All beings—including rocks and rain, corn and coyotes, as well as the Great Spirit—have intelligence. In *Flight of the Seventh Moon*, the American Indian shaman Agnes Whistling Elk teaches Lynn Andrews how to listen to rocks: "Rocks are very slow and have sat around from the beginning, developing powers . . . Rocks can show what you are going to become. They show you lost and forgotten things."[23] The Great Spirit of the

American Indians is linked to the spirits of all beings, including rocks. When asked if the tree had a consciousness, Martin Buber responded, "I have no experience of that."[24] Susan Griffin writes, "Behind naming, beneath words, is something else. An existence named unnamed and unnameable."[25] There is a human tendency to name this unnameable with personal language, to believe that It cares as we care. I imagine, but I do not know, that the universe has an intelligence, a Great Spirit, that It cares as we care. I imagine that all that is cares. Sometimes I feel I hear the universe weeping or laughing, speaking to me. But I do not know. What I do know is that whether the universe has a center of consciousness or not, the sight of a field of flowers in the color purple or the rainbow must be enough[26] to stop us from destroying all that is and wants to be.

NOTES

This essay grew out of discussions in my class "God and the Prehistoric Goddesses" at the Harvard Divinity School and was presented as a public lecture in the Divinity School's Women's Studies and Religion Program on 4 March 1987. Constance Buchanan, Gordon Kaufman, Naomi R. Goldenberg, Judith Plaskow, and Mara Keller provided helpful comments on earlier drafts.

1. See "Finitude, Death and Reverence for Life," in my *Laughter of Aphrodite: Reflections on a Journey to the Goddess* (San Francisco: Harper & Row, 1987).
2. Gordon Kaufman, *The Theological Imagination: Constructing the Concept of God* (Philadelphia: Westminster Press, 1981), 226, 215–16, 225. Kaufman's modern post-Kantian perspective caused him to overstate the separation between divinity, humanity, and nature in Hebrew religion, but he is correct in stating that the Hebrew conception of Yahweh as ruling nature through a covenantal relation with humanity represented a fundamental departure from earlier views of the relation of God, humanity, and nature.
3. Susan Griffin, *Woman and Nature: The Roaring Inside Her* (New York: Harper & Row, 1978), 227.
4. Ibid., 226.
5. Ibid., xvii.
6. Ibid., 227.
7. Ibid., 1.
8. Ibid., 226, 227.
9. Ibid., 226.
10. Gordon Kaufman, *Theology for a Nuclear Age* (Philadelphia: Westminster Press, 1985), 35, 35–36, 44–45, 41, 44.
11. Ibid., 20, 28. See my critique of Kaufman's theological program in "Embodied Thinking: Reflections on Feminist Theological Method," in *Journal of Feminist Studies in Religion* 5 (Spring 1989).
12. Kaufman, *Theology for a Nuclear Age*, 37, 46.
13. Alice Walker, *The Color Purple* (New York: Pocket Books, 1982), 178.
14. Frequently stated in public lectures. See *The Holy Book of Women's Mysteries* (Los Angeles: The Susan B. Anthony Coven #1, 1979), 9, 11.
15. Kaufman, *Theology for a Nuclear Age*, 59, 50.
16. Ibid., 52.
17. Walker, *The Color Purple*, 178–79.
18. Paula Gunn Allen, *The Sacred Hoop: Recovering the Feminine in American Indian Traditions* (Boston: Beacon Press, 1986), 60.

19. Simone de Beauvoir, *The Ethics of Ambiguity*, trans. Bernard Frechtman (New York: Philosophical Library, 1948), 135–36.
20. For the particular dangers of an ethic of self-sacrifice for women, see Valerie Saiving, "The Human Situation: A Feminine View," in *Womanspirit Rising: A Feminist Reader in Religion*, ed. Carol P. Christ and Judith Plaskow (San Francisco: Harper & Row, 1979), 25–42.
21. Kaufman, *Theology for a Nuclear Age*, 44.
22. Allen, *The Sacred Hoop*, 60.
23. Lynn V. Andrews, *Flight of the Seventh Moon: The Teaching of the Shields* (New York: Harper & Row, 1984), 52.
24. Martin Buber, *I and Thou*, 2d ed., trans. Ronald Gregor Smith (New York: Charles Scribners' Sons, 1958), 8.
25. Griffin, *Woman and Nature*, 190.
26. Ntozake Shange, *for colored girls who have considered suicide when the rainbow is enuf* (New York: Macmillan, 1976).

Ritual as Bonding

Action as Ritual

STARHAWK

Rituals are part of every culture. They are the events that bind a culture together, that create a heart, a center, for a people. It is ritual that evokes the Deep Self of a group. In *ritual* (a patterned movement of energy to accomplish a purpose) we become familiar with power-from-within, learn to recognize its *feel*, learn how to call it up and let it go.

The pattern of the movement of energy in a Craft ritual is based on a very simple structure. We begin by grounding—connecting with the earth. Often we use the Tree of Life meditation. Then we cleanse ourselves, perhaps with a meditation on salt water or a plunge into the ocean, taking time to release our pain and tensions through movement or sound. The circle is cast: separating the ritual space and time from ordinary space and time, as we invoke the four elements. We invoke the Goddess and the God, and whatever other powers or presences we wish to greet.

Then we raise power by breathing, meditating, dancing, chanting. The power is focused through an image, an action, or a symbol. We may enter a trance together, taking a journey together into the underworld. After the power has reached its peak, we return it to the earth, grounding it through our hands and bodies. Then we celebrate with food and drink and take time to relax and be together. Finally, we thank all the powers we have invoked and open the circle, returning to ordinary space and time.

Rituals create a strong group bond. They help build community, creating a meeting-ground where people can share deep feelings, positive and negative—a place where they can sing or scream, howl ecstatically or furiously, play, or keep a solemn silence. A pagan ritual incorporates touch, sensuality, and humor. Anything we truly revere is also something that we can ridicule respectfully. The elements of laughter and play keep us from getting stuck on one level of power or developing

---

Starhawk, feminist and peace activist, teaches at several San Francisco Bay Area colleges. She travels widely lecturing and giving workshops. In San Francisco she works with the *Reclaiming* collective, which offers classes, workshops, and public rituals in the Old Religion of the Goddess. Her latest book is *Truth or Dare: Encounters with Power, Authority, and Mystery*.

an inflated sense of self-importance. Humor keeps kicking us onward, to go deeper. . . .

In a large group, especially one consisting of people who do not know each other well, we cannot reach the same level of closeness—nor can the power flow as smoothly—as in a small group. Yet larger rituals can also build community, and they have an excitement and an air of festivity that small coven meetings cannot attain. When bonding occurs in a larger group, and a Deep Self is formed, the energy may move by itself in the same way it moves in a small group. . . .

There are many factors we have learned to be aware of in planning large, open rituals. A ritual can alienate as easily as it can empower.

The first element to plan carefully is grounding. For a ritual to be powerful, we must start grounded, stay grounded, and end grounded, because the power that we raise comes into our bodies through the earth, and then returns to the earth.

We always begin a ritual, or any act of magic, by breathing together, by visualizing our connection to the earth and our connection to each other. Most often we use some variation of the Tree of Life. One of my favorite visualizations follows:

TREE OF GENERATIONS

Breathe deeply, from your belly. Let yourself stand loosely but firmly planted on the earth. Straighten your spine, and release the tension in your shoulders.

Now imagine that your spine is the trunk of a tree that has roots that go deep into the center of the earth. Let yourself breathe down into those roots, and let all the tensions and worries you bring with you flow down with your breath and dissolve into the earth.

Feel the way our roots connect under the earth, how we draw power from the same source. The earth is the body of our ancestors. It is our grandmothers' flesh, our grandfathers' bones. The earth sustained the generations that gave birth to us. As we draw on their power, the power of the earth, as we feel it rise through the roots in our feet and through the base of our spines, let us speak the names of our ancestors—of the ones who came before us, of the heroines and heros who inspire us . . .

And feel the energy of the earth rising into our bellies as we draw it up with our breath, feel it rise into our hearts and spread out from our hearts up through our shoulders and down through our hands. Feel it move around the circle through our hands—feel how it connects us through our breath. As we breathe together—breathing in, breathing out—we link ourselves together, and we speak our own names . . .

And feel the power rising up through our throats, and out the tops of our heads like branches that sweep up and return to touch the earth again, creating a circle, making a circuit. And the branches are our children and grandchildren, the generations that come after us, and we feel them intertwining above our heads, and we know that they are not separate from us, and that, like us, they too will return to earth. And we speak their names . . .

And through the branches, through the leaves, we feel the sun shining down on us, and the wind moving, and the moon and the stars shining down. And we can draw in the power of that light, draw it in as a leaf draws in sunlight, and feel it spread down through all the twigs and branches, down through the trunk, down through the roots, until we are filled with light, and as the light reaches the roots, we feel them push yet deeper into the earth.

And as we relax, we feel the connection, the ground beneath our feet, and we know that we cannot lose that ground.

Whenever energy is raised, we ground it, return it to the earth, by touching the earth. Sometimes we place our palms on the ground; sometimes we crouch down and release the power through our entire bodies. We may ground the energy periodically during a ritual, and we are careful to ground it thoroughly after the cone of power is raised. Otherwise, we are left feeling nervous, anxious, unfinished—and the excess energy easily turns to irritation with each other.

The cone of power is raised at the point in the ritual when the energy we have drawn up through our bodies spirals upward into a cohesive whole, reaches a peak, and then dies down. In a large ritual, the energy needs a clear focus, something easily seen or heard, and understood.

Not everyone in an open ritual will be familiar with the techniques of moving energy. However, if a few strong people shape the power, others will sense its rise and fall. The cone can be directed visually if we throw our arms up in the air. When some people do this, others will instinctively do the same thing, and the energy will follow everyone's body movements. When we touch the earth to ground the energy, others will naturally imitate these actions too. Again, the flow of energy will follow our movements.

In a large, open ritual, language is also crucial. Words that are abstract and New-Age buzz-words drain power, and they cause people's lips to curl. Far better to say, "Let's hold hands and breathe together" than, "Let us have an attunement." William Carlos Williams's famous dictum to poets, "No ideas but in things," is a good guide for ritual-makers as well—since magic is the language of *things*. The metaphors we choose reveal both our spirituality and our politics. We should be careful not to reinforce dualism by focusing on light to the exclusion of dark.

If we wish people to participate in chanting and dancing, then the songs we use must be so simple that they can easily be picked up on the spot. The words must be understandable; nothing drains energy more than a large number of people fumbling with an unfamiliar name, unless it is stopping the momentum of the ritual to instruct people.

When ritual is used in a situation that is not religious, such as a political demonstration, we need to be sensitive to the different needs and perspectives of all the people who may be involved. Religious trappings, the Goddess's names, even the word *Goddess* itself may offend many people and cause dissension. But if we speak of the *things* and people that embody the Goddess, that are manifestations of power-from-within—the earth, air, fire, and water, natural objects, each other—we speak a common language that can touch everyone, no matter what her/his philosophy or ideology.

RITUALS AT THE DIABLO CANYON BLOCKADE

The rituals my affinity group, Matrix, facilitated in camp and in jail at the blockade attempting to prevent the opening of the Diablo Canyon nuclear power plant in California put everything I knew about open rituals to the test. We wanted to share the power of ritual to create a group bond, but we were also aware that most people in camp were not Goddess-worshippers, or interested in becoming Witches. We were very sensitive about not *imposing* our religion on anyone—yet we did want to *share* the experience of magic.

Rose and I were the first members of Matrix to arrive at the blockade, the day after the alert was called. For several days, affinity groups gathered at the campsite, waiting until enough people were present to begin the blockade in force. During the waiting period, we took part in nonviolence trainings, helped with the work of the camp, and facilitated informal workshops in ritual. At one workshop, we planned a ritual collectively for the night of the full moon. It was very simple in structure. The main symbolic act would be to join our hands together in the center of the circle, reflecting the image on our camp buttons: joined hands across a stylized nuclear power plant, surrounded by a red circle that was crossed by a diagonal line (the international symbol for *no*).

We knew that because the underlying structure of the blockade was circular and nonhierarchical, no ritual we attempted to lead could work. Although we had a plan, we knew that, at most, we could facilitate and channel the group's strong, spontaneous energy if it arose.

As always happens, things did not go according to plan, yet everything we intended happened. The full moon rose while people were cooking and eating dinner. It was so fat and beautiful over the hills that everyone began howling, chanting, and banging on pots and pans. We had planned the ritual for much later, but friends came and told us that people were gathered down in an open field, waiting for the ritual to begin.

We went down, announcing the ritual as we went. I found myself deeply grateful for Rose's presence. In a structure so strongly oriented toward collectives, no one person alone could have worked a ritual. I am by nature a shy, introverted person (although I have often been accused of overcompensating), and my first instinct in large crowds is to wish I could disappear. Rose, however, has flair for the dramatic. She combines a warm heart with a striking appearance. She has very short, hennaed hair, clothing in bright, contrasting colors, and a resonant voice. Together, we made an effective team.

In the field a crowd of more than a hundred people was gathered, singing, and some musicians played guitars. We had, of course, no lights, no sound system. We could not even have candles because of the extreme danger of fire—there were no props.

Our plan had been to start with a Tree of Life meditation, and build this into a visualization of a circle of protection that would surround each person, each affinity group, the camp as a whole, and even the police and workers we would face on the blockade. We were going to invoke the elements with a simple chant, do a spiral dance, and build power.

However, the power was already built before we began. We asked the musicians to get people into a circle, thinking that this would quiet them so we could begin. But as soon as the circle formed, people began dancing inward in a spiral. I looked at Rose, and she looked at me. We both realized that we needed to abandon our expectations. I knew that if I could put myself in the silent place that I can find in my own coven, and let the inspiration arise, the ritual would work. I also knew that I couldn't relax that much. But the dance was moving inward— and we had to do something. So we joined it. As it became a tighter spiral, and the musicians ducked outside it to avoid being squeezed to death, we began a Native American chant to the elements:

> The earth, the water, the fire, the air
> Returns, returns, returns, returns.

People picked up the chant; it grew in power, becoming an expression of our purpose at the blockade, our commitment to a return of the balance of the elements. Someone picked up the beat with a drum. Suddenly, spontaneously, *everyone* joined hands and moved together, just as Rose had envisioned in our planning. We were swaying and chanting with our hands entwined, and I slipped into the twin consciousnesses that a priestess develops, let myself go into the power, lose myself in it—in the exhilaration of it—and yet consciously remain grounded in order to keep the power grounded. In fact, I finally began to sing a Tree of Life vision above the chanting. Rose also began to sing a vision, and soon others' weaving voices carried words and melodies above the chant.

At last we grounded. As people sat on the ground, we led the meditation we had planned, and then we asked people to speak of their visions for the blockade. Although hearing people's visions can be moving, after a while the descriptions usually begin to deteriorate into spiritual or political catch-phrases. When we felt the energy begin to dissipate, we thanked the powers we had invoked, and started the group singing. The faithful musicians kindly led the singing as we slipped away. The ritual was over.

Chaotic and backward as it was, Rose and I loved it. While some people who took part were frightened by the intensity of the energy, I suspect that most people also loved it as one loves a big, shaggy, clumsy dog who is terribly good-natured but cannot be trusted near breakable china. Certainly, people seemed to want more exposure to ritual. Weeks later, after a long, painful, all-day meeting, the decision by consensus to end the blockade included an agreement to have a closing ritual.

The closing ritual took place at the new moon. Members of the nonviolence trainers collective asked me to facilitate. Most of the original members of Matrix had gone home, including Rose. This ritual followed the usual structure more closely, although three weeks on blockade had made me an expert at letting go, and I was prepared, I thought, for anything.

We met in an open space under the central parachute. The trainers rigged solar-powered lights so we could see each other. We sang while people were gathering, and then grounded with a Tree of Life meditation.

"In my tradition," I said to the gathered crowd, "we begin by calling in the four directions and invoke the elements of earth, air, fire, and water. I'd like to do that if it's okay."

The group murmured its agreement.

"Shall we do it formally, or just by chanting?" I asked.

"Formally," several people cried out. I then called for volunteers to call in each direction. These four people spoke the invocations. Two seemed to be from pagan traditions, and two from Native American traditions. Yet together they cast the circle. Again, I realized how easily the traditions fit together. The words and symbols may differ, but the thought-forms are the same.

We began a spiral dance, singing:

> She changes everything she touches,
> And everything she touches, changes.

As I began to unwind the spiral, I felt an impulse to make it a kissing spiral, one in which we kiss each person with whom we come face-to-face as we dance. We rarely do this in large, open groups, because many people find it threatening. That night it seemed right because I thought there were about fifty people gathered—a good size for a kissing spiral.

However, while we were invoking and dancing, the spiral had grown. What I didn't realize, until we began unwinding, was that there were about two hundred people in the dance.

We danced, and chanted, and kissed and danced and kissed until we were nearly dizzy or half-way into some other state of being. The situation was funny, but the hilarity only seemed to deepen the power. The spiral unwound, snaked, opened out, and threaded back. The chant went on and on. I began to fear that the energy would dissipate before it could be drawn into a cone. Then it changed. We began to sing:

> We are changers,
> Everything we touch can change.

The chant affirmed our purpose, affirmed the strength of the groups going out the next morning, on the last day of the blockade. The power built. We drew together in a tight spiral again, swaying, chanting, and singing in free-form melodies and wordless harmonies until the power peaked. After we grounded, we sang the names of the affinity groups who were present. Again the singing was both funny and beautiful. Chanting, "Mother Earth," can be solemnly spiritual; chanting, "No nukes, Hold the Anchovies," demands an appreciation of the absurdities of life. . . .

THE EQUINOX RITUAL

The oak trees of the back country around Diablo Canyon are the oldest oaks in the world. I don't know who told me that, or where the information came from, but I believe it. The oaks stretch around us and above us, high and sheltering. There are about eighty of us hiking on a secret path in the back country near the plant, a path that our guides have scouted. We are dressed in our darkest clothes, greens and blues, so that we can blend into the brush when helicopters fly over.

I am tired. Or rather, I am in a state beyond tiredness, between waking and sleeping, brought on by broken sleep and bad food. I am sustained now by energy that is no longer physical. In this state, the trees, the earth, come alive. They speak. They are angry, and we can let ourselves be pulled by the currents of their deep earth power. This must truly have been a sacred place to the Indians, for it feels like an open crack between the worlds, a place where even in bright daylight we are half in the underworld.

In my haze, I begin to see the whole blockade as a giant hex on the plant, an elaborate ritual. It has its own rite-of-entry, nonviolence training. Our way to the camp was secret—like the secret of the labyrinth. First we checked in at a site in the nearby town; then we were handed a map that guided us in a roundabout, circular fashion to camp. . . .

A group of us hike into the back country. In a surprise action on the morning the Nuclear Regulatory Commission is scheduled to grant the low-power testing license to the plant, some of us will block the seven-mile-long road that leads from the main gate to the plant at its midpoint. This will catch both the workers and the police off-guard. When the first contingent of thirty people is rounded up, another thirty will appear suddenly a little further down the road.

Some of us are climbing up the hill because the next day is the eve of the autumnal equinox, and we are determined to celebrate it within sight of the plant. Our ritual will be a political action, a threat to the plant's security, an expression of defiance. It will assert—on a day when we know hundreds of our people will be arrested—that we are still here, that we are loud, and strong, and will come back in force. . . .

For two days, we hike intermittently, eating cold foods because fires are both a security and a fire hazard in the back country. We sleep huddled together under thin blankets because the police are confiscating property and not returning it, and we do not want to lose our good sleeping bags. We hike in the dark and in the hot sun, as the logistics of our secret journey requires.

Finally, as dusk is falling on the eve of the Equinox, the guides lead us over a hill onto an open ridge. The fog-dipped coastal hills roll softly away from us. Below us lies the plant, square, hard-edged, and out of place, like a bad science fiction fantasy cartoon imposed on the landscape. In this place where the earth stretches out her arms and rears her soft breasts, this plant is the emblem of our estrangement, our attempts to control, to impose a cold order with concrete and chain links.

The sun is setting. We sit on the hill and eat our meager dinner, chanting:

> We are all one in the infinite sun
> Forever, and ever, and ever.

A helicopter flies by. It does what can only be called a double take, and returns. On the third pass, some members of the group moon it. That seems to be the signal to start the ritual.

We gather in a circle on the ridge. The helicopter flies around it, as if to seal it for us. In the center is a living tree the Sabotniks affinity group has brought to plant in the back country for a member of their group who was killed during the summer in a highway accident. We plant a flag they have made—a black one for anarchy, for the power of the dark, that is embellished with the pentacle of the Goddess. Some of us have brought offerings—I leave an abalone shell on the hillside.

The ritual is loose and wild. Dark falls, and as we feel our power and our anger rise, we break from the circle, line up on the ridge, shine our flashlights down on the plant, and scream. We yell out curses. We want them to know we are here, shining our flashlights down, to draw their searchlights playing over the hills. We are banging on pots and pans, pointing our anger like a spear.

Hiroshima.

Nagasaki.

Three Mile Island.

No Diablo!

We can think of no worse forces to invoke.

The power peaks, at last, as power always does. We send it down to find the plant's weakest spots, the fault lines within its structure-of-being. We ground, and open the circle, and pick our way slowly, silently, in the dark, back to where we have made our camp.

We wake at three in the morning and hike down the hill in the dark, to plant the tree and to climb over the fence onto the grounds of the plant, breaching their security. Again, the police arrest us.

As Kore returns to the underworld, we return to jail. We celebrate the Equinox once more, among women. But just as Kore emerges in the spring, we know that we shall also return to the hills, to this blockade or another one, to whatever action we must take to bring about the renewal of the earth.

Our Equinox ritual was only one small action in the larger ritual of the blockade. It was another step in a dance of many actions, many rituals, many focused powers.

After the blockade ended, new problems were suddenly discovered in the plant. Blueprints had been reversed; structures had been built wrong; equipment had been inaccurately weighed. The safety violations were so grave that the Nuclear Regulatory Commission took back the license it had earlier granted. At this writing, the power company is embroiled in audits and litigation. No fuel rods were loaded, and still the land is uncontaminated.

So the blockade succeeded—not by physically stopping the workers, but by changing the reality, the consciousness, of the society in which the plant exists. Not the blockade alone, but the years of effort and organizing that preceded the blockade, created that victory.

The ritual, the magic, spins the bond that can sustain us to continue the work over years, over lifetimes. Transforming culture is a long-term project. We organize now to buy time, to postpone destruction just a little bit longer in the hope that before it comes, we will have grown somehow wiser—somehow stronger—so that in the end we will avert the holocaust. But though power-from-within can burst forth in an instant, its rising is mostly a process slow as the turning wheels of generations. If we cannot live to see the completion of that revolution, we can plant its seeds in our circles, we can dream its shape in our visions, and our rituals can feed its growing power.

As we see the Goddess mirrored in each other's eyes, we take that power in our hands as we take hands, as we touch. For the strength of that power is in the bond we make with each other. And our vision grows strong when we no longer dream alone.

[Editor's note: Diablo Canyon nuclear power plant is now functioning, but the blockade has been added to our collective memories.]

Ideology and Social Change

SHARON WELCH

As we in the women's movement encounter a time of backlash, defeats, and dispersal of energies, it is certainly appropriate to examine what causes the defeat of social movements.[1] What has led to serious setbacks for women in the past? What internal and external factors are thwarting us now? And, most importantly, how can we use our social location as thinkers and theorists, feminist thealogians and theologians, to do something about it? The questions motivating this inquiry are quite simple. What is the role of theory in movements for social change? What does it mean to take seriously the Marxist maxim that the point of our philosophy is not to interpret the world, but to change it?[2] This essay is also motivated by a further observation and question. I would argue that feminist thealogians and theologians, like others in the women's movement, are developing theoretical precision at the expense of political power. Internal theoretical debates all too often drain our energies, leading to personal animosity and internal division. How can our theoretical and strategic work remain rigorous, grounded, and politically effective?

I have found a model for such empowering work in the writing of Toni Cade Bambara.[3] In her novel *The Salt Eaters*, Bambara describes a black community's struggle to combine intellectual, political, and spiritual forces in work for justice. Bambara takes as one model for political work the soaring, healing beauty of jazz. I contend that our theoretical and strategic work can also be a soaring, healing manifestation of "sheer holy boldness."

She could dance right off the stool, . . . her head thrown back and singing, cheering, celebrating all those giants she had worshiped in their terrible musicalness. Giant teachers teaching through tone and courage and inventiveness but scorned, rebuked, beleaguered, trivialized, commercialized, copied, plundered, goofed on by half-upright pianos and droopy-drawers drums and horns too long in hock and spittin up rust and blood, tormented by sleazy bookers and takers, tone-deaf amateurs and saboteurs, . . . underpaid and overworked till they didn't know, didn't trust, wouldn't move on the wonderful gift given and were mute, crazy and beat-up. But standing up in their genius anyhow

---

Sharon Welch is Associate Professor of Theology and Society at Harvard Divinity School. She is author of *Communities of Resistance and Solidarity: A Feminist Perspective* and *A Feminist Ethic of Risk*. She is active in the peace movement and the women's movement.

ready to speak the unpronounceable. On the stand with no luggage and no maps and ready to go anywhere in the universe together on just sheer holy boldness.[4]

As we are grounded in community, our theoretical work is an exercise in "sheer holy boldness." What gives our theoretical work its power is its basis in a community of resistance and its resonance in the lives of women also struggling for liberation. Our work is itself the product of liberation and furthers and evokes liberation in others. It is a naming of reality, a framing of strategies by people who were formerly controlled by men and male institutions, defined by men and male philosophies and theologies. As we resist the continuous attempts to limit us strategically and theoretically, our intellectual work is itself political.

It has been of enormous importance for women to realize that different societies have different gender ideals and to formulate in analytical terms the relation of those ideals to material conditions in other societies, and it is equally important to realize that the ideals of women's unique spiritual character have survived a century of dramatic alterations in all dimensions of Western culture. These ideals have even survived in socialist countries, where the capitalist conditions Rowbotham describes do not exist. Because these gender ideals have lasted through economic, social, and political change, feminists have come to see, as Biddy Martin puts it, that struggles "over the production, distribution and transformation of meaning" are at least as crucial as "struggles over economic and political power."[5]

Our location in universities, colleges, and seminaries can also be utilized politically. Feminists have described the challenge of developing styles of education that are genuinely liberating.[6] In this process, theory is both important and relativized. In teaching, the most important concern is to support the process of theorizing and not the mere exposure to "correct ideas." I find it difficult, yet essential, to avoid the trap of more traditional educational methods, the use of theory as a form of social control. This takes several forms, all ways of containing and eventually destroying the boldness of students. One obvious strategy is the smug reminder that a student's ideas—whether critical or constructive—are not new, and giving the long list of all those who have already formulated a similar notion with, of course, greater sophistication and rhetorical power. Another way of preventing boldness is encapsulated in the aversion to "reinventing the wheel." Theories are taught in their final form, and the complex process of engendering them, moving through the requisite understanding of particular forms of oppression, particular visions of liberation, is ignored.[7] I think we would do well to take as a model for our work one that is used in some elementary education.[8] Students are actively encouraged to reinvent the wheel— they are given the problems that lead to creating a formula for finding the area of a rectangle, the volume of a box. By creating the formulas themselves they understand the mathematical theory more thoroughly, and, as a not so incidental side effect, gain confidence, boldness if you will, as thinkers. The fact that the formulas they derive are not new, the fact that others have reached the same conclusions, can be presented after the fact as confirmation of the students' work, as an affirmation that they are not alone or crazy, outside the bounds of communal discourse.

There is another aspect of the deadening effects of theory that I wish to examine. All too often we repeat the mistake of generals, and spend an inordinate amount of energy fighting the last war, focusing on how women were defeated in the most recent wave of feminism, avoiding those mistakes and missing what is going on now. It has become a truism that the strategy of nineteenth and early twentieth century women, the appeal to women's superior moral nature, was faulty, easily subverted and used against women.[9] While the idea of "True Womanhood" did serve as the source of unity and the moral grounds for the move by reformers into the public sphere,[10] it was easy for men to dismiss women on the same grounds, agreeing that women's morality is different and, for that very reason, belongs at home. Women's attempts to challenge public practices with virtues derived from the home were disregarded as naive and sentimental. Micaela di Leonardo provides a concise summary of this argument and its failing:

The activist stance based on the concept of women's strengths as "moral mothers" has a venerable feminist history. Through the manipulation of images of women as morally superior mothers and wives, nineteenth- and early twentieth-century feminists claimed the right to enter the public world as moral reformers and "social housekeepers." Second-wave feminist scholars have shown how this ideological strategy provided short-term gains, but a long-term stalemate for women. Using the Moral Mother image to enter the public world also meant that it would be used against women to push them back into the home.[11]

Leonardo argues that appeals to women's nurturing ability are flawed theoretically (relying on the "culturally ubiquitous sexist, homophobic, and sentimentalizing constructions of motherhood") and strategically (all traditional constructions of femininity and motherhood "cannot be transformed, and will always be used against women to push them back into full responsibility for home and children—and second-class citizenship").[12]

Leonardo's analysis, while accurate in many respects, leaves something crucial out of the equation, the power imbalance between women and men, and the power imbalance between female reformers and the social structures they challenged. The theories of many female reformers were used against them, yet it is simplistic to assume that the cause of their defeats was inadequacies in theory. As we look more closely at the record of the past, it is clear that even those women whose theories were more "sophisticated" were defeated. Linda Schott describes the defeated, albeit superior theoretical perspective of the Women's Peace Party (WPP), founded in 1915.

> The goals of the WPP differed crucially from the goals, as we currently understand them, of other women's reform groups. Those groups urged women to participate in the public sphere in order to reform social conditions that might endanger the welfare of the home. WPP members, on the other hand, worked to integrate women and men and their respective values into the public sphere.

> Because the WPP identified men with the acceptance of war and women with its rejection, the only logical method of abolishing war was to integrate women into the previously male-dominated public sphere. The WPP believed that its goal, unlike the goal of other women's reform groups, would be achieved only through a basic restructuring of society.[13]

The Women's Peace Party avoided the error so often identified as the cause of women's defeat, the appeal to reform the public sphere because of dangers to the home, yet they were defeated as easily as other women's groups. Schott goes on to name the external causes for the defeat of the Women's Peace Party. "The failure of that vision to materialize was due less to faults in the theoretical basis for women's action and more to the powerful, structural barriers of a patriarchal society."[14] The defeat of the Women's Peace Party and other women reformers was not primarily due to the inadequacies of theory or strategy. They were, quite simply, outmaneuvered. Men had greater economic and political power, more control over newspapers and publishing, and thus more control over popular perceptions. Any theory, any strategy, any definition of woman could be turned against feminists.

The lessons of history can be instructively applied to the present, not in the form of avoiding the mistakes of an earlier era, but in the realization that any theory or strategy can and will be used against us. It is not surprising, therefore, that a strategy and theory ostensibly different from that of the nineteenth and early twentieth century reformers is also being defeated. I have in mind the defeat of the Equal Rights Amendment. The authors of *Rites of Passage* analyze the various reasons for the defeat of the ERA.[15] Joan Hoff-Wilson argues that the struggle for the ERA represented a turn from a more relational feminism (a stress on "biological as well as socialized differences between women and men," and the advocacy of "a social or group approach for improving the socioeconomic condition" of women)[16] to a liberal feminism based on individual rights (with its stress on "obtaining the individual political and civil rights held by most men").[17] The danger with this latter strategy was its inability to provide a clear argument for women working together. It was vulnerable to attack from the quickly exploited popular sense of womanhood, of common female identity, invoked by those working to defeat the ERA.

In attempting to avoid the errors of the past, therefore claiming no significant differences between women and men,[19] liberal feminism, ironically, finds that very strategy used against women. The laws that now claim to be sex-blind (no-fault divorce and child custody) reinforce male privileges and work against women, and the attempt to gain equal rights for women was seriously damaged by the right making an appeal to women's identification as women, claiming that identity would be destroyed by feminists. The feminist attempt to offer a woman-defined female identity was not as successful.

The political ferment around feminism has not ended, however, with the ERA's defeat. The struggle for a fundamental transformation of society continues on many fronts. As intellectuals we face a particular threat: we are being colonized in the way the intellectuals of any marginalized group are managed, allowed to achieve theoretical precision at the expense of political relevance. In our society the very definition of academic work, especially the emphasis on "objectivity," precludes work that is directly political. For women, as for other oppressed groups, the subtleties as well as the divisions of intellectual debates serve to distance us from other women, from women inside the academy who become opponents on theoretical grounds, from women outside the academy who aren't interested in many theoretical debates. This colonization is dangerous in itself and its damage is heightened as theoretical debates become the arena of horizontal violence, waged with the fierceness of life and death struggles, as though the correct theory, the right strategy would save us. It is tragic when our empowerment defeats us—empowered to name reality, yet encouraged by the standards of academic work to phrase our concerns in a way that makes it difficult for women outside the academy to hear us. Emily Culpepper has reminded us of the danger of framing our discussions in conversation with male theorists, thus learning again a vocabulary and systems of little relevance to most women.[20] Fighting one's way out of Freud, Marx, or even my favorite—Foucault, can easily become all encompassing.

Those of us who are feminist thealogians and theologians are engaged in exciting, potentially revolutionary work. As we develop a new vocabulary for the sacred, as we create new ways of living faithfully, we challenge the arrangements of power and desire central to our patriarchal society. Our work is multifaceted, complex, and not easily harmonized. There are significant differences among us. Some women work within established religious traditions—Jewish, Christian, Islamic—and others choose to work outside, creating feminist spiritual communities, many drawing from earth-bound religions. Still other women are developing a feminist spirituality within marginalized "folk traditions," especially Native American and African traditions. Just as our location for theoretical work varies, the content of our thealogical and theological proposals is often sharply divergent. The danger or appropriateness of referring to the Goddess as Mother, or God as Mother, is a matter of heated debate. Those women who base a feminist ethic on women's connection with nature often find themselves at odds with those who begin from more explicitly political categories.

The theoretical and strategic differences among us are real and worthy of careful discussion and much mutually challenging and transforming work. It is somewhat ironic, but our differences are less fruitfully explored when we make too much of them, rather than too little, assuming that the discovery of the single correct foundation for ethics or the single most appropriate metaphor for the sacred would free us. Misplaced theoretical fervor arises as we forget that what defeats us is not incorrect theory per se but brute force, coercion, and social control.[21]

The struggle against patriarchy is not an easy one. Any theory or strategy can be used against us. Sandra Harding makes a similar argument, giving the example of divergent tendencies in feminist theory that are equally susceptible to subversion. Post-modernism harbors dangers of a relativism that enables dominant groups to dismiss as relative challenges to their power, and a "feminist successor science" (development of epistemology free from gender bias) may provide "yet another set of rules for the policing of thought."[22]

This could seem grim, but my conclusion is not pessimistic. I see it rather as a call for suppleness of mind, clarity of vision and purpose. We can think, organize, and act with greater focus given this awareness, doing our theoretical work well, but holding it lightly, valuing the human connections it serves more than the cerebral connections it makes.

This recognition can free us for boldness in our theoretical work and strategy planning. Realizing that there is no strategy without risk of being outmaneuvered, no theory without the possibility of subversion, we can freely experiment with different forms of thought and action.

While there is no sure foundation in such intellectual work, it is possible to lessen our chances of defeat. Just as theory separated from community can be most easily distorted, theoretical work grounded in community offers a better chance for political success, and this for several reasons. If demonstrated faulty, incomplete, or even distorted, the base remains for engendering other theories, other theologies and thealogies, and future resistance—the experience from which critical thought is developed. Also, the very process of creating theory, including thealogy and theology, can be empowering, a process (to use Nelle Morton's language) of hearing others to speech.[23]

With this approach to theory we can be bold ourselves and recognize the boldness of women in the past. Even if our work is later used against us, the process of developing theory can be generated in such a way that it creates the matrix for responding to such threats. As we take our own voices seriously, as we name this world with women outside the academy, as we value the process of naming as much as the result, our theoretical work can be (to use another image from Toni Cade Bambara) a way of "sporting power" for others.

Knock and be welcomed in and free to roam the back hall on the hunt for that particular closet with the particular hanging robe, coat, mantle, veil or whatever it was. And get into it. Sport it. Parade around the district in it so folks would remember themselves. Would hunt for their lost selves.[24]

"Power" for intellectuals does not require developing a final theory of oppression and liberation but is found in bold attempts to understand, analyze, and name, utilizing the resources of a resisting community.

NOTES

1. My analysis is an application to the women's movement of the work of Frances Fox Piven and Richard A. Cloward, *Poor People's Movements: Why They Succeed, How They Fail* (New York: Vintage Books, 1979).
2. Karl Marx, "Eleventh thesis on Feuerbach, Notebooks of 1844–1845," in *Writings of the Young Marx on Philosophy and Society*, ed. Loyd D. Easton and Kurt H. Guddat (Garden City, New York: Doubleday, 1967), 402.
3. Toni Cade Bambara, *The Salt Eaters* (New York: Vintage Books, 1981), 265.
4. Ibid.
5. Marilyn Chapin Massey, *Feminine Soul: The Fate of an Ideal* (Boston: Beacon Press, 1985), 28; Biddy Martin, "Feminism, Criticism, and Foucault," *New German Critique* 27 (Fall 1982): 3.
6. Katie G. Cannon et al., *God's Fierce Whimsy: Christian Feminism and Theological Education* (New York: Pilgrim Press, 1985).
7. My analysis is dependent on the work of Paulo Freire, *Pedagogy of the Oppressed* (New York: Seabury Press, 1970).
8. Glenda Lappir et al., *Middle Grades Mathematics Project: Mouse and Elephant, Measuring Growth* (Reading, MA: Addison-Wesley, 1986).
9. See Nancy Cott, *The Bonds of Womanhood: "Women's Sphere" in New England, 1780–1835* (New Haven, CT: Yale University Press, 1977); Mary Ryan, *Womanhood in America, from Colonial Times to the Present*, 2d ed. (New York: New Viewpoints, 1979), 135–50.
10. Barbara Epstein, *The Politics of Domesticity: Women, Evangelism, and Temperance in Nineteenth-Century America* (Middletown, CT: Wesleyan University Press, 1981); Karen Blair, *The Clubwoman as Feminist: True Womanhood Redefined, 1868–1914* (New York: Holmes and Meier, 1980); Jill Conway, "Women Reformers and American Culture, 1870–1930," *Journal of Social History* 5 (Winter 1971/72): 164–77.
11. Micaela di Leonardo, "Morals, Mothers, and Militarism: Antimilitarism and Feminist Theory," *Feminist Studies* 11 (Fall 1985): 602.
12. Ibid., 613, 615.
13. Linda Schott, "The Women's Peace Party and the Moral Basis for Women's Pacifism," *Frontiers* 8 (1985): 23.
14. Ibid.
15. Joan Hoff-Wilson, ed., *Rights of Passage: The Past and Future of the ERA* (Bloomington, IN: Indiana University Press), 1986.
16. Joan Hoff-Wilson, "Introduction," in *Rights of Passage*, 5.

17. Ibid., 5, 3–7, and Kathryn Kish Sklar, "Why Were Most Politically Active Women Opposed to the ERA in the 1920s?" in Hoff-Wilson, *Rights of Passage*, 25–43.
18. Jane Dehart-Matthews and Donald Matthews, "The Cultural Politics of the ERA's Defeat," in ibid., 44–53.
19. Joan Hoff-Wilson, "Introduction," in *Rights of Passage*, 6, referring to Carroll Smith-Rosenberg, *Disorderly Conduct: Visions of Gender in Victorian America* (New York: Knopf, 1985), 252–305, 358 (n. 127).
20. Emily Culpepper, "New Tools for Theology and Ethics: Writings by Women of Color," *Journal of Feminist Studies in Religion* 4 (Fall 1988).
21. I am dependent here on the work of Piven and Cloward and their argument that the causes of the defeat of social movements can be found in the coercive power of the state, as well as in any theoretical or strategic failings of resisting groups (see p. 102 of *Poor People's Movements* for an example). While I find Piven and Cloward's analysis of social movements convincing, I am not in agreement with their proposed strategy—a cadre of organizers producing mass disturbances in key sites. They persuasively argue against the value of membership-based national organizations as a vehicle for continuing social change, but do not address, or see, another option—the creation or sustenance of *local* communities of resistance.
22. Sandra Harding, "The Instability of the Analytical Categories of Feminist Theory," *Signs* 11 (Summer 1986): 656–57.
23. Nelle Morton, *The Journey Is Home* (Boston: Beacon Press, 1985).
24. Bambara, *The Salt Eaters*, 266.

New World Tribal Communities

An Alternative Approach for Recreating Egalitarian Societies

CAROL LEE SANCHEZ

In a holistic cosmogony the profane is sacred, and spirituality is applicable to every mundane aspect of our daily lives.

Most people with a developed consciousness would agree with that statement, yet many continue to search for spiritual groups or organizations that will provide a framework for spiritual practice. In the major Euro-Western and Oriental-Eastern social structures, spiritual frameworks have become religious orders or organizations that functioned quite well for many people through the agrarian period. The advent of a highly sophisticated scientific community that consequently produced a runaway technology has caused an ever-widening gulf between "daily life" and "spirituality" among discerning educated people, particularly in Europe and the United States. This chasm is more than separation of church from state; it is separation of "Self" from "Spirit" or animating Life Force. Literally thousands of people are seeking "spiritual guidance" in many different ways by joining religious movements, new age groups, eastern religions, or returning to traditional Christian churches, and many still find themselves to be unfulfilled— fragmented rather than whole.

How can everyday spirituality and the practice of it be achieved in a fragmented, often polarized, contemporary society? How can we transform the desire to incorporate spirituality in our daily lives into actions that continuously and consciously connect us to the Life Force that infuses and animates all we know of our present reality(ies)? In my mind, these questions revolve around attitude or approach. The Western and Eastern approaches and teachings are based in agrarian

Carol Lee Sanchez taught American Indian and Women's Studies courses at several major California universities from 1976 to 1986 and has conducted workshops on Tribal Communities annually in Europe since 1983. She lives in Santa Barbara, California, where she and her husband operate their Contemporary Indian Art Gallery.

social structures and have not incorporated "modern" science and technology into their philosophic underpinnings. It is this omission that is causing the stress, pain, and dichotomy conscious and intelligent people are experiencing today.

When I became aware of this stressful dichotomy in myself, I returned to the beliefs and attitudes of my own tribal background and began a study of American Indian Tribal practices that still exist throughout North America. The long history of the survival of my Tribe (and other Tribal peoples in the Americas and elsewhere), my early Tribal upbringing, and my own life experiences all tell me that the contradictions between agrarian-based patriarchal religious teachings and our daily lives are causing extreme emotional, mental, and psychic pain that makes us sick—that fills us with dis-ease. As Tribal people, we are taught that when we no longer acknowledge our Spirit connection to everything we get "out of balance" and become sick—dis-eased or filled with dis-ease. If we continue to remain disconnected from the things we depend on for survival, then they will leave us and we will suffer because we can't survive without them. The only way to get rid of our dis-ease and get healthy again is to "walk in harmony and balance" with "all our relations" in our universe.

Based on intuitive understandings of the body structure, its necessary attunement and balance on this plane, and its multidimensional reality in microcosm, Tribal peoples always acknowledge their physical relationship to their place. The sense of place is incorporated formally into ceremonial activities, and informal acknowledgement is an integral part of daily life. These understandings have been handed down from antiquity through the oral teachings of Tribal elders of each generation and are reaffirmed through the contemporary visions, dreams, and experiences of traditional Tribal peoples. The teachings, which include the shared visions and experiences, are about being in touch with All That Is, being aware of everything and connected to everything in order to "walk in balance and harmony."

Most non-Tribal people rarely, if ever, consciously and consistently acknowledge the sacred aspects of their daily lives and therefore tend to be unaware of these connections. Because of this lack of awareness they are often filled with despair as the world of human activity around them appears to be filled with ever-increasing horror. It is my firm belief that it is contemporary Western thought and belief systems that have placed us in such jeopardy and caused the separation of all we know and acknowledge into the sacred and profane. I also believe dominant Euro-Americans waste the resources and destroy the environment in the Americas because they are *not* spiritually connected to this land base, because they have no ancient mythos or legendary origins rooted to this land. At best they revere the lands of their spiritual or ancestral origins. Euro-Western cultures in particular have embraced the monotheistic teaching they say was "authorized" by their male God that grants humans dominance over all things "not human." A corresponding teaching invests this male God with dominion over all things humans can possibly know, think, or do. Mainstream Jewish/Christian/Islamic thought systems are founded on the premise that a single Almighty Spirit Being authorizes and informs human thought and action, leaving the rest of "God's Creation" to be used, abused, and destroyed according to human whim and desire. Euro-Western thought systems place humans above everything that exists and hold them responsible only to God for not getting along with each other and for not worshipping him exclusively.

The values of Euro-Western and Tribal thought systems are in direct opposition. Tribal peoples have an attitudinal perspective that regards all things in the known universe to be equally sacred. To Tribal peoples, humans are only a part of The All (and an insignificant part at that) although humans seem to have more special abilities than other species and elements have. Tribal peoples assume all things have their own unique abilities. Even though other species, plants, animals, our solar system, and the stars beyond are different from humans, we believe they are sacred and to be honored as much as humans. To honor is to hold in high respect, to revere. To revere is to venerate, and it is this important attitude of veneration that produced many "perfected cultures" in the Americas. It is this way of thinking and being, handed down for thousands of years according to the oral traditions of many Tribes, that separates Tribal peoples indigenous to the Americas from non-Tribal peoples.

It is my premise and proposal that the first and most important step back to "health and harmony" is for all non-Tribal Americans to acknowledge and become thoroughly familiar with the indigenous spiritual frameworks of *this* hemisphere and establish a connection to *this* land base where we were born. The wise and prophetic teachings of our Tribal ancestors, where consistently adhered to, have sustained Tribal communities in the Americas through European conquest into contemporary times. The next step is for non-Tribal Americans to acknowledge their own connections to *this* land (through birth or adoption) and to revere this land base more than they revere an abstract notion of freedom symbolized by their Declaration of Independence, their Constitution, and the flag that flew over their conquest and disenfranchisement of approximately forty million native peoples.

Currently, at the end of the twentieth century, we are faced with many contradictory life-styles, social structures, and ideologies. Our inner selves truly know what is appropriate for each of us—yet our external reality presents so many possible choices we become confused and sometimes feel quite powerless when faced with the immensity of the present global situation. Because of our sophisticated global communications networks, none of us is able to escape the many national and international issues that directly affect our continued survival on this planet. We are on the threshold of the third millennium attempting to deal with the myriad results (both rewarding and horrifying) of our dash into progress. We, the people, are inevitably responsible and I believe it is the duty of each of us to do something about the present global reality. The peace/anti-war/anti-nuclear arms movements, the concern for world hunger and world health, the environmental protection groups, and others, all demonstrate that many people do care and are doing what they can. For some of us, however, becoming a "frontline activist" is not sufficient. Many activists maintain a negative attitude, a continuous focus on everything that is wrong, that is harmful and hurtful to self, creatures, and environment. Over a period of time many activists suffer "burnout," long for a different world, and drop out because they accurately perceive themselves to be "out of balance."

My own level of "imbalance" pushed me out of militant activism and caused me to question militant materialistic approaches to problem solving. I wanted to focus on the beauty and positive aspects in my life while at the same time accepting my human responsibilities to *do* something—to find another way. I asked myself how I could be spiritually whole again ("loving my neighbors as myself") and acknowledge global realities of hunger, starvation, brutal oppression, enslavement, nuclear armaments, dangerous nuclear and chemical waste products that were created by my neighbors. I wanted to transform my thoughts into everyday actions that would keep me consciously connected to the Spirits of all things while seeking better wages and living conditions, equality of the sexes in the home and the workplace, equitable healthcare, childcare, and old age security at the same time. Simply stated, I was determined to discover for myself how mundane everyday spirituality and the practice of it could be achieved in the fragmented, often polarized contemporary society in which I lived. In my mind, possible solutions to these questions and conflicts could be achieved through focused thought combined with an attitudinal perspective that honors and reveres all things.

I have found the Tribal framework and process to be a useful model for introducing groups of people to the possibilities of creating contemporary egalitarian social structures. Before I share the elements of this Tribal framework and process, I want to touch on several points that motivated me to explore Tribal structures of the Americas in depth and create the cross-cultural Tribalization process I began to use in the classroom.

Several years of teaching American Indian history and oral literature to non-Indian students, who were unable to understand how American Indian Tribal systems functioned and how American Indians approached every aspect of their daily lives in a spiritual context (Spirit connected to everything and therefore related to everything), led me to develop some unconventional teaching methods. I wanted my students to perceive these Native cultures through the attitudinal perspective of Tribal peoples. During this frustrating period, I had a long conversation with Paula Gunn Allen on our Tribal oral traditions in an attempt to articulate a teaching strategy that would communicate the significance of these oral traditions to non-Indian students. Paula and I understood that our sacred and semi-sacred origin stories literally connected us to our "living" environment and that this connectedness forbade us to plunder thoughtlessly and carelessly or willfully destroy our lands, its elements, and creature inhabitants. This important relationship to our land base is transmitted to all Tribal peoples through our oral traditions—the origin stories, the migration stories, the histories of the people—told and retold throughout our entire lives.

It was during this extended discussion that Paula and I realized that Euro-Americans (as the dominant ruling race) had no sacred origin stories—no land-based mythos—rooted in the Americas. We realized that the conquerors and immigrants (both forced and voluntary) had no ancestral lineage that had loved, valued, protected, and cared for this land base, these homelands to hundreds of native Tribes. The immigrants brought these Western values with them along with their plants and animals, displacing those already here. They continued to revere symbolic homelands (which in most cases were not even their ancestral lands) for over four hundred years, paying no heed to the delicate ecological balance maintained by the natives. The latecomers scoffed at the pagan, heathen native peoples who lived with and treated plants, animals, insects, fish, fowl, and elements as their relatives. Because of my early childhood Tribal experiences, it is my premise that the lack of a land-based mythos and sacred connection to the ecological systems of the Americas has allowed the Euro-American immigrants to rape and plunder these lands without regret or concern. For today's generation it is almost too late to repair the damage, to restore the delicate balance.

This premise was the initial impetus that prompted me to propose to my oral literature class that we emulate an American Indian Tribe and create our own oral traditions modeled on the oral literatures we were studying. After articulating their own personal family histories in traditional Tribal forms, these students became involved more intimately with Tribal literatures. Many students stated that their own personal outlooks and attitudes had been affected in positive ways and others felt enriched through participating in the creation of a Tribe. Encouraged by these positive student responses, I continued to use modified versions of what (at that time) I called "Tribalizing" as a teaching strategy in certain classes I taught in American Indian Studies.

Through reading Indian biographies and through conversations with other American Indians living in urban areas, I discovered that those of us who grew up in American Indian communities are indelibly imprinted with a thought system and a set of values and attitudes that are nearly impossible to erase. We are connected to our Tribes in ways that are very difficult to describe or explain to non-Tribal people. It is partially because their non-Tribal values are directly opposed to our Tribal values that they seem unable to understand our underlying attitudes. This results in a great deal of miscommunication between us.

Another revelation that emerged out of these conversations both dismayed and gratified me. It was evident that those of us who are tribally connected at birth and living away from our home communities often cannot explain, to ourselves or to others, what causes us to feel so much anxiety and personal anguish regardless of the economic comfort or "success" we may have achieved in "the outside world." Our Tribal connection is so deeply internalized that we don't recognize or acknowledge that the weakening of those ties is a primary cause of our mental, emotional, and psychic imbalance. We (Indians) agreed that "going home" stabilizes us again, reestablishes our sense of being in balance and connected to everything. We agreed that being *connected* is fundamental to the mental health of Tribal people. This insight led me to the conclusions that (1) long-term separation weakened our Tribal connection, which in turn made us "sick," and "going home" allowed us to regain our feeling of wholeness; and (2) that Tribal peoples are empathically connected (though I didn't have that term then) to each other *and* all the elements of their environment through empathic transmissions from the Tribe.

Empathic imprinting of Tribal values and attitudes affects us in both adverse and beneficial ways. When confronted with the alien, antithetical set of values, attitudes, and beliefs held by Euro-Americans on a daily basis, most Tribal Indians were/are unable to compete or succeed in dominant culture institutions and social structures for any length of time. This explained why "traditional" Indians (our definition of those raised in Tribal traditions on reservations or within interdependent nonreservation Indian communities) frequently dropped out of school, left jobs and extended social activities among non-Indians, and just disappeared for an indefinite period of time. My own life pattern reflected this same behavior to some extent. The knowledge that I was imprinted with Tribal values, and beliefs that I had been unable to eradicate, submerge, or modify, forced me to rethink my attitudes about myself, my daily life, and the American society in which I lived and worked. It was important for me to balance and harmonize both ways within myself. Once I unraveled what was Indian and what was non-Indian in my own values, attitudes, cultural upbringings, and biases, I was able to identify (and accept) which set of values affected my approach toward the various aspects of my own life and by extension, the Tribal principles my Indian students, Indian colleagues, and I held in common—although we all came from different Tribes.

From my first oral literature class in 1976 until now, my "Tribalization process" has gone through many modifications and variations. In some instances, a variation was necessary because of the subject matter of a particular course I was teaching; in other instances, modifications depended upon the "chemistry" of a particular group. Creating Tribes among non-Indians also posed certain problems for me because the basic framework that I was using could be viewed, from my perspective, as coming dangerously close to proselytizing: the imposing of my traditions on others rather than a unique approach to learning. Our Tribal way is not to impose our beliefs and values on "outsiders." I had to find an acceptable method for transferring the attitudinal approach that comes directly out of my Indian background without imposing my ways on others or breaching the Tribal integrity and taboos of my Tribe—or any other Tribe. Since I may not disclose my Tribal rituals, ceremonial activities, or anything determined by my Tribe to be private and privileged information without the express permission of the Tribal Council, I had to be careful what I taught. It was and is not my intent to "Indianize," proselytize, or disregard Tribal restrictions, but to present an alternative framework in which groups of people can create and formalize what we create into a spiritual community structure that is functional in the daily lives of the group who creates it. Consequently, for all the reasons I've given, plus a deep desire to "turn on" as many people as possible to loving all the creatures on our planet and to care again about our planetary environment, it became imperative for me to identify the general principles of Tribal structures.

Moving from a teaching strategy that provided an avenue for non-Indian students to understand the worldview of American Indian Tribal peoples to the identification of distinct Tribal principles has been an extended but rewarding journey for me. When I discovered the general underlying principles that are the foundation upon which all Tribes have created their own social structures and developed their own unique identity as Tribal entities, I knew I could share this knowledge. this alternative, with others whose vision for peaceful global coexistence was similar to mine. This "process" of sharing these principles has also allowed me to share the experience of my personal heritage without breaching Tribal restrictions or "making Indians" out of anyone. It has been my experience over the last five years that when these principles are acknowledged, accepted, and agreed upon, groups of people are able to maintain a coherent and cohesive Tribal social structure. These "mini" communities have reinforced my vision of the very real possibility for peaceful coexistence within a multiracial, multicultural, global society. Although the idea of community is as old as human habitation on the planet, community has come to mean various things in different cultures throughout the course of human action and inter-action. A Tribal community connotes an interconnected group of peo-ples made up of loosely connected families or clans having a common attitude that is rooted in a substantial and consistent spiritual frame-work.

Now I face the most difficult task, and that is to describe, in writing, just what creating a contemporary non-Indian Tribal community is all about and how it is done. Because I am more Indian than I am Cau-casian, I expect all social structures or frameworks to be flexible and adaptable because that is the nature of all living things. I have no step by step formula but rather a basic framework that contains some general Tribal principles that inform the process of creating contem-porary Tribal communities.

During the first meeting with a group of people, I formulate a small number of objectives or outcomes based on the overall vision and basic intent of that specific group. Working with several dedicated groups of people in Europe, over a three-year period, has proven to me that a bonded modern Tribal community is a consistent outcome, but the steps taken to reach that stage were as varied and different as each group was. I have given fifteen workshops in four European countries, and the few times I predetermined in linear fashion just what I was going to do each day, spontaneous and creative interaction was im-possible. When I remained open to the group dynamic, remained "tuned in" and balanced, the five to ten days of living under one roof with comparative strangers was effortless and incredibly enriching. With that said, I will share some of the elements that I have introduced into previous workshops. Some workshop groups incorporated all of these elements, and some focused on only a few but with a greater depth of experimentation and practice.

The New World Tribal process is intentionally designed to provide groups of people with a loosely structured method in which they can rethink some of their culture's social and technological processes and philosophies and compare them with Tribal principles, philosophies, and social structures. They may examine their beliefs about the rela-tionships between humans, creatures, plants, and elements. They may decide what they want to change about the global reality in their own sphere of activity and how they can accomplish the changes in their own daily lives. Sometimes we explore alternative modes of thought, expression, and being, which we are free to adopt and experience in the moment.

For a long time, I began the workshops with the telling of our per-sonal family stories: who our people were/are, where they came from, and how we each came to this place where we gathered together. We acknowledge our ancestors by acknowledging their contributions to us, to those they knew, to the place(s) where they made their home(s). We do this in the old way. The people sit in a circle and each individual tells the history of their people to the group. The only rule I impose here is that when telling their stories, the group members must name their people according to the important talents or aspects they demonstrate(d) during their lives. They must also give descriptive names to the cities, towns, or regions (the environmental surroundings) where their ancestors were born and migrated to and from. While this origin story is going on, one or two members of the group are asked to take notes, recording the highlights of each person's personal story. This will later be organized into the origin story for that particular group. The first part is a personal migration story, the honoring of one's ancestors and the addition of these historical experiences to the new group the individual has joined. The next part is the combining of all the migration stories into a Tribal creation or origin story, thus remembering where the people came from and how the people came to be. Using various elements and principles as our foundation, we create an alternative contemporary community. This new community can then experiment with reconnecting the everyday to the spirit within and outside ourselves, if and when a specific group willingly agrees to do so.

One of the major goals of my work is to share my vision of planetary harmony and coexistence among all peoples, all creatures, all elements, all plants, all stars, all of everything we are cognizant of that resides outside our individual selves. The mini-Tribal communities in Europe have developed social and spiritual guidelines, practices, and ceremonies that they determined should be formalized and incorporated into their daily lives.

Tribal peoples around the world honor and therefore celebrate life in all its aspects, its disasters along with its riches, and so I always suggest that as a group, we formally acknowledge some important aspect of our current daily lives by ceremonially celebrating it. The groups choose what they wish to celebrate and how they will do so formally. I have participated in naming ceremonies for infants and renaming ceremonies for adults, ceremonies dedicated to the changing seasons, to the cleansing of rivers, to the thoughtful appreciation of nearby forests, to the sharing of our human energies with a grove of dying trees. I have listened to newly created birth songs, baking, shopping, driving, and working songs, peace chants and ceremonies, women's power chants and songs, and men's power chants and songs. I believe it is time to create new songs of acknowledgement as well as ceremonies that include metals, petrochemicals, and fossil fuels, electricity, modern solar power systems, and water power systems. I also believe it is very important to make sacred, to acknowledge the new ways and elements in our lives—from nuclear power (which is buried in our Earth and activates our Sun) to plastics to computers. It is time now, again, for the entire world to honor these Spirits, these new molecular forms in order to restore harmony and balance to our out-of-control systems and in particular, to our modern technologies. If hundreds of thousands of "just folks" would do this, it is possible for a daily ritual to take place in cities and towns and rural regions that could produce the same astonishing results that the Pueblo peoples of the Southwest produce when they dance for rain. Every year the Pueblo people dance, and, if they are all in accord, if they all have the proper attitude and harbor no ill will against anyone in the Tribe, then it rains—without fail. Since I come from these people, I know it is possible to be connected to the living Spirits of our planet, for we are truly all one.

Before I give a workshop, I write to participants suggesting that they keep a journal for several weeks before our meeting. The following excerpts from my letter suggest ways that—through journal keeping—we can begin to create a different set of attitudes as we act in and respond to daily life.

The first section of your journal should be on *plants*—leave enough pages to write at least a half a page every day about your plant. Buy or find a new plant—even if you have some at home now. Become very aware of this plant and write about it at the end of every day or first thing in the morning for at least one week. Talk to it; listen to it; notice its growth, its every change. Notice if you are distracted when you think about your plant, or if you don't pay any attention to it, ask why you didn't notice. Note when the plant tells you to water it or to move it into the sun or take it out of the sun. After the first week, draw a picture of your plant and notice what it does, or how you feel when you do this. I don't care whether you can draw or not . . . just do it and see what happens. Record everything that happens during this process.

In the second section of the journal, write about your *animals*, cat or dog if you have one. Write about how you relate to wild animals and creatures. What do you feel when you see a spider, or a bee, or a bird? What were you thinking when you noticed them? How did *they* respond to you? Write at least a half page about creatures every day. Talk to insects, try to understand them. Listen to everything around you. Yes, in the city also . . . not just in the woods or in the country. Pay attention to the plants, trees, birds, dogs, cats, insects—especially in the city. Listen to them. Send your thoughts to them. Notice what animal or creature seems to appear the most in your daily doings. Meditate about it. Write your thoughts down about why you think what you think about creatures—birds, animals, fish, lizards, insects—whatever kind comes into your daily life.

The third section of your journal should be called *thoughts*. In this section, write about your day. This should reflect your attitudes, your wishes, your feelings toward or about things that happened to you. Do this section before you go to sleep and write just what comes to mind—the high points of that day. Also write your questions down—things you want to know more about. Once you move from an "intellectual mode" into a "connected mode," your daily activities will reflect this shift of focus and attitude, and you will begin to sense a new relationship to your environment and all the living things within it.

The fourth section should be your *daily routine*. It should describe and only describe what you do regularly each day. Do this the first week, then skip a week, and then do it the following week and so on. In this section you will note what time you get up, the first thing you do when you get out of bed, and the succeeding actions as you get into your day. The exact order in which you do your daily routine is the purpose of this section. Keep track of the food you eat each day for at least one week.

The fifth section will be your *dreams*. Dreams are a very important source of information for us—from ourselves. They are empowering. It is important for European and Euro-Americans to establish a relationship to their dreams not only from Western perspectives, but from Tribal perspectives as well. I suggest you include current dreams that disturb you or seem to be prophetic to you, as well as vivid dreams you remember from your childhood—one that scared you or one that made you feel good or important.

Create a *house altar*. You can choose a special corner in your house where you can place a small table for this purpose or use a ledge, the mantle of the fireplace. Your house altar should hold things you have found out of doors along with special gifts from loved ones. These things will remind you they are gifts from the bounty of mother earth and all her children. A pretty rock, a leaf, feathers, branches, or sticks, and by all means things that have special significance to you. A special cloth, a piece of metal, a pin or earring or something decorative—whatever feels to you belongs on your altar. When you look at the things you've placed on your altar, or when you read what you've written in your journal, give a thought to technology. Think about lights, running water, flush toilets, cars, airplanes, buses and trains, and don't forget computers. Think about how we might make ceremonies to incorporate them into our spiritual context. We must make our daily lives *sacred*—and I know there is a way to do it.

I look forward to the coming into being of new attitudes that can begin to heal our planet and her atmosphere. I look forward to the possibilities of conscious people coming together into communities intent on peaceful coexistence. Communities founded on honor and respect for themselves and all living things—aware of their integral interdependent relationships with everything in this solar system and beyond—are already existing in small enclaves around our planet.

They await the birth of similarly focused communities to assist them in the work of reestablishing the tenuous balance of our precious global ecosystem.

Imagine an entire city of people waking and rising together at 5:00 or 6:00 A.M. and the first thing they do is sing themselves—body, mind, and spirit—into the day. The next conscious thought they hold in common is loving goodwill towards all other living things; they do this with an attitude of support for balance among all things and their human place among them. They send out this loving goodwill while visualizing all the creatures, all the plants, all the elements, and especially all the microorganisms (bacteria, viruses, molecules, and atoms) that plants, creatures, and humans depend on to keep the balancing machinery working. Then suppose this city of conscious people has previously agreed, through the media or some central forum, to focus their next waking thoughts in unison on a particular issue such as the abundance of safe, clean waters for the survival of all life forms in their region, country, or continent, or their precious planet Earth. Picture, if you will, this city of people singing to the water Spirits of bubbling brooks and streams, of laughing happy rivers filled with water life, of saltwater seas and oceans filled with saltwater life. Hear them, in your mind, singing this water song as they are imagining pure sparkling waters in quiet pools and lagoons, breathtaking waterfalls, crystal clear mountain waters that taste sweet and cool, and as they continue their water song they visualize the great seas and oceans and all the planet's life-giving waters to be free of pollutants. When these conscious people complete their water song they go about their daily activities knowing that by shifting their focus to loving their world, to loving their city, their town, their air, their water, and the other life forms they depend on for continued existence, they will bring healthy life-supporting conditions back onto this planet, into their region, into the experience of their daily lives.

They can know this, because small groups of Tribal peoples have done this for thousands of years and continue to focus their thoughts in just this way to this day. However, they need help with this self-imposed responsibility. They need a great deal of help because all around them they are being overwhelmed by pollution and the fear-filled and negative thoughts focused on these current unhealthy conditions. Tribal people know it is possible to change the planetary conditions because their ancient traditions and personal experience have demonstrated this to them. Because of their continued conscious daily practices, I believe that *if we can think it, it is possible* and when we, "the people," create a vision with good intent, then it will *become*. Perhaps you too will dream about this possible event, and in dreaming about it, begin to bring it into your daily experience in some measure. Once you know this is possible from your own personal experience, then

perhaps you will add your thoughts of good intent to mine and believe
in this possibility, this vision, with me.

I leave you with my prayer for inspiration and guidance.

> I add my thoughts of Good Intent to your thoughts
> That your Life may be peaceful and content;
> I add my breath to your breath
> That your road may be healthy and long;
> I ask our Grandmothers
> To watch over you
> And lovingly guide you
> As you walk through your days.

Credits

DATE DUE

OCT 2 1 1989	OCT 1 6 1991	
NOV 0 4 1989	APR 1 5 1992	~~RESERVE~~
Nov 18 1989	9/7/92	~~FEB~~
DEC 1 3 1989	APR 0 2 1993	~~REL 228~~
DEC 1 9 1989	JUN 2 9 1993	MAY 0 2 2001
JAN 0 9 1990	FEB 1 3 1994	APR 1 0 2002
FEB 0 5 1990	MAR 0 8 1994	~~RESERVE~~
FEB 2 6 1990	APR 1 9 1995	~~NOV - - 2002~~
MAR 1 9 1990	FEB 2 0 1996	~~Res 316~~
APR 0 8 1990	MAR 1 7 1996	APR 2 2 2004
APR 2 4 1990	APR 1 8 1996	JAN 2 4 2005
MAY 1 4 1990	OCT 2 8 1996	
OCT 0 2 1990	R 2 1 1997	MAY 1 5 2006
MAR 1 3 1991	~~RESERVE~~	FEB 0 6 2007
PR 1 9 1991	~~APR - - 1997~~	MAY 2 9 2009
11-25-91	~~Res 316~~	
FEB 0 4 1992	DEC 0 1 1998	
FEB 2 2 1993	APR 1 5 2004	

GAYLORD   PRINTED IN U.S.A.